Empathy

If Quality matters why doesn't the Customer?

By

Professor Mohamed Zairi

Empathy
If Quality matters why doesn't the Customer?

ISBN 978-1-906993-27-6

1st Edition 2012

Published by:
European Centre for Best Practice Management
Holly House | Spring Gardens Lane | Keighley | BD20 6LE | UK
Tel: +44 (0) 1535 612060 | Fax: +44 (0) 1535 605318
Web: www.ecbpm.com | Email: books@ecbpm.com

Cover Design
Upstart Design & Media
Media House | 25 Aireville Crescent | Bradford | BD9 4EU
Tel: +44 (0) 1274 591199 | Web: www.upstartdesign.co.uk
Email: upstartdesign@blueyonder.co.uk

Printers
Inprint + Design Ltd
WB07 Richmond Building | Carlton Street | Bradford | BD7 1DP |UK
Tel: +44 (0) 1274 235757 | Web: www.inprintdesign.com

Tenderness and kindness are not signs of weakness and despair, but manifestations of strength and resolution.

Kahlil Gibran

Contents

List of Figures

List of Tables

Project Team

Researcher Contribution	**Vahid Saremi Shahab** *Research Associate*
Project Management	**Nidhi Narula** *Projects Manager and Creative Catalyst*
Typing and Proof Reading	**Sara Dawe** *General Administrator*

Acknowledgements

The preparation of this manuscript could not have been made possible without the significant help of the core team at the European Centre for Best Practice Management. It is therefore essential to recognise the following individuals for their vital, unique and comprehensive contributions. Sara Dawe for typing the dictated text and helping prepare the manuscript, Nidhi Narula for technical support and general co-ordination of the manuscript, Vahid Saremi Shahab for being a key contributor by assisting with the research and developing some of the thinking.

Dedication

The heart of a mother is a deep abyss at the bottom of which you will always find forgiveness.

Honoré de Balzac

In loving memory of:

My Mother,
My Father,
My Brother, Rachid

An ounce of blood is worth more than a pound of friendship

Spanish proverb

Empathy is considered a mirroring or vicarious experience of another's emotions, whether they be sorrow or joy.

Centre for Building a Culture of Empathy

Empathy

Chapter 1: Introduction

Does Quality Really Matter?

This book has been written to highlight once more, the importance of total quality management in bringing real transformations to the world of business and commerce. A lot has been learned over the last 60 or 70 years through the use of the principles and tools of total quality management:

- A clear focus on defects, errors and aspects of products and services that displease the customer can be positively tackled.
- The practice of continuous improvement through the constant search for potential solutions to problems does help organisations, not only in fool proofing, optimising their practices and processes but also continuous improvement gifts and boost in terms of building competitive capability.
- A quality culture can be established through the focus on people by engaging them, empowering them and allowing a climate of team work to develop.
- Closer relationships between the focus on quality management inside the organisation and the external impact it generates from the point of view of customers and economic benefits to the organisations can be positively established.
- A sustainable path of an organisations future aspiration can be clearly mapped and preserved through the adoption and preservation of quality management.

In all it can be said that quality matters and throughout the years several studies have attempted to demonstrate the tangible benefits of quality management and also to prove that quality is not a fad but rather is a science that can be taught, applied, enhanced and maintained. Early studies were conducted by the Japanese Union of Scientists and Engineers (JUSE) by focusing on winners of the Deming Prize. This study by JUSE was conducted in the early 1980s and has proved that firms that adopt quality management diligently and systematically are more likely to perform better than the rest of their respective industry sectors. The first study conducted in Europe by the European Centre for Best Practice Management (Zairi & Letza, 1994a; Zairi & Letza, 1994b; Zairi & Letza, 1994c; Zairi, Oakland, & Letza, 1994) has also demonstrated that European organisations that have been pioneering with total quality management have clearly demonstrated better financial results than their respective peer groups and across all the industry sectors. In recent years a more significant research has attempted to counter the attacks voiced towards total quality management as a failed management concept. This study focused on the US context using a large sample and has concluded that stock prices of quality award winners are significantly higher than the rest of their peer groups. The award winners tended to outperform their benchmark portfolios by 34% and this was translated, in the sample, to the equivalent of 669million USD (Hendrick & Singhal, 1999). Other studies have also led to similar positive conclusions (Levine & Toffel, 2008). This study looked at the ISO9000 standard of quality management systems. This system which has been embraced by over 900,000 organisations in 170 countries has had a remarkable effect on organisational performance and their competitive capabilities. In order to validate other researchers claims, mainly through "proponents claim that quality programmes such as ISO9000 and ISO9001 improve both management practices and production processes, and that these improvements translate into increased sales and employment (unless productivity gains outweigh sales increases). The latter benefits are magnified if customers interpret the adoption of ISO9001 or other quality programmes as a signal of high quality products or services. To the extent that greater employee skill and training are required to develop and implement procedures to improve procedures, the theory of human capital suggests that employee's earnings should rise as well. Finally, ISO9001 can improve worker safety through the identification and elimination of potential hazardous practices, development of a formal corrective action process, and institutionalisation of routine audits and management reviews. Some critics suggest that formalisation and documentation of work practices can negatively affect employees, such as by reducing skill requirements or increasing cumulative trauma disorders". The study in Levine & Toffel (2008) has concluded that ISO adopters have higher rates of corporate survival, with significant sales and employment growth and wage increases that exceeds the groups of non ISO9000 adopters. The study also found that organisations that achieved ISO9000 registration are more likely to report no injuries as far as health and safety is concerned and this is measured by workers compensation claims in the years following adoption.

Several other studies have demonstrated that quality does really matter and has significant impacts in several areas. The study which focused specifically on small and medium sized enterprises (SME) and using data from the Australian Bureau of Statistics (ABS) has concluded that quality has significant impact even on small businesses (Watson, 2003). Another study in the US has found that ISO9000 adopters achieve significant improvements in financial performance. The study has also concluded that careful implementation of quality using ISO9000 does also lead to intangible benefits (Corbett, Montes-Sancho, & Kirsch, 2005). The following benefits were also identified by another study:

- Productivity gains;
- Improvement in profits;
- Cost reduction;
- Reducing waste;
- Aiding survival through the recession;
- Improving staff motivation;
- Facilitating elimination of procedural problems;
- Improving awareness of procedural problems;
- Better management control;
- Aiding induction of new staff;
- Improving customer service;
- Improving efficiency;
- Consistency across sites;
- Gaining new customers;
- Keeping existing customers;
- Using standard as promotional tool;
- Improving market share;

- Increasing growth in sales;
- Increasing customer satisfaction;
- Reducing exposure to fraud;
- Reducing staff turnover;
- Reducing barriers to international markets;
- Reduced need for quality audits by customers (Buttle, 1997).

A study that compared samples of organisations that have ISO9000 and the Baldridge Award in the US have similarly concluded that although some demonstrate that financial gains have been achieved it is however more significant that organisations subscribing to the concept of quality management can achieve long term organisational improvement instead of the immediate monetary benefits (Wilson, 2004).

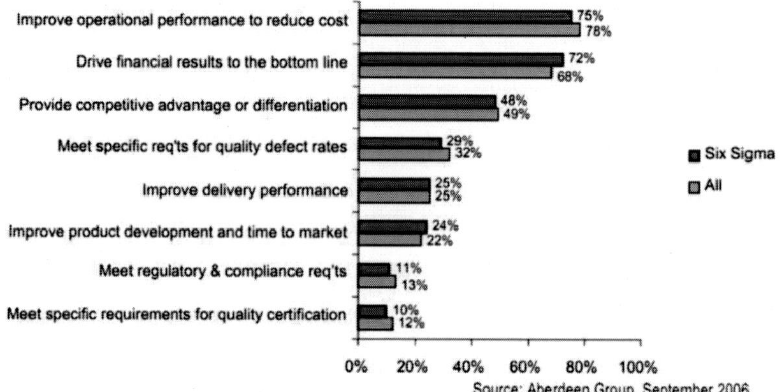

Figure 1: Pressures driving quality initiatives

Source: (Aberdeen Group Inc., 2006)

The report published by the Aberdeen Group Inc. (2006) focussing particularly on the application of six sigma philosophy together with other quality initiatives has demonstrated that organisations tend to apply the various tools and techniques of quality management primarily for economic benefits and enhancing the bottom line. Although the intention is to strive for competitive advantage as a long term desire, it is however the case that organisations look in the short term for financial benefits.

As Figure 1 shows the sample surveyed demonstrated that their use of quality management either in the form of six sigma or other tools and techniques is primarily for tangible, economic benefits with the aim ultimately is to strive for zero defects and producing the perfect products and services that will satisfy customers and therefore deliver a competitive advantage.

In total it has to be acknowledged that quality does matter. Survey after survey led to the establishment of a consensus on the importance of quality from different perspectives:

1. The derivation of a wide variety of benefits – organisations that tend to invest in quality management in the form, for instance, of ISO9000 certification or the use of six sigma or the implementation of continuous improvement for long term purposes tend to do so for the following reasons:
   - To make it easier to satisfy customer needs;
   - To have better management control and reporting;
   - To drive continuous improvement;
   - To minimise problems and failures in product and service quality;
   - To create better awareness within the employees about quality;
   - To use for instant ISO9000 for marketing and sales promotion;
   - To have increased credibility;
2. The engine of quality management is process improvement and process optimisation. Aspects related to enhanced productivity, the delivery of reliability and consistency in products and services is a base line fundamental requirement for any organisation. The following are the reasons why quality tools and techniques are used in the context of process improvements:
   - To increase productivity;
   - To build consistent, repeatable processes;
   - To have a common quality standard and system;
3. In relation to employees quality management has been acknowledged to be a key driver for enhancing individuals performance but also it a motivating tool in a variety of ways. The

following are reported reasons for implementing quality management in relation to the human element:

- To ensure that employees know what to do and how to do it;
- To enhance communication amongst employees;
- To create clarity in job specification;

4. Quality management enables organisations to get close to their external stakeholders and particularly to identify closely with the community at large and in particular in relation to aspects of CSR. The following are some of the reasons that were advanced by organisations adopting total quality management:

- To contribute to the quality of life in general by ensuring improved health and safety;
- To reduce environmental impact;

5. The main reason for implementing quality management is the customer. Most organisations invest in quality programmes so as to impact positively on customer satisfaction and ensure that they remain close to their customers. The following are reasons for implementing quality in the first place:

- To reassure customers and consumers that the provision of quality products and services is guaranteed;
- To differentiate quality organisations from their competitors and therefore keep customers for the long term;
- To reassure customers that service delivery, recovery through complaint analysis and satisfaction are primary objectives of the provider organisations;
- To deliver better quality products and services and new innovations through driving continuous improvement.

Whilst the question on the value of quality management has been answered empirically and scientifically speaking and in view of the fact that the final impact of quality management has eroded, not in terms of whether quality works or not and whether it delivers the intended outcomes. It is rather the case that the life-cycle of growth and development of quality thinking and its growth in terms of uptake has meant that its final value has decreased vis á vie the customer. Across all the sectors of the economy quality at its baseline is considered to be a mandatory aspect that the customers would expect the provider organisations to have in terms of standards and to commit to in terms of philosophy. Its value as a differentiating philosophy does no longer generate the same appeal. Most products and services have similar features, most of them have guaranteed performance, have similar functionalities and deliver similar benefits. Rather than therefore diminish the importance of quality it is important just to acknowledge its critical importance as a foundation for modern competitiveness. If on the other hand quality is neglected the whole engine of organisational performance and competitiveness is severely undermined. Substandard products and services will not be accepted by the customer, negative reactions from the customer to receiving low quality standard products and services will lead to their dissatisfaction and these dissatisfied customers will lose faith quickly and will switch to competitor organisations. Ultimately the credibility and reputation of organisations that are neglectful in terms of their co-commitment to quality enhancement and quality management will severely damage their reputation externally and will start to signal the extinction of those organisations. The answer therefore is ... quality does matter.

Does the Customer Matter Much More?

Having explored the importance of quality management at great depth it now becomes important to ask the questions:

- Where are the new sources of competitive advantage that organisations can derive?
- What aspects must they focus on if quality is taken care of?
- How would they compete in the modern economic context driven by technology?

The answer to all these questions is that modern competitiveness has to focus on the following:

- Customer centric practices and the adoption of customer experience as a key driver for competitiveness;
- Transformational thinking for building meaningful relationships with customers through their positive engagement;

- Using innovation as the key driver for value as opposed to previously continuous improvement for delivering quality as a key driver;
- Moving away from mass customisation towards individualised experiences;
- Measuring competitive impact using customer related dimensions as opposed to products and service dimensions only;

A focus on products and services and an optimisation of the value chain using quality as a key driver is what can be referred to as a push system. It means that the customer is passive and is recipient only. This conventional model is no longer sufficient at an age where the customer is curious, inspired and wanting to be positively engaged in shaping their own experiences and determining their own needs. The previous focus on customer satisfaction as the trump card for delivering long term loyalty is no longer valid and organisations must now learn to focus on the following:

1. An understanding that the economics of loyalty are more related to the delivery of outstanding customer experiences which can create advocates who can then commit longer term and promote the brands they are loyal to, to others.
2. The design of customer experience has to be from an outside in perspective – it means that the push mechanism does not work and a pull mechanism has to be adopted where the customer is put in the driving seat for interacting with the brand and shaping their own experiences.
3. The concept of design and deliver – it means that experiences unlike products and services are one off and everything has to be based on the commodity and perishable aspects of transactional relationships. With the ability of replenishing the needs and through innovative thinking and allowing the customer to redefine, redesign and indulge in their own experiences this will be the best source and best approach for securing a competitive advantage.

In order to understand the difference between the pull system versus the push system it is perhaps to relate customer experience from the point of view of what goes on in the minds of the customer. Most organisations tend to focus on what is referred to as the utilitarian and hedonic customer needs. Whilst this is important from the point of view of offering the customer good value and high efficiency in terms of cost, customers do however expect to be involved for other reasons. According to a report published by Bain and Company (Springer, Azzarell, & Melton, 2011) customers use both sides of their brain to evaluate what they receive from the provider organisations. The left brain is what is referred to as the rational side but more importantly customers now are using their right brain for emotional reasons. Hence the claim that can be made in this manuscript that "whilst quality belongs to organisations, the experience belongs to the customer".

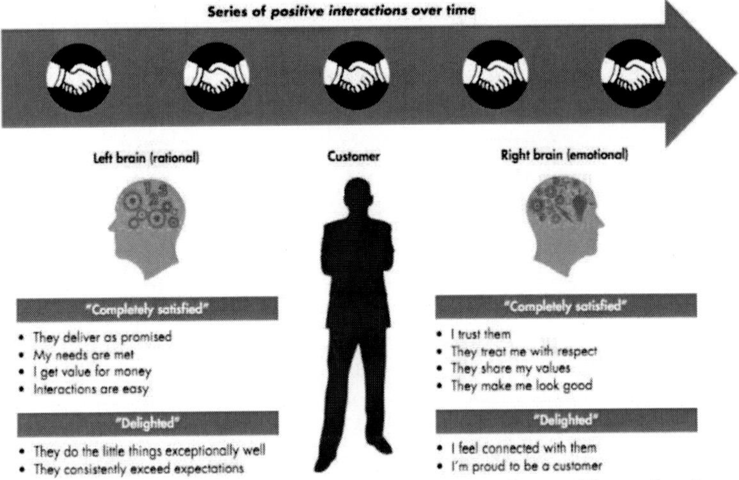

Figure 2: A series of positive interactions goes beyond "completely satisfied"

Source: (Springer, Azzarell, & Melton, 2011)

The report argues that the experience can evolve over time or as customers gradually start to evaluate interactions with their preferred provider. The positive evaluations of the various interactions will lead in time to the customers becoming attached because they trust the brand and through a positive process of engagement and empowerment the customers will be more likely to shift their attention towards the right brain (the emotional side) as opposed to the left brain (the rational side) which they can expect because they trust the brand which can completely satisfy them.

As Figure 2 illustrates the extended life-cycle of a customer relationship using the experience as the pull mechanism puts the customer at the front end when it comes to the pull mechanism and this therefore makes the customer important in a modern business context and makes quality and the push mechanism a foundation for delivering superior customer experiences. It is true that the advent of the internet has enabled organisations to look at new possibilities of empowering their customers in shaping and delivering unique experiences. Various studies have demonstrated that unique customer experiences tend to be based on having ongoing, two way conversations between the provider organisation and the customers but also that the positive impact on loyalty through active customer engagement is triggered by the following:

- Ensuring that engagement activities are done through various channels to allow the customers every opportunity to identify with and engage with their provider organisations.
- To invest in the front end aspects of customer engagement (ie. portals and web sites) to make it easier for the customer to identify with the brand and communicate with the provider organisations concerned.
- To provide the customer with the opportunity to manipulate, design and co-create and deliver their own unique experiences.
- To encourage high levels of active participation so that the customer works towards the long term identification with a brand and therefore will look at different levels of fulfilment through long term relationships.

A survey conducted by Forrester Research (2008), has identified that a large number of organisations that have effective engagement strategies use both on line and off line components (Figure 3).

Furthermore the organisations that have effective engagement strategies rely significantly on the internet for communicating with their customers and empowering and engaging them (Figure 4).

"Would you categorize this strategy, program, technology, or tool to enhance customer engagement as online, offline, or both?"

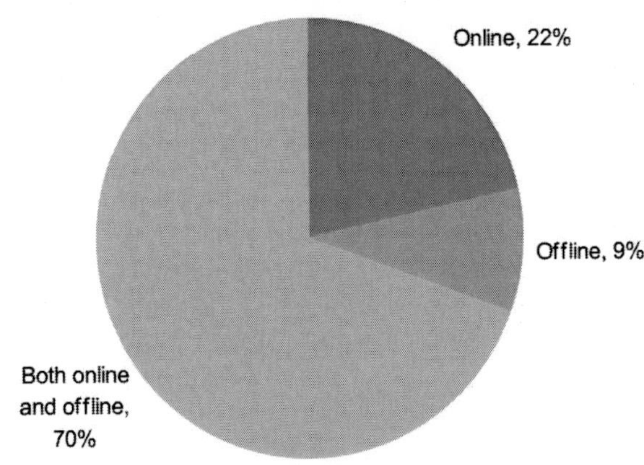

Base: 213 global executives involved in customer engagement

Figure 3: Most firms' top engagement strategy has online and offline components

Source: (Forrester Research, 2008)

"Does your company currently use or participate in any of the following types of interactive / digital technologies or tactics to enhance your customers' engagement with your company or brand?"

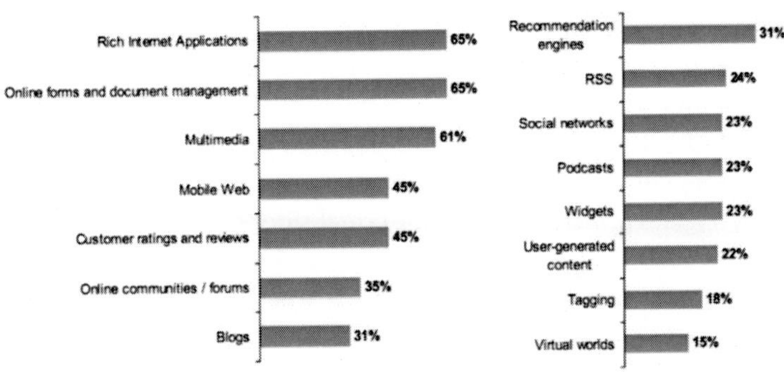

Base: 213 global executives involved in customer engagement

Figure 4: The most-used digital technologies make websites more engaging

Source: (Forrester Research, 2008)

The pull system is therefore a great opportunity for using quality as a foundation and a launch pad for giving meaningful individualised economic and tangible value to customers but also to delivering long term competitive advantage through loyalty. As Forrester Research (2008) argues organisations that take time to focus on customer empowering and engagement are more likely to derive competitive benefits because of the following reasons:

- The customers are more loyal – it means that if the most common goal of the organisation is customer engagement then the pursuit of high levels of loyalty will become real.
- It is a fact that loyal customers spend more, replenish their experiences more and seek for upgrades and new ideas – organisations that spend significantly on customer engagement drive with increased sales and extension of their profit targets.
- Loyal customers tend to recommend the brand to others – research has clearly demonstrated that a word of mouth consumer recommendation does have direct impact on sales turnover and profit enhancement.

The Loyalty Connection – The Service Delivery Challenge

Whilst the internet is a 'magic wand' for making the impossible happen in so far as delighting customers and retaining them for a very long time it is however the case that whilst quality has improved significantly in many respects the service delivery remains a critical challenge. This is due to the fact that the parameters used for designing service delivery processes, creating service delivery standards and measuring service performance have on the whole looked at the customer from the point of view of transactional relationships and not from the customer experience point of view which significantly includes the emotional side. Loyalty in this sense is not an outcome of service delivery but rather has to be considered to be driven from a strategic perspective and has to be understood from its holistic aspects.

A survey conducted by Thompson (2005) has identified loyalty as a repeat by a behaviour in its simple terms. Other customers have however, looked at loyalty from the point of view of advocacy and more importantly the reported emotional commitment to the relationship as a critical aspect of describing loyalty. High levels of customer satisfaction come down the list in so far as critical importance is concerned (Figure 5). Once that loyalty is recognised triggered by emotional aspects as opposed to the left brain rational aspects that deal with the functional aspects of products and services and the fulfilment of utilitarian and hedonic requirements emotional aspects are more in the hands of the customer because they belong to the pull system. A poor understanding of how customer service in a experience context has to be driven can have an extremely negative implications on an organisations long term competitiveness.

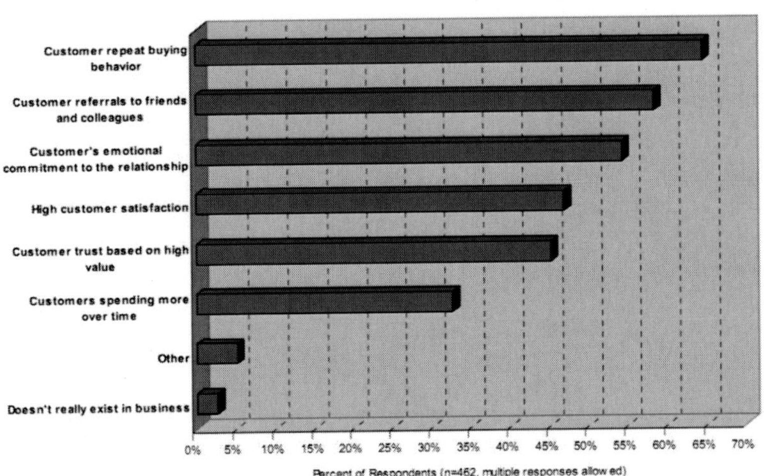

Figure 5: What is customer loyalty?

Source: (Thompson, 2005)

The study highlighted in Thompson (2005) has also identified that the primary reason why customers switch is poor customer service, followed by quality and price. More significantly however is the perception that the customers have on service provision which is totally out of sync with provider organisations beliefs and designed processes and standards (Figure 6).

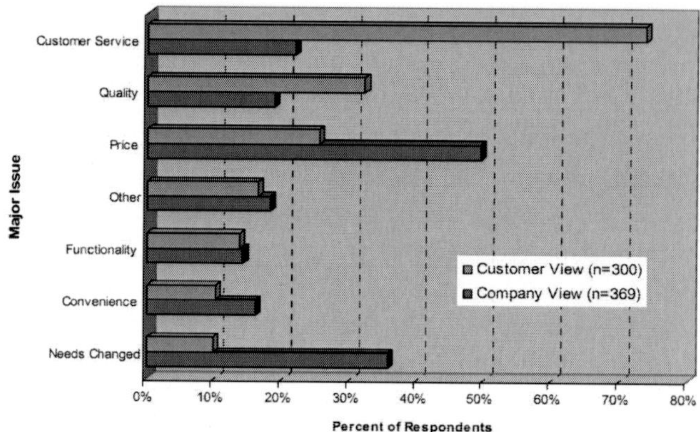

Figure 6: Why do customers leave?

Source: (Thompson, 2005)

The perception that customers may have on customer service can have severe economic negative impact as identified by a global survey (Genesys, 2009). This survey looked at consumer attitudes towards customer service and has led to some significant findings in terms of consumer behaviour, actionable steps to improve customer service, and businesses as from the customer experience. Nearly 9000 consumers were surveyed with a minimum of 500 customers per country.

The following countries participated in the study:

- Australia
- Brazil
- Canada
- China
- Czech Republic
- Germany
- Italy
- Mexico
- Netherlands
- New Zealand
- Poland
- United Kingdom
- India
- France
- United States of America
- Russia

These are the key findings:

- The cost of poor customer service in the 16 key economies is 338.5billion USD.
- The average value (in one year) of each customer relationship lost to a competitor or abandoned is 243 USD.
- The greatest satisfier across all countries was competent people to assist in any channel – this was listed as number one factor.
- The percentage of consumers who would welcome proactive engagement to improve their experience through extended offers or helping during self service transactions is 86.4%.

It is clear from the global study mentioned in reference 12 that service delivery remains to be a critical aspect of differentiation but more importantly it has to be defined in a new way. Customer experience as a pull system will require the understanding and the development of new dimensions of evaluating service delivery. Empathy will be the glue that will link the extended life-cycle of serving customers in the future.

It is expected that the push system of a conventional value adding life-cycle will gradually be replaced by a pull mechanism through increased empowerment and engagement of customers and the focus on total customer experience management as opposed to the prior development of products and services with customers being passive and pushing them out into the market through active promotion and marketing initiatives.

The Empathy Engine

This manuscript therefore seeks to take the quality debate well into the 21st century by highlighting the importance of the inspired customer.

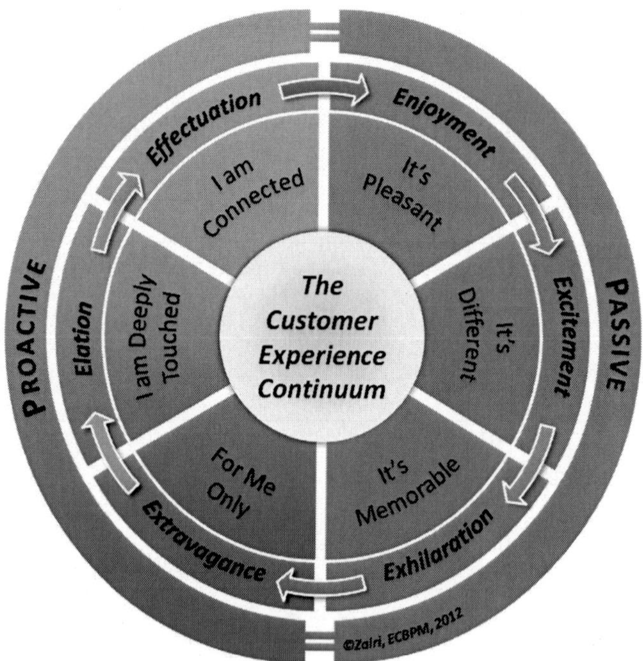

Figure 7: Empathy engine

There are implicit aspects that relate to what conventionally used to be important and new explicit aspects that need to be highlighted:

- **Implicit aspects** – quality management will be an implicit consideration because it is now the licence to practice – it is almost impossible for organisations to succeed in the modern business environment unless they are well equipped with systematic processes that define their value chain, consistent and reliable quality standards that they can make pledges with an offer to their customers and the demonstration that they can be trusted and relied upon in terms of providing to customer expectations, fulfil needs and requirements on a regular basis and manage speed and responsiveness.

- **Explicit new aspects** – the pull system of customer experience is the holy grail of modern competitiveness. This means that a clear understanding of what drives customers from the point of view of the right brain; emotional perspective in defining their individualised experiences will become a pre-requisite. The quality standard of the future is to perhaps consider the following (Figure 7):
    - Customer experience management is a holistic concept that has a continuum of customer engagement and empowerment opportunities.
    - The aspects of customer experience where the customer involvement is at a minimum are all related to the experience representing a small scale aspect of experiencing pleasure for instance, being delighted with a unique occasion such as having a meal in a new restaurant to a level of excitement where the customer indulges in something new such as a bungee jump or an aspect of exhilaration where the customer has been entertained in an endless way to create permanent memorable occasion.
    - Aspects of customer experience that has a continuum of engagement. In this context the customer is gradually involved in defining, designing, determining and enjoying their experiences. This includes a level that is referred to as extravagance or 'for me only' where customers can design their own requirements using the brand, for instance a unique individualised haircut, their own watch or the car that nobody else has. There is a level that is referred to as elation (I am deeply touched) where the customer indulges in an experience that they could never dream of having the opportunity to consume. For instance the customer playing in a live concert with their most favourite band to a live audience.
    - Lastly a level called effectuation (I am connected) where the customer uses the brand for spiritual needs, where they feel connected and where they are making a statement well beyond their utilitarian, hedonic or emotional requirements. For instance Harley Davidson bikers.

Figure 7 illustrates several possibilities where customer experience can be localised, defined or allowed to progress. The most significant aspect of this continuum of customer experience is that the customer matters more than quality and that the emphasis on allowing the pleasant aspects of an experience to take place and measuring them in a rational, systematic and meaningful manner can only lead to long term loyalty and commitment. Through the practice of empathy the various possibilities of giving unique and extraordinary customer experiences will become possible.

Professor Mohamed Zairi
Executive Chairman Zairi Institute
Juran Chair in TQM

Empathy is trying on someone else's shoes - Sympathy--wearing them.

Unknown

Chapter 2: The Meaning of Empathy

Introduction

Customer empathy is very different from the regular, routine provision of customer services. The products and services are the transactional aspects that the customer expects since they would have paid for them. By honouring the contract between a provider and a customer in terms of fulfilling their needs and providing goods to the customers satisfaction will not necessarily lead to full blown relationship and certainly will not raise the concept of empathy at all.

Over many years organisations have tried to extrapolate the concept of customer loyalty from measuring customer satisfaction and gathering information retrospectively on the outcomes from transactional relationships and the fulfilment of basic needs. In many cases the confidence that organisations build from analysing data that is favourable and ratings of customer satisfaction that are positive. Many assumptions have been made that those ratings signify there is an attachment that the customers are expressing and also there is evidence that the customers are making a pledge not to switch and to remain with their existing providers. This of course cannot be the case and customer loyalty is a challenge that needs to be examined separately and has to be based not on the transactional relationships but on the intent of the provider organisations in building meaningful, long lasting and rich relationships.

Is it therefore the case that customer empathy should be linked to the provision of routine, transactional goods and services or is customer empathy an approach that needs to be adopted beyond the contractual obligations and the provision of basic fulfilment needs and requirements? Many people have defined customer empathy as the art of looking at the transactional relationships from the customer's point of view. By empathising with the customer through seeing how they feel, what frustrates them, what levels of anxiety they experience and basing this on how the firm deals with customers and reacts to customers' anxiety this will create an empathy oriented approach. It is however limiting to link customer empathy to the reaction in relation to goods and services provided. In many cases however empathy is required beyond the transactional needs and more for the process of reassuring the customer in dealing with their emotional and physiological states which may not necessarily be directly associated with what they have received in terms of products and services.

In a sense empathy is at its basic level living the experience of others and feeling and understanding the state of other people. Empathy should not be confused with compassion and kindness which are human gestures that can be afforded to any person. Empathy as described by some has two dimensions to it. Mapping the other persons experience and trying to highlight the emotions, thoughts and reactions whether positive or negative they would have experienced and the other dimension is to look at the persons state of mind, psychological state and the implications of the experience that they have gone through in terms of the behavioural attitude. So unless the sensory elements of empathy are in existence it will be difficult to jump to the inference of dealing with a person concerned and trying to show them empathy.

The Key Components of Empathy

Hanson, (2007) suggests the following aspects to empathy and its understanding.

1. Empathy has visceral attunement and conceptual understanding. These work together. It means that the sense gives someone gut feelings about the state of the other person and the thoughts about that person tell us where to look in our gut.
2. Empathy does require individuality – it is possible for instance that we can empathise with someone but we wish they would act very differently. Empathy does not mean that the person has to forego their own rights or interests. We can ride above our own persona to be more empathetic. We can let the other person experience flow through our awareness knowing that we can still let it in and still remain standing intact and whole.

3. The awareness of how it is for the other person can be communicated in some way often non verbally and tacitly. For example through subtle facial expressions or postures that may mirror the other persons.
4. The most important thing is that the expression of empathy gives the other person the sense of feeling felt which is important for the recipient.
5. The expression of empathy is also about the interaction needs. It conveys the vital signal that the message has been received. It serves the purpose of calming the other person and helping them feel better.

Hanson, (2007) suggests that empathy has evolved in two major steps. He refers to the mental aspects of empathy and the sensing aspects.

- **The mental aspects** - this involves neurological processes. By learning about the circuits in our brain this can create empathy. We can use the mind to activate those circuits and thus become more empathetic. In other words we use the mind to change our brain to benefit our whole being.
- **Sensing** - this is concerned with how it is for other people. It is linked to the front part of the insula on the inside of each hemisphere of the brain. There are two insulae. These light up when we feel the emotional components of pain ourselves (such as distress, fear, anguish) or when we see another person in pain. It is interesting that the more important that person is to us and the more we care about them, the more our insulae activate when we know that person is in pain. There is also another sensory aspect linked to the brain which is called the anterior (frontal) referred to as cingulated cortex (ACC). This also is a trigger mechanism to demonstrate how much we care about the other person, in other words the more empathetic that we are the more the insula and ACC light up in response to the pain of others. There are also neurons called miraneurons which activate when we do an action and when we see other people doing that action.

In summary the insula, ACC and miraneurons produce simulations of the experience of others inside our own brain. These occur automatically as hard wired by evolutionary reaction. In other words when we see or even just imagine other people suffering, feeling and doing the brain automatically generates a virtual experience within ourselves of something close to what the other person is experiencing. For instance the phrase "I feel your pain" has become a bit of a joke, but it is literally true.

Hanson, (2007) concludes that "more than anything else, empathy is the glue that joins us all together. By extending the circle of your empathy beyond us to include them, the whole world becomes your home".

Other researchers such as social psychologists have conceptualised empathy as an approach that has two strands (Lawrence, Shaw, Baker, Baron-Cohen, & David, 2004).

- **Cognitive empathy** – which is the intellectual/imaginative apprehension of another person's mental state.
- **Emotional empathy** – which is an emotional response to the emotional responses of others. The emotional empathy has also been labelled as affective empathy. Emotional responses to others mental state has also been classified.
  - **Parallel** – the response matches that of the target for instance feeling fear at another's fright;
  - **Reactive** – which involves going beyond the simple matching of affect (such as sympathy or compassion).

Lawrence, Shaw, Baker, Baron-Cohen, & David (2004), argue that despite the fact that several scales have been developed to measure empathy from the point of view of emotional or cognitive it is however still extremely difficult to establish precisely how the other person thinks or how they feel precisely.

Concept of Customer Loyalty and Emotional Satisfaction

Having argued their case previously about the difficulties associated with the measurement of customer empathy and also its wider understanding there are however several attempts to use empathy in a context that is directly linked to customer service. According to a study published by booz&co. (2007) referred to as The Empathy Engine industries, for example, the banking sector according to this study is using the concept of customer loyalty and emotional satisfaction for instance.

There is a belief that in accordance with the report that the best customer services can generate a measurable impact on customers emotional satisfaction and if customer emotional satisfaction ratings are positively high it is assumed that the emotionally charged interactions will increase the value of the purchases from the banking sector and this will lead to loyalty, as Figure 8 illustrates.

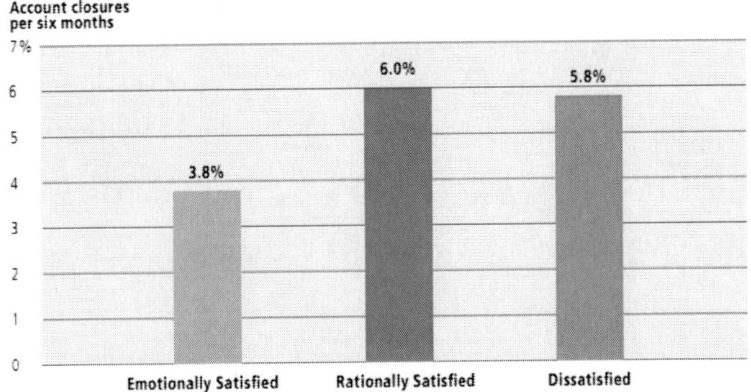

Figure 8: Attrition rates of bank customers

Source: (booz&co., 2007)

In the case where emotional satisfaction is low the attrition rates is expected to be high. On the other hand if emotional satisfaction is high the purchase commitment of the customers in their banks is significantly high (Figure 9). The assumption in this case that emotional satisfaction can be measured easily is perhaps debatable. The emotional aspects of customer experience are ones that are not necessarily easily expressed and cannot be linked to the measurement of customer satisfaction which is based on retrospective, historical gathering of data that is directly linked to products and services. Furthermore to assume that customers who express satisfaction are spending more to loyalty outcomes this will also be a debatable statement and needs to be validated.

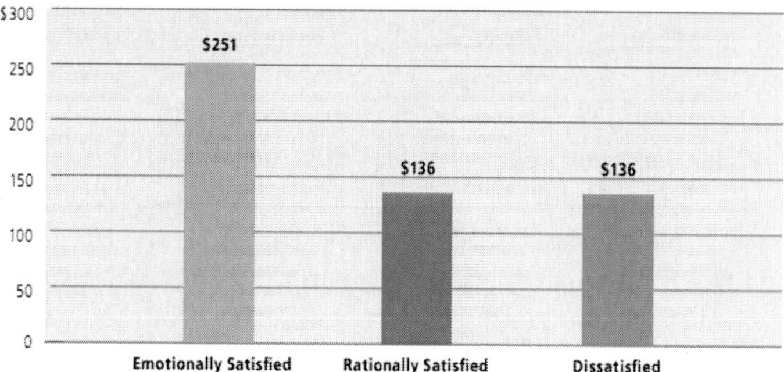

Figure 9: Average monthly spending by credit card customers

Source: (booz&co., 2007)

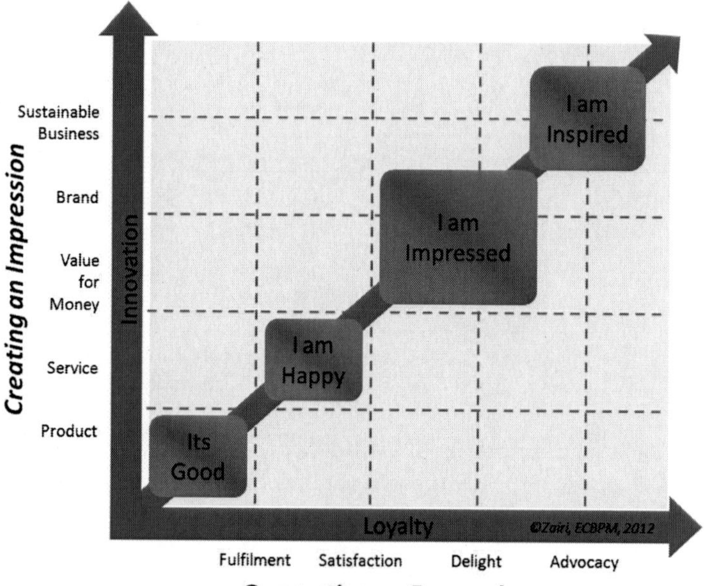

Figure 10: The Customer Loyalty Continuum and the Path to Emotional Attachment

The Customer Loyalty Continuum and the Path to Emotional Attachment

In order to understand the context of empathy and emotional attachment it is necessary to look at the process from the following viewpoints:

1. Emotional attachment is not a reaction on a snapshot basis to one individual experience. It is a cumulative set of experiences over a period of time that will be based on creating foundations of dependency, of trust and commitment. As Figure 10 illustrates, for instance, loyalty is expressed as an evolution process based on a sound evaluation of experiences that occur over a long period of time.
2. At the very base line those experiences are evaluated from a point of view of dependency and trust. For instance, the confidence that the provider organisation can fulfil the needs of its customers with high quality standards and to their expectations. These two foundations represent the fulfilment or contentment with its experiences and the satisfaction which is an evaluation which is consistent throughout time.
3. Once the foundation of dependency and trust is in place the relationship can be safely and confidently assumed to be sound and therefore the expectation is no longer treated with suspicion but rather is one where delightfully outcomes can ensue and furthermore the regular experiences of elation and delight will raise the level of loyalty well beyond the transactional relationships and the value based relationships into a state of non conditional relationships where the customer plays the role of advocate.
4. The processes that provider organisations need to go through in order to create the right emotional reaction by creating a meaningful impression is to foolproof the provision of transactional relationships in the form of products and services using the engine of innovation for driving the delightful experiences and therefore the emotional reactions from their customers.
5. The target therefore is not to limit customer experiences from the point of view of quality, reliability, dependency and building

trustworthy relationships but is to raise the bar by getting the emotional attachment through replenishing the customer with unfulfilled needs and unique experiences that can impress them and building this momentum towards what can be referred to as a spiritual state where the customer feels that they are inspired by the brand and inspired by their provider organisations and therefore can play the role of advocacy.

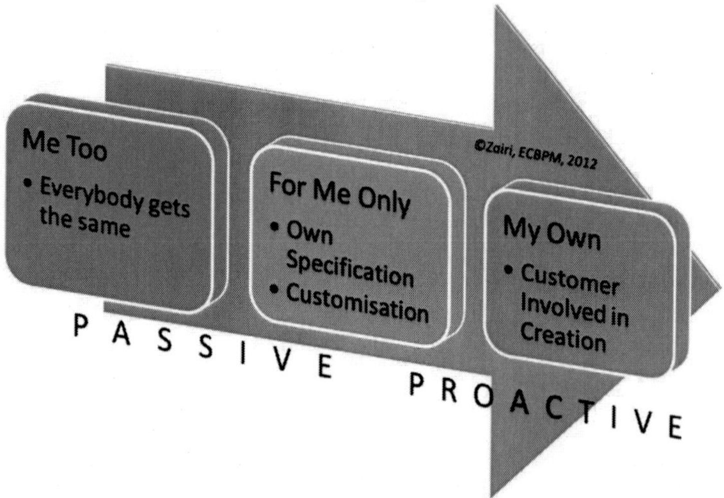

Figure 11: Customer Orientation – An Extended Approach

There has to be a radical approach that needs to be taken in order to create the emotional attachment and extending the life-cycle of customer experiences from a passive approach to a proactive one. This means that it is not sufficient for provider organisations to optimise their quality approaches and focus on delivering their unique products and services with some elements of customisation only. By stretching the concept of customer orientation through the empathy mechanism and getting the customer to be a partner in designing their own experiences and deriving their own benefits and outcomes in a proactive way this will generate the extended customer experience that will deliver the emotional satisfaction outcomes that are desirable (Figure 11).

Understanding Empathy – The Broad Perspective

The pursuit of understanding empathy and its measurability is more likely to continue unabated. Not only is the concept a complex one to grasp and therefore to map and effectively manage but also there are different parameters and trigger mechanisms that lead a customer to react emotionally in a particular way. It is therefore suggested that an integrated, broad approach to defining empathy will help in designing useful tools for measuring the reaction of customers and particularly by targeting dimensions that are associated with the mindset of the customer and also their emotional aspects.

- **Redefining the value chain and creating a customer orientated transformational thinking approach** – this means that the conventional life-cycle of customer experience that is directly associated with the provision of products and services needs to be redefined. It means that real customer value should be the focal point as what is expected and what is desired is the 'for me only principle' where customers can generate their own experiences and therefore derive the value that will seek to achieve. It also means that there is a need to go beyond customer experiences and work on the principle that loyalty can only be derived from inspiring the customers and working beyond reliability, dependability and trust.
- **Offering customer driven innovation –** this means that provider organisations have to accept that unique, highly customised experiences can only be fuelled by innovation in a radical way. Off the shelf concepts and available products and services will not inspire customers and certainly will not give them an experience that can trigger a positive emotional reaction.
- **Using the philosophy of customer is king –** this means to have the courage and the ability to involve customers proactively and to engage them in a meaningful manner.
- **Customer engagement and empowerment** – the proactive approach of driving the value chain from the point of view of the customer and putting them in the driving seat will very likely generate high levels of loyalty, retention and will certainly inspire the customers and create the right emotional outcomes.

- Addressing the customers directly through the principle of customerisation as opposed to customisation. This can be done through a one to one marketing philosophy.
- Integrating the customer from a holistic perspective and not just capturing their voices through sporadic and irregular market research means as the conventional philosophy used to advocate.
- Creating the DIY customer by enabling them to create their own experiences and furnishing them with all the ingredients that they would require for the achievement of high levels of satisfaction and a positive emotional reaction.
- **Using the philosophy of customer experience re-imagination –** this means that the evaluation of customer experiences needs to be looked at as a one off event and the traditional concept of improvement, optimisation and slight enhancement will no longer work and the use of blank sheets of paper to re-imagine new experiences will probably become the norm.
- **Customer empathy –** empathy is feeling the customer, sensing their reactions, recognising their power of thinking, avoiding aspects that may upset them and respecting them from the point of view of what they want. Whilst as it has been explained in the previous sections a good understanding of what customer empathy really means is useful. It is however important to translate this into philosophies and strategies that can be implemented at work in order to generate high levels of loyalty, retention and emotionally satisfied customers. The following ideas may help in this context:
    - Appointing customers as gurus – this means that the input from the customer and the customer influence in the way experiences are conceived and prepared for consumption is more likely going to succeed and deliver the outcomes that can be expected.
    - Letting the customer really feel that they can manipulate all of the ingredients provided to them for generating their own experiences. This means that provider organisations should secure their data and allow the customer to be a partner in a totally independent manner.

  - Instead of the deficiency philosophy of complaint handling in association with the delivery of products and services that tended to be the norm previously, organisations that are really practising customer empathy need to work on recovery plans from the point of view of the relationship side as opposed to the transactional aspects of products and services.
  - Building knowledge based resource centre with ideas, suggestions and evaluations from the customers.
- **Using customer value continuum for sustainable competitiveness** – this means that a radical approach where the customer defines the business and determines the priorities will become the norm. By having some of the following concepts in place:
  - **The use of the customer centric commerce mentality** – this means that organisations would have to be truly customer centric and not add the customer as a bolt on element to a traditional business mind set.
  - **Customer based brand** – redefining branding concepts and strategies so that they are not directly linked to products and services, but they are customer centric in every sense.
  - **Using total loyalty management as a core strategy** – as Figure 10 illustrates the continuum of customer loyalty is worth pursuing. The building of solid foundations in the way as figure shows will be useful to create the total loyalty management strategies.
  - **Measuring emotional satisfaction** – this means that all of the dimensions that are measured are truly reflecting what customers think and how they feel as opposed to capturing their reactions to existing products and services indicated in Figure 8 and Figure 9.

Figure 12 illustrates the various stages of evolution that organisations need to go through in order to create customer empathy and building a sustainable formula for competitiveness where the business parameters and the value chain are all redefined entirely to reflect the customer in spirit, as a partner, as a recipient and as an advocate.

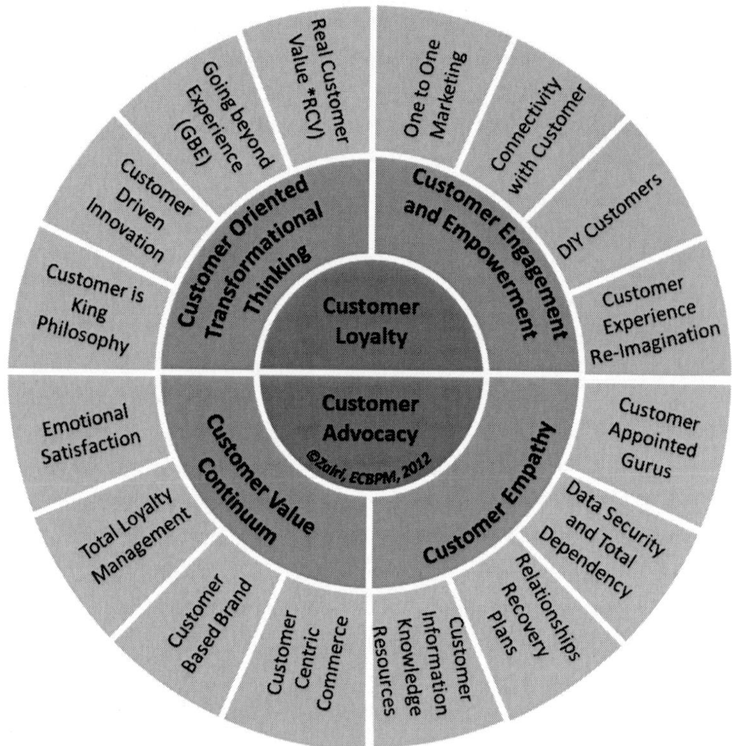

Figure 12: Customer Focus Process

Can Emotional Satisfaction Be Measured?

Original research conducted at the European Centre for Best Practice Management (ECBPM) using on line business transactions and customer experiences has led to the development of a measurement method (referred to as XQUAL) capable of measuring emotional satisfaction. As Figure 13 illustrates the model is based on the following premise:

- The quality perspective is the trigger mechanism for generating customer emotional reactions and expression of satisfaction with experiences. In this context the model has extended the measurability of quality through an extended life-cycle perspective by evaluating aspects that are related to the pre-purchase stage. This is an important consideration since the pre-purchase stage is the stage at which the customer will determine the value they would wish to derive from the experience and the outcomes that would like to see happen. In addition quality in the XQUAL model is to be measured at the purchase level and an extended level of post purchase for evaluating the fulfilment of requirements and the delivery to the expected standard.

- Unlike the traditional measurement of customer satisfaction as a snapshot, retrospective means for evaluating experience levels in the XQUAL model the satisfaction is presented as a continuum of levels which suggest that the delight aspects are based on fulfilling different levels of satisfaction. The assumption is that an enjoyable experience has to have as a base line the fulfilment of the expected needs. In the traditional customer satisfaction surveys the dimensions of measurement are all related to the fulfilment of basic needs. This is a major shortcoming in so far as the design of measurement tools which lead to the dangerous assumption and the extrapolation that high level of customer satisfaction with fulfilment of needs would automatically lead to loyalty and retention. The XQUAL therefore has added new dimensions where the customer expresses their enjoyment in various words and reflecting the perceived aspects of what the experience has done for them. The high level of measurement of customer satisfaction that can lead to delight is one where the customer acknowledges their delight by assessing the pleasant aspects of the experience.
- The contribution that XQUAL has made is adding what is referred to as the continuum of loyalty measurement as outcome measures. This fills the gap in terms of measurement tools and there is no extrapolation from measuring at the basic level of customer satisfaction to assume that loyalty will ensue. The continuum of loyalty measures dimensions of trust and the dimensions that are considered by the customer to be critical and which will lead them to prefer to maintain their relationship with specific provider organisations, leading to the measurement of advocacy. Total loyalty at the spiritual levels where the customer

identifies strongly with the brand and can reflect elation and strong emotional attachments.

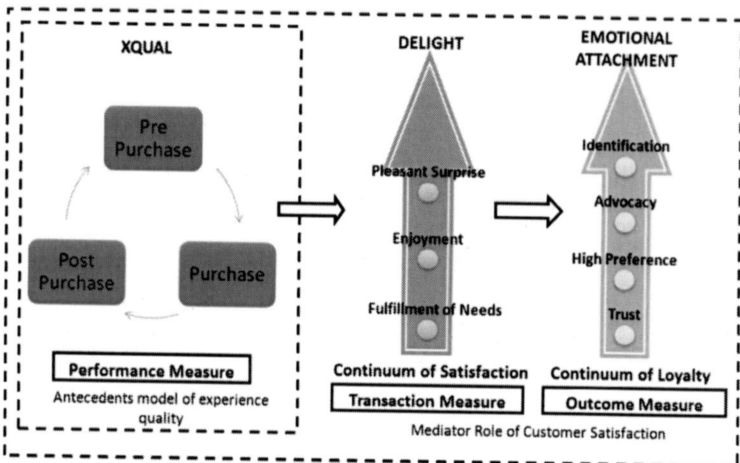

Figure 13: Experience Measurement in the Online Environment

Source: (Zairi M., 2009)

The XQUAL model can therefore be considered as a model that reflects the customer orientated approach from a total perspective.

- By extending the concept of quality and not limiting it to products and services but generating an evaluation and a measurement of quality through the experience life-cycle that includes two extremely important phases. The pre-purchase aspects where the intention is being made and the post purchase aspect where the experience can be immediately evaluated.
- The extension of measuring customer satisfaction and taking it away from the traditional assessment of compliance with need fulfilment into true and proper assessment of experience in the form of assessing the emotional enjoyment that the customer can express directly and the effect that enjoyment and emotional fulfilment on creating the delight state.
- The direct link between customer satisfaction as a continuum and therefore as an approach that needs to go through different levels of maturity through creation of foundations that can lead to true loyalty through emotional attachment.

- The measurement of customer loyalty as an outcome measure from the point of view of trust and preferences in terms of inner feelings and emotional experiences and the true intentions of the customer from the point of view of being proud and acting as advocate to the brand of their preferred supplier and identifying with the brand far away and above the baseline levels of products and services to perhaps a spiritual level.

Empathy

Empathy is like giving someone a Psychological Hug

Lawrence J.

Chapter 3: Empathy – A Personal Story

Introduction

I had to wait precisely ten years to recount this personal story. I thought that time would assist with healing and would provide the opportunity for turning the page and moving on and forgetting the incident that occurred in October 2001 and involved my mother who passed away in 2006.

When planning this manuscript and trying to precisely understand the true meaning of empathy I wanted to make sure that I do understand the concept and before embarking or writing this chapter I took time to look at over 5000 incidents where people have had unfortunate experiences which disrupted their travels, spoilt their experiences, created hardship and challenges for them, destroyed dreams and hopes and worst of all, inflicted unnecessary pain and agony that people have had to endure over years to come.

The following chapter includes a collection of such incidents and particularly focuses on how the individual concerned expressed their true feelings and how they were reflecting on the outcomes of their terrible ordeals and bad experiences.

The case of my mother is perhaps no different to the millions of bad experiences that people encounter in their lives. It is perhaps unique from two point of views:

1. At the time when the incident happened my mother was suffering from the beginning of Alzheimer's and it is perhaps fortunate, in a way, that she could not understand what was going on during the bad experience and certainly she would not feel the negative outcomes through lack of empathy that she would have suffered.
2. From my point of view, as her son, the situation is perhaps unique in the sense that I may have tried to mirror precisely what my mother would have gone through and I may have been

obsessed with the notion that there was hurt and there were loads of negative emotions that she would have felt. I may have also tried to believe that the nonsense that occurred with her situation would have caused further pain and anxiety.

The Alzheimer's Situation

Back in 2001 my mother started to have a form of dementia referred to as Alzheimer's disease. This is an illness where the brain cells start to deteriorate. My mother started to have progressive damage to her brain and started to exhibit symptoms such as memory loss, for example losing track of time, regular disorientation and sometimes strange behaviours. This illness which is ravaging leads ultimately to the person's death and until today there is no cure for it. It leads to the shrinkage of the brain through accelerated deterioration of the brain cells through the build up of protein. It is thought that dementia is very prevalent in women (67%) particularly in elderly people.

My mother was however cheerful and at the time of the incident she was still conscious of the important things in her daily routine and was still communicating effectively. She was still mobile, albeit on a limited basis. She was still keen to travel on her own and wanted, at the time, to make the most of her remaining years and travelled on a regular basis to visit her children who lived in different parts of Algeria except myself where she needed to travel a little bit further to spend time with me and her grandchildren.

Background to the Case

My mother came to stay with us in August 2001. She had a fabulous time and built up very happy memories with my children (her grandchildren). Eventually the time came for her to travel back to Algeria. In order to make her travel smooth and minimise the level of inconveniences I organised for her to travel to Tunis where my brother was going to meet her and drive her back home. Home being in Algeria, but very close to the Tunisian border. This more or less would have minimised the travel distance and therefore would have avoided the complexity of transferring to another flight and transiting via Algiers which is 700kms from where my mother lived. Furthermore I made sure through the British Airways travel office that the "meet and assist" service was booked for my mother on departure and also during the landing at Tunis. The flight duration was just over two hours and this would not have caused any anxiety or irritation as far as my mother was concerned. She had taken the same flight a couple of times previously and everything worked very smoothly.

I drove my mother to Gatwick Airport, overnight since her flight was on the 7th October 2001 out of Gatwick/Tunis. She was expecting to take flight BA6944. The flight was due to leave approximately at 9.30am on the 7th. We arrived at Gatwick with ample time and whilst waiting for the meet and assist service to collect my mother I sat with her and we had breakfast together and a very nice chat. She was telling me how much she had enjoyed her stay and that she was going to miss the children very much. She was cheerful and beaming at the prospect, on the one hand to go back home and see her other grandchildren but at the same time she was excited by the prospect of telling them about the wonderful times she had here and the happy memories she was taking back with her.

As the boarding time approached the meet and assist service was deployed and a wheelchair was provided for my mother and with an agent taking her for the immigration and customs formalities and preparing her for boarding, I said goodbye and wished her a safe and pleasant flight and gave her some instructions on what to do before boarding and reassured her that on landing she would have access to the same meet and assist service. Not having slept overnight I was anxious to drive back home (4 ½ hours driving distance) and have a long sleep and well earned rest. At the time I did not have the use of a mobile and would not have been contactable. As soon as I arrived back home my son, Adel ran into the yard telling me something had happened at Gatwick and that his grandmother did not make it onto the flight and they had held her somewhere safe and had asked if I could go back to Gatwick to pick her up. There were no additional details that Adel could have given me and the feeling of confusion and extreme exhaustion was overwhelming, particularly that I could not comprehend the reasons she did not make it to the flight and I feared something worse had happened and which would have stopped her from travelling. I did not have time to seek answers and there was certainly no phone number I could have called to seek some clarifications and some explanations. I hardly had the time to wash my face and decided to return by train, since it would have been very unsafe for me to drive back having had no sleep for nearly 15 hours.

I took the train, changed in London for Gatwick and eventually made it to the area where my mother was being kept. She was extremely tired because she also had not slept, very confused, upset but extremely relieved and pleased when she saw me. She was not in a position to give me an account of what had happened and I did not wish to find out at the time. A member of the British Airways staff who looked after my mother gave me a brief account of the incident and immediately upon signing the necessary documentation I told my mother that we would be going back to the house and we will be travelling back on the train. This is now the account of the incident itself.

Once my mother made it through to immigration and customs to catch the flight BA6944 to Tunis on the 7th October 2001 the agent who took her, in the wheelchair, created the confusion by communicating with her in a strange way which created some confusion in my mother's mind. She assumed that he was telling her that she would be boarding a different flight to the one that she was supposed to take. This confusion together with the fear and her loss of confidence and her inability to communicate made her refuse to board the plane. The more persistence there was from other staff who were speaking to her in a strange language that she could not understand the more stubborn she became and the more determination she had to refuse leaving. After a considerable amount of time the decision was made to leave her behind in order not to delay the flight and therefore inconvenience the other passengers. She was then transferred through the travel care staff of

British Airways to keep her in a unit which is purpose built for cases such as this. Having therefore assumed that the reason why she was left behind was due to her confusion and stubbornness to board the flight caused of course by her inability to communicate and also perhaps her illness I accepted this fact and was therefore apologetic to all those concerned and just wanted to put this unfortunate matter behind us. My mother and I left Gatwick to return home until such time that I would take her back myself.

Letter to Mr. Rod Eddington

My brother called me from Tunis and I explained what had happened. But I was shocked and horrified when he told me that the British Airways flight supervisor in Tunis had shown him a report that was prepared by the British Airways duty manager at the time in Gatwick and was heavily critical of my mother's behaviour. I urged my brother to fax me a copy of the report and I was extremely upset when I read the exaggerated comments and the misleading facts which were full of inaccuracies. I spent hours pondering about the situation and an incident which I was ready to forget as an unfortunate experience started to prey on my mind as a major issue. I ended up writing a long letter to Mr Rod Eddington who at the time was the Chief Executive Officer of British Airways. It took me four hours to write this letter, perhaps the longest time I have spent in front of my computer crafting a three page letter. The following paragraphs are extracts from the letter I wrote to Mr Rod Eddington.

Dear Mr Eddington
Re: Flight BA 6944 – Gatwick – Tunis (Mrs Salha Zairi)

The purpose of this letter is really to report to you an incident which was rather unfortunate and quite distressing. I have spent over a week pondering on whether it would be a good idea to formally write this letter. Under normal circumstances, letters of complaints would have been sent directly to the Executive Club, but perhaps on this occasion, I felt that the matter was serious enough, so please forgive me for taking the liberty to write to you directly. I do appreciate the demands on your valuable time but I do hope that the matter I have raised gets considered at BA's senior management level.

My mother who is 77 years old came to stay with us for a month, inbound from Tunis on flight BA 6945 to Gatwick, on 9th September 2001. Despite the fact that a wheel chair and the meet and assist service were strongly requested because of her physical condition, her inability to speak English and her failing eye sight, no assistance was provided what so ever on her arrival. The matter was then reported to BA's Travel Shop in Leeds who organised her PTA ticket, and their response was wonderful and very apologetic. My mother was due to fly back to Tunis on Sunday 7th October, outbound from London Gatwick on flight BA 6944.

Rather than bore you with the specific details of the incident itself, which I believe are included in a report under the PAX concerned (i.e. my mother, by the name of Mrs. Salha Zairi), I would like to highlight the following:

- My mother did not make it on the flight concerned and I have to say, that I DO NOT hold BA responsible for this. She refused to board the plane because she got confused and the more people were trying to help her and persuade her to get on the plane, the more stubborn she became. Fear, confusion, loss of confidence and her inability to communicate (despite the services of an interpreter), meant that the decision was made (quite rightly so), to leave her behind in order not to inconvenience the other passengers. Unfortunately by that time I had left Gatwick and drove back north with the belief that she was on the flight and well looked after. Meet and Assist was organised for her in Tunis, and my brother was to meet her at the airport and drive her back home;
- The Travel Care people at Gatwick looked after her extremely well despite the very difficult circumstances they had to deal with. Once alerted by Gatwick police, I had to travel back to Gatwick to collect my mother and take her back home with me;

I have been apologetic to all those concerned and wanted to forget this unfortunate matter, until my brother rang me from Tunis to alert me to the fact that a report was written, explaining what had happened. The report was compiled by the Duty Manager at the time, by the name of Celia Mongahane. The content of the report was highly critical of my mother's behaviour and in some parts contained some exaggerated facts and many inaccuracies;

Once again I am **not** writing to justify my mother's behaviour which of course was odd and incomprehensible. She is old, vulnerable and can get confused very easily. However what I would vehemently contest, are the inaccuracies in the report and the inflated remarks which have been so hurtful to both my family and myself:

1. The Duty Manager wrote that I had REFUSED to pay for the extra baggage weight that my mother had. This is not true at all. I had paid £53 and have the Excess Luggage Ticket to prove it. My mother had 34 kg in total and no hand luggage.
2. The Duty Manager wrote that my mother (according to her own account), was forced to travel to Gatwick and was put in a car against her will. First of all, my mother could not communicate with the various people involved, including the interpreter who was specifically brought in to assist. She came for a month, has enjoyed her stay and although we begged her to stay a bit longer, she decided that she wanted to go back.
3. There are many other inaccuracies and hurtful remarks in the report itself which I wouldn't like to refer to. I am sure that this is accessible to your good offices and I will leave the detail of what has been written for your own assessment. As one of your loyal customers, it saddens me to see the level of damage that some irresponsible staff (thankfully a minority) can do to harm the reputation and credibility of BA. Furthermore, these 'let downs' are felt no more so than at the front end of your business, where BA staff in Travel Shops such as your Leeds office, work so frantically to gain customers and bring in new business to your organisation. I have nothing but praise for the people I deal with at Leeds, who organise all my flights, hotel accommodation and even make my holiday arrangements. The service is friendly,

personalised, with a caring attitude, passionate staff and an immaculately professional approach.

Against this background however, are 'isolated' incidents such as the one I have decided to report, which unfortunately, because of the irresponsible and careless attitude of some BA staff, threaten to wipe out all the good work that everyone else does. I would like to continue having faith in BA, in its commitment to service excellence, its gentle and caring approach and the good value it provides to all of its passengers. After all, paying customers are the purpose of BA's existence, even if sometimes they are a bit difficult to deal with, such as the case of my mother.

By taking the decision to write to you directly, I felt that a candid account of what had happened on the 7th October in relation to flight BA6944, would alert you to some of the alarming cracks in your service provision process. I am therefore making a passionate plea to you and to the senior management team to investigate matters such as the one I am reporting and to take appropriate measures for preventing customer upsets from happening.

I hope that BA will bounce back to remain 'the World's favourite airline', despite the current business difficulties and the tense political climate. Some reassurance on your commitment to continue providing quality service to your customers will go along way to convincing me that what had happened was an isolated, sad and unfortunate incident which hopefully will not re-occur again. However the question of mis-information and quoting inaccuracies, threatens the credibility of BA's integrity, core values and guiding principles. This of course cannot be allowed to happen and no misuse of authority should be tolerated.
END

The British Airways Positive Response

To be fair to British Airways this matter was taken extremely seriously at the highest level and I have received a personal letter from Mr Rod Eddington who assured me of BAs commitment to dealing with the issue fairly and thoroughly and also pledging to recover the level of service and in particular vis-á-vie my mother's future travel. I have also received a letter from Mr John Patterson who was the Managing Director of GB Airways, the BA agent operating out of Gatwick and flying into Tunis. I have attached this letter as it demonstrates how BA at the time was committed to service recovery and has taken the matter so seriously.

BA honoured its commitment and when the time came for me to travel, with my mother out of Gatwick to Tunis she received all the necessary assistance and courtesy that BA staff gave her and she enjoyed the flight and had a very pleasant and memorable experience.

The Stigma that Lack of Apathy Causes

Ten years on I continue to ask myself several questions as to what prompted the duty manager at the time to exaggerate the facts and demonstrate such unnecessary hostility. What was there to be gained from tarnishing the image of a frail, elderly woman who could not even communicate properly? Why demonstrate such levels of apathy towards a customer even if they are difficult to deal with? Are British Airways' staffs not trained to handle such situations which I am sure occur on a frequent and regular basis?

I have continued to ask several questions and to describe precisely what emotions I have experienced I decided to put them together in Figure 14.

- Initially when I read the report from the duty manager I felt anger and hurt that a responsible person, representing BA, would exaggerate facts and produce an exaggerated account of an incident.

- I also felt frustrated by the fact that I was not able to challenge the content of the report and have a conversation with the duty manager herself.
- I felt disappointment in that the promise of the quality service was not honoured and that I had to suffer the consequences on behalf of my mother.

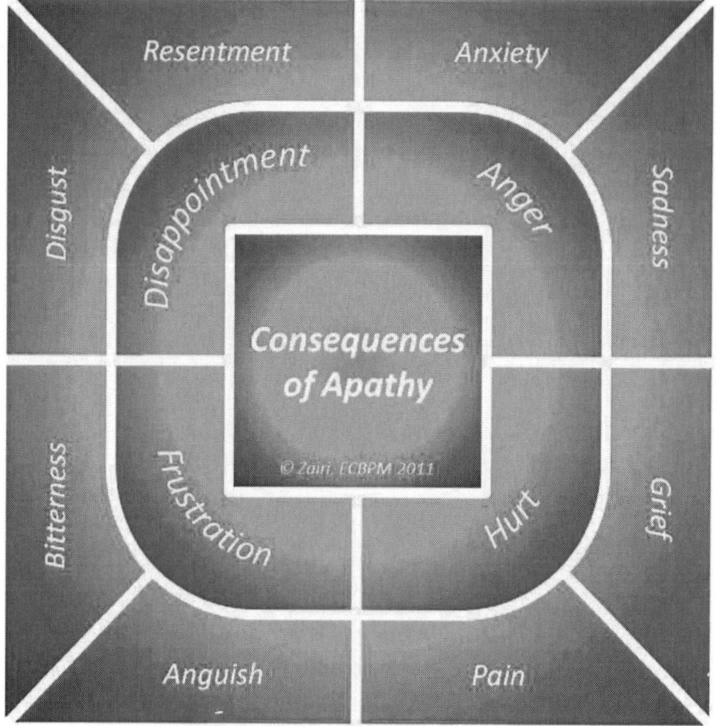

Figure 14: Consequences of Apathy

Over the years other emotions have been felt which include the following:

- Sadness at the unfortunate situation because the scars do not go away and this is felt even worse now that my mother is no longer with us.
- Anxiety about the fact that responsible people could inflict pain and cause grief due to their insensitivities, their carelessness, their apathy and their bias.

- The pain, anguish and resentment is perhaps a normal occurrence and with time that tends to subside and becomes irrelevant.
- The disgust and bitterness over the whole situation were not necessarily evident and particularly upon receipt of the positive letter from the leadership of British Airways this created a lot of reassurance and gave me confidence would have been dealt with properly and certainly gave me the confidence to trust BA and travel to Tunis with my mother and provide her with a pleasant and enjoyable, memorable travel experience. Certainly this was the case.

I wanted to define empathy through this personal experience and also I wanted to emphasise with every single incident that I have read in preparation of this manuscript. I know now that there could be some extremely isolated case of exaggerations and unfairness from people who complain but on the whole I feel for the customers, I know they are real and I empathise with them and I hope that this personal account will make every single person working with customers and responsible for delivering customer service to learn more about empathy and understand how people feel and how much hurt an incident can cause them and treat them fairly and professionally and to demonstrate understanding, compassion and positive helpfulness.

Our Ref: TR/MA10971/JP
14th November 2001

Professor M Zairi
18 Park Drive
Heaton
Bradford BD9 4DT

Dear Professor Zairi,

I thank you for your most informative letter of 12th October. I understand that British Airways are dealing with your concerns relating to the lack of assistance and the matter of delayed luggage. A copy of your communication has been passed to me as GB Airways operate flight BA6944 to Tunis under a commercial franchise agreement on behalf of British Airways.

We do try hard to ensure that our customers receive a high level of service at all times, and I was most concerned to learn that we have failed to meet your expectations in relation to the comments entered into the reservation of your Mother Mrs Zairis and I thank you for the opportunity to address your concerns.

As I am sure you will appreciate it is almost impossible to ascertain the exact sequence of events from the time Mrs Zairi checked in to that of her collection by your good self. However, we do investigate very thoroughly any complaints we receive and a full investigation into this issue has been conducted and where necessary the appropriate action taken.

I have read your account of events with some dismay and offer my unreserved apologies for the report that you feel contained inaccurate and hurtful comments. I do expect our staff to perform their duties in a courteous and efficient manner at all times, especially those performing a customer service role and can assure you that no offense was intended.

In view of the above it was kind of you to take the time to enlighten me regarding the positive aspects of your experiences with British Airways - a gesture that is greatly appreciated.

I fully understand that your faith has been somewhat shaken but I do firmly believe that this was indeed an isolated incident and I have every confidence that this experience will not be repeated.

Should GB Airways be your preferred choice for your Mothers travel on future occasion please do not hesitate to contact my Manager of Customer Relations - Tania Robinson and she will do all possible to ensure that Mrs Zairis journey is trouble free, as we all would wish.

Yours sincerely

John Patterson
Managing Director GB Airways

GB100141

operated by
GB AIRWAYS

The Beehive Gatwick Airport West Sussex RH6 0LA
Tel (Switchboard) 01293 664239 Direct Tel 01293 664
Direct Facsimile 01293 664

Registered Office as above Registered in England No. 2294109

Photography is an investigation of both the outer and the inner worlds. The first experiences with the camera involve looking at the world beyond the lens, trusting the instrument will 'capture' something 'seen.' The terms shoot and take are not accidental; they represent an attitude of conquest and appropriation. Only when the photographer grows into perception and creative impulse does the term make define a condition of empathy between the external and the internal events.

Ansel Adams

Chapter 4: Empathy – The Customer's Plight

Introduction

Since the inception of total quality management organisations all over the world have been striving to create better focus on their customers, to provide them with high quality products and services, to develop meaningful relationships with them and to ensure that they maintain high retention rates through proactive strategies and value adding propositions that will continue to lure customers towards them and generate high levels of satisfaction and loyalty. As a result of the growth in quality uptake and the belief that by focussing on quality improvement organisational outcomes in terms of customer satisfaction and competitive capabilities have been verified, validated and accepted as the norm in all the industry sectors be it the public or private sectors.

Over the last five or six decades we have therefore seen significant improvements in quality to almost perfection in most of the industry sectors. It is very rare nowadays to speak about the challenges that product quality or service quality raise in organisations. Equipped with a thorough understanding of the philosophy of total quality management and using existing knowledge and competencies in terms of driving quality improvement and having access to a wide variety of tools and techniques that can generate meaningful solutions, most organisations have learnt how to deal with defects, how to recover services and how to ensure consistency, reliability and generate dependability vis á vie their customers. So, what is the issue therefore if quality did matter and does matter and the diligence and discipline of organisational systems in driving in an optimum manner their value chains in order not to upset their customers can be verified everywhere ?

It is true that whilst quality has improved and is considered to be a prerequisite for modern competitiveness a customer matter may not necessarily have been dealt with in the same manner. Organisations tend to devote a significant proportion of their energies and efforts in fool proofing quality of their products and services. Furthermore, they have mastered the art of managing complaints and dealing with deficiencies and trying to maintain relationships with their customers through a recovery mechanism. The measurement of the customer has in recent years raised loads of questions.

1. Does the measurement of deficiency in terms of logging in complaints and dealing with them automatically lead to customer satisfaction and customer loyalty?
2. Is the measurement of customer satisfaction through service questionnaires in a retrospective manner an indication that customers are really happy and will demonstrate their loyalty?
3. Is having the front end processes such as a CRM system a guarantee that real customer relationships can develop and high levels of customer retention can follow?
4. Are the measurement tools being currently utilised meaningful enough to capture what the customer really feels and whether they are committed to a long term relationship or not?

To answer all of these questions there has to be return to some fundamental considerations that can address what is important to the customer and how the customer really feels.

The Customer Is Real

In order to appreciate the psychological and emotional feelings of customers and how they feel, how they consider their relationship with their suppliers in the form of providers of goods and services the voice of the customer has to be captured in the first instance and analysed much deeper than hitherto has been the case. All organisations around the world have immense amounts of information in the form of letters of complaints from their customers. The question really is the extent to which due consideration is given to how the customer really feels or whether the customer does really exist?

- The process of complaint handling is a mechanical approach for tracking deficiencies in the provision of products and/or services and investigating whether the provider organisation is at fault or not.

- In the event that a drop in the standard of service quality has been demonstrated, the provider organisation uses various means available in terms of replacement or warranties.
- It is rarely the case that provider organisations study the deep effect that their failures have had on their customers from the point of view of emotional or psychological implications.
- The obsession in the provider organisations therefore is to maintain quality standards that they believe in and they have invested in creating in the first place. The commitment from top management is to ensure that there is zero deviation from those standards of quality that they have established in their organisations.
- There is a widely applied supposition that the process of recovering the service or correcting errors in the quality system through replacement of goods or services or giving the customer a recompense in the form of warranty claims is sufficient enough to lead the customers to be satisfied and therefore to become loyal.

The whole purpose of this manuscript is to ensure that the discussion does not centre around quality as a key driver for service excellence or for impacting on customer satisfaction. This debate has been thoroughly considered and does not need to be put under any further scrutiny. It is accepted that quality does matter and is the core engine for value creation and for delivering economic and competitive benefits to organisations. It is also accepted that quality is the driver for customer satisfaction and a thorough and systematic discipline that is used on a daily basis to generate value to customers will ensure that trust in the delivery process can be established and therefore creating meaningful relationships that can lead to loyalty and retention. What is at stake however is the lack of consideration of the customer from the point of view of the emotional and psychological effect that take place if quality fails and if provider organisations do not use empathy in a meaningful manner.

In order to really appreciate that the customer is real and to highlight the level of anger, frustration, anguish, despair, disappointment and disillusionment that takes place a thorough examination of personal accounts on what has happened to them (customers) has taken place. Over 5,000 complaints have been studied in order to capture the inner feelings and disappointments of customers in the light of them being let down and the consequences that they had to endure as a result of being let down and not receiving what they were expecting from their providers.

The following sections will present firsthand accounts of customers in different parts of the world and representing various key sectors of industry.

Customer Bad Experiences – Hotel And Hospitality Sector

Incident 1: The story of a couple who booked into a hotel and found the owners to be extremely rude, aggressive and were not capable of running a hotel. This booking was for an overnight stay and on arrival they were shown a room without any private facilities, upon complaining they were told that this is their problem and not the hoteliers. This was followed by other let downs where at the dinner they had to wait 45 minutes for a meal. Upon complaining they were told they were trouble makers and if they were not happy they could leave. Eventually they put up with an inedible meal and retired to their room.

Reaction 1: The hoteliers were rude, aggressive and unhelpful. We could understand if we had been aggressive but this was not the case. This is not a place to go to and stay in. There is absolutely nothing to recommend it and it is not a cheap holiday option.

Incident 2: The case of a couple who needed to have an overnight stay to enable them to go to Stansted Airport early in the morning. They booked a room only to find it was absolutely disgusting. Although the bed had fresh bedding the shower and hand basin did not look as though they had been cleaned for months. They were so unhappy that they spent time ringing around on their mobile to try and find alternative accommodation without success. They did not shower or wash and just went to sleep in the room. In the morning they left without having breakfast because they guessed that the kitchen would not be clean. Their experience was exacepated by the fact that the main road was busy and this did not help their quality of sleep. So overall, they had no evening meal, no decent place to wash and there was no drinking water in the room. It was one of the dirtiest places they have ever visited and they believe that it should not have even one star never mind three.

Reaction 2: This hotel needs to be removed from the listing.

Incident 3: This relates to a bad experience that was ignored by the manager owner of a hotel. There was disappointment in the room where the guests stayed. There was no telephone or telephone book in the room, the air conditioning was not plugged in and did not work because it needed an extension cable. The guests had to buy a fan which they plugged into the extension cable to keep the room cool. There was no running water in the bathroom sink, just a trickle and sometimes only a drip. There was a light bulb broken in the lamp near the TV which was also replaced by the guests using one from the bathroom, allowing them to see at night. The lamp had to be plugged into the extension lead to work properly. The pillow case on the second bed had blood on it that did not belong to either of the guests. They were worried by the end whether or not the sheets were clean. As they were tired and it was late at night they did not check on the cleanliness because they just needed to sleep.

Reaction 3: Huge disappointment for being ignored by the manager owner of the hotel who did nothing about the situation, the only thing done was to fire the maid. The guests were never so disappointed in their lives.

Incident 4: The guest spent a night at a hotel near Gatwick; he had regularly used hotels for business and normally used this particular hotel. The guest checked in the room at 4.30pm and then went to a meeting in a nearby hotel. After finishing the meeting he arrived back to his room at 10.30pm where he went straight to bed. After undressing and washing looked on the floor and nearly stepped on a cockroach, it was 11pm by that time. He tried three times between 11pm and 11.15pm to reach reception via the telephone, there was no answer. So he dressed and went down to personally inform them that he was not looking forward to spending a night with the creature. The manager did not even bother to see him, just informed the girl on reception that there was nothing they could do and no other rooms in the hotel were available, they only offered him a free drink. He returned to the room and decided that he would not be able to sleep so he waited in the bathroom for the cockroach to reappear and then caught it. He called the reception and the same girl came up and took one look at the bug and the guest was moved to another room within 10 minutes with a lot of apologising along the way. This was not the girls fault and it was the manager who was totally to blame for not listening.

Reaction 4: I do not know why I was not believed, I certainly do not make a habit of lying (unlike the hotel manager about there being no other rooms available) and I finally got to bed at midnight which was, for me, late and as a consequence I was extremely tired the following day in the meetings I had to attend. The inconvenience this has caused me today and last night was unacceptable.

Incident 5: This is an incident at a hotel in Tunisia. Supposedly being a four star hotel but according to the guests concerned they would not even rate it as one star. It was an all inclusive restaurant which had flies with the meals. The room was full of a whole colony of flies. The flies would sit on the plate; the salads were put out two hours before the restaurant opened. No covers, so basically the flies had already had their feast on the food before they were served. The rooms were very dirty. The hotel's staff were not English speaking so the guests felt isolated. This was supposed to be their honeymoon.

The entertainment was nonexistent unless you spoke a different language.

Reaction 5: The guests were extremely disappointed and would never stay at this hotel again.

Incident 6: This is the experience for a family 30 year reunion. They decided to stay at a hotel where all the family members would congregate. They rented 50 rooms for either three or four consecutive nights. The big disappointment was due to the following issues:

- Blood stained linen;
- Dirty floors;
- Full trash cans - never emptied;
- Total reckless regard for the do not disturb sign;
- Bad attitude and communication problems of the hotel personnel.

Reaction 6: This was a huge disappointment and to say we were disappointed is a severe understatement.

Incident 7: A family of six booked three rooms with en-suite facilities at a hotel. The hotel was scruffy; the outside had a heap of rubbish in the car park. The front access was full of cigarette butts that had obviously been there since the smoking ban, a brush and pan to sweep them up would be an idea. There was no reception area, you walked in to the bar and to go behind to bar to access the poorly lit, filthy staircase, there were loads of stairs and passages that went everywhere, eventually to the bedrooms. The rooms were filthy, dusty, dirty, the drawers full of goodness knows what, the ventilation in the en-suite was absolutely clogged up with dust and grim. You could hardly sit down on the loo. Below the bedrooms was a restaurant with a ventilation shaft which drew all the smells straight into the bedrooms. We complained to the staff first thing in the morning, they shrugged and said they were new. When we came back that night the only room that had the beds made and the sink cleaned, obviously due to many complaints, was ours.

Reaction 7: Extremely disappointed.

Incident 8: A couple booked a hotel via the internet. The information received told them the hotel has recently refurbished to a very high standard. The first room had filthy curtains and all shredded around the bottom, the bed spreads were absolutely disgusting and dirty, the shower worked like a dripping tap. They complained immediately by informing the receptionist about the recent refurbishment, mentioning that the information provided to them immediately after the booking confirmation. The receptionist shrugged her shoulders and offered them another room which was marginally better, except that the wall light was hanging from the wall onto the headboard, the telephone table was broken. Having returned to their homes and checking the hotel web site they noticed that all the other complaints were from people from overseas.

Reaction 8: It made one feel ashamed to be British. We are very surprised the place has not been condemned as not fit for purpose.

Incident 9: This is an account from an experience in a hotel in Florence, Italy. The experience was described as horrible. The party concerned were bitten by bed bugs with the classic trail of bites, a girl in the group develop a huge allergic blister from one on her foot. There was dried blood on the sheets and the girl on the front desk was extremely rude and put out all the time.

Reaction 9: Please let people know this is an awful place to stay in Florence. The floors were so dirty too, if you walked with bare feet they were black within minutes.

Incident 10: The people concerned were in a five star hotel which they booked for the second time. They did so because they enjoyed their stay the first time. To their surprise the second experience was not so exciting. The room was hardly ever cleaned, the domestic just closed the terrace door straightened up the bedding and handed out grey towels. These towels and the bathrobes should have been white. If they asked for fresh towels the old ones are folded nicely and placed back in the bathroom. The room smelt damp at all times. The air conditioning was not working and when reported to the reception they were told to close the terrace door. When on the beach the staff would run drinks around the guests, the gazebos and sun beds that they had been provided with were some uncomfortable and the staff concerned looked for bribery in order to provide the facilities.

Reaction 10: Please take our advice and do not book this hotel. Although people should make up their own minds regarding where to stay. Most of the people that we met and talked to said they would never return. We will not recommend it to anybody. We have been very disappointed.

Incident 11: The complainants made the reservation of two suites. They called a few days afterwards to ascertain if they could have adjoining rooms with the originally requested king beds. They were given adjoining rooms for smokers and the staff told them they would de-smoke the rooms. They arrived in the hotel, the rooms smelt horrible, the pillows, bedspreads, carpets, curtains and closets. They requested everything changed that the hotel was willing to change. They washed the bedspread; they did not have any more pillows. One of the ironing boards and all the clothing smelt and when they left for home every item of clothing that was unpacked, whether it was worn or not, had to be sent to the cleaners because they smelt of cigarette smoke. In addition to these problems the carpets were dirty; the TV had tons of nicotine on it. Everything was washed with soap; the cloth cylinder chair was dirty and showing more than normal wear and tear.

Reaction 11: We all have allergy problems and this stay made this problem worse.

Incident 12: The guests checked in a hotel and during the whole night they could not sleep well. They felt that there was something biting them. Never had this experience before so they thought it was just mosquitoes. Until the early hours of the morning they found so many small black bugs on the sheet and the pillow. There were more than 100 bites on the husband's arms, legs, neck and the back and also all over the body. They were able to kill a few of them and at that time they did not even know they were bed bugs. In the morning they went to the front desk to complain about this the lady said they had to wait until the manager turns up. So they waited for an hour then the manager called the receptionist to say he would be late because of traffic. They were asked to fill out a form and she confirmed that it would be passed onto the manager. She said the manager would call. Because they had to catch a cruise ship they left without seeing the manager. On return from their cruise they saw the manager who said he never got any complaint form, he insisted that they should have a doctor's letter to prove it was bed bugs and he said he would not do anything to solve the problem.

Reaction 12: This is really ridiculous and we have never seen such bad customer service before. We guessed from the beginning they already knew that it was bed bugs but they just wanted the thing to be ignored. This is our worst travel experience and we felt so upset. We still have the pictures of the bites. Until now the bites are still there and it still feels uncomfortable. After we got back home we sent an email to the hotel manager until today we did not receive an acknowledgment of our email and certainly no answer. This hotel has a very bad reputation and we will publish our bad experience and let people know never to go there.

Incident 13: An experience where the guests found the housekeeping deplorable. When they arrived at the hotel the lobby was full of people waiting to check in. The rooms were not ready for some and when they got to the room, it had not been cleaned. They spoke to house cleaning staff but they could not speak English. Having complained about their experiences they did not get a clear answer.

Reaction 13: We have complained and no-one did anything about our plight. Needless to say we won't recommend this hotel and/or stay here again.

Incident 14: Experience of guests who booked a two star room on the internet and paid 150USD for the two nights. Upon arrival there was no reservation so the hotel charged them 100USD for the room for two nights. They contacted the agency that booked them the rooms on the internet three times by phone and several times through email and they are still out 250USD for a bad experience.

Reaction 14: They are still calling but to no avail so far. The hotel swears they did not charge us. We will never use the on-line agency again and we want to get the word out there so that others are not ripped off as we were.

Incident 15: A family travelled with aged, disabled parents. They were informed that the hotel does not serve alcohol. If there is a need for alcohol the hotels next door will be able to provide them with this. The hotel did not provide them with anything and they had to make their own beds, no-one was available. There were no cooked meals so everybody had salad; there were only hot drinks in the rooms. There was no entertainment and for the remainder of the week the family made up games in the evening. There was no other normal entertainment which as expected would be in the form of singing, dancing or even a game of bingo that would be the norm. The father, aged 80, and physically disabled from polio as a child became ill after struggling with a disabled shower that had no wall grips to hold onto. His family heard him scream and become upset. His wife, also disabled, assisted him to walk gingerly with walking sticks. The family paid in full and left a day early.

Reaction 15: The hotel staff offered to change the mattresses but these were so uncomfortable for some. The sun lounge which should be a place to enjoy, watching passers-by in the sunshine, had flies hanging above our heads where no-one had cleaned the area. The cushions on the wicker furniture were worn away and threadbare.

The hotel lift was so smelly that we tried to avoid it as much as possible. The whole building was tired and drab and so boring. Yet proudly three AA stars are prominently displayed on the outer walls overlooking the car park. We feel that the hotel management should have informed us about the restrictions they have in their licensing arrangements and certainly an assessment of the disabled facility is without doubt essential. It is also important that health and safety officers should make a visit.

Incident 16: The guests checked in a hotel in Palm Springs after reading in the Los Angeles Daily News the following quote: "we redefine luxury as it exists, taking the dissonance and flair of arrogance out of it". This was a quote from the General Manager of the hotel concerned. He also said "we deliver the unexpected." We were charged 400USD for one nights stay, even though we cancelled in advance. When we wrote to the General Manager he argued that the hotel has a seven day cancellation policy. Although we had medical documentation to justify the need to cancel the General Manager still refused to acknowledge this.

Reaction 16: I would say this is not only arrogant, but downright thievery and the General Managers ability to deliver the unexpected is accurate as he charged our credit card for a stay we didn't even make. The General Manager is in a business that should provide high quality customer service in an effort to establish high marks for his property retail loyal customers, but instead, his obvious arrogance demonstrates his ignorance of good customer service and potential repeat business.

Incident 17: This experience at a hotel was so bad that the complainants asked for their money back and drove three hours to get home. They felt that they would rather do that than stay there, having had to endure the inconvenience that follows: this experience, which was absolutely awful, started with them being taken to the basement where the room was. The toilets and bathrooms (which were communal) were dirty, mouldy and had no locks on them. The floor was all coming up, electric sockets were hanging off the wall, there was dirty laundry and rubbish bags piled all over the place, there were holes in the wall, the communal kitchens (for people who stay longer than a night), were thick with dirt and the whole place stunk like it had gone off. It was dingy and horrible. The guests went to reception and asked for their money back only to be told that as they had already paid and a receipt had been issued they would not give a refund. After several arguments and with the threat of calling the police, trading standards and environmental health they were told that they would get their money back.

Reaction 17: In our opinion this hotel should be closed down as we would hate for anyone to have to stay in such a hovel.

Incident 18: A parent and their son stayed four days and three nights at a hotel. They discovered black coloured markings on the bed sheets. They also noticed similar markings the morning prior. Initially they thought it could have been due to a small cut that happened the day before. To their horror they discovered small bugs on the pillowcase and on the sheets. The larger bug was smashed on the pillow which resulted in a large blood smear; at this point they pulled the sheets to discover other bugs. The mother commanded her son to get out of the bed, when his sheets were pulled back she discovered bugs in his bed. So immediately she called the front desk who sent housekeeping and the maintenance personnel to the room. The housekeeping manager and the maintenance person moved the son to another room. The mother called to speak to the hotel manager and was told he could not be reached. She asked if the hotel had a policy in place to deal with bed bugs. The hotel manager called to apologise and mentioned that the hotel never had this problem before and that he would have to investigate before confirming the presence of bed bugs in their room.

Reaction 18: This horrific experience led the mother to write a letter to the Florida Department of Health to investigate this matter and to ensure that this is prevented in the future.

Incident 19: This is the experience of a family who had a function. After the function everybody was tired and went to sleep. When they arrived at the hotel the room was open, the bed and linen stripped from the room and the husbands clean shirt was in the trash can. The maid was cleaning the room and they told her they didn't check out yet and asked her what she was doing. Having asked reception they were told that the maid had knocked at the door and since she did not get an answer she assumed that they had checked out. By the time the problem was solved it was almost time to check out. They asked for an extra hour for the inconvenience and were told they could only have half an hour. They wouldn't put the linens back on the bed or give clean, new towels. They went home to avoid a scene and made their complaint with the hotels customer service department. When they arrived home to their horror they were contacted by the hotel accusing them of taking all the towels and linens. They contacted customer services back and they were also told that they stole shelves out of the mini fridge.

Reaction 19: We had a valid complaint, we rented that room until 11am and they should not have sent the maid to clean it. They tried to accuse us of stealing towels and later changed it to shelves from the mini fridge before they realised that it is the maid who stripped the place. So we feel violated, robbed, slandered, lied to and told our freedom of speech is why they don't care and what the hotel does to us. Rude staff and they can lie, steal and slander guests and you can't do a thing about it.

Incident 20: Guest was staying at a hotel when he arrived he was embarrassed. He was harassed by the security personnel; he was followed to the elevator and questioned in front of other guests as to why he was in the hotel. He was asked for his ID and prevented from going upstairs to his room. This was after it had been established that he was a guest there. He was also denied getting a cab until several other guests who came after him had been accommodated. The General Manager of the hotel was there when the two security guards and the desk clerk were insulting him and he did nothing. The same thing happened last year when he was staying there. He has written letters to their corporate offices but all they did is refer the matter back to the General Manager of the hotel.

Reaction 20: The guest has suffered extreme embarrassment and humiliation. Guests at the hotel have witnessed him being followed and questioned by security, when he complained to the security supervisor the guard stood back and laughed at him. He is paranoid when he has to leave his hotel room and paranoid when he returns. Every time he goes into the lobby on his way out of the hotel he is given a hard time by one employee or another. He is extremely depressed about this. His whole trip has been ruined. He can't concentrate on his work, worrying about what is going to happen next. He is a victim of racial profiling.

Incident 21: A family has booked a two day stay at this hotel. Upon arrival they noticed right away how dirty the entrance was. The desk employee was friendly at first and told them they could not get a king/suite room because they booked the room using a point system. So they went to their king size room thinking they could only get a bed in there for their son. To begin with the room was not very clean and too small for a single bed. They called the manager and he promised to try and do something about it. After 45 minutes they went downstairs and the receptionist said they had organised an additional room for them. After switching rooms they noticed the air conditioning was not working correctly. From there on everything went downhill, the first morning for breakfast the food was not very good. The room was not cleaned the first night although they put the sign on the door. The shower curtains had mould on them.

Reaction 21: Extremely disappointed and we will not stay there again.

Incident 22: The guest forgot his back pack containing work papers and camera in its case at the hotel where they stayed whilst attending a meeting sponsored by one of the Federal Agencies and he stayed at one of the rooms especially booked for attendees of the meeting. When he first called to determine where his belongings were and whether they had been handed in to reception was told his name was not on the records. Eventually they found a record which said the belongings were in security including the camera. They would ship them. When the bag arrived the camera case was in the back pack but not the camera, batteries, instruction materials and battery charger. The digital camera still had stored in it the photos of his 21st wedding anniversary. They accused him of lying and that he wanted another camera. He made a police report and then worked with the claims department. The claims department did say that they were not liable and reported that their records indicated that the back pack had not been handed in for several hours; they would not release their records sighting propriety information. The camera case still contained his business card but the hotel made no effort to contact him. They claimed that all had been secure in the security office and that he must have had his camera and that it could not have been stolen. With assistance and continuing efforts the hotel continued to claim no liability. He has since purchased a new camera but had the emotional loss of the 21st wedding anniversary photos which cannot be replaced. He asked for an expense paid vacation to replace the lost photos but they said they will cover the camera only. They did not mention that the instruction materials, batteries, memory card, battery charger were also stolen.

Reaction 22: I believe that the hotel management is negligent and not being truthful nor transparent and that their actions encouraged theft by their employees. I am gravely upset and disappointed. I cannot afford to place my camera, not committing a scam for them to replace it as suggested by their insurance agent. This is insulting. I have never been treated so shoddily by a hotel establishment.

Incident 23: Guest stayed at a hotel for one night. He started to notice a red mark on his wrist, he just figured it was a bug bite and not a big deal until it started to spread up his arm. Over the week it spread to other parts of his body. Over the following week he noticed it had started to spread to his legs, stomach and back. He went back to the Doctor who told him he had scabies. They asked if he had travelled recently or stayed in a hotel. The only place he had stayed in the last month was the hotel in question. The incident started the day after he spent the night there.

Reaction 23: I am a very clean individual and to have this happen was just simply disgusting and horrifying. I was not allowed to go to work because I was told I was heavily contagious. I needed to treat myself with insecticides to get rid of the mites living under my skin. I lost a days' work (unpaid) and have monstrous red bumps and streaks all over my body. I had to pay for a Doctor's visit and medication. I was left with enormous spots, streaks, and welts on my entire body. I find it hard to concentrate at work because I am so itchy.

Customer Bad Experiences – Banking Sector

Incident 1: A customer went to his bank about a credit card finance charge having paid all the charges he wanted to find out why he was being charged excessively. He was upset because the company told him that the charges were legitimate. He asked the customer service representative if she was sure about that and she said yes.

Reaction 1: I think the bank may not be fair. They are driven by making money from their customers.

Incident 2: Customer deposited 20,000 dollars into his bank account. The limit on this bank account was 25,000 dollars. The bank needed to verify the cheque and so they did. However, they put a hold on the cheque, weeks passed by and the cheque was still pending in the bank account. Customer called the bank and he was told that the cheque was still on hold. In the meantime the new account established was closed and the bank would not justify why that happened. To his shock and horror not only his bank account gets closed but also that of his sisters, brothers and wife's account were also closed. The bank argued that all of these bank accounts were fake and that the information that was sent was not real and it was forged. On top of this they told the customer that the account was not open under his name or social security number. The enquiry they pulled was under his credit report. This was a frustrating experience and he is still fighting this nonsense.

Reaction 2: My accounts are closed as are my brothers, sisters and their spouses. The bank has given no kind of reason for the accounts being closed except that is a fraud account.

Incident 3: Customer purchased a pool with his credit account. He received notice that the interest rate on the revolving credit accounts was increasing from 13.99% to 24.99%. If he wanted to avoid the increase in the interest rate he had to send written notification. This would close the account and maintain the lower interest rate and the same monthly payments. This will prevent the bank from charging anything else on his account. At some stage in the future he will send the written notice with a desire to opt out of the rate increase. The next three payments had the higher interest rate. After repeated calls to the bank he received apologies and the bank said that the rate will be lowered and the extra interest credited to his account but nothing has changed.

Reaction 3: My wife has been very distressed over this. Money is very tight right now anyway the extra (no matter how seemingly small) has an effect on our finances. I have had to dedicate hours to this problem – that should never have happened and at worse should have taken the bank 30 seconds to correct in their system. I can't help but wonder how many thousands of people this has happened to. How many just gave up and are now paying the higher rate and how much money is the bank making from this oversight.

Incident 4: The customer wanted a fax confirmation that his loans are on deferment to complete a mortgage application. This was supposed to be a very simple request which the bank refuses to fulfil. They constantly lie to pacify him and their customer service supervisors are not empowered to help resolve this simple complaint. Having contacted the bank he was told that this request would take 24 – 48 hours to send the fax. When no fax had arrived he contacted the bank again and escalated the issue to a supervisor, who said he would rush the request and it will go out immediately. Since this did not happen he spoke to another supervisor who repeated that the time frame was confirmed and they would rush it to him.

Reaction 4: I am at my wits end with this; none of the supervisors will permit me to talk to a manager or anyone higher than their positions. They constantly contradict each other regarding whether they (or anyone) can contact the letter writing unit and they refused to escalate my complaint to their superiors. If I had known how bad their customer service is I would have requested a different lender. It has taken them eight days so far to send the fax and if I ever receive it, it will have been the longest fax in the history of mankind. I have made an offer on a house and must get this paperwork in to the lender to approve the mortgage. This is the one piece that is holding back the process. If I do not close in the timely fashion I will lose this house and potentially the deposit which I have already paid not to mention the fees for the inspection and mortgage application.

Incident 5: A customer has been trying to add information to her card so she can pay the bills online. Her frustration is the added extra security measures for this process. The first time she tried to add the information she forgot her security code so she called the customer service and went through a horrendous process to get a new security number. Once the code has been changed which was not an easy task she was still unable to add information so that she can pay her bills electronically. So she went through a painful process of calling the bank again in order to change the security number which she did. Then they transferred her to another customer service representative who was supposed to help her add the additional information and details. The representative told her that they could not help add the additional information online. This was because she was blocked in again from adding the additional information to her card. So they asked her to wait an additional 24 hours.

Reaction 5: This is the most ridiculous process I have encountered in a long time. Online account access is supposed to make my life easier yet for the last week I have had nothing but aggravation. Suffice to say I am doing my best to open a credit card with another bank so that I can transfer my balances. An incredible amount of time was wasted. Time is money particularly for me since I get paid by the hour. We won't even discuss the frustration and aggravation that was caused by this debacle.

Incident 6: Customer was a victim of having his identity stolen and over 7000 dollars in charges placed on his card and he got very little help from the bank. He had to ask for a list of all the fraudulent charges. Over a period of a month he called several times to have the charges sent to him in order to look them over and mark the ones that were not applicable. He never received the list and was a nervous wreck forced to make exorbitant payments he could not afford and no one seemed to care at all. When finally he received the mess cleared up he was left with a higher balance. The bank had all these commercials and advertisements on the TV about someone having someone else's voice and personality and how they bought all kinds of things the person on the commercial never would. I had been a customer of the bank since 1969 and never made a habit of making large purchases.

Reaction 6: The bank has put me into a very nerve wrecking position and not in a very good state. Do I have a way of making the bank pay for their neglect and mistreatment? I was a very nice person until this happened then everyone acted like I was a real cheat. I had never missed a payment and my record was impeccable and they know it.

Incident 7: The customer paid his last payment on a truck loan. Since then he has been called by the collectors who faxed him a copy of the cancelled cheque three times. On calling back to confirm receipt he was told it was illegible and that he needed to go to the branch. He was told he made some errors in filling in the cheques which led to the cheques being lost. He was irritated by the fact that the bank did not know how to process their cheques and could not research payment issues. They were unable to track the payments and he was treated with condescending tones and insults about writing cheques.

Reaction 7: I am currently being reported negatively to the credit bureau – in error. I lost a home improvement loan for gutters as a result. After the third harassment in a row on the last call to the bank I had to take nitro-glycerine for my heart.

Incident 8: Customer has been trying to contact his branch which supposedly is meant to have working hours from 7am. – 7pm. but no-one seems to be taking their calls. They have been trying to work payment arrangements and have been constantly harassed by the branch.

Reaction 8: I have high blood pressure and these threatening phone calls have made me quite ill.

Incident 9: A complainant applied for a student loan and was told it would take 3-5 working days to receive acceptance of the loan. Having not heard anything after three weeks he contacted the bank but got no answer. Eventually he spoke to someone who told him they did not receive the fax that he was supposed to send four days prior to the application being considered. He was asked to fax it again, which he did. He was also asked to contact the supervisor with no reason given. Eventually when he spoke to the supervisor he was very rude and repeated this same scenario about the fax not having been sent. He sent the fax and the bank still claimed that had not received it, so he was transferred to a manager. At this time he was frustrated and upset because his college term was due to start in two days and he still did not have the money. The bank told him there were processes involved and that it was going to take another week before he receives his money. He explained that he had already waited several weeks and that he needed the money before his college term commenced. He also explained that without the money he could not register for his classes and therefore could not go to college. He was told he will get the money in 3-5 working days and eventually his father had to intervene to give him his mortgage payment to pay for tuition. He still did not receive his loan or any word from the bank about progress. He has no idea when he will be receiving it, now he has a debt of 1700 dollars because of the banks negligence. If he does not get his money shortly his father risks losing his house.

Reaction 9: Very frustrated and very upset about the humiliating treatment.

Incident 10: Customer asked for payment deferral and the bank confirmed that they would give it to him. He even received the paperwork and was asked to fax back the forms once filled in. The bank told him that having received the paperwork the deferral would be approved but he needed to fax the form with his signature on it, which he did within 24 hours. Two months later he was showing as past due and therefore the confirmation was not confirmed. Having phoned the bank he was told that they did not have a record of a deferral and that his payments were due and if he did not settle promptly the case would be turned over to the credit bureau. He faxed the information again but this time to a different number followed by a phone call to a supervisor who could follow up with the case.

Reaction 10: This has caused me tremendous stress and frustration mainly because trying to communicate with the bank is like next to impossible.

Incident 11: Customer went to close his bank account. The manager wanted to know why he wished to close the account. He explained that he was tired of paying a 10 dollars service fee for months because he did not maintain an average balance of 4000 dollars in the account. The bank manager during the whole conversation insisted that it was the customer's fault that led to the situation. First by not following up with by contacting somebody at the bank to find a better suited account and he ignored advice received via a telephone call to move to a better account type.

Reaction 11: Regardless of my reasons I found this manager's attitude and approach to me to be offensive, aggressive and rude. The very reason I wanted to leave the bank. I understand in most cases they are supposed to make a modest attempt to change a person's mind from closing an account. But this was just arrogant and rude. Although I was extremely frustrated for a few hours I am just happy that I am no longer a customer of this bank.

Incident 12: Customer went online to pay for an amount due which was applied after midnight and he mistakenly assumed that the statement date referred to the month he received the bill in. He found out that you can only pay the balance of the statement online and nothing exceeding that amount so as to pay any additional amounts that have accrued since. He has to wait 3 business days in order to make another payment. He raised the issue with a supervisor by saying since the technology available should allow him to make more payments without the silly restrictions. He was told that he can only pay the balance by waiting until the next statement he receives which meant that he would never clear the backlog of payments.

Reaction 12: I have never encountered such imbeciles and robotoids in my entire life. I have my mortgage with them and I will be paying that off very soon. After which I will write a scathing letter to the President of the bank and present the horrific dealings with them. I would also make sure I will use my word of mouth advertising to make sure no-one else is taken in by this monster bank.

Incident 13: A couple opened a cheque and saving account. The savings were set up for the future. A few months after one of them lost their job and were laid off so they had to do loads of transferring of funds between the two accounts the bank converted their saving account into a cheque current account but did not tell them they removed the future savings facility. They were charged 350 dollars for all the draft fees even though there was money in the other current account.

Reaction 13: Because of this I cannot afford to pay day care this week for my two children, more than likely I will lose the job I have currently because of the other bills we have to pay. What is worse is my husband works for the bank.

Incident 14: Customer who is the step-father of the complainant received a dividend from a company he is associated with. He receives regularly an amount that he deposits in his account in good faith. He went to the bank when he could not use his ATM card and was told to wait until the next day because the full details were not available. After that he was told that the cheque he tried to deposit was fraudulent and he is unwelcome to do business with the bank. The funny thing is that his family's trust is through the bank and he has to receive funds for that.

Reaction 14: It sickened me because he is an elderly man and just received a loan which is supposed to be sent to his account. He cannot pay for the home he put a deposit for because he cannot have the loan deposited into the account and he may lose it. It was embarrassing because he did not know the cheque was fraudulent if that is truly the case. It could have caused him a heart attack from the severe stress that he is suffering from. It is unbelievable they could do this to an elderly man.

Incident 15: A customer has just recently opened an account at a bank. He wanted a paperless account so he opened an online account. This was supposed to direct deposits and transfers. First he was given the wrong routing number and his payroll cheque was lost, in limbo immediately after that. He had to get a new cheque from his employer. Having deposited the amount again he was told that the money would be available at a specific time. He checked his balance as told and it was still negative. He immediately called customer service and they told him the funds were on hold. He went to the branch where he made the deposit and he was told that his account was put on hold due to suspension. He could not get a straight answer and the customer service representative was very nonchalant and rude. He was assured that the money would be available at a specific time; needless to say there was no deposit as told.

Reaction 15: I was distraught at this point because my hard earned money is being held without any real reason. I called customer service again and spoke to somebody who implied that the money that had been deposited was somehow bogus and proceeded to interrogate me as to where the money came from. I was left feeling like a liar and a thief, I then spoke to a supervisor who said that they were verifying the funds and in the meantime the amount would be held by the bank. I have bills that are outstanding that are not being paid due to this and the bank said they would send an apology letter to the bill collectors. As of today there is no assurance that my money will ever be released to me and I am beyond devastated. I have my receipt for the deposit made but it means nothing because the bank will not even acknowledge it. I am physically sick and emotionally crippled because of this.

Incident 16: Customer opened a small business account at a bank. He was unaware that his previous bank did not clear a dispute he had with them. He made a cash deposit of 1000 dollars to the new bank, which was accepted. The teller said he had to call customer service, which he did. He was informed that his account had been closed due to an alert (which was an error) from their system which posts messages regarding problem accounts to all banking institutions. Having spoken to three different customer service representatives to ask why they had accepted his 1000 dollars cheque in the first place and whether he could go back to retrieve the amount, they rudely told him no and that he had to wait 15 days after the account was officially closed to receive a cheque from the bank. In the meantime his office rent cheque will be returned.

Reaction 16: I am a one person business and cannot afford to lose 1000 dollars. But I am missing my money; I am risking my relationship with my office landlord. I was never treated so rudely in my life by all three representatives. I was treated like a common criminal and by the way my previous bank admitted their error and will now clear my business name out of their system. I also have to come up with the money for my office rent from somewhere as the silly bank has my money. A caution everyone not to open a small business account with this bank, they are the most difficult, rude, corrupt organisation I have ever dealt with.

Incident 17: A couple had a joint account, they don't make any purchases on the debit card, nor do they write any cheques. They prefer to withdraw money from the ATM and use cash. The husband has direct deposits set up through his employer and faithfully every Wednesday night the money enters the account but is only accessible the following day. There have been times when the automated machine would say that there are available funds for example of 150 dollars and if a cheque is written for 151 dollars for instance the next thing they know is that the bank, for exceeding the amount, in this case, 1 dollar will charge 35 dollars. Also this situation has happened previously when an excess of 1.95 dollars was made and the bank charged 35 dollars. The question is: is this not illegal? The couple did some research on what could be done about it.

Reaction 17: We barely have enough to eat on any given week having a combined employee salary of between 300-400 dollars a month. We have two kids at high school and parents we have to help with their needs. It is not fair to work 10½ hours per day, 5-6 days a week only to realise you are just working to barely survive and pay overdraft fees. They say they start from the largest item and work their way to the smallest amount that is theft no matter how the bank twists their words, theft is theft. So if I have 15 dollars on Monday and I make a 5 dollar purchase on Monday with my debit card and write an 11 dollar cheque on Tuesday and it clears on Thursday the bank says they cleared the cheque that was written on

Tuesday, on Thursday and the debit card purchase then becomes an overdraft because it is processed on Friday. I have called them, complained and complained why I feel that the charges were unfair, they refuse to credit the fees back with a quick follow up for being a loyal and valued customer of the bank. Loyal I am, valued not hardly. Several occasions where this incident has occurred in the past two - three months also we have been hit with no less than 200 dollars in overdraft fees. This is on a weekly basis it seems we then cannot pay our vehicle insurance, card notes, loans or utilities. We are always behind on our bill payments.

Incident 18: The customer has been with his bank for several years, she is not happy about the charges she has incurred from the bank. Not only do they charge amounts for depositing money into the savings account but they also charge on transactions made causing overdrafts on her account. When trying to complain the customer service representatives were rude and dismissive and she was told to learn how to keep a register on her cheques that she signs.

Reaction 18: I am a single mother of five children. They are taking my child support that is directly deposited into their account; they should be ashamed of themselves. I have photocopied my statement and have sent the customer complaint to the Attorney General. I have had enough of them using my hard earned money to pad their pay cheques with, I will tell anyone and everyone how horrible that bank is, not that it will do much, but if I keep one person from being sucked into their banking scams, then it is worth it. I am now short of payments that I had set up to be paid via the internet. My children's savings accounts have been raided of their birthday money and my savings account has been depleted to cover the bank fees. I have lost time to hang on hold only to be disconnected. I have lost pay to fight with the representatives of the bank to no avail since I could not get anything resolved over the phone.

Incident 19: A customer had a bad accident a year ago. He could not pay his mortgage or any other bills. Now he has recovered and has a better job but the bank would not work him to help him pay them back. They want all or nothing at all. He has 4000 dollars and the bank won't take it and that is almost the whole balance he has and the bank still refuses to take it.

Reaction 19: I am 61 years old, have pets and I am worn out and ready to walk away from it. I am working full time and trying to pack. My daughter is having trouble with her pregnancy and my mother is gravely ill. I don't know whether I am coming, or going. I am lived here for three years and have lots of stuff to liquidate and I have offered the bank 4000 dollars and they won't take it. No-one can figure the problems out.

Incident 20: Customer is frustrated with the charges that he has incurred from his bank. He claims they are costing him a fortune that he cannot afford. For many years he used to call the bank to enquire about the overdraft fees and the rearrangement of purchases on his account. Sometimes he was told he would receive a call back which never happened. This year he was told the charges are placed in order from largest to smallest at the day end due to customer complaints in the past concerning non payment and since there are insufficient funds on items such as mortgage payment that customers prefer to have paid as a priority as opposed to a smaller charge on their account for that day. The customer was not happy with this policy and was told that the process was soon to be changed due to increased customer complaints. He has also sent email correspondences in the hope to receive a more accurate solution or answer to the successive charges. He never received an acknowledgement or a response to his query.

Reaction 20: The consequences of this led me to being broke most of the time. Having utilities cut off. Not having Christmas or food money. This is my account but I cannot access any of it. They placed a fraud alert on my account because of increased spending the day prior to Christmas Eve. Not having all of my house payments because they charged me 5 overdraft fees in one day. Not having what I need when I need it for my children.

Incident 21: Customer had a cashier's cheque to cash that they were really off. Having explained to the staff at their bank branch, when they arrived, and she asked how long it would take for the cheque to clear. They told her that it takes 2 days maximum and then she can have the cheque cashed. Having waited 2 days she contacted the bank and they told her that the cheque was on hold in the account but it looks good and it will be cleared. She still mentioned there could be a problem later if they don't check properly and through their reassurance she assumed that being a cash cheque it will almost be foolproof. Then after about 1 week she received a statement which informed her that the money was charged back because the bank could not collect the amount. After explaining the case again to the bank manager they said it is not their responsibility to chase the amount from the other bank where the cheque was issued.

Reaction 21: I am upset that the bank takes no responsibility even though I took every precaution to make sure this would not come back to me. I am appalled that after I explained my suspicion they didn't tell me to wait at least a month to be sure. I felt that they did not bother listening to me and are so quick to say they are not responsible. This has created the biggest strain ever on both my family and my relationships. They are refusing to temporarily freeze my account and waive any overdraft charges. This will hurt my credit because I don't know how or when I can pay this back even though it is a mistake on the banks part that led us here and it is the banks because of the promise I received and the precautions I took. I just bought a ring for my girlfriend hours before I found this out and what was supposed to be the happiest day in my life has turned into one of despair and hardship. This problem with the bank has caused me severe depression and anxiety and I feel that life cannot be good or the same for a very long time without some serious help.

Customer Bad Experiences – HealthCare Sector

Incident 1: This is a case of the complainant's adult daughter who jumped out of her second floor apartment window. The paramedics were called and they iced and elevated her feet (she landed on the pavement on her feet). She was taken to hospital where she spent four days. The attending doctor told the mother there was nothing they could for her because the heels of her feet were crushed. She also suffered a break in her neck. The doctor who saw her recommended that she should be taken home because they felt nothing could be done for her. However, the mother took her to two podiatrists since her feet were very, very swollen and had large blood blisters on them. They immediately needed to operate on her feet but because they were not elevated nor were they iced the swelling and blood blisters presented a high risk of infection. However they had two to three week window to help her before it is was too late. Ultimately they operated on her. She got an infection and lost part of the bone in one foot. To date her foot has not completely healed and she is going to have another operation. She recently was able to walk with braces. She continues to have serious problems with her feet.

Reaction 1: Her feet are deformed and she still has to take pain medication. She may need a wheelchair again after her next operation to clean up her foot and remove the pins and screws that are not exposed. This is definitely a case of negligence and we will be filing for a law suit.

Incident 2: The complainant was referring to her husband aged 57 had surgery at a hospital. He caught two infections whilst in recovery and was sent to five different ICUs. He had terrible care. They tried to cover up their errors and they wouldn't tell her much about the infections. Her husband suffered several ordeals which at one point led to his kidneys being shut down due to the infections and he was put on dialysis. He also had to spend a lot of time lying down and has suffered from bed sores and he had to ask for an air mattress. He suffered an additional infection which put him in a coma for 2½ weeks, and while in a coma he got another infection.

Reaction 2: There was much neglect of my husband. He wasn't cared for as he should have been. The rooms were dirty, items would fall on the floor and the nurses would pick them up to use them. Something should be done about this. I think my husband would have come home had it not been for the unsanitary conditions and poor care he received at this hospital.

Incident 3: A woman's husband went to hospital complaining of pain in the chest and stomach and they told him they did not find anything wrong. But the patient knew there was something severely wrong but they let her husband leave without further tests. This led to his death.

Reaction 3: The results of what they did not do I feel caused me to lose my husband which has caused me a lot of anxiety and pain.

Incident 4: Patient reported an infection that was not treated properly by the physicians concerned and certainly not followed up by infection control at this hospital. He was initially treated and declared clear and discharged from the hospital. However, the infection returned two days later, with a vengeance (no preventative medication were given) and he was re-admitted where after one day on a routine floor he was sent to an ICU. He died there, due to this infection.

Reaction 4: The consequence was death because the patient was 80 years old; no one followed this up though there were other cases that happened previously in this hospital.

Incident 5: In 1991 a patient was sent to the hospital for a follow up for two pacemaker operations. These devices eroded out to the surface of the skin six times with one having a faulty battery after only a few months. None of these devices stayed in place. The patient ran a low grade fever for seven years, severe soreness of the chest, severe depression and anxiety attacks. After the operation, for about eight years, he was unable to work because of constant dizziness and chills due to fevers from infections due to the pacemakers eroding out of place. As a result of all the patient has suffered he spoke to another doctor to seek advice on what to do. The doctor thought that due to all the infections he has received the best thing would be to remove the pacemaker. This was suggested to the original surgeon. The economic damage led to the patient not being able to work and losing a lot of benefits. His son and daughter went to bed hungry several times which caused severe emotional damage to him.

Reaction 5: I still have not recovered from the depression and anxiety attacks due to constant fear of death from a heart condition that was never corrected. I am not an educated man. In my terms it would be like a mechanic telling you that you need a transmission in your car. And after seven transmissions were bought and changed and you were charged for several years then were told there was nothing wrong with the original one and put it back in and it works fine.

Incident 6: The complainant's mother was hospitalised for minor surgery. Although the surgery went fine three days later she began to experience nausea and said she did not feel right. They asked the doctor on call to put her on a heart monitor. He refused because he indicated that she was responding normally to the surgery. The next day she felt worse, whilst sitting up in the chair visiting with her friends the nurse came over to her and removed her oxygen.

Reaction 6: My mother complained about not being able to breathe, the nurse was called and she failed to return to my mother's room and when she did my mother began showing signs of distress. She went into cardiac arrest and subsequently was not able to be revived.

Incident 7: The patient was unexpectedly admitted to hospital through the emergency unit and ended up having his gall bladder removed. Two days later they rushed to discharge him when they realised he was not insured. Within less than two weeks of discharge he began receiving collector's calls from the hospital before even receiving the bill. When he did receive the bill they demanded full payment of 14,000 dollars for a two day stay. The patient is unemployed and cannot be attending long term rehab; he doesn't even have a home to live in. They did not counsel him about charity care and to date they did not offer him any discount such as the ones they give to big insurance companies. They have been calling him every day and it still hasn't been two weeks since he was discharged.

Reaction 7: I feel harassed and I know that this is just the beginning and this will further damage my credit. I have given my mother a power of attorney and asked the hospital to call her to try and settle this but can use help. I know that there has been a lot of publicity lately about the uninsured and aggressive hospital collection practices. More damage to my credit if not a judgement and harassment expected. I am trying to slow them down. It is not that I don't want to pay them.

Customer Bad Experiences – Retailing Sector

Incident 1: The complainant ordered a sofa from a store on a buy one, get one free basis. The order was confirmed and the delivery date was set. The delivery arrived on time and it was at this point that the nightmare began. The sofas ordered were advertised as self assembly and one was needed for a narrow boat which was ideal and the other one the complainant decided to donate to a nursing home where his wife worked. On the day of the delivery he dismantled the furniture in the narrow boat, where they lived, and disposed of it. When the delivery arrived there were two sofas, they were not self assembly so this would not have fitted on the boat. The other was a three seater. He complained, by telephone, to the store and was told they would give him a full refund. So he went to the local branch that did not want to know and said they were not part of the company itself.

Reaction 1: To say I am disgusted with their service is an understatement. I have informed them that I will never, in my lifetime, buy another item from them or their related company. I also informed them that I have sympathy with the fellow who drove his Rolls Royce through one of their stores in sheer frustration.

Incident 2: A trolley collector at this store damaged the car of the complainant with a line of trolleys and he then continued on his way. The complainant was in her car at the time, when she got out and called him, he immediately replied that he never touched the car and then was aggressive, shouting at her that it was her fault and came to the conclusion that her car had rolled into his line of trolleys. This was after he had first of all denied any collision. Luckily other witnesses had seen him check the side of the car for damage so she had back up. However, when she went to get the manager who she assumed would be apologetic, was just as rude and refused to acknowledge that any damage had been caused. Once a demonstration using the trolley was done to show that the scratch had in fact been caused by the trolleys, the manager still did not apologise nor did his attitude towards the complainant change. Throughout the conversation he was incredibly rude and acted as if she had done something wrong. She complained to the company about the attitude of these two employees and finally their response was that the manager did not record the incident or had lost the incident form so it was not in their database so they could not take this complaint any further.

Reaction 2: It is no surprise that the manager has lost the vehicle incident form given his attitude on the day. But I don't see why they need that form to uphold the complaint about the behaviour of two of their staff. What they have told me to do, again no apology for losing the incident form, is go back and make another complaint in the store. After the aggressive and hostile attitude of the two men in question do they really think I want to go back and complain to their faces?

Incident 3: The complainant, on the way home, stopped at the local store to buy some groceries. She went to the toilets and was shocked and disappointed at what was confronting her. The three cubicles and hand washing area were all absolutely filthy to the point they could not be used. There was rubbish and toilet roll all over the place, but worst of all there was excrement and blood all over the walls and toilet seats. As there was only two checkouts she waited at one and was going to mention it to a member of staff but then a third till was opened. By the time she had listened to the two cashiers shouting and arguing with each other across the four tills between them she was running late, so had to leave. They were arguing about the new till opener being too lazy to go to the warehouse to get their own carrier bags and leaving the first till with none.

Reaction 3: Up to this point I have never had any reason to even think about complaining about any aspect of the store, but I was truly shocked by this experience. It also made me think if the stores senior managers are happy for the customer area to be like this what must the staff and food storage areas be like.

Incident 4: A complainant went to the local store to do her usual weekly shop. As a sufferer of chronic headaches and recently diagnosed with IBS she decided to get medication for both of these illness at the store as the local pharmacy did not open until later in the morning. She tried to purchase paracetamol and ibuprofen for her headaches and biscopan for her IBS. At the checkout where three members of staff were hanging around chatting about Disney holidays she put her shopping through, but when it came to the medication she was told that she could not purchase more than two types of painkillers. She told the girl at the till that there was only two types of painkillers, paracetamol and ibuprofen, to which the girl on the till replied that the biscopan was a painkiller also. The complainant argued that it was in fact a muscle relaxant or an antispasmodic, the member of staff said that she would have to ask her supervisor. The biscopan was shown to the supervisor, one of the members of staff who had previously been speaking about holidays, she said it was a painkiller. The complainant said it was not. In the end the IBS medications were put through as separate transactions, the mind boggles and she suffered a lot of needless embarrassment.

Reaction 4: I am long standing and good customer of this store but this makes me want to shop elsewhere. Shouldn't the staff be taught to deal with these types of purchases with a lot more sensitivity, why the hell were they allowed to stand around at the tills for so long, chatting about personal things? Is there no canteen for that kind of thing?

Incident 5: A complainant went to his local store with his six foot tall son who is also 29 years old. He had in his basket two bottles of wine and some cans of beer. The complainant left his son at the till and went to look at magazines. Two minutes later his son rushed up to his father in a blazing temper. The woman on the till would not serve him until he showed her some ID. There was a lady waiting behind him who just could not believe what the cashier was asking for. The son thought she was joking when she asked for ID but soon realised that she was not. He then told her what he thought of her and left.

Reaction 5: I myself do my shopping there at least twice a week and have done since it opened. But I can assure you I will never set foot in there again. It is a joke, if you saw my son you would know the reason why I feel so strongly. With staff like her, she makes the shop a laughing stock.

Incident 6: Complainant bought a loaf of thick sliced, wholemeal bread and as she opened the loaf she was horrified to find several strands of hair approximately six inches in length embedded in the slices. There is no possibility that this hair could have been hers as she has just broken the seal. Not only did this deprive her of having breakfast but also prevented her from making sandwiches for lunch. This inconvenience left her with no choice other than to buy lunch from outside.

Reaction 6: I have now lost faith in purchasing any of your products and this incident has now put me off eating bread so far to the point that I am now considering only eating bread that I baked at home myself. I am very disappointed in the breach in the quality assurance of the manufacturing process of this product and have now lost faith in your company because as a consumer I trusted that your product would have been fit for its purpose. This has also led me to believe there could easily be other more serious contamination. I would not wish any other consumers to experience what I have been through, i.e. having strands of hair wrapped around their fingers. I have retained my receipt and will now be contacting the store for a full refund and will also be notifying the local food standards authority.

Incident 7: The complainant felt frustrated after noticing lowering standards in her local store. She realised the shelves are poorly stacked, quite often items are missing for several weeks. The food quite often is out of date and most recently a loaf of bread purchased from home bakery when unpacked it was two days past its sell by date. She returned it to the store and was given a refund and the young lady at the customer services counter did not even apologise or indeed speak to her. The floor is quite often dirty and the added frustration was the fact that the staffs restock their shelves during the busiest times of the day with cages strewn all over the place and this presents a health hazard. She also noticed that the staffs don't smile anymore.

Reaction 7: Perhaps a mystery shopper would be a good idea to get some of these issues addressed.

Incident 8: The complainant went for her shopping trip in the local store, as usual. As a treat for her children she decided to buy a box of the stores all butter flapjack squares. Over the weekend the family decided to have some of the flapjacks and to her horror and disgust found that after biting into a flapjack she was chewing on a large sharp metal shard which she promptly spat out. She had a cut inside her mouth. She kept all the metal, packaging, remaining flapjacks and prevented anyone else from eating them. She then contacted the Environmental Health to ask for advice on how best to deal with the situation and they advised that all the evidence ie. the metal, the packaging and the left over flapjacks be kept for their own inspection. She felt that something needed to be done to prevent others from possibly doing the same so she called the stores' help line to advise them of what had happened and to ask them to remove from sale any remaining boxes of the same batch.

Reaction 8: As a loyal customer of this store and spending an average of £150 on her weekly grocery shopping with yourselves I would have expected to receive a decent standard of customer service. However your customer service personnel could not care less. I can assure you that this will not be the end of this matter and I would also like to add that it is lucky under the circumstances that it was me who ate this particular flapjack and not one of my young children. I will await the visit from Environmental Health and let them deal with the issue as they obviously took it as seriously as it should be.

Incident 9: The complainant had an unfortunate incident where, through no-one's fault, a spillage on a pair of trousers in the store where she normally shops. The matter was dealt with efficiently and courteously by customer care, who made a record of the incident on their computer. She was told that she did not need a record as it would stored on their computer and told to take her trousers to be dry cleaned and return with the receipt and it will be reimbursed. She returned to the store a few days later with the receipt making a round trip of 10 miles. Unfortunately no record of the incident could be found. The duty manager who dealt with the query decided that she should be reimbursed for the dry cleaning but when she asked for mileage he was rather dismayed. She (the duty manager) did suggest £2 but the complainant was not happy with this and 32p/mile was agreed upon.

Reaction 9: The reason I am writing to you is that I was far from happy with the manner in which I was dealt with by the duty manager. She ignored me until negotiations for mileage came up and I felt I was being a nuisance. I am a loyal customer to your company, 74 years old who can ill afford to pay for unnecessary petrol money. If the young lady in question hopes to progress up the management ladder at your company she needs to improve her customer relations technique.

Incident 10: The complainant feels very frustrated because of the attitude of the grocery store that he normally goes to. He feels sick and tired of staff coming across disinterested, rude and arrogant. He went to his local store recently; he was looking at the newspaper stand, reading a few of the headlines and deciding which one to purchase. One of the staff members was obviously busying himself stacking the top half of the stand with magazines then tried to lean past the customer as he was looking at the papers. He let the first time go but he did exactly the same again. So on the second occasion the complainant said "excuse you" and the staff member looked crossly at the complainant and just said "what?" The complainant told the staff member he had leant right across his personal space without any regard for him or any other customer, but he just muttered under his breath and turned away. The complainant immediately went over to the staff member and said how rude he thought they were and asked for his name. The complainant then went to find a manager to complain relaying his concerns regarding this rude and arrogant man. The manager assured him she would speak to him. So the complainant continued his shopping trip and went back to the manager who gave him a pathetic excuse for the employees terrible behaviour. As he left the store the employee concerned just scowled at the complainant.

Reaction 10: I will never ever go back to this store again as the customer service is just non-existent. I have shopped in this store for the last 25 years and have obviously spent a great deal of cash in there. But I will now go elsewhere. Also the quality of fruit and vegetables is also appalling to match the appalling staff.

Customer Bad Experiences – Telecommunications Sector

Incident 1: A customer who lost his dial tone phoned up the provider to report to the fault line. He was told that the fault maybe due to the exchange and the line would be fixed within 2 days. Although it was corrected the fault reappeared again, several months later. This time around it was not easy to rectify because the customer changed providers for line rental. After long conversations he was told they could not find any faults and it may be better to call an engineer. When the engineer arrived he disconnected the phone from the socket, plugged in the analogue phone he had with him, punched some numbers twice (it did not work the first time) and the line was back. When he was asked what the problem was he said no idea and for this service the customer had to pay £99. The handset is okay tested on the other line in the house and it was working fine so there was no faulty equipment. All was working fine for several weeks and then bingo one day the phone lost its dial tone again. This time round the customer decided to do some research and see how this keeps reoccurring. He was told through a user group that since there is no fault detected in the sockets and plugs in the house then the defect would be coming from the provider itself. Armed with all of this knowledge he rang the providers' customer service and was repeatedly bullied into inviting again, another engineer to check the equipment in order to say the line test is okay.

Reaction 1: I am exhausted by all of these problems and although the provider says that no dial tone at the test socket means no fault of mine I am still pushed to fix an engineer to come out and I am very much afraid of doing so because it will happen again. No idea what the problem is and this time charged £116 as they had increased the rate.

Incident 2: Customer rang the provider to see if they could have a phone line connected to their new flat. He was told he needed a new phone line installed, costing £124.99. He tried to argue the case that he could not afford it outright so he was given the option to pay the

£124.99 over six months by direct debit. So on this basis he agreed to have the phone line fitted and requested monthly billing on direct debit and for the number to be ex-directory. He then gave the bank details and instructed them to take the payment. He was expecting to receive a letter of confirmation but it never arrived so he rang them the day before the original installation date to which they said they had never received an order from him and had no record of the call. He was furious as he is already waited 3 weeks for the line to be fitted and they could not tell him why the order had been cancelled even though he was given an order number. They also demanded that he pay a £25 deposit again to which he refused, eventually they agreed to use the £25 from the original order. He reordered the phone line provided it was under the same conditions as the previous order, he was convinced that would be the case and he was also told he would receive £30 compensation credited to the amount due for the inconvenience. He was assured the engineer would come about 3pm. since he could not be released from work before 2pm. when he arrived there was a note under the door saying the engineer came today at 2pm. but nobody was at home. He rang the provider and was given a new date for the installation. The engineer came on the due date and fixed the line but to the customers shock and horror a bill of £164.99 was sent, he immediately rang the provider to find out whether there had been a mistake. Surprise, surprise they had no record of any previous conversation and were no longer offering to split the bill over six months. They had no record that the customer had requested a monthly bill in with the instruction to keep the number ex-directory. He was asked to pay £75 straight away (over the phone) and for the balance to be split over three months by direct debit. He refused to pay the £75 on the basis that he only agreed to the line being fitted based on the fact that it could be paid for over six months. After several arguments on the phone with a manager they reached an agreement to allow payment to be spread over six months and to change the account to monthly billing and ex-directory. A week later he received the final notice that demanded payment within 7 days so again he called the provider to see if there was a mistake and again they had no record of any conversations, nor had the account been changed to ex-directory or monthly billing. By this time the customer lost his temper and told them to take the phone line out. They demanded payment of £56 over the phone and then four monthly payments of £36 which would have meant paying them £240 in total. So he refused and asked to speak to the manager again. He then agreed the original terms again and this time promised the following:

- A credit of £30 on the account;
- To change the account to ex-directory;
- That no late payment fees would be charged to the account;
- That the provider would agree monthly billing plans;
- That the direct debit team would call within 3 – 4 days to set up the direct debit.

Reaction 2: I had never had any intention not to pay the provider what I owe them but I am only prepared to pay them on the conditions they offered to me at the time I placed my order. I refused to ring them again as I feel I would be wasting my time but don't know what to do next. I am concerned that I have such a large debt to my name and that the company with whom I ordered are completely ignorant to treating customers fairly.

Incident 3: Customer has had a problem with his provider so the phone had interference and the provider said the line was okay. Since then he purchased three new phones, all of them with the same problem, same story from the provider and they did nothing. He then had a problem with broadband and when contacting them their technical department was through a call centre in another country where the engineers could not even speak proper English. So they could not convey the message and could not understand what they were saying to them. Having spent approximately 35 hours on the phone trying to get the problem solved without any success they lost all the emails and the correspondences sent to them.

Reaction 3: They have lost all my emails dating to 2003 which included all mine and my wife's previous hospital appointments and the future ones. We are both disabled and pensioners; also very important emails were lost.

Incident 4: A customer runs eight houses for others enduring mental illness. Recently they received a call from a telecommunications provider who spoke to one of the residents asking them if they wanted broadband installed. The resident was pressurised to say yes although the contract was in the customer's name. When he rang the provider to query the broadband charges he was told it was an 18 months contract and that they had to pay to have it cancelled. They then received a bill of £438.48 which the customer disputed. He was very frustrated with the provider.

Reaction 4: I think the company's treatment was appalling, it is clear that the agreement was with a resident who had neither the authority nor the mental capacity to deal with a pushy salesperson, the contract should have been cancelled immediately.

Incident 5: This customer has had an outstanding issue with his telecommunication provider going back to 2004. He feels he has been fobbed off and a cursory look at the issue has not resolved it. He moved from the Hebrides back to Edinburgh and whilst waiting to move into a house in April 2004 he wanted the phone transferred to the new flat across town. Having spent time explaining this to his provider and after several phone calls, months in advance to ensure there would be no loss of service. He checked that the new flat had a working landline and no fault was detected on it. He was only moving area by a couple of miles. He was assured on several occasions that the new service would go on within an hour of leaving the first flat, certainly the same day. This was very important for the customer concerned who has a life threatening condition and will not live so long, his close family relatives were in Australia and the only one resident in England was his mother who was in Australia at the time. The day of the telephone allocation to change the line to the new flat came and there was no service. The customer was hospitalised for an operation, when he came out of hospital he was extremely weak and was to rest with plenty of bed rest for a minimum of three months. He could not leave the flat, nor walk about in the flat because he had lost several pounds of weight and would pass out frequently. For three months he had no phone service and the provider wanted to charge £190 for an engineer call that was not necessary and never had been. The distress of these months was so bad that instead of recovering from the operation within three months he did not heal up and was physically unwell for fourteen months. He is now in need of counselling for depression brought on by this experience in 2004. He was unable to walk and was too tired to sit up for long with post operative pain and fatigue. He would try to get through for hours in order to get help and when he was connected to customer services they refused to deal with anyone other than the bill payer, even though he was authorised to do so (his helper). The customer was due to get phone and broadband because in his previous flat the dial up internet service was appalling and he was constantly cut off due to poor signal whilst web browsing.

Reaction 5: I was angry, frustrated and very frightened that I had no way to contact anyone. Not even a doctor or nurse in case of problems and the stress caused me to be re-hospitalised for a few days only a week after the operation. I did not know how I would be able to eat. To top it all I was billed for three months line rental without even be connected and when I requested that this would be reimbursed to me on other occasions I was told I was in credit and so would not pay the next quarter. This is absolute rubbish because my line rental is always deducted from my bank account by direct debit and I have never had the money refunded to me. Rather than someone juggling figures and saying I have not paid in advance, when I have. I have never got over the intense fear and isolation and worry about feeding myself and getting help that I went through the first three months in my new flat without a phone to reach the outside world. I had indeed worried that my line would not be connected and that is why I asked for assurances and checked that everything would go ahead as scheduled, this did not happen. The tardiness in connecting my line was also meant a delay in email for when I was stronger, to not only contact family in Australia but restart my search and self promotion/networking for commissioned work, self employed to my cost. I asked again, once and for all, to take notice of the serious consequences that poor management which is certainly not technical caused me to have to go through this ordeal without the support of a voluntary charity (whose remit it was to help me move in, not health related in anyway) I would have possibly died from complication, accident or injury or even neglect and starvation for want of a phone. That I had even paid for in advance.

Customer Bad Experiences – Airline Sector

Incident 1: A customer who was travelling on a round trip found himself stuck on both legs of the journey and because the flight arrived late it caused him to miss the connecting flight. Asking for help at the desk he was ignored and did not get proper customer service. On the return trip the flight was cancelled and he found himself in a ridiculously long line waiting at the customer service counter with three agents helping passengers. It was around noon and the lines were moving at a snail's pace when one of the agents got up and left, probably to have lunch. It took an hour and a half to get to the counter and when the customer got there he was booked with a connection to where he wanted to go. When he asked if he could get a direct flight as the one originally scheduled he was told to take it or leave it.

Reaction 1: I got the clowns name and the airline concerned has some really considerate customer service representatives.

Incident 2: On a return flight from Atlanta to Las Vegas this couple, with an eight month old niece, had to sit trapped on a flight while workers tried to fix the air conditioning system. It was 90°+ outside and probably 100°+ inside. Another passenger asked if they could go back inside and wait in the cool of the terminal. He was told the door was shut and no-one could exit. One of the passengers asked for ice and a paper towel to help keep the niece cool. They were told the crew were serving first class passengers and someone would be back after the flight had taken off. One hour later the flight took off. The flight attendants started serving up the aisles but the couple concerned were ignored. When asked why the crew passed them by without serving them the air hostess just laughed.

Reaction 2: After contacting the airlines' customer service department about this their response was about being competitive in an industry and they hoped future flights would be more problem free.

Incident 3: A customer had the misfortune of his flight being cancelled. First of all the airline announced a two hour delay and about an hour prior to the revised estimated take off time the flight was cancelled. Although they provided accommodation the luggage handling left a bad taste in addition to the poor planning of the flight scheduling in the first place. Whilst the airline did not provide the passengers concerned with a reason for the cancellation judging by the number of people waiting to reclaim their luggage it might have been due to load considerations. What was disappointing was the front line customer facing team who were insensitive and rude to customers already inconvenienced by their poor planning. The attendant who issued the vouchers informed all the passengers to reclaim their bags and said they would be put out on the carousel in half an hour. When the bags did not arrive well past an hour later the customer concerned together with a few others asked the attendant for a status update. To his dismay he mentioned that the bags may or may not be delivered and if they did they had a four hour window for them to bring them onto the carousel. The customer informed the attendant that the supervisor of the airline had said it would be a half an hour wait and the attendant said they plainly were lying. When the customer insisted on speaking to a manager the attendant refused and accused him of being rude. After much persuasion the customer was put through to the attendants' supervisor who did not have a clue either or pretended not to have a clue.

Reaction 3: What baffles me is the lack of planning on top of the appalling customer service.

Incident 4: Customer went to the baggage claim department to report damage to his suitcase – a wheel had come off. The attendant was extremely rude for no apparent reason other than possibly having a bad day. When told that the wheels are not covered the customer asked what the exclusions were and aware that there was even a list that could be referred to. The attendant said that she was not going to read the whole list and suggested that the passenger concerned looked at the list for themselves. The passenger asked if there was a phone number where she could contact someone the attendant responded rudely "can you not see I am entering the information in, wait and I will give it to you".

Reaction 4: If this is the kind of callous rudeness I am subjected to this airline will never be on my list again. I have flown twice since then using other airlines; I have a plan in place. I don't appreciate being treated like cattle.

Incident 5: Customer has been waiting for two months for a refund and after a number of phone calls, emails and faxes he was told to wait another two months to get a refund for a return flight. The customer needs to use this ticket for the remaining value at least. Initially he called the reservation department who told him that the fax enquiry would have gone to the customer service department. After waiting one month they finally responded by email. They told him it was forwarded to the Refund Department, so he called them and was told that the customer service department were looking into this.

Reaction 5: I cannot even get hold of the customer service representative who sent me the email responding to my original letter. I cannot believe the service. They said "it is their job to please their customers" if you read their logo this is a bunch of lies. They are cheap but the flights are expensive.

Incident 6: This is a complaint about a honeymoon that was completely ruined. The couple booked a flight with reserved seats, seven months in advance. It was supposed to be a direct flight and they found out at the last minute that the flight was over booked and had no reserved seating. The gist of the complaint is:

- Two days of honeymoon ruined;
- The couple got "bumped" from four flights in total;
- They were left completely stranded in Honolulu Airport with no way to get to Maui;
- They had to purchase tickets for 400dollars through another airline to get to Maui;
- The airlines customer service had a 2 ½ hour wait time that day;
- They arrived in Maui twelve hours later than scheduled;
- The airline offered them a gift basket as a condolence.

Reaction 6: Disappointed and very upset.

Incident 7: Customer left her bag on a flight, she knew exactly where on the plane and what flight it was left on. She did exactly what they said and filled out a online claim form but she also wanted to speak to someone at the airline. She knew the bag was there and was adamant to speak to someone. She was given several telephone numbers but no one ever answered them. One number said that "due to high call volume no one can answer the call".

Reaction 7: I called all the numbers at all hours, they cannot always be busy. It was my purse and I am very concerned about it, but no one at the airline is.

Incident 8: Passenger who is a gold traveller with the airline concerned was upset at being charged baggage fees, not having priority boarding and no preferred seats because the airline did not recognise his status. He was told that when they put his numbers into the boarding pass it recognises the number but no elite status is shown to them. He has been trying to contact the airline on the phone for hours and hours. The airline says that they will try to fix it but the problem still persists.

Reaction 8: As you can guess I am very frustrated with all of this, my name spells the same everywhere and I do not have any middle initials.

Incident 9: Customer was upset because the airline charged them for excess baggage to the tune of 400dollars. The bags were overweight and he had asked a friend to pick them up from the airport. Upon arrival back from the trip one of the Samsonite suitcases was locked. The airline said it was locked by the TAA Inspection of bag section. However there was no evidence of this. The customer felt that if the TAA had a problem with the bag it would have been held or tagged as a problem. He explained this to the airline and told them he was a disabled veteran and lived alone and had no way to get his bag back to the airport for help. Their reply was that they didn't do it and cannot help him. He tried to contact the TAA through various means without much luck. Several weeks afterwards he went back to the airport and the bag was still locked.

Reaction 9: I have no family in the immediate area to take the bag back to the airport. As a disabled veteran and retired post master I remember prior to using this airline that I gave them ample time to give a solution to this problem. As we all know at times they deliver bags that didn't arrive on the passengers scheduled flight and have to drop them off. I think they should have picked up my bag and taken it to the airport and had the section that locked it, unlocked and returned to me. I still don't know if all my items are there. I really don't want to have someone destroy a Samsonite suitcase that costs us 100dollars.

Incident 10: After purchasing a ticket for her elderly parents the complainant reported that her parents had to delay their trip for three days due to a medical issue. When the tickets were purchased she was told that with a doctor's note she would be entitled to a refund on the old tickets to the tune of 300dollars and the original economy plus fee 176dollars. They ticket was rebooked and a letter was written claiming the old ticket value, without any response. A follow up was done and again no response. Finally now that her father has passed away she spoke to someone and they promised to send an email request. Unfortunately the airline has been holding onto this money for the last six months with no indication that they will ever pay it back and all the claimant received so far was some lame excuse that it would be sent on.

Reaction 10: My newly widowed mother cannot understand how a company could do that. I told her that it is not all companies but this airline clearly does not care for her and likely does this all the time and people just give up. I should know, for many years I was a premier executive member of an airline and was frustrated with their customer service a few years ago so switched to another airline. After this experience it will be a cold day in hell before I fly again with this airline.

Incident 11: The passenger was returning home having attended a family funeral. The flight was from Chicago to Indianapolis. She was travelling with her 82 year old mother returning from her sons' funeral. She requested a wheelchair and was told the flight will be boarded via metal steps but that her mother would be boarded first via a ramp. When the passengers began boarding she was informed that the ramp was delayed so her mother was seated at the gate whilst all the other passengers boarded the plane. No wheelchair ever arrived; her mother suffers from severe spinal problems plus other ailments. The complainant herself is diabetic with also other complications. Both of them ended up walking up a long hot ramp onto the plane. On entering the plane, which is by now full of passengers, they had to make their way back to the rows where their seats had been allocated. On reaching their seats and opening the overhead storage compartments they found it was loaded with someone else' luggage and a box. When they asked why someone else' luggage was there and if possible could it be moved, the stewardess stated loudly and rudely it is first come first served. They were both told that they need to put their carry ons under the seat, she tried to explain to the air stewardess that the seats didn't have enough space for the carry ons to go underneath, to which the air hostess once again replied loudly and rudely "put your luggage under your seats".

Reaction 11: I was very upset with the stewardess' attitude and treatment of myself and family. I then said I hope no-one else buried their brother/son today to which she stated "I did, my mother". I then asked for her name and she stated very flippantly Priscilla, she then actually spelt it out, letter by letter loudly, I then said, quietly, thank you Priscilla. I do not think I have paid so much money to be treated so rudely and thoughtlessly in my entire life, I ended up crying for half the trip. I absolutely feel that we experienced blatant discrimination due to age and disability. I was publicly humiliated as I have never experienced before.

Incident 12: Passenger was connecting to another flight and his travel suitcase was delayed so he immediately went to the airlines' baggage office to find out what had happened to his luggage. He was told that the wrong tag was attached to his baggage and it had been sent somewhere else. The local agent opened the baggage delayed report and placed an electronic request into the airlines system to make sure that the luggage was forwarded to the hotel where he was staying. He was also asked to call the airline premier desk in the morning and ask for assistance. He was provided with a toiletries kit for the overnight stay in Boston. The following morning he washed some clothing items and contacted the premier desk asking for assistance. He had a very important job interview that he had been waiting for, for almost six months. So he had to go for the interview and resumed trying to call the premier desk afterwards only to be told that the luggage had not in fact been located and was considered to be missing. Eventually he was able to determine that the bag was still located in Boston airport and had not been taken to the hotel address as instructed. He was not pleased to hear this and was informed by the unit concerned that the luggage was not going to be sent within immediate effect.

Reaction 12: Following delay after delay all the attempts failed, as usual. Poor customer service.

Incident 13: A customer was travelling with her three year old daughter and had to face the abusive behaviour of the flight attendants. Although she travels regularly she felt extremely humiliated this time. The abuse happened several times during the flight and was also directed at her three year old daughter and that was why she was extremely irritated. During the serving of beverages she was completely ignored and she assumed that this was just an oversight, when she asked for beverages the flight attendant was very rude. During the course of the flight when the seat belt sign was off the three year old was sleeping, partly on her seat and partly on her mother's lap. The mother was holding her tightly and the belt sign was not on. The flight attendant came to the passenger and yelled at her, "how old is your child – put her on the seat". The mother replied that she is in her seat, but her head and part of her body is on the mother's lap. She is just three and cannot sleep properly in her seat like others. The mother also pointed her to some other passengers and politely mentioned that some other folks are also holding their children and the flight was moving slowly with the seat belt sign unlit. In response the air stewardess yelled "if everyone wants to die, you want to die too?" the complainant felt very hurt, disgusted and insulted. Finally during taxiing the daughter started to cry, needing the rest room but on asking for help the attendant yelled at her "sit down and control your child". The complainant agreed that it is not allowed to move during taxiing but she should not have yelled at her. Once the flight stopped properly the mother tried to talk to the attendant but she said she would rather have a sick child than a dead child.

Reaction 13: I never expected this from a major airlines non-stop international flight. I always admired this airline but this experience makes me think twice about the airline and future travel plans with this company.

Incident 14: This couple had to endure aggressive behaviour from one of the flight attendants who was mean and rude. During a flight from Houston to New Orleans the attendant would come and slam the seat back to the upright, take off position and scolds the husband for endangering the people behind him. The seat was upright. It may have been down one click, the attendant then barks at the wife for her purse strap sticking out from under the seat. The flight was an hour late for takeoff. Instead of the customers feeling irritated and in a bad mood the attendant felt that this has inconvenienced him more than the passengers. He slams the drinks down and then splashes them before they finished drinking. He was asked, in a nice voice, why the flight was delayed and whether the plane had engine problems. So he shouts at them that there was no problem, the plane was late, they noticed that he had no name badge and so politely asked him for his name. His eyes glared at them and he asked them what their names were so they told him and he went to the front and came back with a passengers list and circled their names. They asked him again for his name and he mumbled in reply. They started to think that this was abnormal behaviour and that this flight attendant was unstable. The wife, who as a medical professional has worked with mentally ill people for over thirty years, they came to the belief that this is a case of someone who is a grenade with a loose pin. They pretended to sleep the rest of the way to New Orleans.

Reaction 14: This guy is a huge problem. If he tried this attitude with the wrong person there would be fireworks. I bet he was already in conflict with other passengers.

Incident 15: The complainant whilst flying from Austin to Houston to then continue to Calgary was told at the gate that her carryon bag would have to be checked for the flight. When she got to the plane there were other bags the same size as hers and there was still room in the overhead stores for her bag. She was also not told that she would not get her carryon bag back until after the flight which had always been the norm in any other flight she has taken.

Reaction 15: Expecting to keep my carryon bag with me I had left my medication and jewellery in it, this is where the airline recommends you carry such possessions. My jewellery was in a small blue box in the top, outside pocket; the box was small as I only took one change of earrings and one necklace. When I arrived in Calgary everything was gone.

Incident 16: The complainant had been trying, over six months, to book online a trip using their air miles. Eventually they called the reservation centre for help. They were told there were no seats available, when looking at the seats available there was always empty cabins or one seat taken. The couple were booking six to eight months in advance.

Reaction 16: I would like to express my revulsion at the airlines policy towards the usage of frequent flyer miles. My wife and I have been trying to book a trip to Hawaii for late 2010 using our mileage. Even though the flights are wide open for first class seats we are always told that no seats are available for mileage. All we are told is that a seat is available going but not returning. Buying a one way ticket is more expensive than a round trip. My wife and I have been reluctant but loyal customers and it is frustrating to be constantly blocked from using our points.

As we have no immediate experience of what other men feel, we can form no idea of the manner in which they are affected, but by conceiving what we ourselves should feel in the like situation." The emotions of the spectator will still be very apt to fall short of the violence of what is felt by the sufferer. Mankind, though naturally sympathetic, never conceive, for what has befallen another, that degree of passion which naturally animates the person principally concerned.

Adam Smith

The Theory of Moral Sentiments (Sympathy)

Chapter 5: In Search of Empathy – The Art of Complaint Handling and Resolution

Introduction

The Japanese Quality Movement, over the years, has worked with various levels of quality mindsets and used the levels for driving continuous improvement, enhancement and optimisation. One approach that was used was negative quality or deficient quality. This means that the baseline and the foundation for a total quality management philosophy is dealing with deficiencies and therefore managing complaints and handling disappointed, frustrated or even angry customers. This has to be a fact that must be acknowledged and there has to be an understanding that unless the foundation quality or negative quality is optimised to be fool proofed and to become totally reliable customers will always demonstrates their anger and frustrations. At least this is the case in relation to the core aspects that traditional organisations tended to hold onto. Customer complaints is accepted by the vast proportions of businesses as a welcome opportunity for optimising their processes and minimising their errors and also for conducting root cause analysis and clearing out obstacles that hinder their drive for excellence and also that create negative impressions within their customers. The only shortcoming perhaps is the fact that many customers still do not complain. As Figure 15 indicates the tip of the iceberg is considered to be the norm in most industries in so far as the percentage of customers who complain. It is estimated that in some industries as much as 50% do not complain. In relation to customers who complain this can be seen across many industries. The airline industry, for instance, complaints are linked to the whole life-cycle of travelling be it booking, checking in, baggage handling, flight delays on landing and taking off, online services such as seating, food and in-flight entertainment and staff attitudes amongst others. In the hotel industry, for instance, similar complaints are linked to booking, staff attitudes, cleanliness, noise levels and dirty rooms, customer being overcharged, bed bugs, services generally speaking and value for money etcetera.

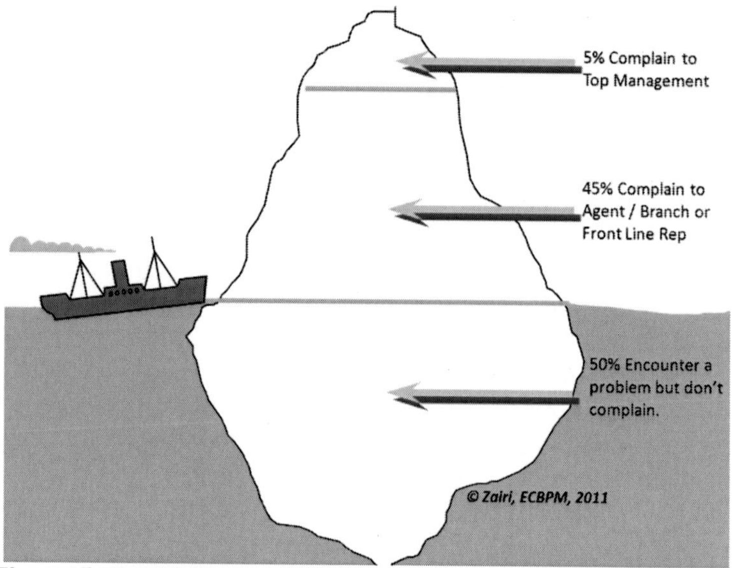

Figure 15: Tip of the Iceberg – The Hidden Truth of Customer Complaints

In the financial industry, for instance, it has been found in the UK by the Financial Ombudsman Services (FOS) (Butterworth, 2009) that the banking industry in the UK is still falling behind in terms of providing satisfactory services to their customers. In particular the focus was on the five biggest banks which accounted for more than half of all the complaints the FOS received. They registered over 3000 each during the six months of the year when the investigation was carried out and this was considered to be a jump of 22% year on year. The Ombudsman Service found that 70% of complaints were about general insurance products, 61% relating to banking and 41% about mortgages. This was considered to be a wakeup call for the banking industry and a pre-cursor for getting them to focus on better customer service and handling their customer's complaints more seriously.

In the health service, for example, the Parliamentary and Health Service Ombudsman report (2010) has detailed how complaints are being handled for the satisfaction of patients (Figure 16) and what investigations were subsequently carried out in order to put things right (Figure 17).

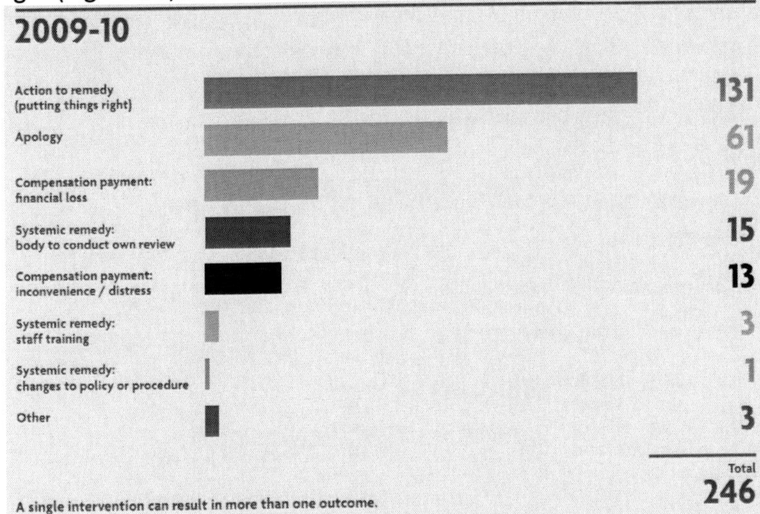

Figure 16: Intervention outcomes
Source: (Parliamentary and Health Service Ombudsman, 2010)

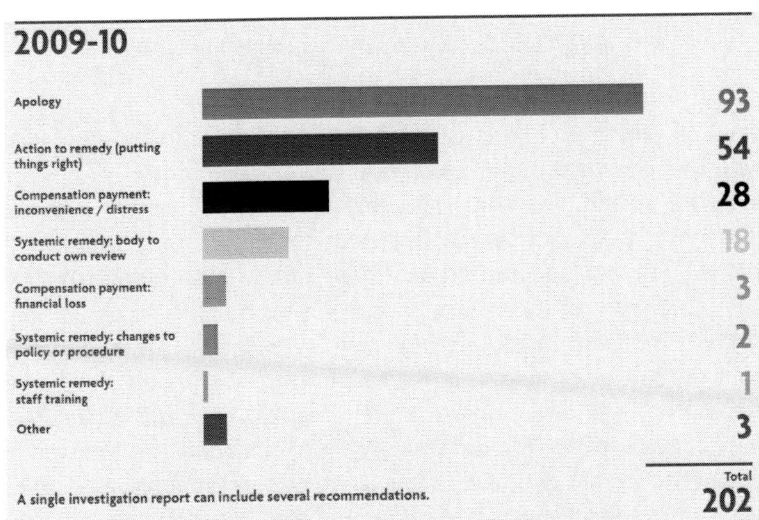

Figure 17: Health investigation recommendations
Source: (Parliamentary and Health Service Ombudsman, 2010)

It has however, to be acknowledged that the tip of the iceberg phenomenon still continues even with the level of increased commitment in relation to handling customer complaints and also the attitude that has become more pervasive in accepting complaints as an opportunity for improvement and building good rapport and solid relationships with the customers. Many customers still do not complain and this is across most of the industry sectors (Figure 18).

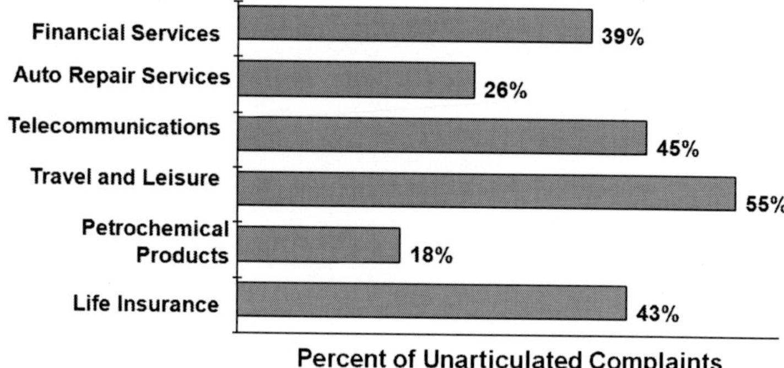

Source: The results are from a 1994 cross-industry research study by *The Service Impact Group*, a network of leading experts in service quality and quality improvement.

Figure 18: Complaints pervasiveness by Industry Sector

The correlation of customers committed to maintaining their links with their provider organisation that has let them down is depicted in Figure 19 and it demonstrates that the cycle of recovery in terms of service disappointment safe guards the relationship and allows the relationship and the commitment of the customer to remain positively solid. In most cases it can be found that across various industry sectors, customers who generally speaking feel satisfied with the service or who have their complaints dealt with effectively, are more likely to demonstrate their propensity to buy again from the same supplier. In a sense customer satisfaction and customer dissatisfaction are two sides of the same coin. It is not to be assumed that one is the inverse of the other. The lack of complaints does not necessarily indicate satisfaction however; the presence of complaints is a partial indicator of dissatisfaction. By measuring the voice of the angry customer and focussing on customer complaints and dissatisfaction using a variety of tools this will ensure that there is a continuous commitment to foolproof the transactions and ensures that quality is at an optimum level and value branded is to the satisfaction to the customer.

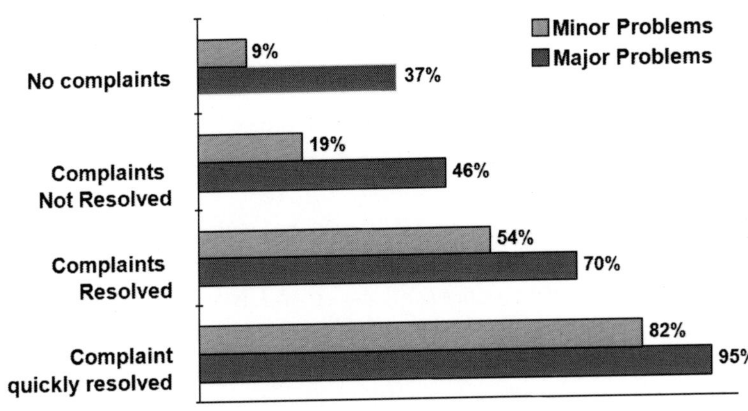

Source: The results are from a 1994 cross-industry research study by *The Service Impact Group*, a network of leading experts in service quality and quality improvement.

Figure 19: Impact of speedy complaint resolutions on buying intent

The Importance of Using Complaints as a Lever for Customer Satisfaction

It is acknowledged across the board that satisfied customers are more likely to tell others about their positive experiences. Dissatisfied customers are more likely to tell more people about their unfortunate experience. Here are some examples across various industry sectors:

- In the packaged goods industry, satisfied customer tells 4 – 5 people about their experience. A dissatisfied customer will tell 8 – 9 people about their negative experience.
- In the automobile industry, a satisfied customer will tell 8 – 10 people about the experience. A dissatisfied customer will tell 16 – 18 people about their negative experience.

- 30% of customers with problems complain to the direct provider of the product or service.
- 2% – 5% of customer complaints are voiced at the highest level within the organisations that are providing goods and services.
- 20% – 70% of customers will not do business with their providers if they are completely dissatisfied with the way their complaint was being handled.
- Only 10% – 30% of customers with problems who do not complain or request assistance will do business with their provider organisations again.
- The average business spends 2 - 25 times more on average to attract new customers than it does to keep old ones.

In a sense a complaint is a statement that customer expectations have not been met and perhaps a sign of belief if received positively that the organisation concerned cares and is willing to crack the situation. By getting useful feedback from customers this could be used as a direct measurement of how well the organisation is doing. Quality improvement has to be driven by an opportunity to fix what goes wrong and rectify negative situations in order to repair customer relationships perhaps sometimes the only way of finding out where a problem is and whether there are problems is to receive complaints. The following quote by Rhymer Rigby is useful: "complainers will no longer accept the 'you will have to speak to the manager who isn't around at the moment' approach". They want an answer now – or next time they will go elsewhere. David Garvin said "high quality means pleasing customers, not just protecting them from annoyances". The drive for customer loyalty has to come through an internal commitment to optimisation, eradication of problems, fool proofing of our processes and delivering consistency, reliability and high quality goods and services for the customers. This will liberate organisations to focus more on value orientations and giving the customer more with less. It is now recognised that loyalty is what counts and customer satisfaction is only measuring at the base line level.

- A 1% increase in customer loyalty can result in an average 9% increase in overall profitability.

- Customers who rate an organisation as five on a five point satisfaction scale are six times more likely to buy from the same organisation again than those who rated as a four.
- A 5% reduction in customer defection can result in doubling of an organisations profit.
- 67% of customer defections are due to poor service.
- In various markets of the economy, 70% of customers reduced purchases or stopped buying completely because the provider is not a business to deal with.
- Research shows that if customer enquiries are satisfactorily answered in one or two calls, more than 70%+ are completely satisfied. However, the percentage falls to 10% - a 60% drop – as soon as they have to make three or more calls.
- Many organisations completely change their top 20 customers every three years.
- 65% of new business comes from recommendations from friends and business associates.
- Acquiring a new customer is 6 times more expensive than keeping an existing one.
- The typical customer service support function has more customer contacts each day than any other part of an organisation – and the more opportunities to strengthen or destroy customer relationships. Negatively, and unhelpful or inflexible responses lead to 15 – 20 bad references about the organisation concerned.
- Customers who may never complain, either because they have experienced bad customer service or because the organisation concerned has a bad reputation in this area represent on average, from 35% – 65% of all those experience problems. They usually have the least expensive and simplest problems, yet they have the lowest level of loyalty.
- Research shows that most serious problems leading to customer disengagement are sales related, and almost impossible to recover from. Yet they are often trivial faults such as returning phone calls, failing to meet promises, failing to match requirements.
- Lengthy query resolutions reduce customer loyalty by 25% - 49%, while recurring problems usually lead to customer

disengagement. Research shows that most customers become dissatisfied if queries are unanswered within 5 – 10 days. Yet too many organisations plan for customer query responses of between 10 – 30 days.

- Many organisations throw money away on improving sales transaction technology because they perceive their competitors are doing the same. Fewer take the time to ask their customers what they really value in transaction terms.
- Satisfied customers continue to buy the same products and services.
- It costs more to bring in a new customer than to service an existing one.
- Repeat customers bring in new ones.
- Long term customers are more willing to pay full price for their products or services.

The Ultimate Failure – Customer Defection

Defection occurs for a variety of reasons. It is not necessarily due to major dissatisfaction with a product or service. It is possible that defection is caused by a competitor who has offered additional purchase incentives, a product which is slight better or better value for money. Customers go through periods where they start to question their value for money. This has to be treated as a relative concept and therefore by monitoring on a constant basis customer dissatisfaction organisations can prepare themselves and foolproof the defection of their customers. For example the first sign of slippage in customer retention can be determined by the following metrics:

- The declining and repeat purchase rate;
- A lower buying rate;
- A longer reorder cycle.

It is also useful to use defecting customers who no longer buy the specific products or services in order to establish the main reasons for the decision to switch and what are the attributes that competitors are offering to lure them away? This is not necessarily a strategy for trying to convince customers to reconsider coming back but more to gain intelligence and to use it for making the strategic decisions that will enable the organisations concerned to counter the threats coming from their competitors.

Another way to prevent switching/defection is by benchmarking the views of users of products and services in relation to the brands relative strengths and weaknesses in order to further explore why certain customers might leave the brand concerned and determine how to win over the competitors users as well.

Dealing with customer complaints in order to foolproof organisational leakage in terms of customer defections have to be based on creating a new mindset. This mindset is to create an attitude across the board where the ultimate aim is to satisfy the customer and to find a remedy to the problem by choosing the best communication mechanism and to provide tangible value that is appreciated by the customer. The staff who will handle these challenges must have the right attitude, total confidence in their ability to investigate the problem and seek a solution that is acceptable to the customer. They have to have the right competencies and feel empowered enough to make decisions in order not to lose the customer (Table 1).

Old Method	New Method
Justified	Satisfied
Liability	Remedy
Letter	Telephone
Warranty	Customer Value
Defensive	Confident
Untrained	Trained
No Authority	Full Authority
Clerical	Graduate

Table 1: Dealing with Customer Complaint

In a sense the fool proofing of organisational success in terms of their retention rate of existing loyal customers is to use the complaint resolution process in an effective manner. There are some rules that are considered to lead to effective complaint resolution and also to ensure that there is minimisation of the risk of losing customers:

- To view complaints as feedback that can point out weaknesses and provide an opportunity for improvement. Most of the complaints tend to point towards operational flaws and weaknesses in the value chain.
- To understand that resolution is not always a matter of right or wrong.
- To understand that how to resolve a complaint can require a lot of time and energy over the long term.
- To understand that some people will complain regardless of circumstances.
- To handle complaints in a timely manner.
- The rule of thumb is as soon as possible. Many complaints get worse and harder to resolve with the passing of time. The timely handling of a complaint often avoids a confrontation.
- To listen – listen to the complainers' side of the story. Asking any questions if any details are unclear. Asking them how they felt throughout. This provides a different perspective of the business.
- To make certain that all the facts are available before coming to a conclusion.
- To show empathy. Many complainers simply want to know they are being heard. This does not mean accepting fault or guilt. Think of phrases such as 'I understand why you feel that way. I would feel that way too'.
- To ask them what the organisation can do to make them happy. They may ask for the moon but more often the complainers ask for something reasonable. Use this question because it can often give you the quickest and cheapest resolution. Depending on the complaint, you could also ask what the complainer would recommend to prevent the problem.
- If the complaint is severe enough, set up a damage control plan.
- If the complainer is wrong, determine if a resolution is worth the time, money and energy to prove your moral point. This is why court cases are often settled out of court.
- If the complainer is right let them know you will deal with the matter internally.

- Determine how the problem happened and how it can be prevented.
- Understand that complaint resolution in many industries is a cost of doing business.
- Try to keep personalities out of complaints, look at the issues objectively and try to keep your emotions under control.
- Survey your customers regularly. Most customer complaints are not brought to the businesses' attention – customers just go somewhere else.

Testing the Empathy Capability – How to Handle Difficult Customers

It has to be acknowledged that as human beings we all have limited capacity for tolerating difficult individuals and certainly accepting abusive behaviours and threatening attitudes. However, one of the challenges for organisations that truly believe in retaining their customers and solving their problems is to learn how to deal with difficult customers. By preparing the front line staff who deal with customers psychologically and also by training them in terms of customer behaviour and attitudes and by equipping them with technical knowhow and finally by empowering them to make the right decisions. This will go a long way towards applying the true art of empathy and managing customers generally speaking and in particular being able to handle challenging situations that may involve difficult customers.

Difficult customers are those who may complain about everything. They might also be individuals who challenge an organisation on its own business. Sometimes difficult customers are those who are indecisive and may not know precisely what the issue is or what they want. A small minority may be people who are rude or thoughtless to others. There are loads of people who may want to negotiate a lower price or squeeze more benefits from their provider organisations. If there is not a clear strategy on how to deal with such customers this could create tense moments and can escalate benign and trivial complaints into a severe situation. The following are some of the reasons where organisations find it difficult to handle challenging customers:

- By failing to listen carefully to their view point and to establish therefore whether there is a genuine complaint or not.
- By not using empathy as a powerful method and therefore not being to see whether there is another view point.
- By failing to acknowledge that the customer concerned may be right or at least partially right.
- By failing to negotiate or at least try to achieve a win-win situation.
- By failing to show flexibility.
- By failing to find creative ways to address and solve the problem if there is one, or at least to convince the customer that everything was done above board.

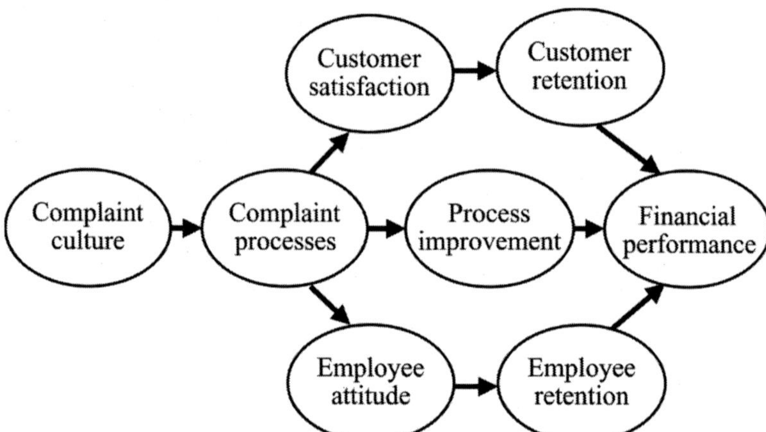

Figure 20: Effective Complaint Management and Resolution Culture

Source: (Johnston, 2001)

As Figure 20 illustrates an investment in creating an effective complaint management and resolution culture will help create customer satisfaction, customer loyalty and will lead to high levels of customer retention.

1. **Promoting a complaint culture** – this means that all employees within an organisation have to understand that the customer may have reasons for feeling upset, let down, disappointed,

frustrated or angry. The psychology of understanding customer behaviour and latitude must be one of the competencies that personnel involved in the provision of customer service and managing relationships must have. A thorough training on customer empathy has to be a prerequisite before facing a customer.

2. **Complaint handling processes –** this means that the process that an organisation promotes and applies for managing its quality levels in delivering high level services and impacting positively on their customers must be based on best practice thinking and must be enabling the positive aspects rather than preserving a defensive and bureaucratic approach.
3. **Focusing on customer satisfaction** – this means that the complaint resolution process has to be in terms of how it impacts on recovery and therefore creating customer satisfaction. This has to have the ingredients that will ensure that the recovery is fool proofing the process internally but satisfying the customer externally so that they remain attached to the provider organisation.
4. **Employee motivation and attitude –** the complaint handling and resolution processes have to enable employees to investigate and hopefully resolve the complaint and have to provide them with empowerment that will build their confidence to go the extra mile and therefore solve the customer problems. This will have the net impact of maintaining employees' positive attitudes and belief that not only the processes within their organisation are working properly but also in their ability to safeguard customer satisfaction and protect the long term interest of their employer organisations in terms of convincing the customers to stay.
5. **To use the complaint resolution process for driving process improvement –** the whole purpose of complaint management is to seek opportunities for optimisation, rectification of what is wrong and fool proofing all the value chain so that there is internal confidence in delivery and external confidence from the customer in terms of trusting the dependable transactions that they receive from the provider of services and products.

6. **Use complaint resolution as an employee motivational tool** - the process that ensures quick and satisfactory recovery on the one hand and which ensures motivation and satisfaction of employees internally will lead to people working through passion, teamwork, high levels of motivation and therefore will ensure that staff retention levels will remain high. On the other hand repeated customer satisfaction through fool proofing and recovering the service will lead to high levels of customer retention.
7. **Driving sustainable organisational performance though employee motivation and satisfaction** - high levels of employee retention together with high levels of customer retention and therefore loyalty will impact on the economics of an organisation and will delivery sustainable financial performance.

The management of difficult customers without empathy and without enabling processes for handling the complaint in the first place and certainly without empowerment will have a direct impact on an employee's performance in terms of quality contribution.

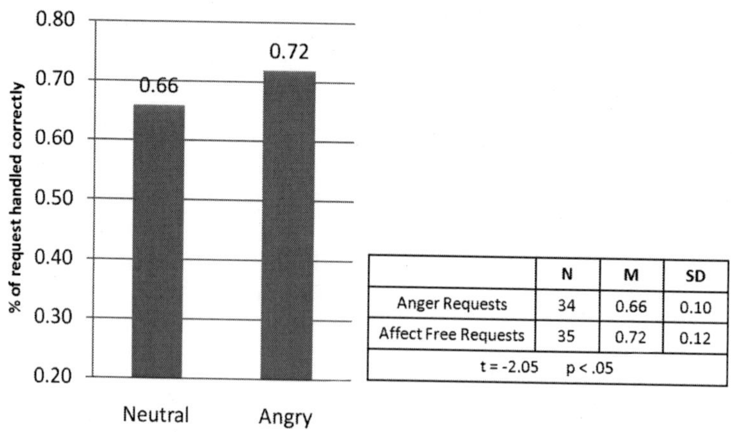

	N	M	SD
Anger Requests	34	0.66	0.10
Affect Free Requests	35	0.72	0.12
t = -2.05 p < .05			

Figure 21: Performance Quality

Source: (Rafaeli, Derfler, Ravid, & Rozillio, 2008)

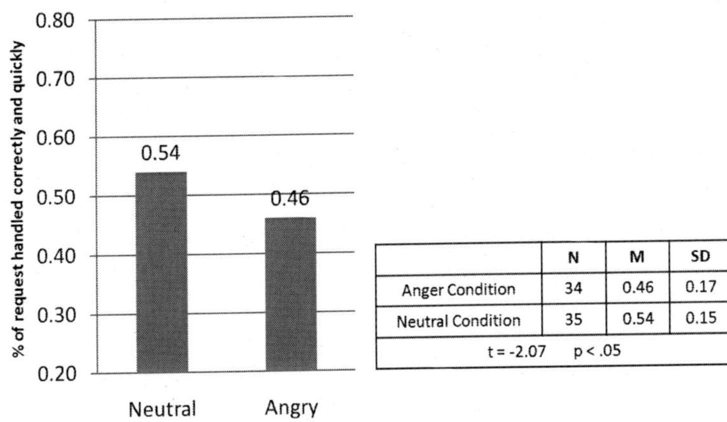

	N	M	SD
Anger Condition	34	0.46	0.17
Neutral Condition	35	0.54	0.15
t = -2.07 p < .05			

Figure 22: Effects on Performance Quality

Source: (Rafaeli, Derfler, Ravid, & Rozillio, 2008)

As Figure 21 illustrates employees who get upset because of their poor training, perhaps, are more likely to produce erroneous work as opposed to a sample of employees who are neutral and do not show the negative emotion to the customer. Similarly, in terms of productivity as Figure 22 shows employees who display emotional reactions to customer anger are more likely to produce less than employees who are neutral to them. In addition, the effect of customer anger on creating residual negative emotions in employees is more apparent in the case of individuals who are poorly trained, not empowered and unable to show empathy as opposed to neutral employees who are confident to handle difficult customers and who know how to demonstrate empathy.

It can therefore be concluded that employees who are not affected by negative emotional exhaustion are able to perform at a much higher level (Figure 23). Research has also shown that the residual effect of negative emotions lingers on and affects the concentration and focus of employees. Participants in a research exercise when asked to engage in an unrelated fun task (Raven Matrices) and after completing the tasks they were asked to resume their work and their performance on the subsequent tasks was measured. As Figure 24 depicts those who were previously angered by showing their emotional side to the customers found it more difficult to complete the task as opposed to the neutral sample. In other words the effect of customer anger continued to linger on (Rafaeli, Derfler, Ravid, & Rozillio, 2008).

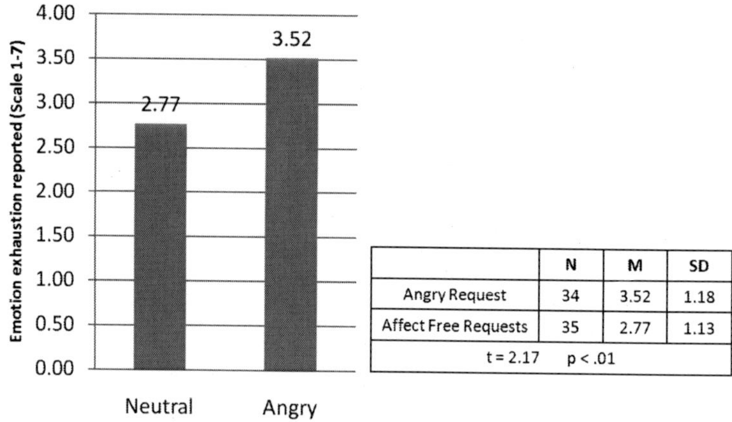

	N	M	SD
Angry Request	34	3.52	1.18
Affect Free Requests	35	2.77	1.13
t = 2.17 p < .01			

Figure 23: Effects on Employee Exhaustion

Source: (Rafaeli, Derfler, Ravid, & Rozillio, 2008)

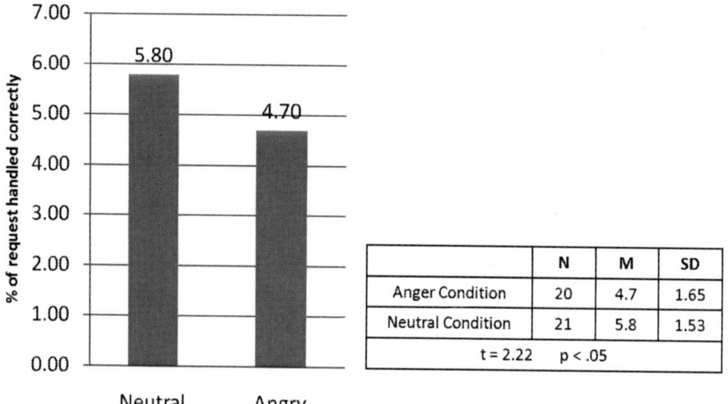

	N	M	SD
Anger Condition	20	4.7	1.65
Neutral Condition	21	5.8	1.53
t = 2.22 p < .05			

Figure 24: Performance on Subsequent Task

Source: (Rafaeli, Derfler, Ravid, & Rozillio, 2008)

The Art of Complaint Handling and Resolution

Over the years various organisations representing our different industry sectors have published guidelines and principles for good complaint handling. This has been a practice within the various industry associations and in the context of public sector these are public bodies that are regulators of how providers operate and are organisations that represent the voice of customers and take responsibility for investigating their complaints. By understanding the various processes that are being advocated by these different bodies and therefore reflecting on how complaint handling is now being considered to be a driving force for improving services, solidifying internal capabilities in terms of quality and consistency and ensuring that the right outcomes are to the satisfaction of customers, wider stakeholders and government themselves.

Example 1: The Parliamentary and Health Services Ombudsman published guidelines on good complaint handling (Parliamentary and Health Service Ombudsman, 2009 and Parliamentary and Health Service Ombudsman, 2010) the process used by the Parliamentary and Health Services Ombudsman is depicted in Figure 25

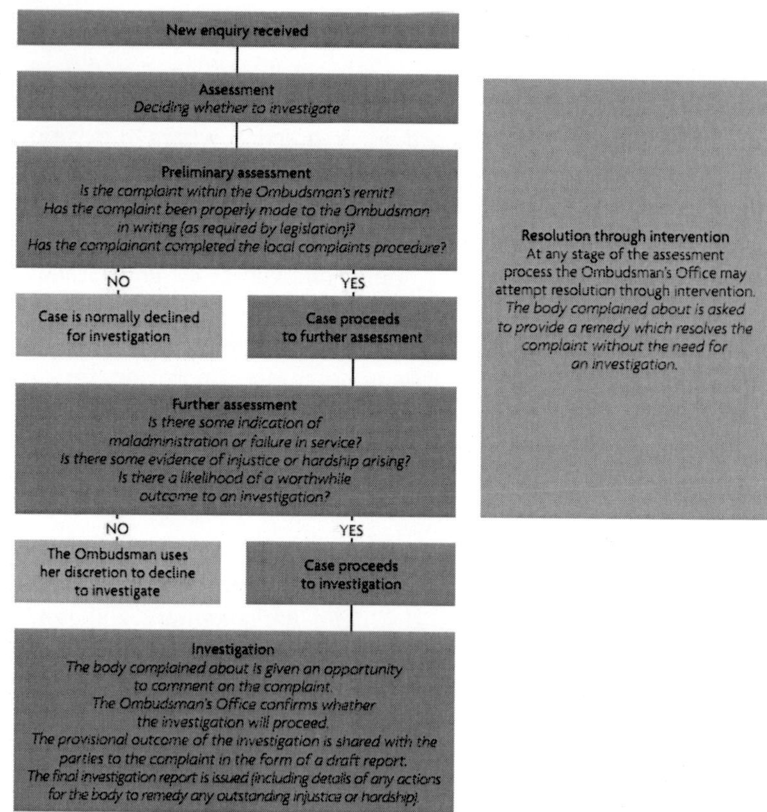

Figure 25: Complaint Handling Process
Source: (Parliamentary and Health Service Ombudsman, 2010)

Figure 26: Complaint Handling and Resolution Process (UK NHS)
Adapted: (Parliamentary and Health Service Ombudsman, 2009)

The process as Figure 26 illustrates is based on six distinctive principles:

1. **Getting it right –** means that the Healthcare providers must act in accordance with the law and regulations on which they have been set up in order to ensure that there is positive leadership that appreciates the importance of good complaint management processes and seeks to establish a culture that has transparent governance arrangements and where roles and responsibilities are clearly defined so as to drive quality improvement and service excellence through the closed loop cycle of investigating deficiencies and fool proofing through root cause analysis and

implementing the right solutions that ultimately lead to the right outcome for the complainant and the public at large.

2. **Being customer focused** – the processes used within Healthcare providers must ensure that there is a front end focussing on customers (patients) and those particularly who complain and that the complaint is using the expectations of complainants in terms of speed, sensitivity, quality, professionalism and the expected outcomes.
3. **Being open and accountable** – means that service standards including the ability of the Healthcare provider to handle complaints are published on a regular basis and that the data is presented in an honest, evidence based explanations.
4. **Acting fairly and proportionally** – this is to demonstrate that the treatment of complainants is done fairly, without any unlawful discrimination or prejudice.
5. **Putting things right** – recognising that there are deficiencies and apologising if and when the case arises. Demonstrating prompt reaction to dealing with deficiencies by finding the right remedies.
6. **Seeking continuous improvement** – using lessons learnt and learning particularly from complaints in order to improve service design and delivery.

Example 2: This is a useful guidebook used by the Government of Canada (2009) and it is a best practice guide on how to deal with complaints using a variety of perspectives:

1. **Complaints** – a critical form of communication. This is to encourage organisations to appreciate that complaints provide abundance in terms of information and therefore enable them to focus on the vital few areas where serious deficiencies exist and where there is the biggest opportunity for improvement. Complaints are also important in terms of ensuring that customers are least affected by deficiencies and poor quality and that the impact externally is much more significant if the focus is not on those aspects that affect the customers directly.
2. **The importance of complaint handling** – the sole purpose of handling complaints is to generate goodwill, loyalty and word of

mouth promotion. It is well accepted that complaint behaviour is not reflecting the total population of dissatisfied customers. By encouraging more and more people to complain this will show the root cause of the problem and therefore the analysis from the data received is more likely to foolproof the problem and help recover the service provision.

3. **Complaints management system is the top managements role** – the importance of managing complaints has to be on the agenda of every executive and has to be reflected in terms of how well their organisations does in terms of enabling and empowering employees to handle customers externally and delivering high levels of satisfaction and retention on the one hand but also the performance of the organisations concerned through the high levels of retention and the economic benefits that ensue.
4. **Customer retentions strategy** – in the long term customer retention is more likely to deliver more tangible benefits and also strategic benefits and is a cost saving opportunity for not chasing after new customers and replacing what has been lost. The management therefore of the existing customer pool and generating long term loyalty is a strategic imperative that top executives have to pay attention to.
5. **Complaint handling staff** – the empathy engine is the magic wand that will enable staff to learn how to preserve customer satisfaction and ensure least defection. The art of managing complaints and finding the right solutions to the existing problems and more importantly those solutions that will lead directly to the customer satisfaction through recovery mechanisms will be a distinctive competitive advantage.
6. **Publicising the customer complaint system** – by ensuring that the system represents the backbone of quality improvement and service delivery optimisation this will make the organisation stronger in the long run. This will also drive every single employee to ensure that the enabling complaint handling management system is the key focal point as it represents the voice of the customer up stream, mid stream and downstream.
7. **Customer complaint resolution at the first point of contact** – the more empowerment that exists and the more encouragement of

front line staff to interact and interface with the customer in order to investigate, assess, design, negotiate and implement solutions that foolproof the complaint and help recover the service and satisfy the customer the more likely the organisation is competitive.

Example 3: The published complaint handling report issued by the Financial Services Authority (2010). This report was published to ensure that the financial services industry takes the customers more seriously and to encourage financial institutions to embed a culture that is committed to treating their customers fairly and positively. "The quality of a firm's complaint handling is an important aspect of this, revealing the extent cultural drivers such as senior management engagement, decision making and staff reward structures are delivering fair outcomes for customers".

The report also states the following: "carried out well, complaint handling presents a valued opportunity for firms to rebuild and enhance their relationships with their customers when something has gone wrong, and to use the information gathered to make changes that deliver fair outcomes for their wider customer base (for example, by changing their product service or sales processes)".

The report states that many of the top and leading banks, in particular, were found to have serious breaches in terms of how they handled complaints and deal with their customers. "We found poor standards of complaint handling within most of the banks we assessed. This resulted mainly from weaknesses in banks culture, particularly their governance arrangements, policies and controls".

The report (FSA) concludes with a process that will enable banks to improve in the several areas highlighted through their investigations and in order to ensure better services, better quality internally and more customer satisfaction (Figure 27).

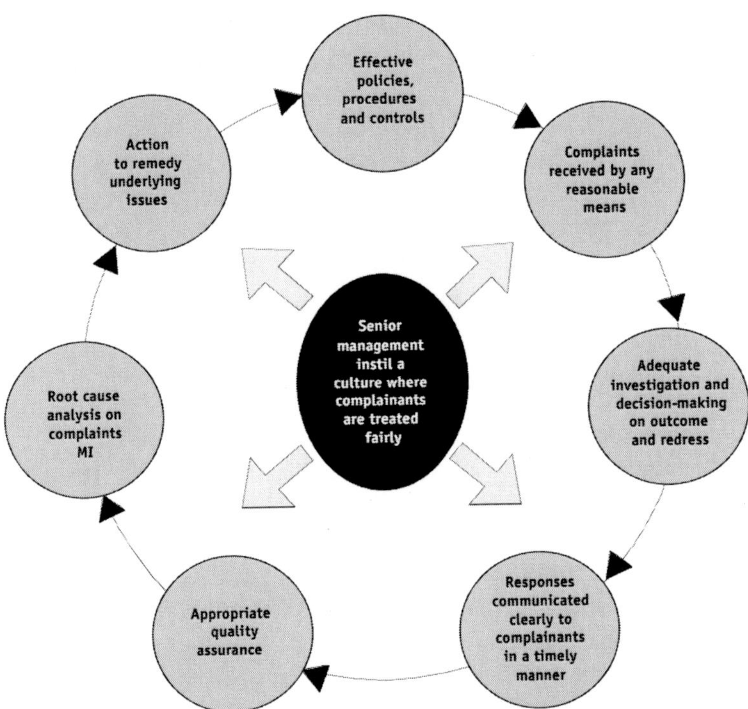

Figure 27: Key Elements of Fair Complaint Handling
Source: (Financial Services Authority, 2010)

For instance, they emphasised the following key points:

1. **Senior management role and responsibility in instilling a culture where complainants are treated fairly** – this means that there is a clear accountability and responsibility of senior managers to get closely involved in the complaint handling management system and embedding the governance structure that they are responsible for, particularly in terms of monitoring standards to help drive the necessary actions and improvement of standards as a result of complaints received.
2. **Effective policies** – procedures and controls for complaint handling – this means that the management system within an organisation has to be focussed on the customer in terms of its policies, procedures and controls so as to enable a fair complaint handling to the levels expected by the customers.

3. **Complaints received by reasonable means** – this means that different channels must be put at the disposal of customers to make complaints.
4. **Adequate investigation and decision making on outcome and redress** – procedures for managing complaints need to lead to a resolution where the deficiency occurs and by putting in place a recovery plan that can guide a predictable and positive outcome as far as the customer is concerned.
5. **Responses communicated clearly to complainants in a timely manner** – this means that the timeliness, quality, speed and professionalism associated with dealing with complaints have to be the norm and the outcomes have to be articulated to complainants in a fair, clear and not misleading way.
6. **Appropriate quality assurance** – this means that the quality handling and management process needs to work well and effectively with continuous improvement to all the necessary aspects in order to foolproof the organisations capabilities internally and maximise the positive outcomes and by minimising unnecessary complaints.
7. **Root cause analysis** – by using data and information in particular feedback from customers organisations concerned can analyse, rectify and foolproof their approaches and processes to preserve high quality standards and ensure positive outcomes with regards to the customers.
8. **Action taken to remedy underlying issues** – this means that the necessary action to remedy any issues internally or externally takes place and any changes that are necessary for policies, procedures or processes must take place based on the identified root cause analysis.

Example 4: This guide is produced by the British and Irish Ombudsman Association (BIOA). As Figure 28 illustrates this guide suggests a process that involves the following steps:

- Receiving a complaint from a complainant;
- Seeking a response from the organisation they complained about;
- Trying to resolve the complaint as quickly as possible;

- Carrying out some sort of 'investigation' to identify the merits of the case, arrive at a conclusion and provide appropriate redress;
- Feeding the outcome of systematic findings in best practice within the organisation.

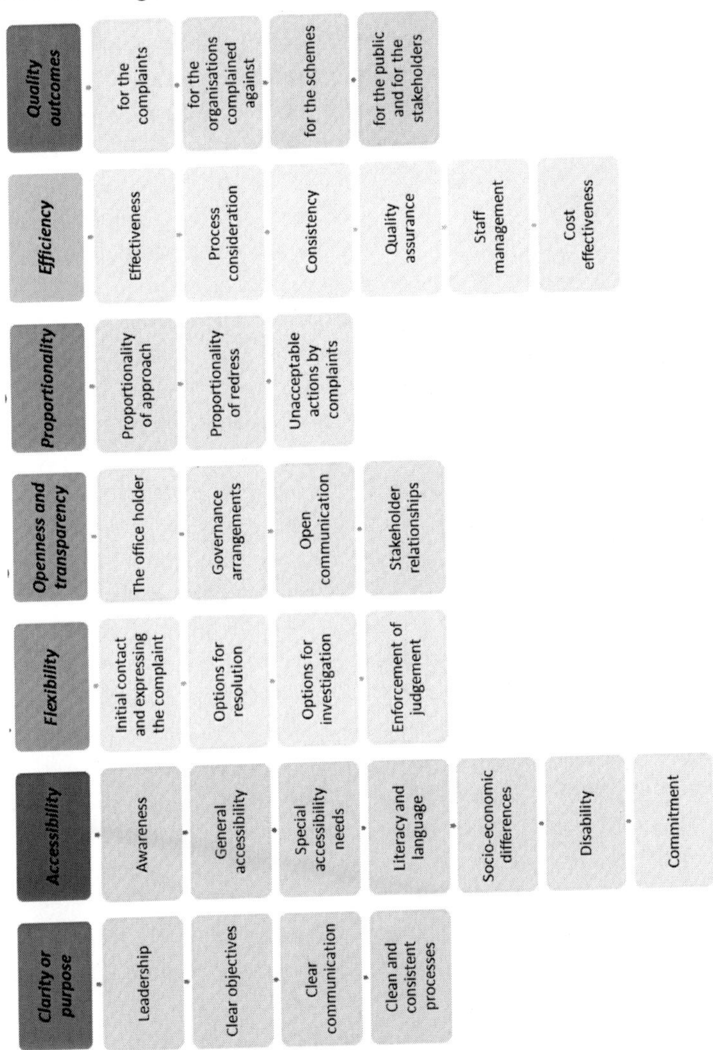

Figure 28: Generic Complaint Handling and Resolution Process
Adapted: (The British and Irish Ombudsman Association, 2007)

The seven principles that are depicted in Figure 28 and on which this guide is based include the following:

1. **Clarity of purpose –** means that the organisation has clear roles and responsibilities in so far as the management of complaints is concerned and in particular the role of leadership in driving the process of customer empathy and dealing with deficiencies through complaint handling resolution. It also means that there are clear objectives and clear communication through openness and transparency and there is reliance on solid policies and processes for handling complaints. "Consistency must not equal complacency. The schemes service should be regularly reviewed in the light of feedback from complainants and organisations within its remit, to ensure that it continues to meet changing demands and circumstances. Schemes should continue to look for improvements in service provision and be prepared to learn from and assist others".
2. **Accessibility –** in relation to health services, open and available to all who need it. By creating awareness through various promotional means and by providing general accessibility regardless of age, social group or gender. In particular by focussing on special access ability needs and by handling issues related to literacy and language. By enabling wider accessibility this may also include social economic differences and understanding the wider social issues associated with age, gender, race, culture etcetera. By appreciating the importance of disability and making staff aware of sensitivities associated with physical and mental disabilities and illnesses. By showing commitment to the schemes of health care service provision. "Genuine commitment accessibility is more than just a matter of ensuring disabled access, induction loops, providing leaflets in various languages etcetera. It is about proactively 'opening up' – widening access, literally and metaphorically – for all kinds of people who might not otherwise have the knowledge, confidence or ability to complain".
3. **Flexibility –** the use of policies and procedures that are responsive to the needs of the individuals. This means right at the onset the initial contact and expressing the complaint by making

that the scheme in place does address their particular problems. By having in place options for resolution which means that the in-house complaint handling procedure has been able to resolve a dispute. In particular to allow a settlement to take place by mediation or conciliation before investigation begins because the cost will escalate and the irreparable damage will become very significant. This scheme does also have to have the capability for allowing investigations which will enable the complainant handlers to speak to other parties, is appropriate. Lastly the need for enforcement of judgement for the scheme to make recommendations that are binding on the organisations concerned. "Whenever recommendations are made to an organisation, its response should be recorded and the implementation of any recommendations monitored. The scheme can then explain what has happened, both to the complainant and where appropriate, publicly".

4. **Openness and transparency –** providing public with information in order to make the service very transparent and therefore gets rid of demystification. For the leadership to exercise their authority to create confidence and demonstrate their independence in so far as complaint handling is concerned. By putting in place governance arrangements that are based on best practice and which are geared towards preserving confidence and independence of the scheme. Using an open communication strategy in order to take account of the needs of complainants, staff and other stakeholders. Building stakeholder relationships in order to exert positive influence through a partnership approach towards improving an organisations own service standards and those in similar organisations, "the willingness to work with a scheme and learn from complaints reviewed, requires confidence in the advantages to be gained by demonstrable commitment to good customer service. Whether in the public or private sector, organisations are more likely to understand, trust, and comply with a schemes determination if they have a clear appreciation of its vision and values, awareness of the review process and any mechanisms for assuring quality, fairness and consistency".

5. **Proportionality –** process and resolution that is appropriate to the complainant. To have effective complaint procedures which facilitate total resolution and where appropriate refer complaints back to give the organisation an opportunity to achieve the right outcome? Proportionality of redress should include an apology, remedial action and sometimes financial redress. Dealing with unacceptable actions by complainants means procedures should be in place to allow the investigation to proceed while managing such difficult behaviours. Engagement with complainants can of course be reduced if their complaints are dealt with efficiently and go to a timely conclusion. "The scheme should have clear procedures for responding to a complainant who is particularly threatening. In extreme cases, this may include calling in the police. These procedures should be open and transparent for complainants as well as for staff. They should include a requirement, wherever possible, to make a complainant aware that particular behaviour is considered unacceptable and why this is the case, and to explain what will happen should it continue. It is important however not to confuse such cases with those where special sensitivity is needed, for example when responding to the requirements of some complainants with mental health problems or other disabilities".
6. **Efficiency –** a service that strives to meet challenging standards of good administration. This includes being effective and having credibility in the eyes of the stakeholders. A scheme that has good internal planning processes will rely on its published values, mission statement, clear objectives and performance risk management processes etcetera. In addition process considerations where documented steps and processes can be easily implemented and where information and data can be analysed will reflect a fair procedure and provide opportunities to comment on facts and arrive at the sound conclusion or outcomes. Consistency in terms of referring to previous cases and reflecting sound standards therefore, will help monitor the number and outcomes and can nourish the improvement of the quality of decision making and arriving at sound conclusions. Quality assurance is referred particularly to the process and

guidance on internal complaint handling and redress. Staff management is the life-cycle of recruiting, developing, involving, empowering and recognition schemes for doing good work. In so far as cost effectiveness is concerned its related to driving quality improvement for ensuring value for money at least cost and providing effective outcomes through the scheme that are not just judged in terms of output but also the quality of the outcomes themselves, "the value for money and effectiveness of the scheme should be judged not only in terms of output but also the quality of the outcomes that are delivered. Although difficult to quantify, a scheme can be set to deliver value for money if the outputs and outcomes it achieves merit the running costs of the scheme".

7. **Quality outcomes –** a complaint resolution that leads to positive change. Quality of the outcomes first and foremost for the complainant means that the complainants expression of satisfaction with the scheme and with the outcome in accordance to their expectations. Furthermore quality outcomes for the organisation complaint against itself in terms of the way the investigation took place and due diligence has been observed, case by case and where the scheme operation has proven to work effectively in a visible and transparent way. Quality outcomes for the scheme itself in terms of the lesson learned from the complaints that were handled in order to improve outcomes for the future complainants and other stakeholders. "Schemes must handle complaints in ways that promote their credibility and standing. The aim should be to manage expectations, take into account and respect the feelings of all concerned and ensure no surprises at the outcome". In so far as quality of outcomes for public and wide stakeholders it means holding the organisation responsible for the way it handles complaints and deals with people and also the wider public confidence in the provision of health care services and proactively it will enable the organisations concerned to act as role models for other complaint handlers. The learning can be used as publicity for widening the best practice across the whole sector.

Figure 29: Complaint Handling and Resolution Process (Legal Services)
Adapted: (Legal Ombudsman, 2011)

Example 5: This is a guide issued by the Legal Ombudsman (2011). As Figure 29 illustrates the guide is based on the following principles:

1. **Accessibility** – to ensure that users of legal services can have their complaints heard.
2. **Good customer care** – where the staff facing customers are trained to deal with the customers with sensitivity and empathy.
3. **Customer focus** – to design complaint handling procedures that are clear, simple and customer orientated.
4. **Accountability and transparency** - to ensure that a proper investigation with clear and honest explanations and geared towards finding the right outcomes that complainants can expect.
5. **Acting fairly and proportionality** – means that complainants are treated impartially without any bias or discrimination.

6. **Putting things right** – learning from complaints in order to foolproof the service provision and optimise internal processes.
7. **Learning from complaints** – to use complaints as an opportunity for driving improvement and bringing necessary change for the end benefit of customers.

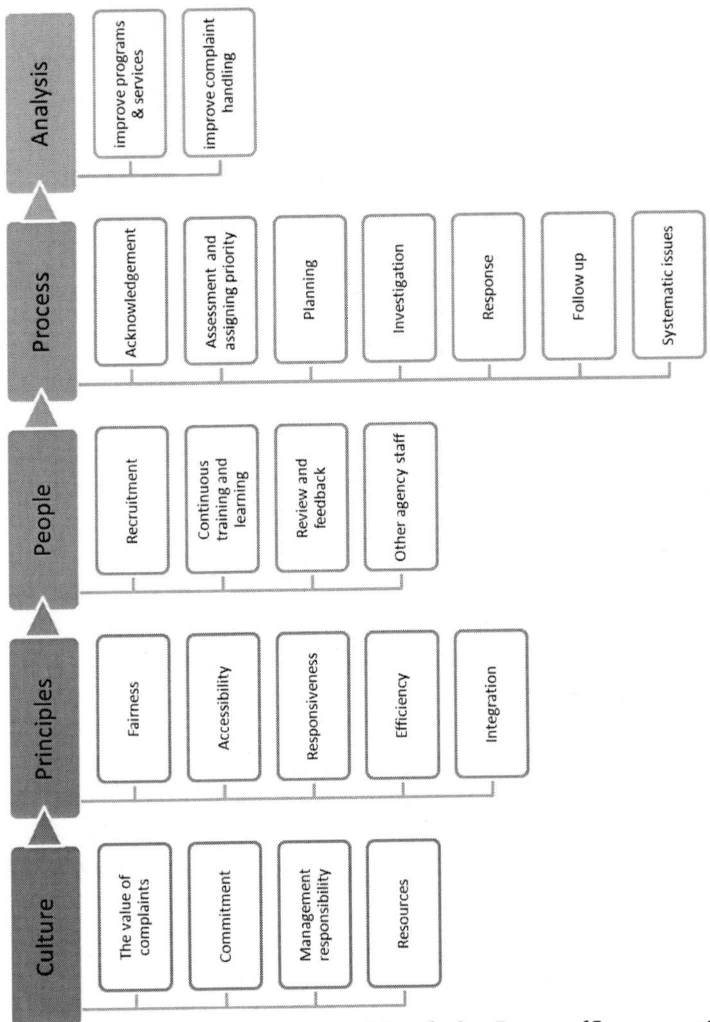

Figure 30: Complaint Handling and Resolution Process (Government Sector)

Adapted: (Commonwealth Ombudsman, 2009)

Example 6: This guide is produced by the Commonwealth Ombudsman and as Figure 30 illustrates the guide is based on five principles which include the following:

1. **Culture** – this means that an organisation has to value complaints and recognise that the challenge is effective complaint handling that will benefit its short, medium and long term competitiveness. By constantly revisiting the policies, service delivery mechanisms and driving improvement this will reassure the external customers on the commitment to have their problems solved, voices heard and complaints resolved to a satisfactory level, but also it will create trust by portraying the organisation concerned as transparent and committed to improvement.
2. **Principles** – this means that the principles of fairness, accessibility, responsiveness and efficiency are core business values and they have to be adhered to and the leadership of these organisations must act as role models and made accountable for these published principles.
3. **People** – ensuring that the individuals who are responsible for delivering service and facing customers have the right skills and competencies together with the positive attitude and the empathy capability for dealing with complainants.
4. **Process** – the complaint handling and resolution process must be reflected in terms of the policies and procedures, not only in terms of acknowledging the complaint quickly but also n how it is assessed and prioritised. The process of investigation and root cause analysis to generate the facts and identify where the failures have taken place and the speedy response to the complainants must be clear and informative. In a case where complainants are not satisfied with the response the process of referral of complaints to higher authority or a different process for further investigation and decision must be clear and documented.
5. **Analysis** – the information obtained from complaints must be used by the organisations concerned to constantly drive the improvement of their services and processes and fool proofing in all critical aspects of their value chain.

The art of complaint handling and resolution is perhaps one of the backbones of organisational excellence in the 21st century. By clearly investing in a solid extended life-cycle process for encouraging complaints and handling them at all stages of the value chain to the satisfaction of customers this can only create more impetus for the drive of excellence and will give the organisations concerned a competitive advantage. It means that the voice of the customer is captured, not just in terms of designing new requirements for products and services, but also that the voice of the customer whether it is an angry voice reflecting frustration, disappointment is also amplified through the value chain to test the areas where the recovery is required and where the deficiency has occurred.

The effective complaint handling resolution process as seen in the various examples highlighted is not necessarily just based on solid policies and processes and procedures but more importantly it is critical factors of effectiveness and success will continue to depend on the human component. This is where empathy will become the most significant ingredient for handling complaints and where the drive for higher levels of customer satisfaction, retention and loyalty will become real.

When someone really hears you without passing judgment on you, without taking responsibility for you, without trying to mould you, it feels damn good. When I have been listened to, when I have been heard, I am able to re-perceive my world in a new way and go on. It is astonishing how elements that seem insoluble become soluble when someone listens. How confusions that seem irremediable become relatively clear flowing streams when one is heard.

Carl Rogers

Chapter 6: Customer Experience – The Umbilical Cord

Introduction

One of the past Chairman of Ford Motor Company, Mr Donald Peterson said:

> *"If we are not customer driven, our car won't be either"*

and the late Gandhi in 1890 said:

> *"The customer is the most important visitor. He does not depend on us, we are dependent on him. He does not disturb our work; he is the purpose of our work. He is not an outsider; he is an integral part of our company. We are not pleasing him in serving him, he pleases us in buying".*

The customer therefore is the raison d'être of organisations in terms of their survival and long term prosperity. Whilst the quality era has provided a meaningful foundation in terms of optimising products and services and creating rapport, trust, dependency and positive relationships with customers none the less the new era takes over from the quality foundation as a baseline in order to compete on new parameters that are defined well above criteria of product and service functionality, service delivery and reliability aspect and economic value.

Pioneers such as Dell Computers who recognised in the late 1990s that getting closer to the customer is critical for the future of their businesses are now reaping out huge benefits. Dell decided to reconfigure its business model (Figure 31) to ensure that the customer is integrated into its business and therefore facilitating the process of building meaningful and long lasting relationships. The model that Dell has pioneered was to shrink its supply chain and build a business that is totally customer orientated.

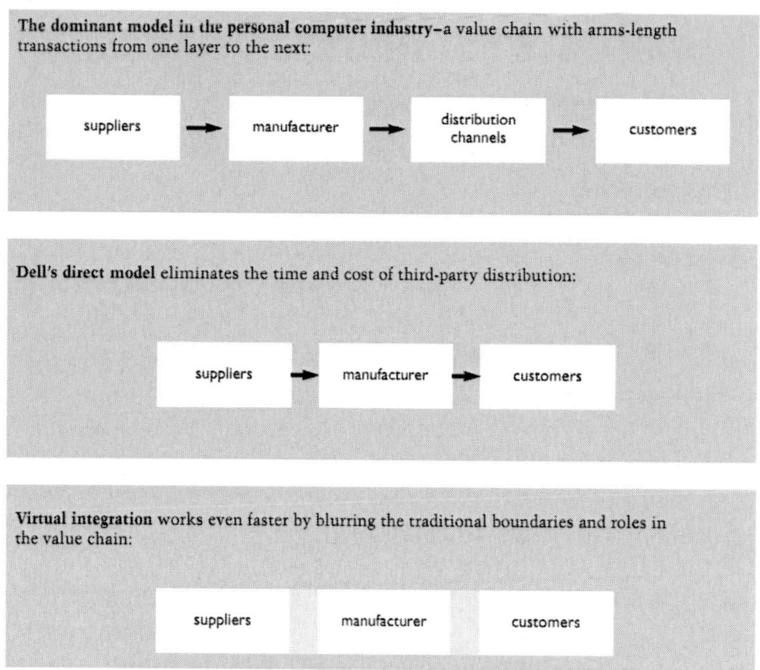

Figure 31: The Evolution of a Faster Business Model

Source: (Magretta, 1998)

As Michael Dell explains

> *"In this business, it is not about inventory you have, but about how fast it is moving through the cycle. I don't want a warehouse of stuff, because it becomes obsolete so quickly. With our model, we start with the customer whose order pulls inventory through the channel. That results in our ability to deliver a desk top computer in three days which is configured exactly as the customer wants. That provides a great deal of value".*

Source: (Pearlson & Yeh, 1999)

The new reconfigured Dell business model referred to as the Dell Direct Model is illustrated in Table 2. Essentially Dell has recognised that the battle of the 21st century is going to be based on providing meaningful and superior customer service and providing unique and individualised customer experiences. Dell built its foundation for business on the following criteria:

- **Priced for performance –** which means driving great efficiencies through a thorough and dedicated quality application in all aspects of the value chain.
- **Customisation –** all of its computers are built to order and ensuring that the 'for me only' principal of customisation is applied so that customers receive exactly what they want.
- **Service and support –** by having a meaningful relationship with their customers Dell has learnt through its extensive knowledge accumulation to empathise with customers and improve on the specific aspects that do matter to each individual customer.
- **Latest technology –** the power of technology has helped Dell integrate its channels of distribution and also shrink its inventory from weeks to days, on average by partnering closely with its preferred suppliers.
- **Superior share holder value –** through the process of driving great efficiencies delivering superior quality and customised value Dell has been able to deliver on a sustainable basis value to its shareholders as well.

Dell's award-winning customer service, industry-leading growth and financial performance continue to differentiate the company from competitors. At the heart of that performance is Dell's unique direct-to-customer business model. "Direct" refers to the company's relationships with its customers, from home-PC users to the world's largest corporations. There are no retailers or other resellers adding unnecessary time and cost, or diminishing Dell's understanding of customer expectations. Why are computer systems customers and investors increasingly turning to Dell and its unique direct model? There are several reasons:

- **Price for Performance:** By eliminating resellers, retailers and other costly intermediary steps together with the industry's most efficient procurement, manufacturing and distribution process Dell offers its customers more powerful, more richly configured systems for the money than competitors.
- **Customization:** Every Dell system is built to order. Customers get exactly, and only, what they want.
- **Service and Support:** Dell uses knowledge gained from direct contact

before and after the sale to provide award winning, tailored customer service.

- **Latest Technology:** Dell's efficient model means the latest relevant technology is introduced in its product lines much more quickly than through slow-moving indirect distribution channels. Inventory is turned over every 10 or fewer days, on average, keeping related costs low.
- **Superior Shareholder Value:** During the last fiscal year, the value of Dell common stock more than doubled. In 1996 and 1997, Dell was the top-performing stock among the Standard & Poor's 500 and Nasdaq 100, and represented the top-performing U.S stock on the Dow Jones World Stock Index.

Source: (Pearlson & Yeh, 1999)

Table 2: Dells Customer Orientation Approach

One of the best and often quoted examples of customer empathy is the Ritz Carlton. The Ritz Carlton has focused on providing unique and exceptional customer experiences which led to the company winning the prestigious Malcolm Baldridge Award in the US. The Ritz Carlton uses its employees as a key driver for unique and exceptional circumstances customer experiences. In order to ensure extremely high service standards the Ritz Carlton recruits and develops individuals so that they fit the company's culture based on the following parameter:

- **Individuals who share the same values and purpose** - by using a careful selection process that focuses on talent and personal values as these are things that cannot be taught. The top management of the Ritz Carlton ensures the close fitness between the individuals and the culture of the organisations.
- **People who care for and respect others** – by learning about individuals in terms of their persona, what drives them, what motivates them and their purpose in life the Ritz Carlton looks for individuals who enjoy and are passionate about helping others. They emphasise the importance of caring and respecting others. but the most important criteria is the enjoyment of being in contact with others whether they are guests or colleagues at work.
- **People who smile naturally** – the Ritz Carlton has the belief that if a person smiles naturally then this is important because this is

something you cannot force. If an employee is happy inside then they are happy outside. If an employee is happy that makes others feel good about themselves.

- **People who seek long term relationships** – employment at the Ritz Carlton means a long term relationship and therefore the criteria for selecting candidates is based on their aspirations to grow within the company and remain through a long term relationship.
- **People who have talent for the job** – the careful selection process chooses the best people in terms of their fitness from the point of view of culture and the philosophy of the Ritz Carlton. This is systematically measured through their behavioural event interviews during the selection process.

The world famous motto within the Ritz Carlton is:

"We are ladies and gentlemen serving ladies and gentlemen"

This exemplifies the commitment to service excellence and providing unique and memorable customer experiences. The Ritz Carlton drives this by emphasising on three steps to providing excellence service:

1. A warm and sincere greeting. Use the guest's name.
2. Anticipation and fulfilment of each guest's needs.
3. Fond farewell. Give a warm goodbye and use the guest's name.

Toyota for instance, uses the 14 principles of the Toyota way. As Fujio Cho, President of Toyota in 2001 said:

"Since Toyotas founding we have adhered to the core principle of contributing to society through the practice of manufacturing high quality products and services. Our business practices and activities based on this core principle created values, beliefs and business methods that over the years have become a source of competitive advantage. These are the managerial values and business methods that are known collectively as The Toyota Way".

The Toyota Way is based on the premise that respect for people is a fundamental value and the drive for continuous improvement is what brings excellence and delivers sustainable results. Quality in so far as Toyota is concerned is based on the following four pillars:

1. Long term philosophy;
2. The right process will produce the right results;
3. Add value to the organisation by developing your people;
4. Continuously solving root problems drives organisational learning.

In the airline business one of the always quoted pioneers in terms of unique customer experiences is South West Airlines. This low cost airline has, over the years, taken on giants who are full service providers and demonstrated that it can compete with them through service excellence and giving unique and individualised customer experiences driven by empathy as the engine. By using quality to drive internal operations and reduce costs whilst not compromising the quality of their services South West Airlines has delivered sustainable profitability to its shareholders whilst maintaining high quality standards (Figure 32). At the same time South West Airlines through its empathy engine and dedication to providing unique and customised and individualised customer experiences has optimised its productivity and delivered higher levels of satisfaction than all the other major airline carriers in the USA (Figure 33) (Heskett, Jones, Loveman, Sasser, & Schlesinger, 1994).

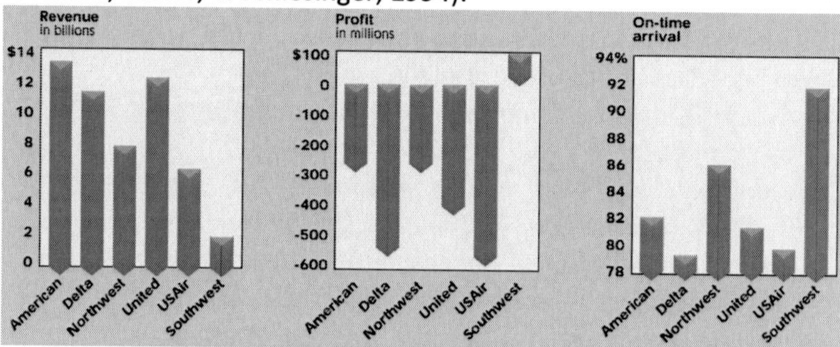

Figure 32: How Southwest compares with its competitors (Economic KPIs)
Source: (Heskett, Jones, Loveman, Sasser, & Schlesinger, 1994)

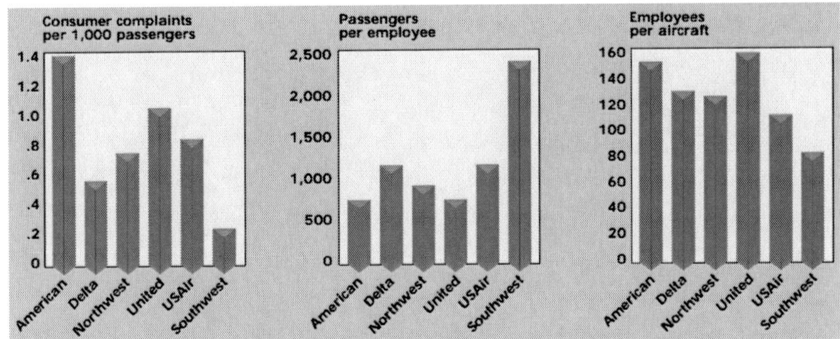

Figure 33: How Southwest compares with its competitors (Quality KPIs)
Source: (Heskett, Jones, Loveman, Sasser, & Schlesinger, 1994)

The mission of Southwest Airlines is:

"Dedication to the highest quality of customer service delivered with a sense of warmth, friendliness, individual pride, and company spirit".

Furthermore South West establishes itself on five leadership expectations (Figure 34). Amongst these five leadership expectations and the most important is their empathy approach which is to encourage people to work hard and dedicate themselves to their best ability and most importantly to use what is referred to as servants heart by following the golden rule and adhering to the basic fundamental principles of the company through putting others first and being proactive in delivering customer service.

Furthermore the fuel for empathy and customer satisfaction in so far as South West Airlines is concerned is to create a fun loving attitude where people do not take themselves seriously and they can celebrate success and enjoy their work by being passionate team leaders.

So quality matters after all and even in times of economic recession it is one of the key messages that continues to be emphasised by leaders of organisations from different parts of the world.

Live the Southwest Way

- ♥ **Warrior Spirit**
  - Work Hard
  - Desire to be the best
  - Be courageous
  - Display a sense of urgency
  - Persevere
  - Innovate
- ♥ **Servant's Heart**
  - Follow The Golden Rule
  - Adhere to the Basic Principles
  - Treat others with respect
  - Put others first
  - Be egalitarian
  - Demonstrate proactive Customer Service
  - Embrace the SWA Family
- ♥ **Fun-LUVing Attitude**
  - Have FUN
  - Don't take yourself too seriously
  - Maintain perspective (balance)
  - Celebrate successes
  - Enjoy your work
  - Be a passionate Teamplayer

Build Great Teams

Identify the right People for the right job
Build and maintain trust among Teammembers
Encourage vigorous debate and dialogue
Gain commitment to shared goals
Seek diversity
Always be on the lookout for great People

Think Strategically

See beyond today's activities
Act like an owner
Strive for continuous improvement
Understand the relationship between current actions and future consequences
Embrace problem solving
Translate broad objectives into specific action plans

Develop People

Know your People
Set clear expectations
Communicate consistently
Delegate responsibility; hold People accountable
Encourage strengths; address weaknesses
Provide timely, candid feedback
Build a bench

Get Excellent Results

Focus on safety, low cost, and high Customer Service delivery
Meet operational objectives
Complete projects ontime and on budget
Maintain a bias for action
Adhere to all internal controls
Demonstrate integrity in all actions

- Be honest
- Be ethical
- Be trustworthy

Figure 34: Southwest Leadership Expectation

Source: www.southwest.com

A survey conducted by the Conference Board (Gutner & Adams, March 2009) has led to the conclusion that quality is considered to be a pre-requisite and a key engine for driving efficiencies and putting businesses back on track as a result of the economic crisis and the external competitive pressures that they face. The report highlights that quality if aligned and put to drive the business can become very influential in driving improvement in different aspects of the value chain. The use of a large number of quality tools and techniques is being used extensively by the members of the Conference Board's Quality Council responses (Figure 35). It is clear, according to this report that quality does still matter and it is an opportunity for CEOs and leaders to respond more effectively to the challenging forces of change and the economic pressures that their businesses might face at the moment.

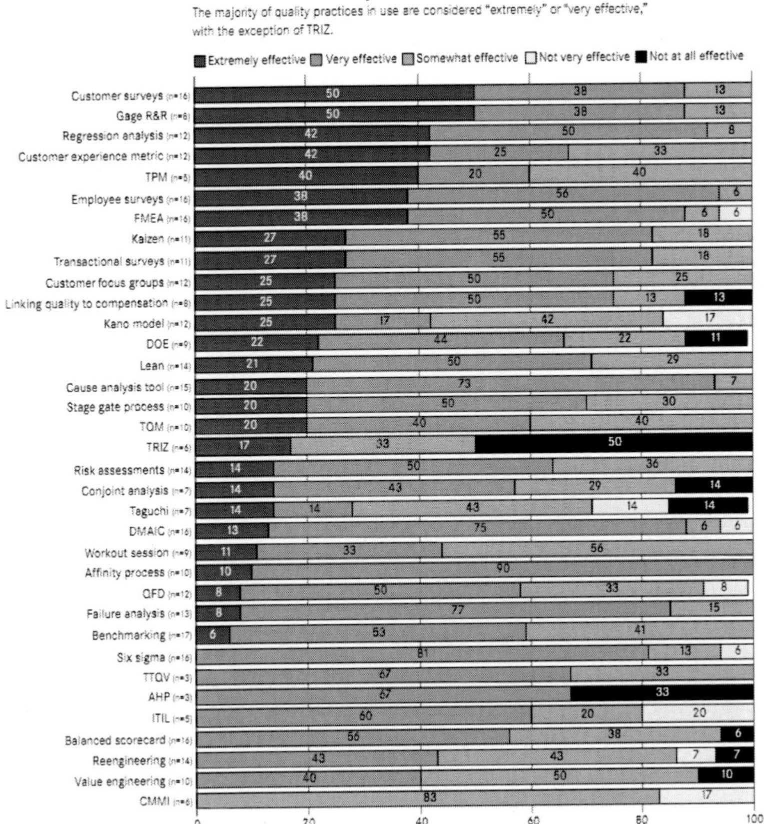

Figure 35: Effectiveness of Quality Practices

Source: (Gutner & Adams, March 2009)

Quality can help them deliver the following:

- To create better focus on customers and commit to strengthen the bonds with their customers through optimising value provision and building meaningful relationships.
- Improving operational excellence and speak to market by creating customised products and services with least cost and maximum value and through innovative means.

- Building the next generation of customer advocates – an opportunity to focus on engaging the customer in order to maintain their loyalty and increase their commitment to the future of the organisation. In a global economy this means that systems thinking and customer empathy will have to be taken more seriously.

Ensuring the Customer is Real – Building Effective Customer Experiences

The move from delivering services and providing high quality products is not a concern that most of the executives and leaders of corporations of different sizes and from different sectors of the economy are focussed on. According to several studies there is increasing evidence to suggest that the main concern at the moment is to create customer experience management as a philosophy for driving the future of business. More and more executives are convinced that there is a direct correlation between an effective customer experience and the drivers of loyal behaviour. The willingness to buy and the reluctance to switch and the likelihood of recommending a provider organisation to others are largely based on the experiences that customers go through.

A survey conducted by Forrester Research Inc. (Temkin, Dorsey, Chu, & Beckers, 2009) has demonstrated that there is a direct correlation between profitability and unique customer experiences on the one hand. And also there is a direct correlation between customer experience and loyalty (Figure 36). It is evident that across all industry sectors customers who receive excellent customer experiences are more likely to be loyal and are more likely to remain with the brands they have faith in and also are more likely to consider repeating the experiences and investing with the same organisations.

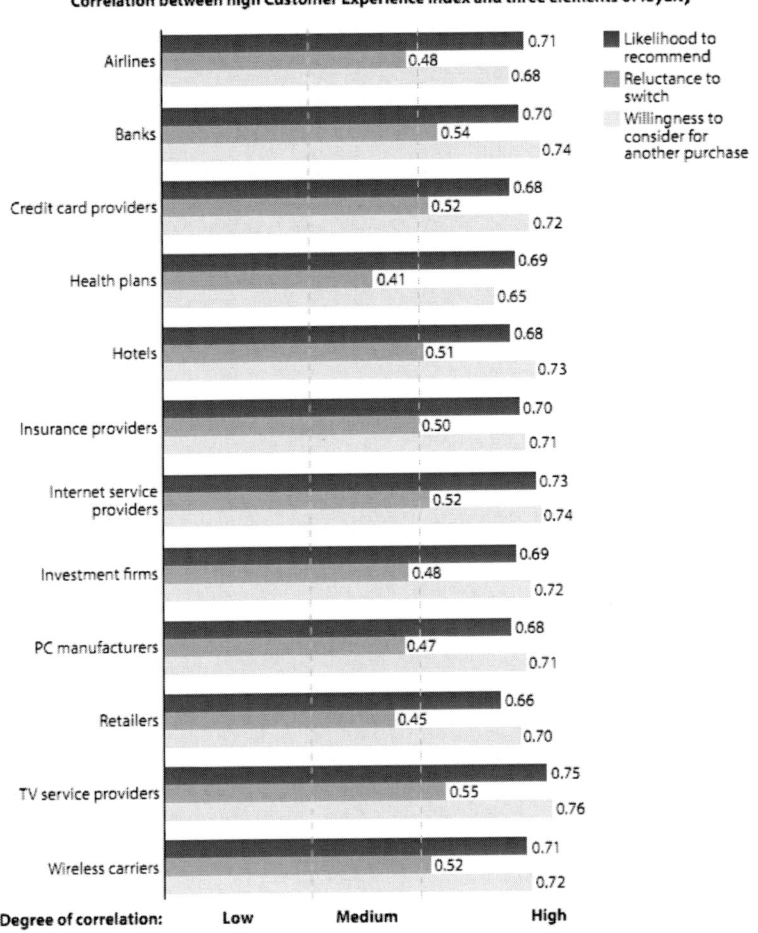

Figure 36: Customer Experience Correlates with Loyalty

Source: (Temkin, Dorsey, Chu, & Beckers, 2009)

Forrester (2008) have also found that customer experiences becoming an important item on the Chief Executives agenda because of the following reasons:

1. It tells them that customer experience is critical to their businesses.
2. It helps them create a clear strategy about where to focus.

3. It ensures that the impact on customers is one that will hit the bulls' eye and deliver high levels of satisfaction.

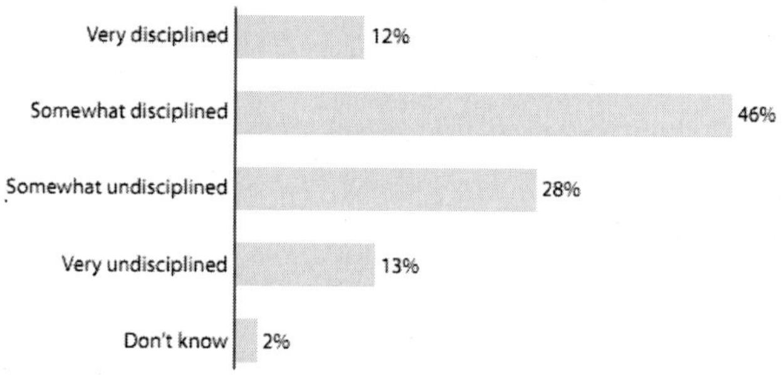

Base: 287 customer experience decision-makers from US firms with annual revenues of $500 million or more

Figure 37: CEM Approach Evaluation

Source: (Temkin & Geller, 2008)

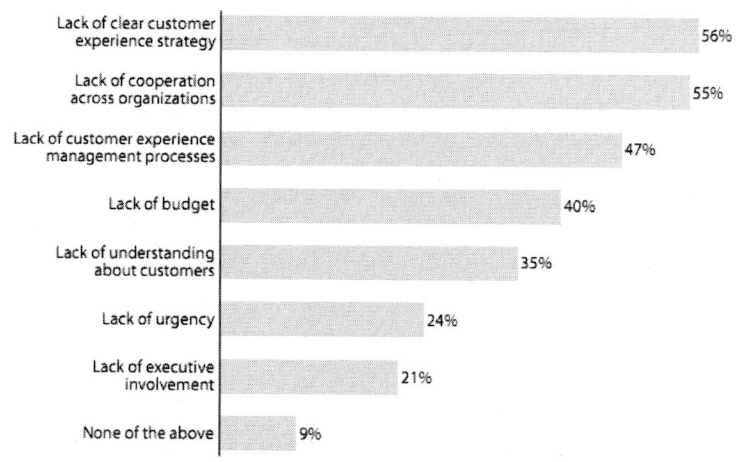

Base: 287 customer experience decision-makers from US firms with annual revenues of $500 million or more

Figure 38: CEM Key Obstacles

Source: (Temkin & Geller, 2008)

The survey by Forrester (Temkin & Geller, 2008) has also found that businesses that do not have the customer experience discipline and clear strategies represent quite a significant number (Figure 37). The reason why these businesses continue to struggle with the concept of customer experiences is quoted to be due to the following key factors:

- Not having a clear customer experience strategy.
- By not creating a seamless value chain in cooperation within the businesses.
- Not having clearly defined customer experience management processes and enabling methods for being customer orientated (Figure 38).

Forrester Research Report (Temkin & Geller, 2008) suggests a very useful blue print for building customer experience excellence through what is referred to as Experience Based Differentiation (EBD). This model is described as follows: "a systematic approach to interacting with customers that constantly builds loyalty". The model is proposed through three key principles:

Principle 1. To be obsessed with customer needs and not with product features.

Principle 2. To enforce brands with every interaction, not just communications.

Principle 3. Treat customer experience as competence, not a function.

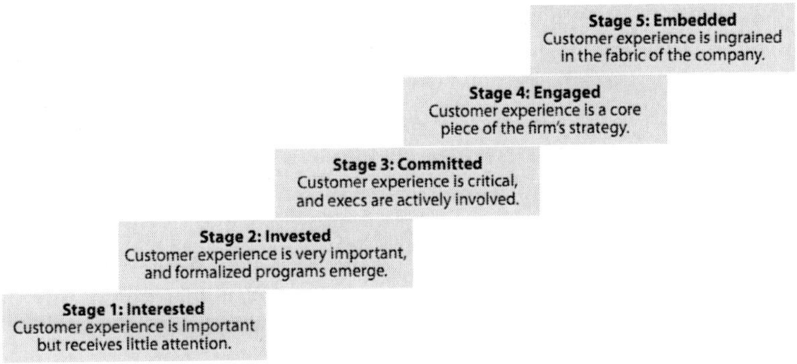

Stage 5: Embedded
Customer experience is ingrained in the fabric of the company.

Stage 4: Engaged
Customer experience is a core piece of the firm's strategy.

Stage 3: Committed
Customer experience is critical, and execs are actively involved.

Stage 2: Invested
Customer experience is very important, and formalized programs emerge.

Stage 1: Interested
Customer experience is important but receives little attention.

Figure 39: The five stages of EDB maturity

Source: (Temkin & Geller, 2008)

The EBD is further described through a five stage maturity model (Figure 39) which helps organisations through regular audits build the foundation and the interest in terms of highlighting the importance of the customer and investing in terms of creating base lines and capabilities in the form of management methodologies, processes and guidelines and getting the leadership committed to driving the business through customer experience. The harvesting stages are when customer experience becomes a core element of the corporate strategy and therefore is quantified in terms of impact and performance outcomes. Lastly the customer experience reflects the culture of the organisation and defines its competitive approaches. There are however big challenges that organisations face when creating customer experience orientation and customer centric way of doing business. It is reported that in the case of businesses that have demonstrated effective competitiveness through customer experience management the focus has clearly been on knowing through depth, rigour and intimacy of external customers. Furthermore successful businesses with customer experience orientations use their brand attributes to drive customer experiences. They also drive the improvement and the optimisation of customer experiences through meaningful reward and recognition system. They have exemplar role model behaviours of their executives who speak on behalf of the customer and who ensure that the customer is what defines the business.

In terms of creating a customer centric culture that delivers repeated and great customer experiences studies conducted by Forrester Research Inc. (Hagen, Manning, & Peterson, 2010) it has been found that there is a disconnect between what organisations wish to achieve and the values they would like to see espoused in the behaviours of their employees. As Figure 40 illustrates there are big gaps between what organisations wish to achieve and how employees are involved in terms of driving unique and meaningful customer experiences. Only 24% of the sample reflects employees who share a consistent and vivid image of target customers. The attributes of the companies brand are not well defined and employees do not understand these key attributes and companies do not the brand to define and drive customer experiences. Only 31% have reported that their companies recognise and reward them for improving customer experiences. Only 40% of senior executives were found to regularly interact with target customers (Hagen, Manning, & Peterson, 2010).

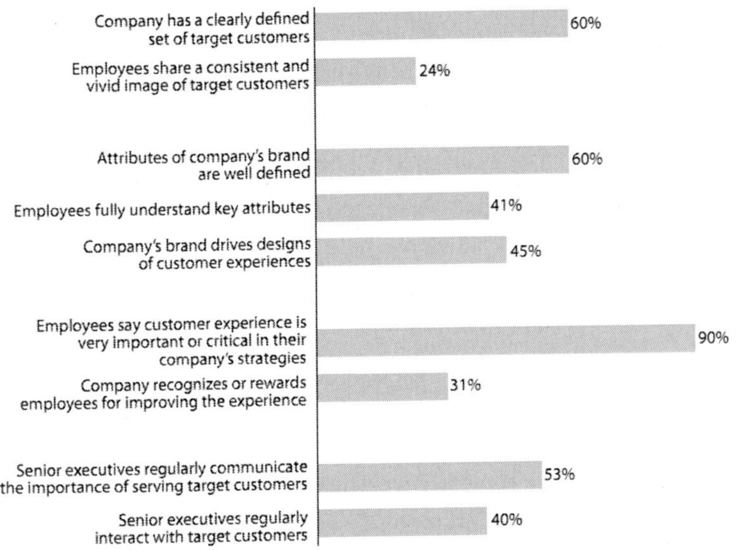

Figure 40: The Disconnect between companies and employees

Source: (Hagen, Manning, & Peterson, 2010)

Customer Experience Management – The Driver for Customer Loyalty

Organisations that have applied the concept of customer experience, over the years, and demonstrated their commitment and determination to building meaningful and long lasting relationships with their customers have started to see the results through the net impact on loyalty and retention even in times of hardship and economic downturn. Perhaps it is useful to see what the customers' perspective is in terms of exhibiting loyalty to their suppliers. A recent study (Thompson B. , 2006) has found the following:

- In order for their providers to earn their loyalty the customers rated the quality of interactions with the organisation they are dealing with as equally important to the quality of the goods or services they purchased. Memorable experiences build loyalty – 31% of customers in the survey recommended the company to a friend or colleague and 19% increased their purchase.
- Well trained and helpful employees are an aspect that is considered to be the top attribute of companies that provide consistently excellent customer experiences.
- Investing in employee training and internet based transactions and support have had a more positive effect in improving customer experiences.

Those organisations that have achieved high levels of customer loyalty and retention tend to have a broad definition of what customer experience means. They emphasise more on interactions with their organisations people, processes or systems. Only a few have intimated the importance of interactions with the product. The leading organisations refer to experiences as including feelings or emotional responses generated by the interactions.

In a sense customer experiences are expected to include all the points in which the customer interacts with a business organisations products and services. For instance in the case of Starbucks the customer interaction will include the anticipation of going to Starbucks, walking up to the shop, opening the door, ordering and paying for the coffee, getting the coffee, sitting down in the atmosphere of the shop to enjoy the coffee. These points of interaction are referred to by SAS Carlzon as the moment of truth. They reflect the points during which the customer is fully engaged with the brand and at which the relationship can succeed or can break. So in a sense customer experience has to be defined more clearly as beyond the tangible aspects of relationship building and relationship management but more on the basis of the perception of the interactions that the customer exhibits with the particular brand. In this sense, perception has to be critical because the customer has to think and feel at the same time about what is happening in terms of their desires and their expectations. The interaction on the other hand is literally dealing with the messages that the brand conveys, the actual use of the products with the service, and the post purchase of the service and the support activity in case there is a problem for instance. Is it important that the brand in the context of customer experience is not necessarily the logo or the marketing communication that organisations spend a vast amount of their money on? In so far as the customer is concerned the brand is the symbol of the organisation and the promise of fulfilment.

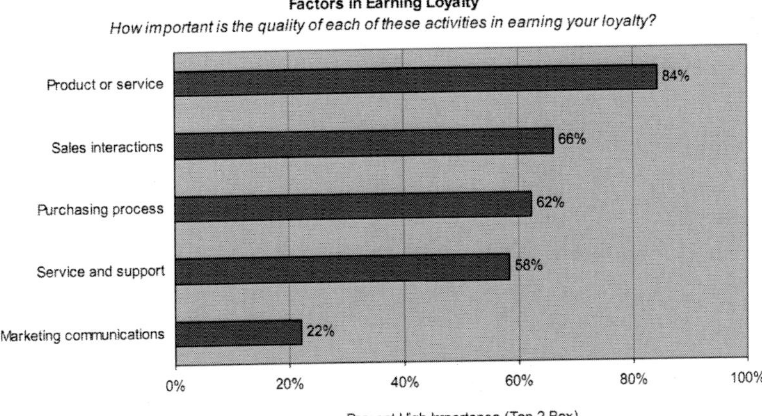

Figure 41: Factors in Earning Loyalty

Source: (Thompson B., 2006)

In order to consider the impact of customer experience on loyalty it would be useful to look at a list of factors that customers consider to be important and key drivers to loyalty. As Figure 41 illustrates customers were asked to rank a list of factors in terms of criticality in convincing them to be loyal to the brands that they are interacting with. The vast majority of respondents acknowledged that the base line has to be the product or the service but also the interactions and the delivery process. Less emphasis was acknowledging the post purchase aspects and least of all is the marketing communications.

It is however important to acknowledge that products and services are still important in driving loyalty but increasingly the emphasis on high quality interactions with people and systems and in particular with e-business are at the same level, if not higher, to the transactional aspects of services, service provision and product provision.

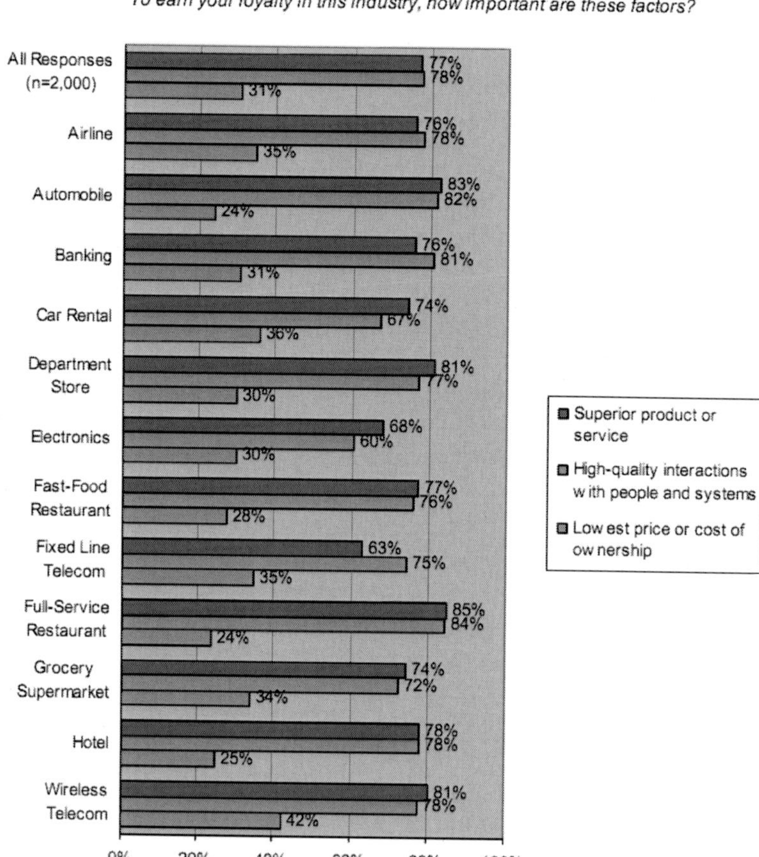

Figure 42: Loyalty Drivers by Industry

Source: (Thompson B., 2006)

A survey conducted in 2006 on-line, with 600 respondents representing 2000 industry settings have reflected on their experiences in determining loyalty drivers (Figure 42). It is clear that an aggregate picture demonstrates that the high quality interaction with people and systems is equal to the importance of superior quality of products and services. Price comes significantly lower. This characteristic has been exhibited across all the twelve industry sectors examined. This therefore conveys an important message that the customer is looking at unique experiences and having the big say in the design, delivery and relationship management aspects. The more opportunity businesses therefore provide for high quality interactions with their customers the more likely that this will drive loyalty. it is an important message for organisations to focus less perhaps on limiting their competitiveness solely on the provision of competitive products and services but work harder by creating new dimensions where winning the hearts and the commitments of customers would become at least an equal parameter for defining their strategic intentions.

As to whether currently organisations are capable of providing unique and excellent customer experiences the jury are still out and most businesses recognise that they have lots of challenges in determining superior standards of customer experience. Figure 43 illustrates, on average less than 30% conviction of firms ability to provide excellent customer experiences. The vast majority of organisations representing different sectors of the economy are yet to find ways and means of ensuring unique, dependable and superior customer experiences.

One of the reasons perhaps why Figure 43 illustrates disappointing statistics in terms of the provision of consistent and dependable high convincing percentages of excellent customer experiences is because of the lack of knowledge in terms of what drives unique customer experiences and what capabilities and competencies organisations would require in order to improve. A recent survey has established that the reason why only approximately between 20%-30% of organisations know the state of their customer experiences success is because they measure it holistically across the channels. Whilst they understand the quality of what drives the experiences and its impact on customer behaviours such as loyalty there are however obstacles in terms of the measurement and particularly the dimensions that are critical in determining the quality of a customer experience.

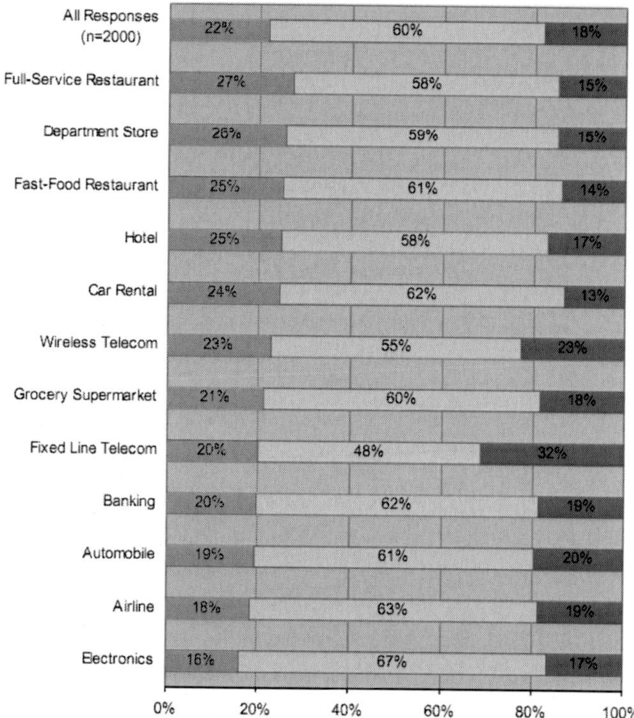

Figure 43: Currently Provide an Excellence Customer Service

Source: (Thompson B. , 2006)

The survey by SAS Institute Inc., Peppers & Rogers Group and Jubelirer Research, (2009) has reported that the most advanced organisations in terms of the sophistication of their customer experience capabilities (60%) are outperforming the competition. The reason behind this is the drive and determination to establish customer experience maturity. As Figure 44 illustrates a customer experience tends to drive competitive advantage through emphasis on building loyalty, dependability and high capability that the organisations concerned can compete with. The outcome of this is the competitive performance results that are significantly different from the lower end of represented by organisations with little maturity to the high end which includes organisations that drive customer experience excellence and maturity in a dedicated and meaningful manner.

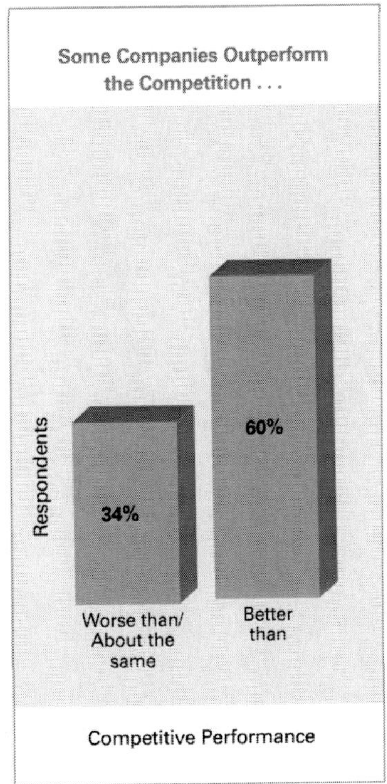

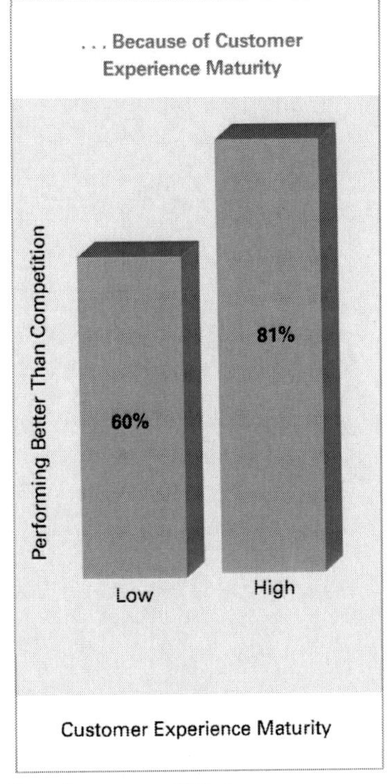

Figure 44: Companies outperforming competition
Source: (SAS Institute Inc., Peppers & Rogers Group and Jubelirer Research, 2009)

The SAS Institute Inc., Peppers & Rogers Group and Jubelirer Research, (2009) study proposes that the reasons why the leading group of organisations that outperform the rest is due mainly to their activities which include the following:

- Good insight.
- Good interaction.
- Significant improvement.
- Dedicated customer orientation (Figure 45).

This study clearly indicates the benefits of focusing on driving competitiveness through distinctive capabilities that are customer related and in particular the specific focus on the Customer Experience.

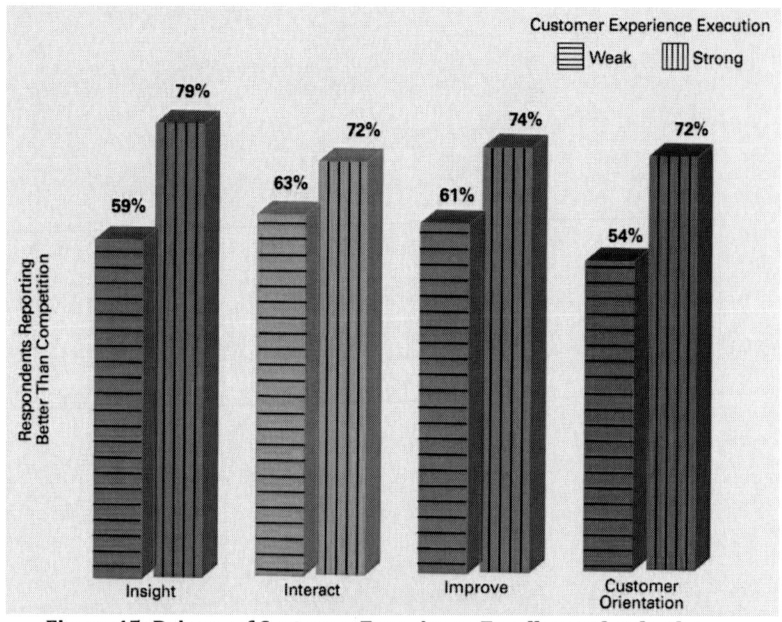

Figure 45: Drivers of Customer Experience Excellence that lead to a Competitive Advantage
Source: (SAS Institute Inc., Peppers & Rogers Group and Jubelirer Research, 2009)

In so far as good insight is concerned it means that these organisations know everything there is to know about their customers and have quality data that they can depend on in making the right decisions and planning for the future for providing unique experiences. One of the respondents has been quoted to say "we have 4000 variables on every customer . . . . we do information audits, have regular cleansing of the full file on a monthly basis, and use some in house bureau tools". They tend to also predict customer behaviour through scenario analysis and calculating the probability of them purchasing or defecting to a competitor. They establish individual profiles on segments of their customers and analyse the data in terms of value and in terms of specific and common needs. They also look at the value in terms of capturing the worth of a customer to the company and in the case of a critical customer the implications of them switching on the organisation itself.

In so far as interaction is concerned the leading organisations tend to interact through various means with their customers and manage and optimise the segments strategies. Using for instance one to one marketing, managing something referred to as the generic customer and looking at the critical aspects of each segment and how to foolproof the relationships with their customers. They have a proactive strategy of engaging high potential customers to ensure that their involvement will lead to real time customer experience evaluations. For the improvement aspects a significant focus is made on measuring and reporting through different methods and using optimisational marketing, planning and investments in order to improve the customer experience. Through primary marketing research using focus groups and other data that can guide in the assessment of personal experiential judgment using advanced analytical tools this will enable them to establish the status quo and make the right decisions.

In addition they use learning and improvement in order to optimise constantly and improve and inject best practice thinking. Lastly in so far as customer orientation is concerned the leading organisations are determined to build one to one relationships with their customers by establishing good customer trust, building a culture that recognises the drivers of customer thoughts and emotional reactions. The customer orientation within these leading organisations does tend to make a difference. The leading organisations use different methods for measuring the impact on customer satisfaction and use customer attitudes and perception in so far as the emotional aspects are concerned. They also recognise there are areas where improvements need to be conducted including for instance the new approaches to gaining customer insight and the tracking of customer behaviour and triggers of their reactions amongst others (Figure 46).

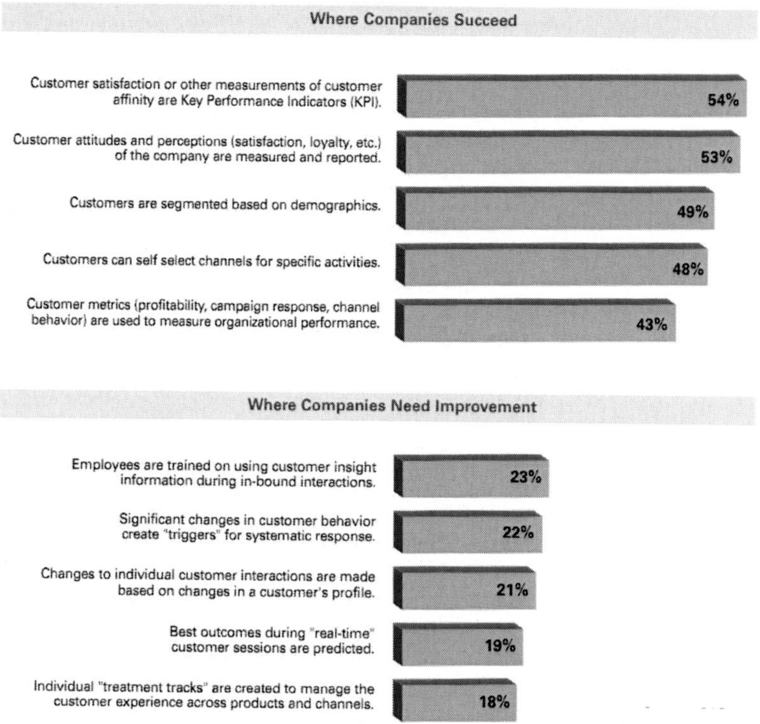

Figure 46: Where Companies Succeed—and Where They Improvement

Source: (SAS Institute Inc., Peppers & Rogers Group and Jubelirer Research, 2009)

The research conducted by SAS Institute Inc., Peppers & Rogers Group and Jubelirer Research (2009), proposes a useful method for building customer experience maturity. This is based on five levels of maturity and this audit tool can help organisations gradually build distinctive capabilities and competencies by moving away from a narrow minded focus on the product and to creating customer centric approach and gradually to developing capability for engaging with the customer and allowing the customer to interact with the organisation and using the intelligence and the customer knowledge that gets accumulated. Eventually meaningful customer experiences can be provided through having integrated customer centric strategies and working beyond by maintaining and sustaining a competitive advantage that is derived from excellence in providing customer experiences that are directly correlated to their loyalty (Figure 47).

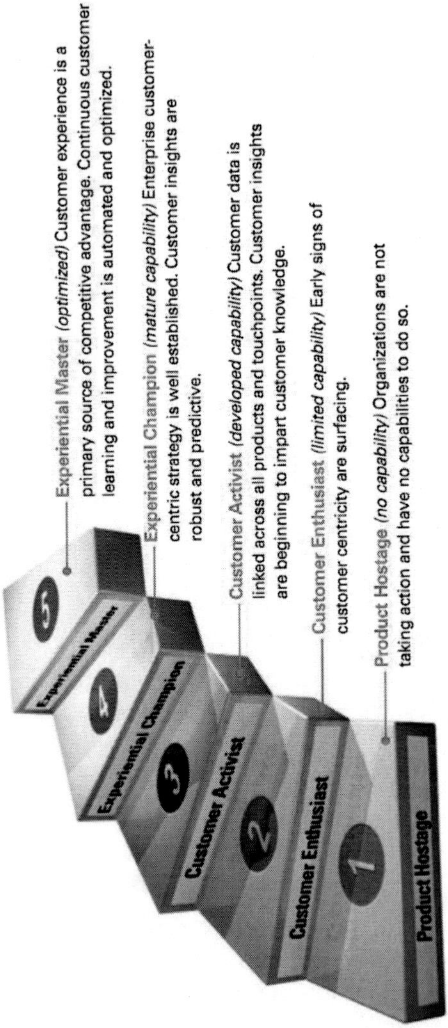

Experiential Master *(optimized)* Customer experience is a primary source of competitive advantage. Continuous customer learning and improvement is automated and optimized.

Experiential Champion *(mature capability)* Enterprise customer-centric strategy is well established. Customer insights are robust and predictive.

Customer Activist *(developed capability)* Customer data is linked across all products and touchpoints. Customer insights are beginning to impart customer knowledge.

Customer Enthusiast *(limited capability)* Early signs of customer centricity are surfacing.

Product Hostage *(no capability)* Organizations are not taking action and have no capabilities to do so.

5 Experiential Master

4 Experiential Champion

3 Customer Activist

2 Customer Enthusiast

1 Product Hostage

Figure 47: Customer Experience Maturity Model

Source: (SAS Institute Inc., Peppers & Rogers Group and Jubelirer Research, 2009)

Useful Strategies for Making Customer Experience Impact on Loyalty

The previous section was extremely useful at least by answering questions on how to build customer experience capability and how to ensure that this can be tracked on a regular basis and built towards a sustainable end that leads to superior competitiveness and high levels of loyalty and retention. What might be useful is to answer the question on what precisely organisations need to do in terms of embracing the philosophy of customer experience management and also building sustainable relationships with their customers by making the business model a viable one.

A report published by IBM Business Consulting Services (2005) and based on extensive research that was carried out by the consulting group has come to the conclusion that customer impact according to 68% of the respondents to the study have generated quantifiable revenue growth based on customer experience management practices. The organisations that have demonstrated competitive outcomes from the adoption of customer experience philosophy are not just basing it on operational concerns but emotional aspects as well. The traditional silo mentality of having marketing, sales, and services departments with individual agendas has been broken down. The business model that these pioneering firms have used is to create a seamless integrated approach where the organisations vision and strategies are defined in terms of customer orientated outcomes and the impact at the front end of the business is the value perception using customer evaluations based on the various interactions (Figure 48). The value chain is based on creating a seamless chain where the interaction of the customer with the organisation is enabled by all possible touch points and vertically to define processes that enable the customer to design their own unique individualised experiences using parameters that are important to them, such as user friendliness, options in terms of functionalities, time efficient, safe and secure, seamless in terms of the various transactions and interactions and defined in terms of the uniqueness of the brand that they are dealing with.

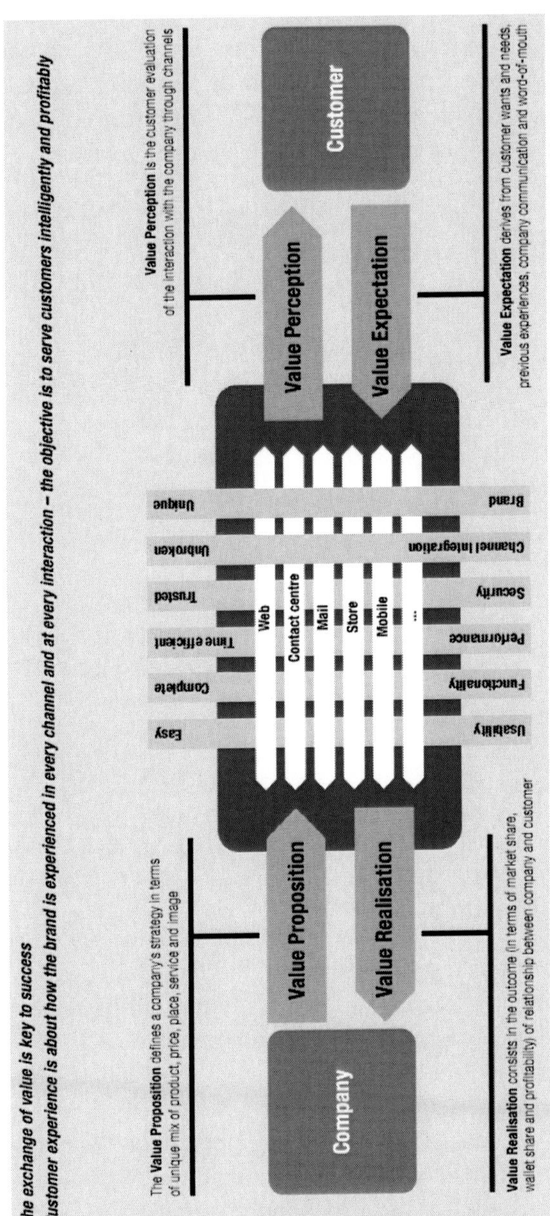

Figure 48: Customer Oriented Value Chain
Source: (IBM Business Consulting Services, 2005)

The IBM study did however demonstrate that 78% of companies that responded to their survey still measure customer experience from functional (transactional and operational) information they have captured. Only 64% measure emotional (bonding) aspects.

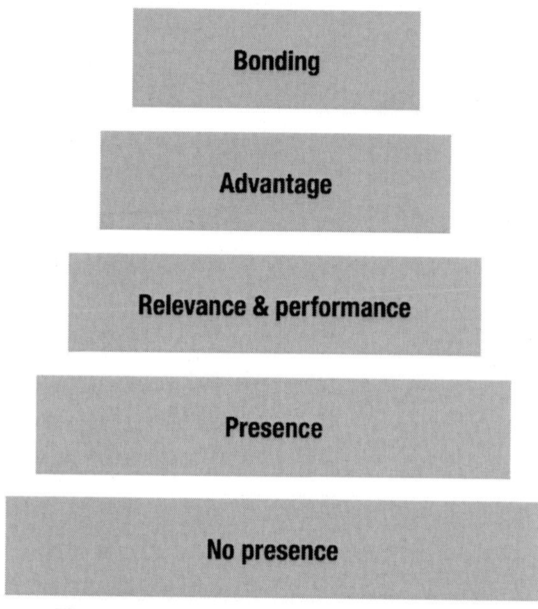

Figure 49: The Emotional Loyalty Pyramid
Source: BrandZ™ and the Ogilvy Loyalty Index, Available: (IBM Business Consulting Services, 2005)

In relation to building the emotional bonding perspective the IBM report (2005) illustrated the useful model (The emotional loyalty pyramid). The model represents a continuum useful for guiding the creation of solid bonding based on emotional loyalty starting with a baseline where the customers have a zero attachment, the progression continues with a development of linkages that makes customers and consumers more aware of the provider's brand. The educational perspective that customers and consumers receive grows their awareness and appreciation of how the brand is fulfilling their needs and requirement. This then leads to a stage where consumers distinguish the brand that serves their needs as a preferred option that fulfils emotional satisfaction and attachment. Finally the strong bonding emerges once the emotional attachment becomes a driving force with a sense of ownership, empowerment and advocacy (Figure 49)

The USA Government used a proactive approach to create excellence in services and therefore encouraged organisations to provide their customers with unique customer experiences using an approach that they refer to as world class courtesy (National Perfromance Review, 1998). This initiative was led by Vice President Al Gore during the Clinton term of office. It was a Federal initiative geared towards creating a focus on courtesy as a critical driver of empathy and service excellence.

PRESIDENT CLINTON'S EXECUTIVE ORDER 12862

"Setting Customer Service Standards"

- Identify customers who are, or should be, served by the agency.
- Survey customers to determine the kind and quality of services they want and their level of satisfaction with existing services.
- Post service standards and measure results against them.
- Benchmark customer service standards against the best in business.
- Survey front-line employees on barriers to, and ideas for, matching the best in business.
- Provide customers with choices in both the sources of service and the means of delivery.
- Make information, services, and complaint systems easily accessible.
- Provide means to address customer complaints.

Bill Clinton

Figure 50: The US Government Customer Service Pledge

Source: (National Perfromance Review, 1998)

The initiative was taken seriously by the national performance review and was supported by the Federal Government through an executive order signed by the then President Clinton, himself (Figure 50). Essentially the purpose was to identify courtesy, best practices and best in class organisations and to highlight the level of commitment to providing service excellence across the USA.

Characteristics Exhibited by World Class Organisations

In the case of leading organisations courtesy was generally considered to be a component within the customer service strategy. Indeed world class organisations tend to exhibit the following characteristics:

- An organisations cultural climate that reflects a commitment to meeting and exceeding customer expectations.
- Senior leaders demonstrating by example the organisations commitment to exceptional courtesy.
- Employees that are empowered to fully meet the needs of their customers.
- Courtesy is practiced by everyone throughout the entire organisation.
- Specific and ongoing training in courtesy is provided within the organisation.
- Formal and informal screening techniques are used to hire employees with exceptional skills in courtesy.
- The organisation establishes systems to measure the value of its services to customers.
- Services are provided seamlessly from the customers' perspective.
- There is zero tolerance for discourteous service.
- All the organisations found that courtesy improves customer loyalty. Furthermore the world class courtesy best practice report has also established that courtesy is expressed through a wide range of respectful behaviours and attitudes. They catalogued the following personal characteristics and behaviour that were repeatedly expressed by the best practice case studies. They

reported them as essential elements of courteous behaviour. These include:

- A willingness to discover opportunities to exceed the customer expectations.
- Sincerity.
- A friendly smile (even over the phone).
- Using the person last name (unless the customer indicates otherwise).
- A neat appearance.
- Proper use of the language.
- Exceptional listening skills (attentiveness).
- A relaxed and natural tone of voice.
- Appropriate eye contact.
- Clear communication at the customers' comprehension level.
- Knowledge about the product or service.

Tips for Improving Courtesy

- Be flexible – encouragement of learning to take lead from customers.
- Take some risks to delight and surprise the customer.
- Practice service leadership – developing a passion for service and then put the passion to work in whatever position.
- Smile your best smile – customers appreciate a pleasant atmosphere. A smile always helps.
- Listen as if you mean it – the greatest compliment to another person is listening to them.
- Call people back – returning calls have a direct relationship to dependability and dependability is the corner stone of good customer service.
- Demonstrate telephone courtesy – the tone and pitch of your voice can assure the caller that you are sincere, friendly and that you are listening.
- Develop a team focus – team work is definitely needed when it comes to improving courtesy.

Empathy depends not only on one's ability to identify someone else's emotions but also on one's capacity to put oneself in the other person's place and to experience an appropriate emotional response.

Charles G. Morris

Chapter 7: Service Recovery – Regaining Customer Confidence

Introduction

As we move well into the 21st century the notion of the enlightened and inspired customer will become more and more real. It is true to say that the previous year of competiveness was dealing with what can be referred to as the world of deficiency. The drive for measurement and optimisation was concerned with improving quality standards, delivering better services and trying to focus on the customer with all the challenges that are created by raising expectations and moving targets. Currently there is the emergence of what can be referred to as the world of delight. Indeed with customers seeking empowerment and positive engagement and wanting to shape their own individualised experiences it is no longer sufficient for organisations seeking to become world class just to remain cocooned and focussing on optimisation of internal quality standards. The school of thought has moved on from being obsessed with retrospective measurement in terms of customer satisfaction or dealing with service recovery through the measurement of complaints and customer dissatisfaction in to a new mind set of measurement that can be referred to as customer loyalty measurement. The latter is more challenging but also is more promising in terms of helping firms avoid switching customers.

The question of whether organisations are well equipped to deal with new challenges is a legitimate one. Furthermore the following question needs to be answered: "if quality matters, why doesn't the customer?" at the end it has to be recognised that whilst products and services are in the hands of the provider, experience is in the hands of the customers. In a sense, customers who wanted to have a big say, be part of shaping their own individualised experiences and want the uniqueness and the choice that most suits the individual needs. It is no longer exciting for customers to imitate what other customers have or what other customers do. In this sense, therefore the measurement that we have grown accustomed to and mainly linked to raising quality, optimising service provision and trying to create consistency and reliability of service provision is no longer sufficient. As Figure 51 illustrates the evolution in terms of customer focus has progressed significantly. It has created a mindset that focuses well beyond products and services and even in the context of individualised experiences customers are now looking for close associations with brands for other reasons than the classical functional and hedonic fulfilments. The word elation probably describes what customers want to feel and experience beyond the expected fulfilment attributes of the products and services and what their providers put in front of them.

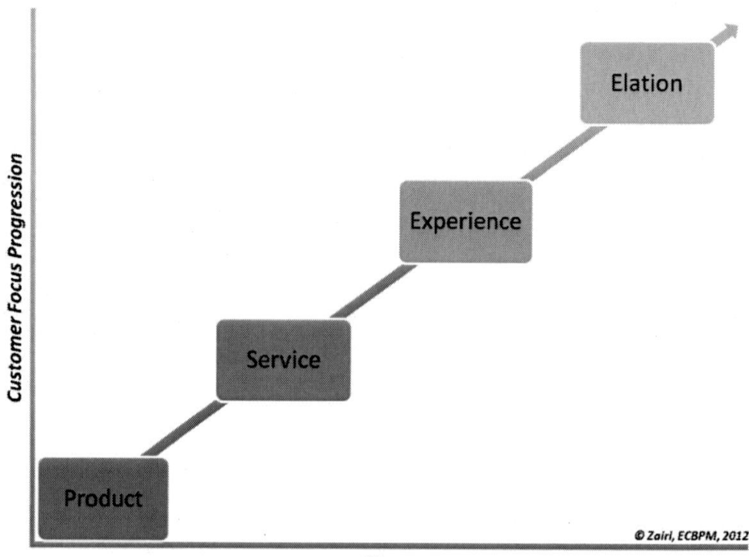

Figure 51: Customer focus – Evolution process

The evolution in customer behaviour and attitudes and how they would like to express their wants and needs in an emerging economy that is highly influenced by technology and enlightened and inspired customers has to be followed by radical change in the mind set of providers of products and services moving from the conventional measurement school of thought that is mainly concerned with products and service evaluation and measuring retrospectively complaints and customer satisfaction (Figure 52) into accepting albeit with serious challenges the new need for measuring loyalty aspects which requires new tools and methods well beyond the tangible aspects of conventional measurement means based on products and service satisfaction. It is also no longer sufficient to extrapolate from the retrospective customer satisfaction measurement into predictive outcomes of customer loyalty and retention. The new pioneering measurement methods will be extremely useful in creating better bonding with customers and will provide organisations with the opportunity to look beyond the measurement of customer experience for instance and to start measure emotions, reactions and the drivers of emotional attachment which ultimately lead to loyalty and elation for advocacy impact.

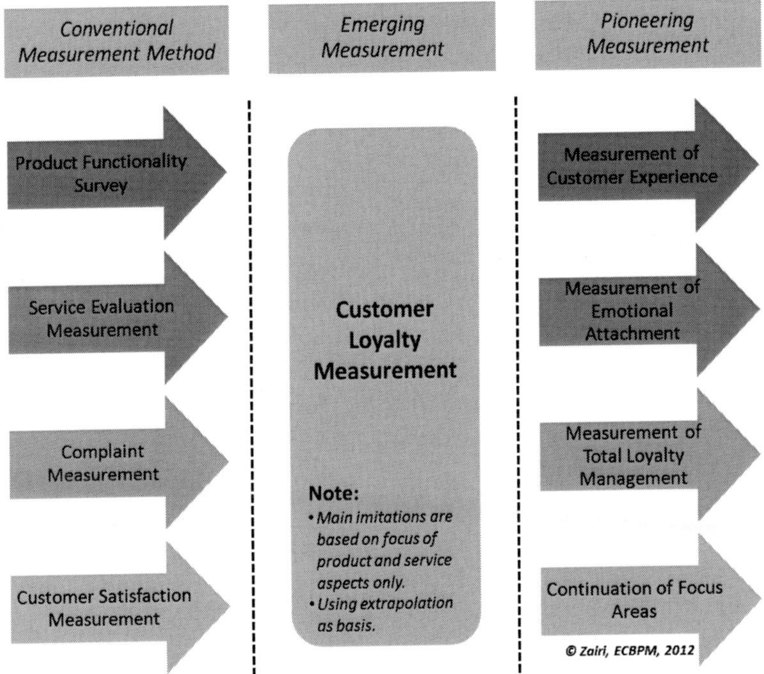

Figure 52: Loyalty measurement – a new integrated perspective

Reconfiguring Organisational Setup for Driving Service Excellence

In the context of a new era of customer enlightenment and inspiration it is important for organisations to reconfigure by being outwardly orientated through customer centricity but operating as an open system with different methods of interaction and driving innovative thinking and their value chain. There are two mind sets that need to be put in place in order to facilitate the growth and development of organisational thinking that can lead to world class status through the notion of excellence in service and excellence in operation:

1. **Building a change driven culture** - The notion of a change driven culture means that organisations aspiring to become world class through customer centricity and the provision of service excellence will have to use a pull mechanism as opposed to the conventional push mechanism. This means that the innovation process is no longer based on the life-cycle that delivers products and services only.

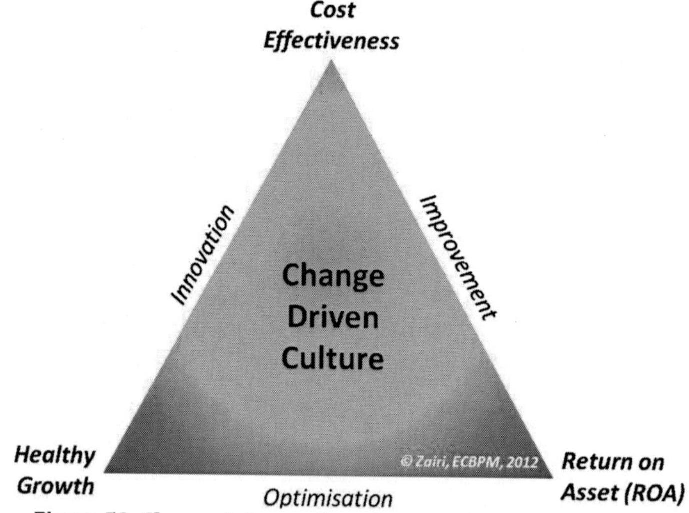

Figure 53: Change driven culture (an organisational internal perspective)

The extended life-cycle process through a change driven culture means that the experience will become the main area of focus and the customer loyalty will become the main expected outcome. This means that organisational thinking which conventionally focuses on continuous improvement through optimisation and enhancement will have to be fuelled constantly by innovation (Figure 53). Innovation cannot be relied upon as a sub set of the conventional value chain but as the main catalyst for driving the value chain and ensuring that the customer is involved throughout all the touch points of the value added activities and that experience has to be individualised whilst products and services have to have sufficient flexibility to be customised. This model will enable organisations therefore to constantly deliver innovation driven fulfilling experiences that are highly rewarding, specifically individualised and providing the positive reactions from customers beyond the satisfaction levels that through the measurement of emotional damages that guarantee future loyalty and retention. The main outcome from this new mind set is that internally organisations continue to do more with less by being cost effective and the outcomes of their performance will delivery healthy growth and return on assets will be one of the measures that will determine how successful they are.

2. **Developing a customer centric culture** – By extending the life-cycle of serving customers organisations would be able to focus on the most critical aspects of delivering customer experiences that are unique, fulfilling, exciting and rewarding both for the customers concerned but also for the organisation itself. This means that the value chain has to be built on aspects that will enable services and experiences to be designed with high quality standards but also with sufficient flexibility so as to allow individualisation and customisation aspects. Furthermore by having a dynamic flexible value chain this will enable organisations to be more responsive in terms of changing needs, changing competitive positions or absorbing opportunities for exploiting new ideas or technological innovation. There are three

driving forces for ensuring that a customer centric culture will succeed.

3. **Delivering value for money –** This means that an experience has in the end got to be measured by individual customers who value several dimensions that may not necessarily be related to products or services but more importantly to what it means to them as individuals.
4. **Empathy –** It means that in an individualised personal experience the customer would like full attention and they would like to be treated as individuals. The notion of creating an experience that can be hailed as "for me only" is one that organisations need to work with more closely in the future.
5. **Dependability –** This means that in the context of delivering extraordinary and excellent customer experiences the process of repeatability of enjoyment and fulfilment will have to be guaranteed and fool proofed. Dependability is no longer reliant on conventional means of preserving quality standards of delivery, reliability, consistency and timeliness but more importantly is the reliability of the value chain from the point of view of customer interventions, involvement and manipulation of different components of the delivery process to suit individual needs and requirements (Figure 54).

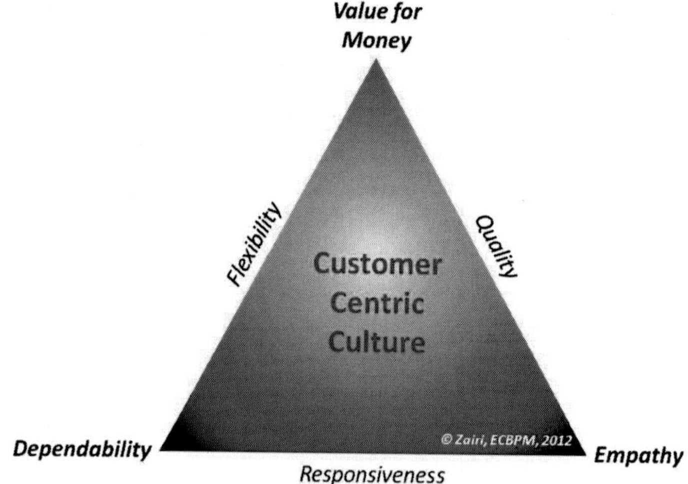

Figure 54: Change Driven Culture (An External Customer Perspective)

The Process of Regaining Customer Confidence

Regaining customer confidence is not necessarily through being effective at having a process for handling complaints but rather it has to be dependent on the following two aspects:

1. **The ability of an organisation to effectively investigate and resolve a complaint to customer satisfaction** – This is a short term measure for fixing what is wrong.
2. **Service delivery capability enhancement** – this means that once the complaint has been resolved the organisation does not stop from conducting investigations and doing root cause analysis for fool proofing processes and its internal capabilities involved in the delivery of services.

The 8R Service Recovery Model

The European Centre for Best Practice Management has developed a process for service recovery and fool proofing which has been used in several industry sectors (Figure 55).

Figure 55: The 8R Service Recovery Model

This process referred to as the 8R model is a closed loop approach for recovery purposes but also for regaining customer confidence. This model starts with the point of dealing with deficient aspects that lead to increased and repeated customer complaints and finishes off with fool proofed mechanism for delivering services that can be used for creating a competitive advantage.

R1. Repair – this stage requires organisations to evaluate the current state of their service provisions and to identify cracks and rectify errors and foolproof their processes and approaches so as to minimise the negative impact on their customers.

R2. Recover – during instances where there is a failure that can lead to an external complaint the recovery stage means that organisations need to identify the reasons why the service standard has dropped and put in place solutions that will enable the recovery process and therefore reinstate and re-establish the previous service state through ensuring that quality standards are unlikely to fall again.

R3. Regain – the recovery process has to be followed by assuring that the quality standard in the eyes of the customer is one that can be trusted and therefore communicating with a customer to validate this fact and ensure that the trust and confidence is still there.

R4. Revitalise – through an independent regular audit process which looks at opportunities for improvement, enhancement organisations need to constantly reinforce their distinctive capabilities for the provision of sound and excellent services and this refreshing aspect will give them the impetus to drive service excellence that can delight their customers.

R5. Rethink – by operating as an open system and welcoming best practice thinking and innovative ideas organisations create an opportunity for re-engineering their service provision capability and building a value chain that is seamless and which can impress the customer beyond the usual metrics of quality, reliability, consistency and dependability.

R6. Realise – the evidence that the service value chain is competitive and can be stretched through innovation as the main catalyst will be measured by the ability of organisations to put stretch targets vis- á- vie the type of services they offer and achieving those targets to ensure that they are leaders in the area that they wish to differentiate themselves in.

R7. Retain – once the service provision value chain is built to deliver competitive outcomes this provides organisations with the ability to drive their strategies with their distinctive service delivery capability that can enable them to achieve a competitive advantage.

R8. Risk management – a culture of service optimisation, service recovery and service enhancement has to be under pinned by a philosophy of risk management. This means that at each stage of the 8R model application the consequences of not attending to what is required and the neglect of exploiting opportunities that can give organisations a big boost in building a competitive advantage through building service capability will show themselves negatively from the point of view of the customer. A risk management regular assessment does therefore help in the following areas:

- If a deficiency in service provision is not attended to the consequences are that the organisation concerned will be unable to deliver to customers expectations and will fall very short from maintaining its minimum quality standards.
- The inability of an organisation to deal with raised complaints effectively and to the satisfaction of the customers will lead to escalation in terms of costs and more importantly to customers defecting.
- If quality standards are not reinstated the customer will lose trust and will ultimately look for alternatives elsewhere.
- If the process of service delivery is not fool proofed and is not refreshed with new ideas the organisations capability to provide a new portfolio of services at a competitive level will decrease significantly.
- The risk of not injecting on a regular basis new ideas and fresh best practice thinking will lead to organisations being left behind at competitive levels and not having sufficient differentiating capabilities that will make them compete effectively.

- Without regular measurement in various forms organisations will not make the best out of their internal capabilities and will not use the right approaches for competing and those include internal service capability but more importantly the customer measurement that really counts which is related to satisfaction, loyalty and retention.
- There will be a significant risk associated with organisations inability to achieve and maintain a competitive advantage through their focus on customers and being excellent at the provision of services and unique experiences.

In all, the 8R model provides an opportunity for organisations to be ready for modern competitiveness and building the right foundation that will allow for the real experiences to be provided and with the full confidence that they can engage the customer in designing their own individualised experiences and derive the benefits that they would wish to have. The 8R model however is meant to focus on service recovery and service enhancement and does not necessarily deal with aspects which are associated with the provision of individualised experiences per se.

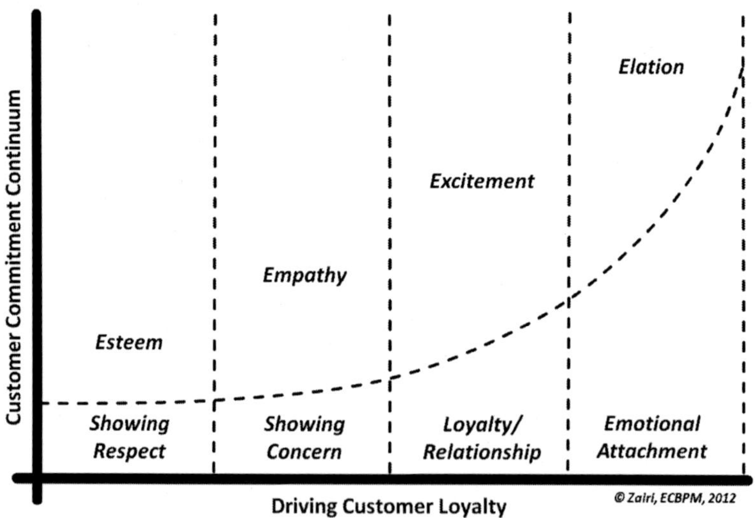

Figure 56: The 4 Es approach – Customer Loyalty Maturity Grid

Working Beyond Service Recovery and Integrating the Customer Perspective

It is suggested that the momentum for creating service excellence has to be followed by a continuum that will demonstrate organisations commitment to their customers through customer centric approaches and through the practices of customer engagement and empowerment. This is considered to be the best strategy for driving customer loyalty and building maturity with time (Figure 56). The 4Es approach reflects stages of maturity in terms of creating total loyalty and ensuring that there is an attachment to an organisations brand:

E1. Esteem – By considering the customer as a partner in creating their own experiences and showing the customer respect in terms of voicing their concerns, wanting to add input or willing to participate in shaping their own experiences this will demonstrate that organisations have high esteem for their customer and that they consider them with deep respect.

E2. Empathy – This means that the professional way to deal with customers on the positive front or when issues are being raised is a demonstration that there is total commitment towards showing **concern** for the customer and wanting, at all costs, to alleviate any fears, remove any issues, ensuring that experiences are not spoilt and most of all give customers the due consideration and the moral support and the necessary levels of empathy that will make them feel important and listened to.

E3. Excitement – Building total loyalty and a long lasting relationship means that each individual experience that customers will go through must generate excitement for them and for them only. This means that an organisations ability to be innovative and to be ready and prepared for engaging the customer towards future experiences with different needs is real and can be afforded with confidence so that it can generate excitement.

E4. Elation – Ultimately customer elation means that the customer who is loyal, regularly satisfied and enjoys every experience they go through will work with a brand at a different level because of their emotional attachment. This stage is described as the elation stage and it means that the brand is represented for other aspects rather than just the usual fulfilment whether utilitarian, hedonic but perhaps spiritual even.

Building Customer Confidence – An Integrated Perspective

It has been said previously that whilst products and services belong to an organisation, experiences do however belong to customers. By focussing on service provision as a driver for delivering excellence and ensuring customer loyalty may not necessarily be a sufficient approach in guaranteeing total loyalty and in the long term high levels of retention. The 8R model is mainly concerned with driving the service value chain as a push mechanism. Through defining the requirements and designing the right portfolio of services and delivering them through different channels and determining the impact that this is generated on customers through a closed loop perspective this can help organisations to build a service provision capability and ensure that there are high quality standards and they could ultimately deliver excellence through distinctive capabilities.

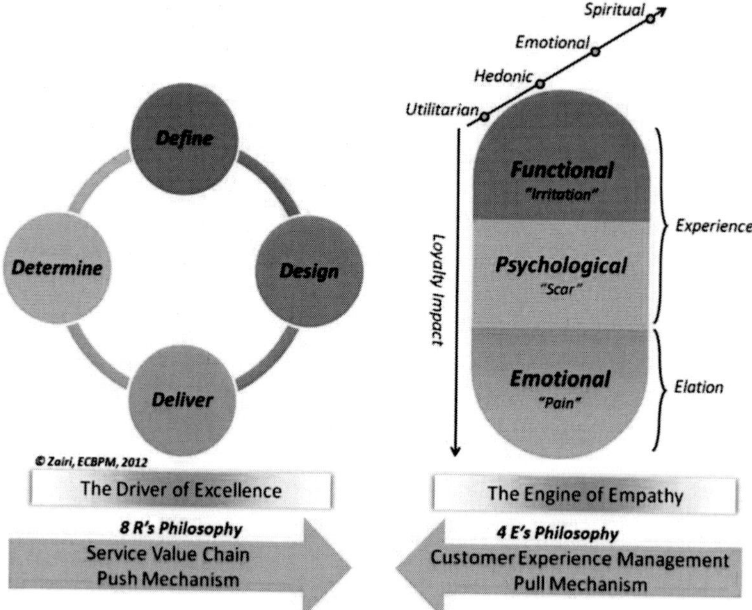

Figure 57: The Impact of Service Excellence in Customer Experience

The notion that service excellence through a focus on giving the best to the customer from the point of view of products and services is sufficient to generate loyalty has been challenged already and may not necessarily be sufficient. There has to be an integration of the internal capability building for service excellence through the push mechanism with an extended perspective that may be external for providing customer experiences pull mechanism). As Figure 57 illustrates there are additional challenges for organisations seeking to achieve long term relationships with their customers and retain them profitably for them and for the organisations themselves. There are several challenges that need to be taken into consideration:

1. The acceptance that experiences really happen beyond the conventional utilitarian and hedonic fulfilment aspects which are closely linked to products and services even though the hedonic fulfilment dimensions are related to customisation of services and products. Customer experience is associated with individualisation of emotional requirements and these needs to be taken into consideration. Ultimately customers may not have any requirements through the push mechanism and they may define their experiences through an association with a brand for other reasons including for example spiritual fulfilments which is the detached process from the provider organisation itself.
2. Customer experience has to be defined from the aspects that have been described but the loyalty continuum reflects that the physiological and emotional aspects matter much more than the conventional functional aspects. The more an organisation emphasises on empathy and closeness to its customers on a one to one basis and being able to provide individualised requirements and ingredients for delivering unique experiences the more likely it will generate high levels of loyalty and retention. The experience becomes real perhaps by creating the "for me only" principle through the fulfilment of functional and psychological needs. The loyalty will be triggered by the emotional mechanism and the wow factor that leads to elation.

Equally the severity of complaints, if empathy is not there, will gradually become evident as the impact travels from functional to the emotional aspects.

1. It is likely that in the context of organisations having a blip for the provision of products and services at a functional level this may cause a slight irritation to the customers and a quick and effective recovery will easily remove any scars.
2. The psychological aspects tend to damage the relationship more significantly as the experience may not be repeated and what would have been a unique and memorable event may become a nightmare so the scar on the psychological aspects is something that has a higher order of severity.
3. The emotional side of loyalty may create enduring pain and therefore may cause permanent damage which the customer cannot recover from and which they will carry for a long time to come. This therefore means that recovery from inflicting emotional pain may almost be impossible to do.

It is therefore suggested that the process of managing customer experiences and building customer confidence through a firm's ability to induce service recovery plans and optimising its service capability is considered beyond the internal aspects of service management. The importance of using customer experience management as a pull mechanism through a thorough understanding o the various levels of experience management and experience evaluation to create total loyalty must be understood and appreciated and in particular, by using the empathy engine for fool proofing failures in customer experience management.

A human being is a part of a whole, called by us "universe", a part limited in time and space. He experiences himself, his thoughts and feelings as something separated from the rest... a kind of optical delusion of his consciousness. This delusion is a kind of prison for us, restricting us to our personal desires and to affection for a few persons nearest to us. Our task must be to free ourselves from this prison by widening our circle of compassion to embrace all living creatures and the whole of nature in its beauty.

Albert Einstein

Chapter 8: Quality Does Matter - Building Service Excellence

Introduction

> *"A smile costs nothing - and in the hospitality industry, it means everything".*
>
> ***Brian D. Langton, Chairman and CEO, Holiday Inn Worldwide***

Customer service is more and more recognised as experience orientated as opposed to product and service orientated. It is very much about the level of care for the customer. There isn't an optimum standard of serving customers and if it comes from the heart there is no better way than evaluating it. The notion that customer satisfaction is the best indication for evaluating the quality of services and the standard to which an organisation should stand proud is no longer sufficient. The process of customer experience is one of enrichment and driven by a firm's ability to go beyond the mere articulation of basic customer needs and requirements. Enrichment is a leap well beyond the conventional paradigms of serving customers through the push perspective. It is more about empathy and using it to drive unique and in delightful experiences.

It has already been established that a dedication to service excellence through delivering unique experiences pays off in many ways. Various studies have already established that it costs more to recruit a new customer rather than serving an existing one. It has already been established that customers who are unhappy with their experiences are more likely to tell more people than those who have enjoyed a positive experience. There is also something that all business will have to face as a challenge and that is a natural depletion in retaining existing customers even if there is nothing wrong with services and even if the customers have been extremely satisfied as a result of their repeated experiences. It is also recognised that 80% of successful new products and service innovations or initiatives come from customers ideas.

Delivering Superior Customer Experience – The Real Facts

Most organisations will make the claim that they are delivering high quality customer experiences. The reality is however different and according to several studies the claims made by a large number of organisations can be easily challenged.

- A survey of 362 firms conducted recently by Bain and Co. has found that 80% believed they delivered a superior experience to their customers. However, when customers were asked only 8% per rated as truly delivering a superior experience.
- The inability of organisations to understand that customer experience is a pull mechanism and the measurement has to right in order to evaluate the individualised experiences as opposed to the push mechanism which is measuring the quality of products and services and the delivery aspects is yet unclear. Back in the 1980s the late Dr Edward Deming, the godfather of quality, did challenge the notion that measuring customer satisfaction is not the best way of assessing customer loyalty. Deming said "what actually makes customers loyal? Simply satisfying them certainly isn't enough". There are of course several shortcomings with the measurement of customer satisfaction. Amongst which are the following:
    - Satisfaction scores measure only past experiences.
    - The tools that are available currently for measuring customer satisfaction such as the American Customer Satisfaction Index (ACSI) looks at value against expectation.
    - Customer satisfaction deals with the rational assessment at a particular point in time.
    - Customer satisfaction does not capture customers' intentions.
    - Customer satisfaction is a poor predictor of customer behaviour.

Similarly the current service excellence measurement models have got some limitations as well. For instance the service – profits chain is a very widely used model for assessing service excellence. It is however, limited since it makes the extrapolation from the measurement of customer satisfaction into customer loyalty without emphasising the importance of the experience side. The service – profits chain model is more of a push model and it lacks the pull customer experience management aspects (Figure 58).

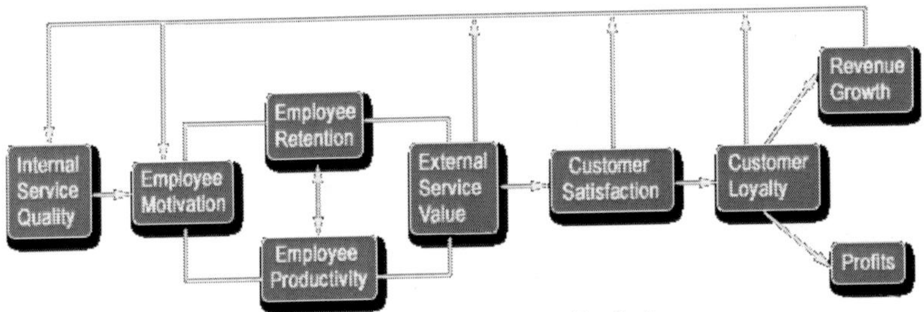

Figure 58: The service profit chain
Source: (J. L. Heskett, T.O. Jones, G.W. Loveman, W.E. Sasser Jr, L.A. Schlesinger, 1994)

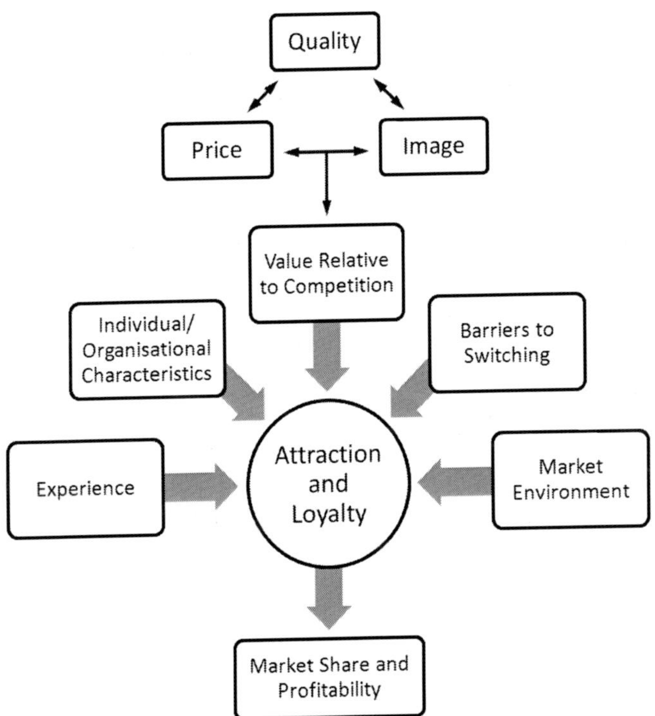

Figure 59: Quality Loyalty - An Integrated Model
Source: (Fredericks & Salter II, 1998).

Another model that has been used which demonstrates some limitations is the customer loyalty model as depicted in Figure 59 (Fredericks & Salter II, 1998). This model is based on the measurement of value from the point of view of price, quality and image. It assumes the impact on attraction and loyalty to the customer is an integrated perspective which evaluates experiences based on the internal evaluation of organisational characteristics and the value it provides in relation to its competition plus the challenges it faces externally, and this assumption is that attraction and loyalty will impact positively on market share and profitability.

Similarly the customer loyalty model described above is unable to depict how customer experience management is driven as a separate pull process as opposed to the conventional service delivery management process which is a push model.

The new era can very much be characterised as the emotional aspect of the customer. As most people recognise experience is the Holy Grail that gives organisations the competitive edge and which sets them apart from their competitors. Several studies have recognised that emotional aspects customer experiences are becoming the driving force for establishing true and meaningful competitiveness.

- In a 2002 survey by UK (CRM) Consultants, 85% of senior business leaders surveyed agreed that, it is no longer sustainable to just differentiate on the physical aspects of the customer experience, such as price, quality and delivery.
- This was further recognised by many other studies which emphasised the importance of managing the cumulative impact on the customers interaction with an organisations brand across all the touching points through what is referred to as the entire customer life-cycle in order to deliver a competitive customer experience that is not just fulfilling in terms of utilitarian and hedonic needs but more expressed in terms of beliefs, feelings and attitudes.

Measuring Customer Attachment through Emotional Experiences

One of the useful tools that have been developed in recent years was done by Gallup. This was referred to as the Gallup measurement instrument (CE^{11}). Essentially this instrument has eleven indicators that tackle customer attachment and loyalty. There are three questions related to loyalty and eight questions related to attachment:

1. **The loyalty questions, these include the following:**
   a. How satisfied is the customer with the brand overall?
   b. How likely is the customer going to continue to choose/repurchase from the brand?
   c. How likely is the customer going to recommend the brand to friends/associates?
2. **The attachment questions these include the following criteria confidence, integrity, pride, passion.**
   a. Confidence:
      - The brand is a name I can always trust.
      - The brand always delivers on what they promise.

   b. Integrity:
      - The brand always treats me fairly.
      - If a problem arises, I can always count on the brand to reach a fair and satisfactory resolution.

   c. Pride:
      - I feel proud to be a customer of the brand.
      - The brand always treats me with respect.

   d. Passion:
      - The brand is the perfect company for people like me.
      - I can't imagine a world without the brand.

The Gallup tool provides an opportunity for measuring customer emotional attachment to a particular brand. As Figure 60 illustrates the study conducted by Gallup has been able to establish the degree of attachment from customer experiences to specific brands covering six different industry sectors. It is clear from Figure 60 that in the airline industry, for instance, the switching and defection likelihood is much higher than other industry sectors.

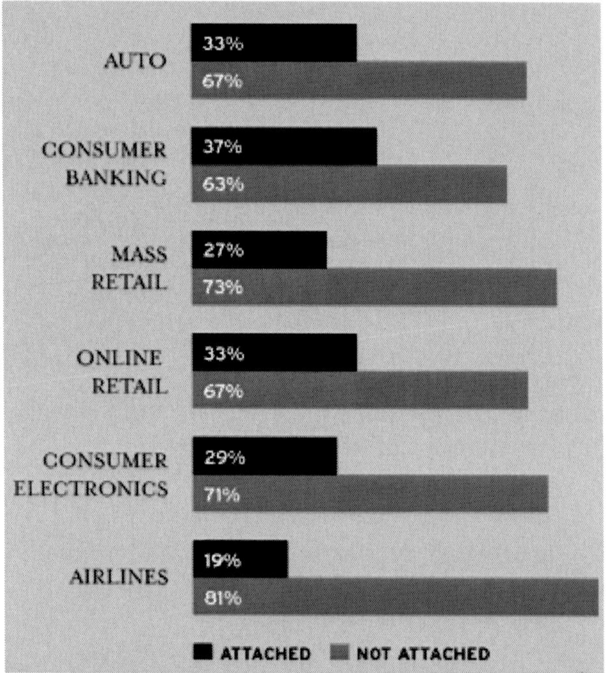

Figure 60: Customer Loyalty Measurement by Industry Sector

Source: Gallup organisation

Best Practices in Service Excellence

There are several organisations often referred to as being excellent in providing services and unique customer experiences, amongst which and covering the airline industry is Singapore International Airline and South West Airline.

Singapore International Airline

SIA is recognised for its consistent, high quality and superior service provision and its commitment and drive for creating excellent standards and competing on the power of services and unique experiences. SIA uses ten ingredients for driving service excellence which include the following:

1. **Clarity and commitment** – this means that the mission statement and core values are used to establish, without question, the quality of service in relation to customers and this is also considered as a fundamental objective and aspiration of the airline.
2. **Continuous training** – SIA uses classroom, on the job or using full scale simulations for all staff members to make sure they are continually motivated to upgrade and improve their performance.
3. **Carrier development** – SIA staff are regularly appraised for performance and more importantly for the potential that they exhibit. It has a fast track for high fliers who are identified early and given opportunities to learn and grow.
4. **Internal communications** – SIA uses different methods of communicating amongst all of its employees, for instance, by relying on newsletters, a monthly magazine, having regular dialogue sessions between management and staff and using staff ideas in action scheme. Furthermore it has some annual business meetings where all the employees are briefed about the company's' direction and strategic progress.
5. **Consistent external communication** – the continual emphasis that the real bottom line is delivering quality service.
6. **Connection with customers** – by using different methods of gathering data and establishing first hand evaluations from their customers SIA uses the rich data and knowledge gained to improve its services and a focus on what matters to the customer. For instance, use of the in-flight service, customer focus groups, reply to every compliment or complaint they receive. They also use a quarterly service performance index.
7. **Benchmarking** – SIA feeds from external best practices and uses new innovations to be introduced for service design and improvement. It also monitors key competitors' progress in order to make sure that it doesn't fall behind.
8. **Improvement, investment and innovation** – SIA is committed to introducing new services and new variants to existing services so that it has the edge over its competitors. They also monitor the level of innovativeness emanating from its competitors.

9. **Rewards and recognition** – SIA has a philosophy of rewarding excellent staff performance by increased pay and promotions. They also have the prestigious award which is reserved for extraordinary acts of truly superior service.
10. **Professionalism, pride and profits** – SIA has built a staff culture which is vigorously committed to the airline, its customers and more importantly to driving continuous improvement incessantly. By emphasising on staff pride and sense of ownership this impacts on SIAs profits which are "the applause we receive for providing consistent quality and service to our customers".

South West Airlines

South West Airlines being a low cost airline has demonstrated that customer unique experiences through service excellence is possible without an over elaboration or investment on the provision of products and services which is the main focus of full service airlines.

What drives South West Airlines are the following:

1. An exceptional organisational model which focuses on maintaining customer relationships.
2. Having customer service at the core of South West Airlines mission which is "dedication to the highest quality of customer service delivered with a sense of warmth, friendliness, individual pride, and company spirit".
3. South West treats employees with the same concern (respect and occurring attitude).

Ritz Carlton

Figure 61 illustrates a useful process used by the Ritz Carlton which facilitates the provision of unique and exceptional customer experiences. This empowerment process demonstrates the level of emphasis there is on empathy as the engine for driving service excellence, unique customer experience and generating loyalty and commitment in the long term.

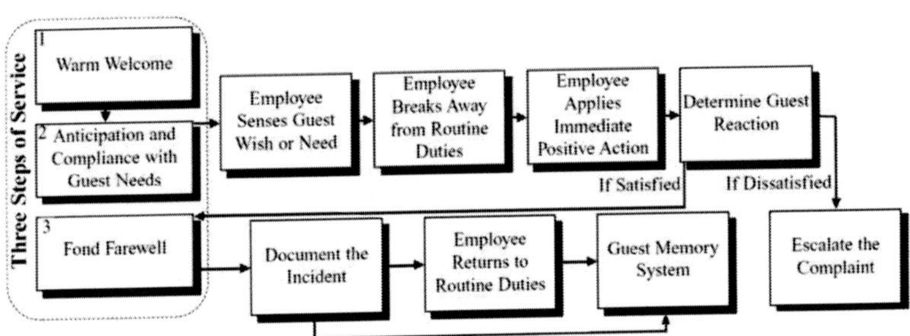

Figure 61: The Basic Empowerment Process
Source: Ritz Carlton, MBNQA Submission

How to Deliver Sustainable Service Excellence

In order to appreciate the different aspects of providing service excellence that leads to unique customer experiences through an integration of the pull and push approaches together the following elements are critical and must be considered one by one (Figure 62).

Figure 62: Drivers of Service Excellence

The model illustrated in Figure 62 depicts key pillars for delivering service excellence

1. **Empathy** - To show empathy is to identify with someone else's feelings. It is to emotionally put oneself in the place of the other. By having the ability to empathise this will be measured directly on someone's trust on the providing person. The dependency on a person's ability to feel someone one's own feelings and identify with them is a powerful process for helping them in the first instance and delivering what is required.

   Empathy includes the following:

   a. **Awareness and acknowledgment** – this stage includes the following:
      - Emotionally expressive people are easiest to read because their eyes and faces are constantly letting us know how they are feeling.
      - Once we have figured out how another person feels, we show empathy by acknowledging the emotion. We may say, for example:
        - I can see you are really uncomfortable about this.
        - I can understand why you must be upset.

   b. **Sensitivity** - this includes the following:
      - A basic guideline for showing sensitivity to someone is to not invalidate their feelings by belittling, diminishing, rejecting, judging or ignoring them. Even just a simple acknowledgment without any real empathy is much better than totally ignoring someone's feelings.
      - Sensitivity also means being receptive to others cues, particularly the non-verbal ones such as facial expressions.

   c. **Understanding and compassion** – this includes the following:
      - When we feel empathy for someone we are getting emotional information about them and their situation. By collecting information about others feelings, you get to know them better.

- As Haim Ginott wrote, "It takes time and wisdom to realise that the personal parallels the universal and what pains one man pains mankind".

d. Conscience – this includes, amongst others, the following:

- Those who are not in touch with their own feelings are not likely to have a sense of conscience. They may feel no remorse, no guilt for causing hurt to others.
- For example, common defences are rationalisation, justification, denial, intellectualisation, moralising, preaching, self righteousness, projection, suppression, etc.

2. Expertise

This includes being competent, confident, service orientated and customer focused. There are two enemies of excellence in service provision, complacency and incompetence. Complacency hampers efforts to deliver unique and memorable customer experiences for several reasons and incompetence is allowing things to fail again for different reasons.

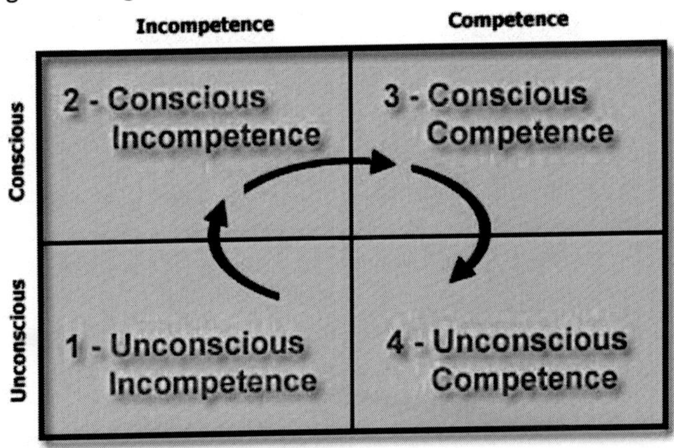

Conscious Competence Learning Matrix

Figure 63: Incompetence/Competence Model

Source: (Cognitive Design Solutions, Inc., 2003)

As Figure 63 illustrates the challenge for organisations to ensure fool proofing in so far as dealing with incompetency is concerned is to understand how far they would like to stretch their employees and making them drive performance improvement in a conscience manner using their full potential. By understanding what blocks them from using their full potential the abilities they have can be unleashed through an effective enabling strategy geared towards making every employee count in terms of performance improvement and making them confident about what they possess in terms of skills and competencies. By giving regular feedback through formal and informal evaluations the unconscious side of competence and incompetence can also be transparently revealed and people can be enabled therefore to become more aware of their stock of competence and other unique abilities that they may bring to the fore or in the case of incompetence it made people more motivated to improve in the areas where they are significantly lacking.

3. **Empowerment** – This key element includes the following:
    - **a.** From a managers point of view it is important that empowerment is used in the right way, for the right reasons and with a clear understanding by all the staff concerned. Empowerment has to be proactive, it has to result in employees taking increased responsibility, making additional positive contributions, bringing solutions and certainly not problems.
    - **b.** From the point of view of employees empowerment means the following:
        - Being given more autonomy;
        - Being left alone to sort things out on their own;
        - Being able to make decisions;
    - **c.** In a sense to empower organisations' need to develop a creativity that people already have and perhaps are not fully utilising.
    - **d.** The motivation is to get people to appraise where they feel able to suggest and offer things, doing things right rather than waiting to be told what to do.

e. Empowerment would mean in the end, an active participation, involvement, accountability, encouragement, setting boundaries and expectations, listening to and acknowledging people's ideas.
f. In its final analysis empowerment is treating people as adults whatever their role is, no matter where they sit in the hierarchy.
g. By creating the process of increasing the capacity of individuals or groups to make choices and help them to transform those choices into desired actions and outcomes.
h. At the heart of the process of empowerment is actions that will help build the individual as a human asset but also to improve the efficiency and fairness of the organisational and institutional context.

4. **Excitement** – This includes some of the following:
   a. Inventions dreamed up by the organisation and geared towards enhancing customer's experiences and adding value by solving problems and issues.
   b. Solving a problem even if the customer did not notice and recognise there is one.
   c. Using a proactive approach that does not wait for customer complaints to dictate what the organisation must do.
   d. By asking questions such as the following:
      - What is the real problem we solve for the customer?
      - How does the customer consume our products or services?
      - What else is missing to perfect the total experience?
      - How can I surprise the customer?

5. **Excellence** – This includes the following:
   a. Having a quest for progress and advancement in quality and performance.
   b. Building superior capability for serving and delighting customers.
   c. Competing on innovative approaches to customer service.

d. Focussing on empowerment and people motivation satisfaction to drive quality and establishing high standards of delivery of products and services. This will lead to repeated customer satisfaction and the minimisation of complaints and which will create trust and dependency and ultimately to helping the organisation achieve its competitive advantage.

Building Sustainable Quality through Service Excellence

The emphasis on service excellence has to be made through the pervasiveness of quality as a philosophy that defines an organisations intention to create unique and competitive offerings to its customers and also to build sustainable distinctive capability for preventing switching and customer defection.

Furthermore the quality drive within an organisation has to reflect the following four different aspects (Figure 64):

1. Improvement and optimisation through the management of deficiencies – the improvement philosophy has to prevent casualness and peoples behaviours and attitudes towards errors, defects and things that might hurt the customer and harm the organisation. Furthermore by emphasising on innovation in improving and raising quality standards this will also help position the organisation as one that is serious about its customers and committed to offering them unique experiences.
2. Building capability and commitment to creating customer centric cultures and service excellence orientation – this means that the main drivers for service excellence are to be based on having excellent human talent, supported by excellent enabling systems, having excellence in leadership and commitment and building excellence in the value chain.
3. Offering unique experiences through front end focus on the customer and creating meaningful relationships through regular communication and addressing their needs more specifically.
4. Creating the pull mechanism for customer experiences through the enablement of customers to be a partner in shaping their

own individual experiences and engaging them positively in this respect.

The process described in Figure 64 is developed by the European Centre for Best Practice Management and is referred to as the 12Cs model for service excellence. This tool is designed for the following purpose:

1. To allow organisations to determine their level of maturity in building service excellence capability across the four different aspects.
2. The audit tool allows organisations to integrate customer orientation in a meaningful way to their strategic planning and to ensure that further development of their value chain and an extension of the customer life-cycle takes place in a systematic manner.
3. To correlate the level of emphasis of the organisation concerned and the outcomes it gets through its measurement tools. For instance, a significant emphasis on the deficiencies aspect will absorb the energies of the organisation by being reactive rather than building a proactive strategy for creating unique and meaningful customer experiences.
4. The weakness in the drivers aspect of the organisation are likely to demonstrate low impact at the proactive level and that is the pull mechanism for creating unique and memorable experiences of the customers.

Overall, this tool has been used in different sectors of the economy and has proven to be useful in assessing maturity levels of service excellence, determining the level of capability in delivering unique customer experiences and is a method for generating meaningful data that can be used for building ambitious strategic plans and driving the customer experience through an integrated perspective. Appendix 1 includes the full tool with the evaluation methodology.

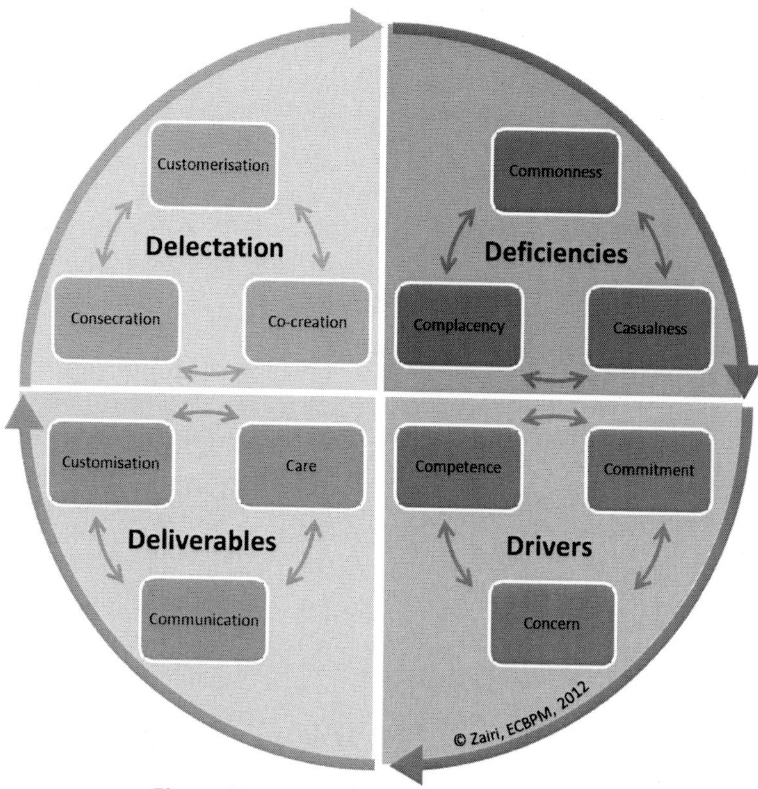

Figure 64: 12 C's Model of Service Excellence

If you could actually stand in someone else's shoes to hear what they hear, see what they see, and feel what they feel, you would honestly wonder what planet they live on, and be totally blown away by how different their "reality" is from yours. You'd also never, in a million years, be quick to judge again.

Unknown

Chapter 9: Customer Empathy Model

Introduction

In order to give proper meaning to the word 'empathy' and extend the practice of customer centricity during an era where the customer is intelligent, inspired and proactive it is important therefore to take a new perspective on what goes in the mind of the customer and ensure that any simulation model of wanting to create positive customer impact and generate sustainable loyalty is feasible and reflects precisely the emotions and the expectations of customers. As we move deep into the 21st century it is more and more the case that customer experience is what would matter in most cases and even in the context of what we previously called commodity replenishment of products and services the concept of value is going to be the predominant currency on which customer relationships can be built with a solid foundation and durable impacts can be generated. The focus, therefore, on quality alone as a means for ensuring that external impact on customers is going to be positive, consistent and will enable the delivery of value will however no longer be sufficient. Most organisations have now gone through the motion of putting their houses in order and minimising negative impacts and disruptions in their abilities to deliver their promises to their customers. Having said that and whilst it has to be acknowledged that quality is important in the minds of most Chief Executive Officers and more and more organisations are diligently applying the principles and concepts of quality management to a large extent the customer is still ignored and the empathy factor is still lacking.

The purpose of putting together the model illustrated in Figure 65 is therefore to guide organisations on how to extend the concept of quality management in a modern business context where the customer is king, truly in the driving seat and using a pull perspective on creating their own unique and rewarding experiences. The model illustrated assumes that there is a solid foundation of quality management that dictates that both products and services within provider organisations are fool proofed in terms of their design, development, translation and delivery. The push mechanism therefore that used to reflect the traditional value chain is now only a partial element of the newly proposed and extended value chain that is more outward in its outlook and where the pull perspective has to be added on.

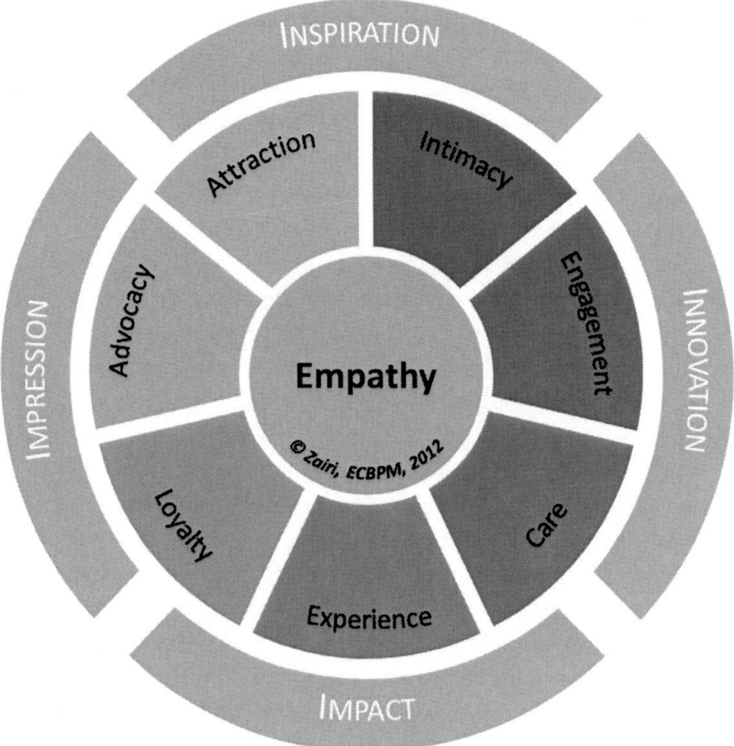

Figure 65: Empathy Model

Empathy Model

The empathy model illustrated in Figure 65 proposes that there are seven critical perspectives that impact directly on creating a culture of total customer empathy.

Customer Engagement

In the 21st century the customer is proactive and these cannot therefore be any assumption of them being the recipient and being asked to assess their level of satisfaction without any direct involvement or intervention in shaping their own individualised requirements or experiences. The engagement perspective is to be acknowledged as a total process where the customer interacts with the provider of products and services in order to ensure that whatever they receive is unique, customised and applicable to their own individualised requirements. Chapter 10 extensively covers the customer engagement process.

Customer Advocacy

Advocacy is a powerful marketing tool which provider organisations must appreciate and indeed the use of the voice of the customer for promoting the brand and reputation of organisations cannot be under estimated. Word of mouth recommendation and the emphasis on providing customers with the opportunity to influence the vision, values, brand and behaviour of their preferred suppliers is in the best interests of the supplier organisations themselves. This form of positive empowerment and involvement of the customers to be ambassadors for the brand, to campaign by helping argue the case and more importantly through positive promotion of the products and services is the way forward and in particular with the advent of new technology in the form of social networking this allows for the opportunity of creating a customer centric approach to external branding and promotion. Chapter 11 comprehensively covers methods and roadmaps on the establishment of effective customer advocacy.

Customer Loyalty

The break through that has happened in previous years by getting organisations to focus away from measuring customer satisfaction in a retrospective manner and to develop proactive strategies for generating long term customer retention and affecting loyalty seems to be on the increase and most of the evidence from various studies seems to suggest that there is a direct correlation between customer loyalty and long term business sustainable performance. Loyalty is determined by an organisations commitment to its customers and by demonstrating that everything it does in terms of capturing the mindset of the customer and re-engineering its internal practices and structures for listening to the voice of the customer and applying dedicated resources for designing, developing and delivering customised solutions to individualised needs and preferences is the means by which loyalty can be generated. Attributes beyond functionality factors of cost, quality and durability have been added on to reflect the importance of customer experience and the need for applying individualised solutions to specific requirements.

The pursuit of dedicated loyalty strategies through the design and implementation for instance of loyalty programmes, the measurement of impact of loyalty internally and externally the open communication strategies with customers to ensure that there is inclusivity in their input on a much wider scale than previously was permissible is a further demonstration that there is a radical shift in the way organisations wish to be seen in the future as customer centric organisations and focus on the experience side of their value chain as opposed to the product and service push that has characterised the practice of most organisations in the 20th century. Chapter 12 illustrates in detail the principle of customer loyalty, road maps for the implementation of customer loyalty, strategies and some best practice thinking on loyalty and retention.

Customer Experience

The notion of customer experience is the practice of individualised preferences and a mindset that provides value for individuals as opposed to great masses as was the case with the traditional mindset of distributing products and services all over the world. An understanding of how a customer experience manifests itself is important and the life-cycle perspective of customer experience is a good starting point for implementing a customer orientated competitive formula. Understanding, for instance, the early expectations and the emotion that a customer goes through in order to choose carefully for themselves their needs and wants, putting the customer in the driving seat particularly through e-business and e-commerce and the reaction of customers having consumed the experience from an emotional perspective and learning how to evaluate it is an extremely critical knowledge base that needs to be applied effectively for modern competitiveness. Chapter 13 covers all aspects associated with customer experience and proposes a detailed roadmap on how to implement customer experience that can have direct impact on empathy.

Customer Attraction

Customer attraction tended, in the past, to be an implicit practice where organisations tended to focus more on the promotion of their products and services and wishing to recruit numbers of consumers that can support the health, growth and development of their profit margin without specifically understanding the nature of the customers that they were targeting and whether they were the right type in so far as long term retention is concerned.

In a highly competitive business environment the acquisition of the right customers as a starting point is an art and needs to be implemented through detailed strategies. Learning about the type of customer and segmenting the customer base through a study on needs, requirements, preferences and potential for converting them into advocates and more importantly retaining their business through loyalty and long term business profitability is what smart, modern management should be all about. Chapter 14 looks in detail at customer attraction and discusses various techniques and models for customer attraction and also suggests a detailed roadmap on how to implement customer attraction practices.

Customer Intimacy

Intimacy is perhaps a direct measure on how customer centric organisations are. It is really about the application of all the knowledge that organisations have on their customers and the competitive market out there and in addition on their ability to convert their value chain to include excellence in terms of consistency, service quality, dependability and right first time impact in terms of immediate satisfaction and dependability from the point of view of trust and long term relationships in the form of loyalty based and value orientated relationships.

By developing a leadership position in understanding the customer intimately and avoiding crisis and disruptiveness to the provision of unique and excellent experiences the approach adopted will give organisations that apply these principles a unique competitive advantage. Chapter 15 covers different aspects of customer intimacy and highlights key principles and also propose a detailed roadmap on how to create and measure customer intimacy culture.

Customer Care

Customer care in a modern business context is not necessarily a task nor is it an activity that can be bolted on into the traditional approach to serving customers and using a product and service push philosophy. Customer care has to directly be related to the real purpose of an organisation and how it creates a set of values that amplify the importance of the customer and drive behaviour at all levels within the organisation on the importance of care and consideration with empathy for the customer. Chapter 16 illustrates the concept of customer care from different perspectives and also proposes a detailed roadmap on how to implement an effective customer care that impacts directly on empathy and which can support the drive of excellence in the provision of customer experiences that impact positively on long term business have and sustainable relationships with customers.

Impression

It has always been said that beauty is in the eyes of the beholder. The final impact that organisations dream of having is creating the right customer impression and impacting on brand reputation and organisational external standing. Brand impact is not a process that is driven internally but it is rather the outcome of all the other perspectives that have been discussed. Unless organisations have the ability to create uniqueness, differentiation and a customised and individualised value impact based largely on their ability to create empathy but more importantly to use customer centric practices with the customer being in the driving seat then brand impact cannot ensue.

The secret of driving customer empathy through generating an impression is to develop a complete understanding of the psychological, emotional aspects of customers in addition to the usually utilitarian aspect of their needs and wants. Chapter 17 describes the concept of customer impression and proposes a roadmap for implementing this concept which can help generate an impact on brand reputation.

Innovation

Innovation is the fuel for generating value in a modern context even in the previously acknowledged world of commoditisation. Indeed since the shift has been to generating customer experiences the raw material will therefore remain innovation and organisation's ability to constantly introduce new ideas, new methods, new products and services and new techniques for getting closer to their customers. This can only happen through building an innovation driven culture which has the capacity of generating ideas all the time and the capability for implementing know how that can inspire customers externally. Chapter 18 covers aspects related to innovation driven customer experiences and proposes a roadmap on how to implement such a practice.

Impact

The bottom line is what matters to organisations that are dedicated to creating what can be referred to as emotionally satisfied customers. The measurement of customer satisfaction in a traditional sense is no longer applicable and can be counterproductive. The retro prospective collection of data that is largely focussing on functionality of products and services is far away from reflecting the truth and is too remote from the understanding of customer experience based value provision.

Current efforts are to provide a broad understanding of loyalty factors with emphasis on individualisation and emotional criteria of measurement and also the impact that loyalty models can have on retention aspects on the one hand but growth in organisational benefits on the other. Chapter 19 illustrates various models that cover the emotional satisfaction methods available and also proposes a detailed roadmap on how to generate long lasting emotionally satisfied customer impact on the sustainable aspects of organisational competitive performance.

Inspiration

The extension of the life-cycle of customer experience management is about replenishing needs and wants for unique customer experiences on the one hand but furthermore it is about generating long lasting impact through delightfulness. Organisations that are totally dedicated to inspiring customers focus on service leadership, for instance, and the unique abilities for applying speed, agility, innovativeness and inspirational thinking that goes far beyond what the norms are and what the art of possibilities can promise. An extension of customer experience management in this way helps maintain organisational competitive leadership positions but also inspires customers to be truly motivated to generate stronger relationships with their existing preferred suppliers. Chapter 20 covers the concept of customer inspiration in great detail and also includes a detailed roadmap on how to implement inspirational strategies for generating customer loyalty and retention.

Learning is a result of listening, which in turn leads to even better listening and attentiveness to the other person. In other words, to learn from the child, we must have empathy, and empathy grows as we learn.

Alice Miller

Chapter 10: Customer Engagement

Introduction

Traditionally, organisations used to provide the type of customer service, which was separated from the core of the business and largely seen as a cost centre designed to minimise overhead and quickly complete interactions; while nowadays, organisations strengthens customer relationships and optimise business outcomes by proactively engaging customers with the ideal customer service experience through any channel. In the 21st century, world-class organisations rise to the challenge of revamping their approach to customer engagement in order to effectively meet changing customers' needs. Organisations are increasingly realising that customer retention and loyalty are important drivers to achieving a competitive advantage, and re-evaluating their customer engagement strategy to ensure a customer service experience that is convenient, competent, specialised and proactive.

A Model for Customer Engagement

Over the past few years, there has been a significant shift in customers influence and power. Organisations are now keen to learn how to harness the power of customer data in digital space and how they too can start to build direct customer relationships. Organisations are seeking to engage with customer through establishing more potential contact points with customers, which provides a greater opportunity to start and build two way communications. The concept of customer engagement increases and customer loyalty based on the delivery of continuous value to customers. Previously, CRM has been widely used by organisations for building two way dialogues with customers; however, most of the relationship has been one way. With the start of social media applications and web-based services, the power of the customer grew. They are now more informed and have the power to express themselves. They can seek out advice and opinions from other consumers that organisations have little or no influence over. These changes, coupled with advances in data processing technologies have led to strategic shifts; a move from relationship plans with customers to engagement plans with customers. Fundamentally, customer engagement is about the use of technology, data, processes and channels to drive value.

4I's Model of Customer Engagement

The focus of customer engagement is not only on the areas of involvement and interaction but also the areas of intimacy and influence. The 4Is model (Figure 66) illustrates the links between customer engagement and four main aspects of customer service management. An effective deployment of customer engagement strategy can make a direct and positive impact on customer experiences. Two of the four main elements, interaction and involvement, are particularly important for getting input from customers and using this input for improving services. The next two elements influence and intimacy can be perceived as the outcomes of the customer interaction and involvement.

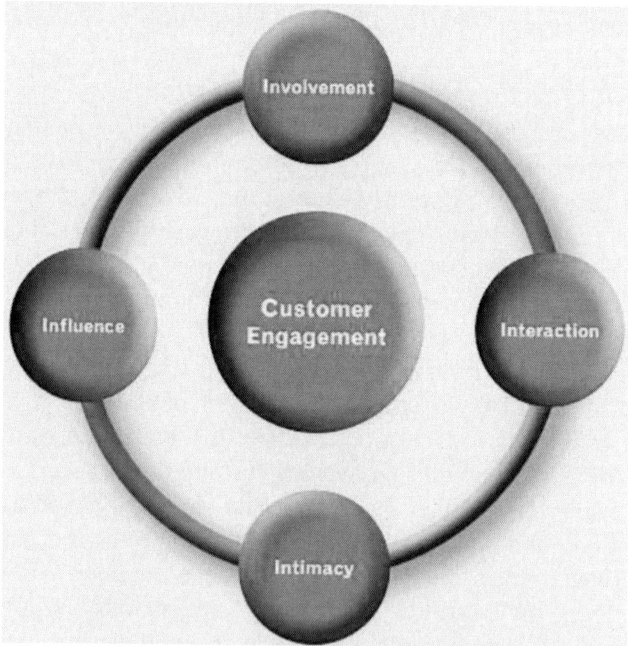

Figure 66: A model for customer engagement

Source: (Experian, 2011)

In order to attract and communicate with customers, organisations require an advanced level of technologies, techniques and best practices. In addition, the need for automation backed by applied decisioning techniques is a must have. A prerequisite for having legitimate interaction with customers is to establish an effective two way conversation with customers. The greatest step will be allowing customers to proactively engage with the organisations and not only that, being able to react to them.

Customer intimacy is about striving to exceed customer expectation and it can be achieved by cultivation of lasting relationships with customers and striving to satisfy their unique needs. For a genuine involvement of customers, organisations should develop and deploy the customer involvement strategy for achieving the following objectives:

- To enhance the involvement of customers in the decision making processes
- To enhance existing customer involvement structure to allow for greater participation
- To empower customers to have greater involvement with and control over the decisions which affect their services received
- To have in place mechanisms for enabling customer views to be taken into account when developing and improving services
- To ensure that customers who are involved have the appropriate training and support
- Customers can highly influence on the way services are designed and delivered if they are genuinely empowered and truly engaged. The possible outcomes can be but not limited to:
    - Improved services that are better tailored to customer needs
    - Improved governance and accountability
    - Greater customers satisfaction

Ingredients for Customer Engagement

Customer engagement requires a long-term commitment and should comprise an organisation structure that tackles the challenges inherent in the following five customer-engagement ingredients: Interactions, Resources, Infrastructure, Processes, and Performance (Genesys, 2009):

1. **Interactions –** Every interaction with an organisation creates a lasting impression on the customers. Today, organisations must strive to successfully manage many different types of interactions; a challenge that is compounded as customers jump channels during the course of a service process. In addition, customers are directly connected with each other through social media, which provides them with an empowering platform to publicly discuss an organisation's services – for better or worse.
2. **Resources –** An organisation connects with customers through a plethora of resources including agents, outsourcers, knowledge workers, at-home agents, back-office, and automated systems. These resources represent the engine for growth objectives and should be optimised for efficiency, effectiveness, and driving the bottom line.
3. **Infrastructure –** Legacy infrastructure and disparate hardware and application systems exist in every IT infrastructure. The challenge is to cobble these individual parts together into a powerful customer engagement machine. The synergy of these assets will support an organisation's customer engagement strategy by empowering every employee responsible for customer service, service delivery, and support.
4. **Processes –** Every customer interaction incorporates an underlying customer process. For example, calling the insurance organisation to file a claim automatically initiates a process involving many organisations across the enterprise. Often these processes are managed independently in the back office through a Business Process Management (BPM) or Service Request system. Unfortunately, many of these systems lack the visibility into resource availability and business priority to meet service level requirements. The challenge is how to ensure that the back

office achieves similar efficiencies as its front-office/contact centre counterparts.

5. **Performance** – Since customer engagement is driving growth objectives, senior executives and business managers are scrutinising customer service operations. Unfortunately, most Key Performance Indicators (KPIs) and reports don't provide the visibility into how the customer experience and engagement impact business outcomes. Performance Management and analytics will increasingly play an important role in helping business executives gauge customer engagement effectiveness and guide the decision-making process.

Tools of Customer Engagement

Organisations are reaching out to customers and tempting them at different levels and in very different ways. Best practices for engaging and engaging customers are: (The Economist, 2007)

- **Be available for customers 24/7** – A key to engagement is to provide customers with more ways to get the information and service they want, any time they want it. Organisations must do whatever it takes to be 'open for business' around the clock. For example maintaining a 24/7 call centre for responding immediately to customers' needs no matter what time of day customers' enquiries are received.
- **Offer a variety of communication channels, and use them to engage in two-way dialogues with customers** – In order to build robust relationships with customers, organisations should support a variety of modes of communication for responding swiftly to customers' enquiries, requests and feedback through all of them. Evidently, customers want access to many kind of communication channels e.g. although email and Web interactions are widely used by organisations and customers, there are many customers who actually prefer postal mail and telephone to obtain information or discuss their concerns.

- **Tailor the method of contact to the type of customer** – while some customers can be engaged by technology; others by the human touch.

> ***A best practice example – Middle eastern global financial services***
> According to the firm's sales director, high-end customers often want extremely personalised service, while others at the lower level of income may settle for a more cookie-cutter approach.

- **Listen and learn** – Organisations can deeply engage customers if they listen to their needs and respond by providing more targeted information or better value proposition.

> ***Example – A Belgian pension fund organisation***
> The organisation has segmented its customers so that it can effectively provide the most relevant information to each segment according to their needs and expectations. The retirement questions of a doctor in his thirties are likely to be very different from those of someone nearing retirement, and the organisation has segmented these communications in a simple, cost-effective way.

- **The customer interaction data** should be used for not only delivering of services but also designing new services.

> **Example – Middle eastern global financial services**
> The financial service organisation's knowledge about its Middle Eastern target market subgroups was derived from customer data and feedback, which are used to help shape product and service offerings.

- **Deliver personalised responses** – Responses that are personalised, consistent and quick stand the best chance of attracting and retaining customers' attention.

> ***A best practice example – Epson, the computer printer organisation***
> Previously, the organisation would have some complaints from customers where they had already sent an email or they sent multiple emails in a very short frame. Depending on which agent picked the complaints up, the organisation may have responded to customer differently. The organisation has identified this problem and it has therefore established an infrastructure by which all the relevant material on the customer's case can be reviewed and the customer given one answer from the organisation, not three or four slightly different responses. This technique has been useful in preventing misunderstandings in another way as well.

Co-creation

Co-creation is defined as "the involvement of Customers in delivery of public services to achieve outcomes which depend at least partly on their own behaviour" (Loffler, 2008). The term co- creation refers to a way of working whereby decision-makers and Customers, or service providers and users, work together to create a decision or a service which works for all of them (Involve UK 2008). It is about governments "working together" with others.

Best Practices while Co-creating

Using the concept of co-creation, organisations now are able to capture valuable insights into the likes and dislikes of a targeted customer group, test different design concepts and design a solution that is far more reflective of customer preferences. It adds a new dynamic to the provider/customer relationship by engaging customers directly into the production or distribution of value. However, because it demands a higher level of trust and accountability both on the parts of the customers as well as the service providers, it is critical that it is approached systematically. One approach that can be adopted has been described:

- **Define objectives** – Before undertaking a co-creation strategy, organisations should clearly define their objectives and determine how they want their customers to affect the value chain.
- **Select the right co-creators** – Not all customers will be good or fit-for-purpose co-creators. It is important for organisation to choose the right customers with the right skills to affect specific elements of the value chain.
- **Be clear about rights and expectations** – Customers need to trust producers not to misuse the information they provide or unfairly exploit the relationship. The service providers need to actively manage customer expectations about how the relationship will evolve.
- **Control the channels** – Service providers can manage their risks by carefully selecting customers to support co-creation, controlling the channels for presenting information or managing co-creation by proxy.
- **Outsource co-creation** – If an organisation does not want to assume the risks and confront the challenges associated with managing co-creation, it can sometimes have a third party manage the community and still reap the benefits.
- **Provide capabilities for co-creation** – Organisations must provide customers with the right tools and training to co-create efficiently and effectively.

- **Manage incentives –** Finally, organisations must provide the right reward and level of rewards for effective co-creation behaviour. In addition to rewarding customers, solution providers can also create sanctions to address the legal risks.

Seeing customers as partners in the creation of value widens the horizon of the organisation in the new knowledge based economy. However, the effectiveness of the process will depend on how much value is created for both customers and solution providers.

Source: (Kambil, Friesen, & Sundaram, 1999)

Co-design and co-creation – A survey This survey can be used to understand the depth and pervasiveness of co-design and co-creation methodology within the organisation.
Have you been involved in a project to develop or improve a service that has included the views of users? • Yes • No
Are there any other parts of your organisation where this type of participatory approach is taken to service design? • Yes • No
Are there any particular reasons why your organisation has not involved users in the development or improvement of services?
Looking to the future, how likely is it that your organisation will begin to involve users in the development or improvement of services? • Very unlikely • Fairly unlikely • Likely • Fairly likely • Very likely
How do you plan to involve users in the development or improvement of services?

Does the project involve new services or existing services?	All services are new	→	All of the services already exist
Which of the following best describes the approach taken in designing the services associated with this project?	No opportunities to make large-scale changes	→	No assumptions were made about what can and can't be changed
What kind of relationship did the project team have with the users during the design?	Minimal collaboration: Users were occasionally consulted if a specific question needed an answer	→	Completely collaborative: Users were involved in all stages
Were the users already known to the project team? • Yes • No			
At what stage of the process, if at all, did the relationship with the user begin?	At the very end of the process: Users were not involved until the design project is finalised by the provider	→	At the very start of the process: Users were involved in the very earliest discussions, even before the main design effort had begun
To what extent, if at all, were users involved in the definition or modification of the design process itself?	To no extent at all: The process was owned by the internal project team, and there was no user feedback regarding process	→	To a great extent: The internal project team and users worked together at all levels to define and refine the process
How much information, if any, were users given about internal design discussions in which they did not directly participate	None: Internal discussions were strictly private	→	All information available: The entire process was open-access to all those involved, whether users or the internal project team

How frequently were users consulted during service design?	Rarely: One or two consultative meetings took place over the course of design	➡	Continuously: Users played a day-to-day role in the design process
For how long did a particular user play a part in the design process?	Single interaction: Each particular user contributed a single comment or set of responses and has no further involvement	➡	For an extended period: Each user followed the design process for a substantial amount or a particular phase of its entire duration
How diverse were the viewpoints which users contributed to the design process?	Not at all diverse: Users are selected to fit specific criteria which match specific design goals	➡	Very diverse: Users were selected using criteria specifically designed to ensure a variety of viewpoints and interests
Which of the following best describes the relationship that developed between all those involved in the design?	Limited: Relationships between individuals were limited to those strictly necessary for the design agenda	➡	Wide ranging: All participants were given opportunities to interact and form a wider community of common interests
To what extent, if at all, did users learn about the service(s) under design?	To a minimal extent: Discussions with the user only covered those specific areas of the service to which they were likely to be exposed	➡	To a great extent: Users obtained a wide-ranging picture of the service and the context in which it is delivered
How much did users learn about the way in which the service was designed?	Only a little: User was given some information about the process if it is necessary to elicit a response	➡	A great deal: Users left the project knowing as much about the design process as the internal project team

Again thinking about the project that you have just described, how important was the existence of a clear design process?	Not at all important: There was no design process – the way to proceed, and the people to be involved, are decided as and when necessary		Very important: The process clearly guides the actions to be taken, and the people to take them, every step of the way
In the project, how clear were the responsibilities of, and limitations on, the internal design team and users, during the design process?	Not at all clear: Responsibilities and limitations varied with no apparent reason		Very clear: Everyone involved was aware of the responsibilities and limitations that apply to him or her
How much weight was given to the ideas and comments of users?	Very little: User comments were only considered in exceptional circumstances		A great deal: User comments were every bit as important as those of the internal project team
What scale of change warranted consultation with users?	Only very small changes involved user consultation		Only very large changes involved user consultation
In your opinion, how clear, if at all, was the communication of the overall vision and direction of the design effort to users?	Not at all clear: Each participant had a different idea of the goals of the design effort and the way of reaching those goals		Very clear: All participants shared the same goals and are working closely together to achieve those goals
How concrete and practical was the focus of the detailed design effort?	Not at all: The detailed design effort remains focused on very generic goals, e.g. 'improve service delivery'		Very: The detailed design effort was focused on the achievement of tangible and measurable goals. For example: reducing the waiting times by 15%

Empathy

In your opinion, did the design process encourage comments from users?	No, never: Comments were always attributable and criticism was viewed unfavourably	→	Yes, always: All comments were welcome and did not reflect on the source, whether named or not
How well did users and the internal project team communicate with each other?	Very poorly: Communication was difficult because users and the internal team had difficulty in explaining their ideas clearly and effectively to each other	→	Very well: Participants used methods of expression which aid understanding and made communication effective, e.g. diagrams, simplified models
How flexible, if at all, were the ways in which participants could contact each other?	Not at all flexible: Contact was limited to a few set times, using one means of communication	→	Very flexible: All participants could contact each other throughout the working day and often beyond, using several different means of communication, e.g. telephone, email, face-to-face meetings and web pages
What level of involvement did participants have in any changes to the way they were involved in the design process?	None: Changes were made without any form of discussion	→	A great deal: Participants were fully involved in both the decision to make changes and their implementation

Are you aware of any other people within your organisation to whom we should speak about this type of participative design?

- Yes
- No

Can you suggest any other public sector organisations that we could speak to in relation to this subject? • Yes • No
What would you say worked particularly well in relation to the involvement of users in the design of this project?
What barriers or difficulties did you face?
What would you say were the main benefits or impacts of using the participative or co-design approach in this project?
Have you measured or evaluated these benefits? • Yes • No
How have you evaluated these benefits?
Do you have any further comments to make in relation to this topic?

Table 3: Model 6 – Regulator Driven

Source: (DEMOS & PWC, 2008)

A Roadmap for Customer Engagement

Customer engagement is a tool to help organisations to make better decisions in providing customer centric service provision. Table 4 contains essential steps, which can be used as a road map for engaging customers.

Engaging Customers	**Issues to be considered**

Define the issue	• What is the specific customers' problem or issue you want to address?
	  ○ Discuss alternatives, solutions, and consequences with the customers and community
	  ○ Be sure that the scope of the problem is appropriate and feasible

Identify the purpose and degree of customer engagement	• Why do you need or want people to get involved in your project?
	• What do you want to accomplish by getting people involved?
	  ○ Do you want to inform people about a project, or help them understand a problem or an opportunity? Do you need more information from customers to make a decision? Primary techniques to inform include public opinion polling, needs assessments, and public hearings.
	  ○ Do you want to get public feedback about a project, program or decision? Do you want to stimulate public debate about the issue? Primary methods used to consult the public include community meetings, Delphi techniques, and roundtable discussions (focus groups)
	  ○ Do you want to work directly with customers throughout the decision-making process, drawing on their expertise to make recommendations? Primary tools to engage the public include dialogue sessions, customer juries, public issues forums, et al.
	  ○ Do you want to create long-term partnerships among participants and community groups that will implement the solutions they create? Primary tools for this goal include study circles and community task forces

<table>
<tr><td rowspan="3">Identify tools for engaging customers</td><td>To inform</td><td>• Interviews and Surveys
• Delphi Technique
• Roundtable Discussions (focus groups)</td></tr>
<tr><td>To engage</td><td>• Public Issues Forums
• Customers Panels</td></tr>
<tr><td>To collaborate</td><td>• Study Circles
• Community Task Forces
• Electronic Methods of Deliberation</td></tr>
<tr><td>Identify individuals and groups that need to be involved</td><td colspan="2">• Who needs to be part of your project in order to accomplish your goals?
  o Identify what your project needs, what it already has, what it is missing, and who can fill in these missing pieces
  o Identify groups and individuals that will represent the diversity of your community, especially those who may traditionally be underrepresented in community efforts
  o Include those people who can influence how a decision is implemented, and who may be affected by the decision
• Remove barriers to customer participation</td></tr>
<tr><td>Develop a plan for recruiting and retaining participants</td><td colspan="2">• Develop a plan for recruiting participants that identify who will be invited, how they will be contacted, and who will be responsible for inviting each group or individual
• Develop or use a system by which people can indicate their interest
• Have a “talent bank” – A file of people who have expressed an interest in helping your organisation can help you fill slots quickly
• Develop an effective reward system for people who are actively participating throughout of the project (service provision)</td></tr>
<tr><td>Create a positive environment for customer engagement</td><td colspan="2">• Continue offering worthwhile experiences and opportunities in order to encourage continued participation
• Establish value statement, rules and protocol for effective discussion and exchanging ideas
• Facilitating meeting
• Frame the issue</td></tr>
</table>

	• Focus on interest not position - a position on an issue is something you have decided upon and is how a customer thinks the issue should be solved or addressed while an interest is what causes someone to decide on his or her position
	• Cooperative problem solving - defining opponents as partners in the effort to find an agreeable solution to all participant
	• Deal with conflict
	• A few suggestions to make the discussion productive:
	  o Be sure to involve all members in the discussion
	  o Encourage accurate and fair communication practices
	  o All participants should listen and raise questions
	  o The discussion should focus on the issues, not the people

Identify evaluation criteria and decide on next steps	• Create benchmarks to track progress toward goals • Celebrate achievements, successes, and remind participants of the role they played in getting to that point • Re-evaluate your action steps in light of accomplishments
Maintain open lines of communication	• Keep your issue fresh in the minds of the community, raise awareness about the group and improve the group's credibility through on-going, regular communication about your group and your group's issues is important.

Table 4: Customer Engagement – A Roadmap

Source (the Center for Rural Pennsylvania, 2008)

Assessment Toolkit: Engagement

Communication

Q1. How well-developed are the organisation's communication channels in order to effectively reach out to its customers?			
Basic	**Developing**	**Maturing**	**Leading**
The organisation has some communication channels but doesn't use them effectively	The organisation uses several communication channels for customer engagement (soliciting, reporting, feedback, publishing etc.)	The organisation has a communication strategy in place to use a multitude of communication channel but there is a lack of integration resulting in some inconsistency and incoherence of the communicated messages.	All the customer communication channels are integrated and deployed to meet overall stated objectives of the communication strategy.

Q2. To what extent do the communication channels allow the involvement of customers?			
Basic	**Developing**	**Maturing**	**Leading**
The communication channels can only be used for one way delivery of messages (broadcasting purposes).	The communication channels allow the customers to seek or solicit information on an on-demand basis.	The communication channels allow the customers to seek and solicit information on an on-demand and real time basis as far as possible.	The communication channels are well-developed to handle all complex multiple-way transactions with the customers and can also be used as a tool for some service delivery.

Q3. How frequently does the organisation communicate with its customers regarding its services?			
Basic	**Developing**	**Maturing**	**Leading**
The organisation communicate with its customers on an on-off basis and rarely and therefore customers are not fully informed about services	The organisation sometimes communicates with its customers with regards to its services.	The organisation often communicates with its customers with regards to its services.	The organisation continuously and on an ongoing basis communicate with its customers with regards to its services, it keeps the line of communication always active and open.

Involvement

Q1. To what extent does the organisation deploy the Voice of Customers (VOC) in designing new and/or improving existing services?			
Basic	**Developing**	**Maturing**	**Leading**
The organisation lacks a proper mechanism for reaching out to its customers; however, it does collect customers' data on an occasionally.	The organisation has a mechanism for collecting customers' data; however, it lacks the required capability for translating this raw information into the customer insight, which can be used for improving services.	The organisation develops an effective mechanism for collecting customer data and translating it into the customer insight; however, the customer insight has been inefficiently deployed due to the lack of a clear deployment strategy.	The organisation has developed an effective mechanism and strategy for approaching to its customers and extracting and deploying the voice of customers for improve the quality of its service provision.

Q2. Does the organisation provide customers with the right tools and training to co-create efficiently and effectively?			
Basic	**Developing**	**Maturing**	**Leading**
The organisation provides customers with limited number of training programs to co-create and hence, the customers are not sufficiently equipped to effectively co-create	The customers have been provided with several training programs in relation to service co-creation; however, most of the training programs delivered are irrelevant and not sufficient for enabling customers.	The organisation provides customers with a wide range of relevant training programs in relation to co-creation; however, the training programs are designed to develop customers' capabilities from basic to intermediate level.	The organisation provides customers with a wide range of relevant training programs, which are designed to develop customers' capabilities to the most advanced level.

Q3. To what extent does the organisation involve customers in the definition or modification of the design process itself?			
Basic	**Developing**	**Maturing**	**Leading**
The organisation controls the entire activity chain and there is no customers' feedback regarding that process of service design.	The organisation seeks customers' feedback with regards to new services or latest service improvement; however, the customers will be approached after the completion of service design.	The organisation involves customers in the process of service design and reactively but continuously seeks customers' information; however, evidently, the customers are	The organisation has proactively sought customers' input with regards to the improvements of the process of service design, which possibly can be made. In other words, the customers have been fully involved not only

		not involved in the decision making process.	in the process of service design but also in the decision making process.

Empowerment

Q1. To what extent does the organisation customise services in accordance with customers' needs and personal preferences?			
The organisation provides one-size-fits-all services to the customers and they are viewed as passive recipients of the services.	The organisation customises the delivery aspects of its services in accordance with customers' needs and preferences; however, it owns and controls the entire process of decision making in relation to the design aspects of the services and does not allow customers to be actively involved in it.	The customers are fully involved in the process of personalisation of services and also they are passively involved in the process of decision making with respects to the design aspects of the services.	The customers are empowered to not only personalise the delivery aspects of services based on their preferences but also being a strategic partner during the decision making process in relation to the design aspects of the services.
Q2. To what extent can the customers influence on the decision making process?			
Basic	**Developing**	**Maturing**	**Leading**
The organisation does not engage customers in the decision making process; however, it	The organisation passively engage customers in the decision making process through informing customers about the finalise decision and	The organisation engage customers in the decision making process through having a customer representative in the meetings; however, the	The customers are actively engaged in the process of decision making. The power of decision making is partially distributed

keeps customers fully informed once the decision has been made.	seeking their feedback	representative is not allowed to actively contribute in the actual decision making.	between customers and the organisation.
Q3. How profoundly does the organisation implement the concept of 'Do it Yourself (DIY)' for empowering the customers?			
Basic	**Developing**	**Maturing**	**Leading**
The organisation has not considered the concept of DIY as a tool for empowering its customers.	The organisation provides customers with the limited range of tools, resources and infrastructure required for an active contribution of customers over the process of service delivery.	The organisation provides the customers with a wide range of tools, the necessary resources and the required infrastructure to actively contribute over the process of service design; however, the organisation lacks to provide a clear strategy and policy to help customers in effective deployment of resources.	The organisation ensures that the customers are provided with sufficient tools and techniques, the necessary resources and the required infrastructure for an effective management of the process of service delivery. The customers are also well-supported with a clear strategy, policy and a set of guidelines, which helps the customers in implementing the concept of DIY in a proper manner.

Empathy is the most revolutionary emotion.

Gloria Steinem,
Revolution from Within

Chapter 11: Customer Advocacy

Introduction

The desire of most organisations is not to just have customers who are satisfied, but to ensure that long term survivability and competitiveness are heavily reliant on their loyal customers. This means that the first challenge that organisations have is to ensure that loyalty exists within their customer base and the loyal customers become the advocate of the organisation's services and products. When the customers become the salespersons for the organisation (word of mouth, reference, et al), the organisation can assume that it is well on its way to long term competitiveness and sustainability. Willingness to talk up an organisation or product or services to friends, family, and colleagues is one of the best indicators of loyalty because of the customer's sacrifice in making the recommendation. When customers act as references, they do more than indicate they've received good economic value from an organisation; they put their own reputations on the line.

However, there are several challenges associated with moving the boundaries of customer loyalty so that future success can be guaranteed. Organisations have to create an open dialogue with their customers and must radically move the momentum from a transactional based relationship, driven from products and services, to experience based relationships which are driven by the customers themselves. Furthermore, the organisations have to adopt an open system, which would mean that the mentality of the "push" would gradually give way to a new paradigm of a "pull" mechanism triggered by customer needs, and customers wanting to cater for their own individual requirements. The theme of customer advocacy, therefore, is a direct consequence of having created the necessary changes and the radical transformation of operating a business with the following characteristics in mind:

- An open system where innovation is based on co-creation and is not under the control of the provider organisation

- The value chain is redefined so that it reflects the voice of the customer at all stages of the value creation and translation aspects
- The key catalyst for ensuring that great, individualised experience is customer engagement and empowerment at all stages
- The communication is defined as a dual dialogue of open sharing, knowledge transfer, education and pro-active efforts, to capture ideas and propose schemes for the future
- The measurability of values is to be radically shifted from the transactional based approach which tends to measure value through economic means into a new mindset where value is measured by fulfilment according to individual customer needs (i.e. beauty is in the eyes of the beholder)
- Trustworthy relationships: This means that trust is a mutual currency that both parties concerned value immensely. From the point of view of the customers, they trust the brand and they trust the provider organisation in catering for their needs for the present and for the future. From the point of view of the provider organisation, this is to trust that the customer will be advocates for the brand and they will promote the interests of their preferred brand, or preferred provider in the best way possible.

Active customer advocates are different from the satisfied customers or the loyal customers in the sense that they are fully committed, with an emotional connection well beyond the typical relationship of customer and supplier. They are the customers with the highest level of involvement--active, vocal and proud. These are the crème de la crème: the people who "live" the brands that they regularly use. Their lifestyle often mirrors that offered by the brand, and they are active in talking about their experiences.

Customer Advocacy at Harley-Davidson

Owners of Harley-Davidson motorcycles who are members of the H.O.G. (Harley Owners Group) clubs around the world, for example, are very visible advocates for the brand. They not only buy the motorcycles, but also they actively accessorise with Harley-Davidson equipment for their choppers, wear a vast array of Harley-Davidson clothing and enthusiastically participate in Harley-Davidson events. Starting with fewer than 50 members in 1983, H.O.G. has grown to more than 800,000 members, more than half of whom attend at least one Harley-Davidson event per year.

How important is advocacy to the organisation? Harley-Davidson does almost no advertising, depending instead upon its community of advocates to purchase both motorcycles and logo gear - and spread the word to others. Customer advocacy has an impact on virtually every area of organisation activity. As John Russell, managing director of Harley-Davidson, Europe, has said: "If it is important to the customer, if it's a good insight, if it's a good point of understanding and connection to the customer, it makes its way into business processes and becomes part of what we do."

Source: (Lowenstein, 2004)

Traditionally, organisations have relied on the “push-pull” mechanism where the organisation designs a product or service to fill a need and then convinces the customers to buy the product or use the service by doing aggressive advertising, promotion, and distribution tactics. But with the increase in customers’ powers and knowledge, the customer-organisation relationship equation has changed, giving birth to a new era of “customer advocacy” which is based on the organisation representing the customers’ interests by providing them with the complete and unbiased information, advice on which products/services are best for them (including fair comparisons with competitors), joint design of products/services, and a partnership that breeds long-term loyalty.

Source: (Urban, 2005)

Business Case for Customer Advocacy

To assess the financial impact of word of mouth advocacy on organisation growth in the UK, the following study, at the London School of Economics in the early summer of 2005, has been conducted. Three measures of word of mouth and one for satisfaction have been calculated.

1. **Word of mouth** - net promoter score, which means the proportion of customers who had actually recommended the organisation they use to others in the last 12 months, and the proportion who had spread negative comments during the same time period.
2. **Customer satisfaction** - the average (mean) customer satisfaction score (out of 10) for each organisation.

Correlations were then computed to see if the word of mouth metrics and satisfaction scores could predict sales growth performance (Figure 67 and Figure 68).

The findings show that organisations in the UK with a high net promoter score, such as HSBC, Asda, and Honda outperformed their competitors in terms of growth in 2004, whilst those with low net promoter scores, such as Lloyds-TSB, Safeway, Fiat and T-Mobile underperformed (Figure 67).

The study reveals that organisations attracting high levels of negative word of mouth, which tended to be, logically enough, those organisations with low net promoter scores, published poorer results – in terms of growth – than those enjoying low levels of negative word of mouth (Figure 68).

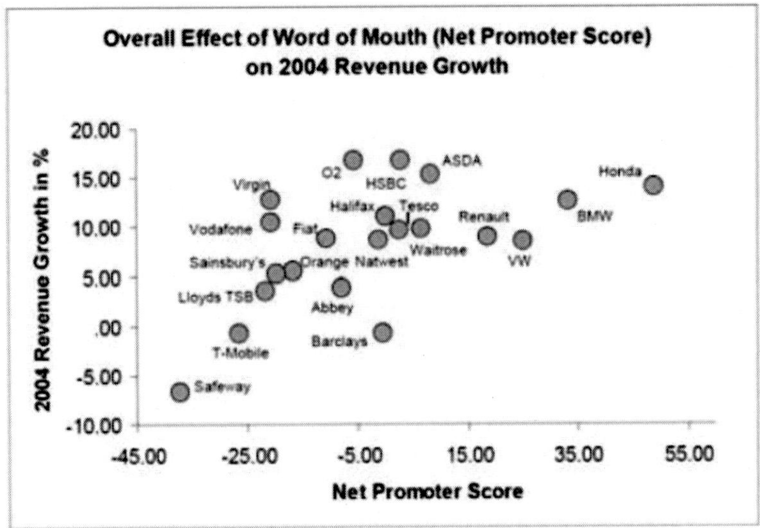

Figure 67: Customer Advocacy Drives UK Business Growth

Source: (Marsden, Samson, & Upton, 2005)

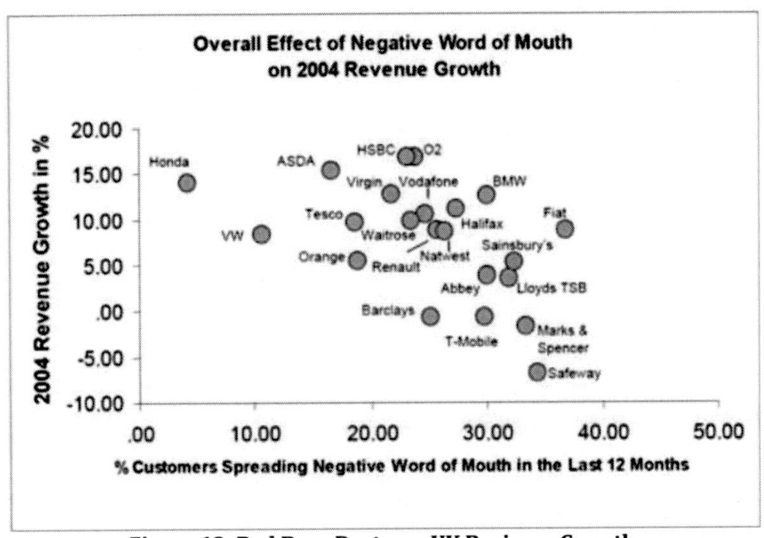

Figure 68: Bad Buzz Destroys UK Business Growth

Source: (Marsden, Samson, & Upton, 2005)

Tools for Optimising Customer Advocacy

It is evident that businesses that build customer advocacy will grow. In order to do so, organisations require proven advocacy optimisation solutions. The following model (Figure 69) entails eight distinct advocacy-generating tools that have demonstrated themselves to be effective in helping organisations to build customer advocacy.

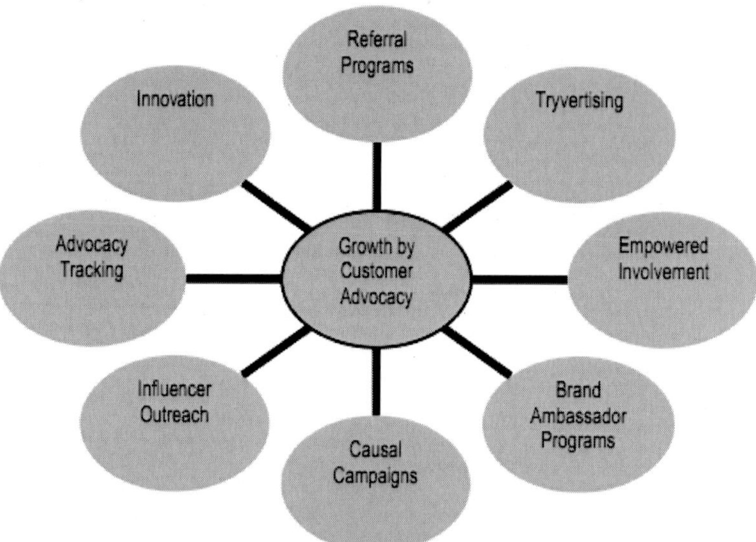

Figure 69: Driving Growth by Optimising Customer Advocacy
Source: (Marsden, Samson, & Upton, 2005)

Model Description

1. ***Referral programs*** – this is the most elementary solution for optimising customer advocacy levels through rewarding existing customers for recommending new customers. This can be done through introducing different rewarding schemes such as customer-get-customer, introduce-a-friend or member-get-member schemes. The type of rewards considered for customers, who become word of mouth advocates, might be varied from cash to gift incentives to discounts on purchases etc. However, this method is typically associated with subscription services within the context of private service; public service organisations

can use similar schemes for motivating existing customers to share their experiences from using a particular service channel and promote a new service or channel to new customers i.e. this can be a supporting tool for deploying channel migration strategy.

2. ***Tryvertising*** – this tool aims at turning lead customers into advocates by giving them sneak peeks of new yet-to-be-launched services. Traditionally, samples of new services were widely available to anyone within the market and consequently, the organisations should have dealt with the substantial cost of service prototyping and marketing. In contrast, Tryvertising conveys the message that organisations should be selective in providing sample of new services to the customers. In order to do so, they require to explicitly identifying lead customers who can potentially be word of mouth advocates and then give this opportunity to them to try new services. This is a win-win scenario for both customers as well as organisations. From customers' perspectives they have an advantage to be among the first users of new services before they become widely available; while from organisations' perspectives this is an effective strategy for optimising customer advocacy. The primary objective of this tool is to use exclusivity and scarcity to turn the 'privileged' trial participants into advocates who then showcase the innovation to others.
3. ***Empowered involvement*** – empowering customers to call the shots on new services, is an advocacy generating tool that harnesses a powerful psychological phenomenon known as the Hawthorne Effect. The Hawthorne Effect is simply the "I did that" effect, the consequence of being asked one's opinion and seeing it acted upon. For example, Think Big Brother/American Idol where audience participation empowers viewers to vote participants off the show. This can be facilitated with Web polls, SMS votes and other innovations in personal communications technology, which means that empowered involvement has become a fast, scalable and cost-effective solution for creating advocacy.

4. **Brand ambassador programs** – this fourth way of transforming customers into advocates is to invite highly valued and satisfied customers to become brand ambassadors. Brand Ambassador Programs work by giving chosen customers special privileges both for themselves and to share with their friends. These privileges may include exclusive offers, special invites, and sneak peeks of new products or inside scoops of brand news. The idea is to give the Brand Ambassador materials that help them promote the brand.
5. **Causal campaigns** – organisations can adopt a good cause as a strategic positioning and marketing tool that appeals to existing and target customers. For example, In the US, when American Express pledged to donate a penny to the restoration of the Statue of Liberty for every transaction made by its cardholders, use of American Express cards in the US increased by 28% and new users increased by 17%.
6. **Influencer outreach** – the sixth way of transforming customers into advocates is to influence on influencers through targeting the mass majority directly who then influence the majority by word of mouth. Influencer outreach programs involve identifying influencers in a target market (using influencer screeners), and then engaging them with tools from the advocacy toolbox to transform them into word of mouth advocates.
7. **Advocacy tracking** – organisations can identify what they are doing right and where there is room for improvement by monitoring advocacy levels through the net promoter score for services and customer-facing departments.
8. **Innovation** – this is a fact that eventually customers will recommend a service when it is worth recommending. The key to driving growth through advocacy is innovation. Using the psychology of word of mouth provides a useful handle on how to innovate advocacy worthy services. The key here is to have service that delivers an experience that exceeds expectations because customers only tend to talk about things that are at odds with their expectations. In other words, service-talk is triggered when the service either exceeds or falls short of expectations. In practice, this means identifying the expectation priorities of a

target market – as opposed to needs or satisfaction – and delivering experiences that exceed those expectations. By identifying where customer expectations can be exceeded, and then by focusing new service development in these areas, organisations have the opportunity to hardwire customer advocacy into innovation.

Measuring Customer Advocacy

There have been many measures that have been used by organisations to measure their customer advocacy quotient i.e. the extent to which the customers will vouch for the excellence in services or products provided by the organisation. However, Fred Reichheld, in his book *"The Ultimate Question"*, stresses on the importance of the single most important indicator. The metric, Net Promoter Score (NPS), since then has become a buzzword in several organisations. At the heart of the matter is that research has proven a very strong correlation between NPS and repeat purchases and referrals. In most industries, this one simple statistic explains much of the variation in relative growth rates; that is, organisations with a better ratio of Promoters to Detractors tend to grow more rapidly than competitors.

NPS, fundamentally, segments the customers in three categories: Promoters, Passives and Detractors. As is evident from the name, Promoters are the loyal enthusiasts who will keep buying and referring others, thereby fuelling the organisational growth. Detractors, on the other hand, are unhappy customers who can damage the organisational brand and impede growth through negative word-of-mouth. Passives are the in-betweeners and are typically characterised as satisfied, yet unenthusiastic customers, who are vulnerable to competitive offerings. Segmentation of the customers through this methodology helps the organisation in adopting targeted and differentiated approaches to building, developing and protecting the brand image of the organisation. But the moot question is how an organisation should actually segment the customers. The answer is surprisingly simple: by asking one simple question — How likely is it that you would recommend

[Organisation X] to a friend or colleague? Figure 70 depicts the segmentation of the customers based on their response to the previously stated question on a scale of 0-to-10 point rating scale.

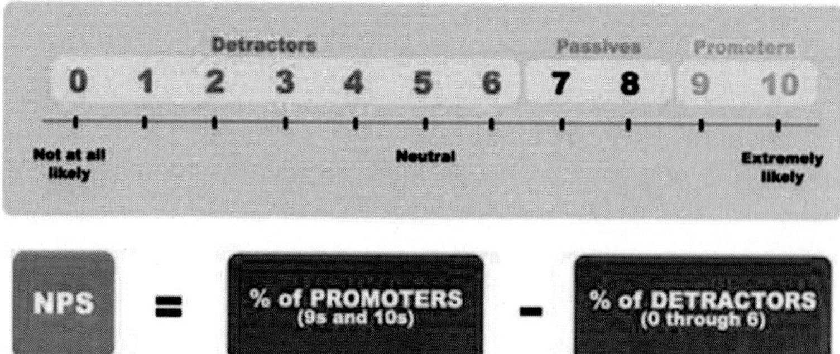

Figure 70: Customer advocacy - Net Promoter Score

Source: (Satmetrix Systems, Inc., 2011)

The organisation's NPS (Net Promoter Score) helps define the organisation's leaders, their organisation's real mission and hold their people accountable for building great customer relationships. In order to improve the organisation's score, there have to be targeted strategies for all the three different segments of customers.

- **"Act upon" the Three Groups of Customers** – Grouping customers into three segments helps the frontline managers in deploying the targeted strategy to increase the number of promoters and to reduce the number of detractors. This makes a lot much sense for the frontline managers than asking them to raise the customer satisfaction index by one standard deviation.
- **Tune Your Organisation's Growth Engine** – As the ultimate strategy for any customer-relationship metric is to help the organisation tune its growth engine to operate at peak efficiency, the NPS scores well in this front because it helps employees clarify and simplify the job of delighting customers and it also allows them to compare their performance linearly across time.
- **Increase Promoters and Decrease Detractors** – The business goal is not only to delight the customers always, rather it is to ensure that there are more promoters on board who buy more and who

actively refer the organisation's products and/or services to their networks. This will ultimately result in a sustained competitive advantage. At the same time, the organisation ought to ensure that the number of detractors decreases on a consistent basis. These are two distinct processes that must be managed, and NPS captures both.

Source: (Satmetrix Systems, Inc., 2011)

The operating model depicted in Figure 71 provides a best practice framework for how organisations collect and act on customer feedback to optimise financial benefits. The key here is to transform the DNA of the organisation to that of a customer-centric one.

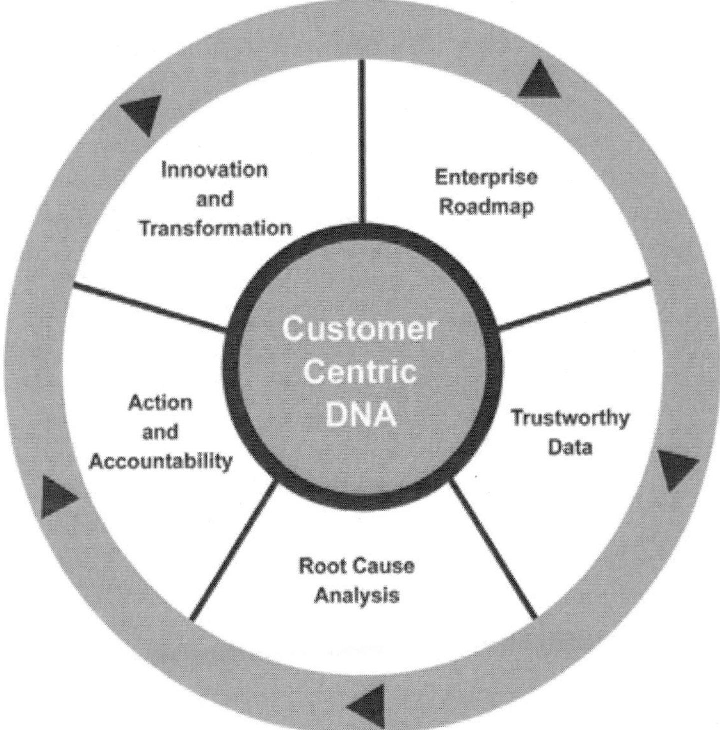

Figure 71: Net Promoter Operating Model

Source: (Satmetrix Systems, Inc., 2011)

The transformation will be led by gathering rich and relevant data, analysing them to develop a robust intelligence and finally using that intelligence to innovate and transform.

- **Create customer-centric DNA –** Two key dimensions with building a customer-centric DNA are executive (leadership) sponsorship and support and organisational alignment. Top leadership is key so that the transformation programmes are provided with the required resources and the focus on customers is treated as a key strategic differentiator (constancy of purpose). However, in order to cascade the vision to the appropriate levels, the necessary alignment and buy-in has to be there so that the customer focus is at the core of the organisation and permeate all decisions.
- **Develop an enterprise roadmap –** Programs are often found to develop at different pace to suit the varied needs at different levels within the organisation. As such roadmap planning should be refreshed based on the evolution of the customer relationship and it should take into account critical customer touch points for the customers' experiences, analysing which ones have the greatest impact on the customers' experience and in which sequence should they be addressed (roadmap).
- **Build trustworthy data –** In order to develop a robust and relevant customer centricity transformation programme, it is important to be prepared to make important decisions based on the Net Promoter Score. If not, the data may not be robust enough and there is a need to ensure that the feedback solicitation process from the customers and from the touch points is robust and intelligent enough to connect the feedback to the specific operational and strategic actions.
- **Identify root cause –** Organisations, often times, wrongly believe that they know their customers inside out. However, not surprisingly, the data has revealed different loyalty drivers. A detailed root cause analysis – supported by a mix of quantitative and qualitative analysis - will enable the organisation and its employees to understand and address the real and relevant loyalty drivers for their customers.

- **Drive action and accountability –** Intelligence without action is worthless. The organisation will have to ensure that the relevant intelligence is provided to the employees in terms of understandable, actionable and timely information. Also, closed loop processes have to be deployed where data is understood, root cause is analysed, and actions are completed, resulting in direct improvement of the customer experience.
- **Enable innovation and transformation –** At the heart of this transformation process is the ability of the organisation to make the right strategic decisions and foster innovations that improve the competitive positioning of the organisation. The organisations, which tend to outperform their competitors, have been found to drive the product and service innovation through an iterative process of listening to customer feedback and making improvements.

Why Customer Advocacy is not enough

However, organisations increasingly adopt their strategies centred around customer advocacy in order to s identify themselves as customer focused; they fail to realise the promised benefits due to the lack of additional information behind their advocacy scores . There are two fundamental questions, which an organisation should strive to properly answer if it is to fully realise the benefits of advocacy. The questions are:

1. What pieces of information do organisations need from their customers to influence advocacy?
2. How can they ensure that information reaches the right employees?

Customer-centric organisations should use advocacy as part of their strategy to improve customer experiences. Customer experiences are created every time a customer interacts with an organisation. Regardless of whether an organisation uses one or multiple channels for delivering services to its customers and responding to the customers' enquiries, customers' experiences are formed at multiple touch points throughout the customer life-cycle (Figure 72)

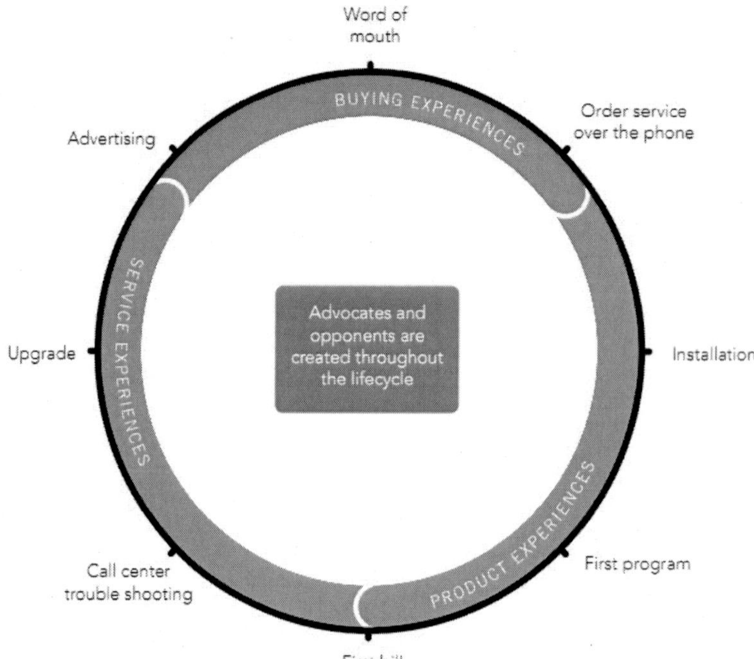

Figure 72: Customer life-cycle (An example)
Source: (ResponseTek Networks Corp., 2008)

Advocates are customers who recommend a business based on good experiences whereas opponents are those who actively criticise it. Figure 73 depicts the ladder of customer experience. Organisations, in order to create advocates, should push customers up the experience ladder. This can be done by consistently delivering the positive experiences that customers expect. They need to:

- Understand which touch points are important to customers
- Understand what their customers' experiences are at each of these touch points and how those experiences affect customer advocacy
- Integrate those experiences into business processes and strategies

Customer advocacy, on its own, only measures whether a customer will recommend a business to friends or family. Its power comes from combining it with additional information about the customer experience: where it happened, when, with who or what. This can organisation in identifying what drives advocacy or creates opponents and hence they can use their resources addressing the customer pain points that matter most.

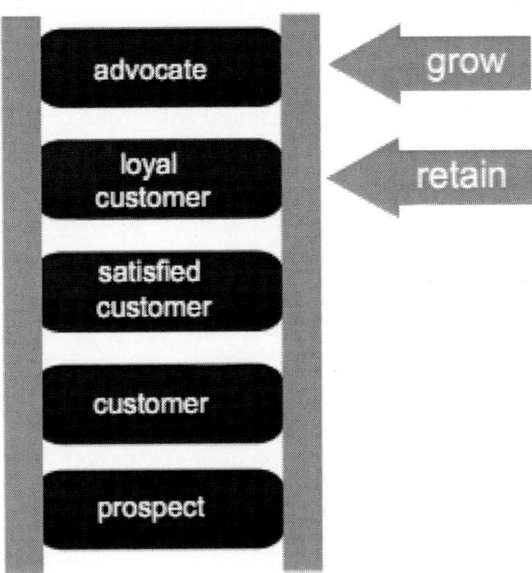

Figure 73: Customer Experience Ladder
Source: (ResponseTek Networks Corp., 2008)

Relationship between Advocacy and Customer Experience Management

Customer Experience Management incorporates the voice of the customer into the business to accelerate improvements that customer's value whereas Advocacy is simply an indicator of the quality of the experience, as evaluated by customers and informed by their expectations of the interaction. An organisation's advocacy score reflects the sum of customers' experiences across the business. CEM provides detail about each experience to pinpoint where the customer has identified gaps between their expectations and the delivered experience, so that the organisations can target improvements and reduce customer defection (ResponseTek Networks Corp., 2008). Table 5 entails three advocacy metrics, which when combined with additional customer experience information; these metrics can be truly valuable.

	Net Promoter Score (NPS)	***Customer Focussed Insight Quotient (CFiQ)***	***Advocacy Index***
Customer Segments	• Promoter • Passive • Detractor	• Advocate • Apathetic • Antagonist	• Advocate • Neutral • Opponent
Method	Customers rate their likelihood to recommend the business from 0 to 10	Customers rate agreement with three statements: • I would recommend this business to friends and family • I would use this business first for future needs • I would stick with this business if offered a competitively priced product/service	Customers indicate whether they would recommend the business on a 5-point scale
Score	-100% to 100%. Scores are calculated by subtracting % of Detractors from % of Promoters to achieve net score	% Advocates	% Advocates

Table 5: Measuring advocacy - Three methods

Source: (ResponseTek Networks Corp., 2008)

Assessment Toolkit: Advocacy

Advocacy as a part of organisation's strategy

Q1. To what extent does the leadership of the organisation view customer advocacy as a mean for achieving sustainability and future growth?			
Basic	**Developing**	**Maturing**	**Leading**
Leaders of the organisation are not aware of the role of customer advocacy in driving sustainability.	Although, leaders of the organisation know customer advocacy has a positive effect on sustainability and growth; they do not believe in the significant impact of advocacy on growth and sustainability.	Leaders of the organisation are fully aware about the importance of customer advocacy in driving sustainability and growth; however, they do not believe it is important as to be incorporated in the organisation's strategy.	There is a mutual understanding and a strong belief about the significance of customer advocacy in driving sustainability and future growth among leadership team. Hence, advocacy is fully incorporated in the overall strategy of the organisation.
Q2. To what extent do managers and leaders promote customer advocacy throughout the organisation?			
Basic	**Developing**	**Maturing**	**Leading**
Promoting customer advocacy within the organisation is not something, which managers need to be concerned about or spend time on.	Managers regularly communicate the benefits of customer advocacy with employees.	Managers are regularly communicating the benefits of customer advocacy for the organisation with employees and also introducing passive	Managers not only clearly and constantly communicate the importance of customer advocacy in organisational growth with employees but also sufficiently

		motivational schemes and programs (for example: incentives etc.) to increase employees' participation in optimising customer advocacy.	empower employees in delivering services, which can ultimately lead to building customer advocacy.
Q3. To what extent does an organisation's policies and work practices facilitates customer advocacy?			
Basic	**Developing**	**Maturing**	**Leading**
Customer advocacy is a missing part in almost most of the policies and work practices, which are related to customer experience.	Customer advocacy has been considered in few numbers of work practices and policies; however, it does not fully support the entire customer experience life-cycle.	Customer advocacy has been incorporated in most of the policies and work practices in relation to enhancing customer experience over the entire customer experience journey.	The element of customer advocacy has been distinctly considered and emphasised in every policies and work practices, which are related to enhancing customer experience over the entire customer life-cycle.

Customer advocacy measurement and management

Q1. How often does the organisation measure its performance in building customer advocacy?			
Basic	**Developing**	**Maturing**	**Leading**
The organisation lacks a measurement system for measuring its performance in	The organisation occasionally measures its performance with regards to customer	The organisation has a clear measurement system in place for measuring customer	The organisation has an effective and distinctly realisable measurement system using a

building customer advocacy and hence, it rarely affords to do so.	advocacy.	advocacy; however, the measurement system uses a limited number of metrics.	wide range of metrics for measuring its performance in building customer advocacy.
Q2. To what extent is the overall performance improvement of the organisation triggered by the results of customer advocacy measurement?			
Basic	**Developing**	**Maturing**	**Leading**
The organisation does not consider the results of customer advocacy measurement as a factor, which reflects the need for service improvement.	The organisation considers the results of customer advocacy measurement; however, it doesn't give priority to this factor compared with other indicators while evaluating the necessity for service improvement.	The organisation considers the results of customer advocacy measurement as a factor along with other factors for determining the need for service improvement.	The organisation sees customer advocacy measurement results as an important and preferable indicator in determining the necessity for service quality improvement.
Q3. To what extent does the organisation strive to optimise the level of customer advocacy through implementing different advocacy programs?			
Basic	**Developing**	**Maturing**	**Leading**
The organisation does not implement any program for promoting and/or building customer advocacy.	The organisation implements limited number of programs for building customer advocacy.	The organisation undertakes wide range of programs for transforming customers into advocates; however, there is an inconsistency	The organisation undertakes wide range of programs for optimising customer advocacy while there is a clear vision for undertaking

		between what the organisation is trying to achieve from undertaking a particular program and what the program is actually designed for.	each program.

Customer experience management

Q1. To what extent does the organisation strive to create a unique customer experience?			
Basic	**Developing**	**Maturing**	**Leading**
The organisation aims at attracting prospects customers.	The organisation aims at not only attracting prospect customers but also inspiring existing customers.	The organisation strives to push customers beyond inspired customers and towards loyal customers by meeting or even exceeding customers' expectations all the times.	The organisation strives to transform loyal customers into advocates, who can promote services, by exceeding customers' expectations through delivering innovative services.
Q2. To what extent does the service delivery management system of the organisation allow personalisation of services, which can create a unique customer experience?			
Basic	**Developing**	**Maturing**	**Leading**
Service delivery management system of the organisation is designed on the basis of	Service delivery management system of the organisation is designed for delivering quick	Service delivery management system of the organisation is capable of incorporating	Service delivery management system of the organisation empowers customers to

delivering passive services and hence is not capable of delivering personalised services.	responses to the customers' enquiries but it lacks to improve future services based on customers' feedback.	customers' feedback about existing services in future services.	personalise the services in accordance with their current needs and expectations.
Q3. Taking the role of customer advocacy in determining the quality of services provided into account, to what extent does the organisation strive to improve the quality of services through excelling in customer experience management?			
Basic	**Developing**	**Maturing**	**Leading**
There is no link between customer experience management system of the organisation and its service quality improvement system.	The organisation separately measure customer advocacy and customer experience; however, it struggles to effectively utilise information collected for improving the quality of services.	The organisation continually seeks information from its customer experience management system at different phases of customer experience life-cycle in order to rightly determine the problem areas so that it can enhance customer experiences and ultimately enhance customer advocacy	The organisation continually evaluate the impacts generated by customer experience improvements occurred at different phases of customer experience life-cycle so that it can effectively identify the most critical areas for advocacy improvement through improving customer experience.

To embrace suffering culminates in greater empathy, the capacity to feel what it is like for the other to suffer, which is the ground for unsentimental compassion and love.

Stephen Batchelor
Confessions of a Buddhist Atheist

Chapter 12: Customer Loyalty

Introduction

Customer loyalty is the proportion of time a customer chooses the same service in a specific category compared to the total number of service orders made by the same customer in that category, under the condition that other acceptable services are conveniently available in that category. Yim and Kannan (1999) believe that two types of loyalty exist based on consumers' brand switching behaviour – the first is hard-core loyalty, which is defined as the proportion of a service's orders accounted for by repeat order the service alternative, and the second is reinforcing loyalty, which is the proportion of the service's orders accounted for by customers who may switch among service alternatives, but predominantly repeat order this product alternative to a significant extent. Khatibi *et al.* (2002) defines loyalty as the strength of a customer's intent to order again services from a supplier with whom they are satisfied.

Renowned loyalty expert, Richard Reichheld, presents a more thorough definition of loyalty "A loyal customer is one who values the relationship with the organisation enough to make the organisation a preferred supplier. Loyal customers don't switch for small variations in price or service; [instead] they provide honest and constructive feedback, they consolidate the bulk of their category purchases with the organisation, they never abuse organisation personnel, and they provide enthusiastic referrals *(Reichheld, 2002)."* Shoemaker and Lewis (1999) discussed loyalty in terms of a customer's attachment to the firm: The customer feels so strongly that an organisation can best meet his or her relevant needs that its competition is virtually excluded from the consideration set. A number of other researchers have presented definitions which encompass the same thoughts as Shoemaker and Lewis. For instance, Edvardsson *et al.* (2000) believe that 'loyalty is a customer's predisposition to repurchase from the same firm again'. While Yu and Dean believe that 'true loyalty, in this context, encompasses a non-random, behavioral response which results from evaluation processes that result in commitment' (Yu and Dean, 2001).

Loyalty is defined here as the enduring psychological attachment of a customer to a particular service provider Butcher *et al.* (2001). This attachment is reflected through:

1. Advocacy of the service to others;
2. Tendency to resist switching to alternate service providers;
3. Identification with the service provider; and
4. Having a relative preference for the service ahead of other competitors.

Similarly the dimensions of loyalty are:

1. Positive word-of-mouth;
2. A resistance to switch;
3. Identifying with the service; and
4. A preference for a particular service provider.

What is Customer Loyalty? – A Survey

The result of CustomerThink survey, in 2007, revealed that 68 percent defined loyalty as repeat buying behaviour; 59 percent as a customer who makes referrals to friends and colleagues; and 56 percent as a customer's emotional commitment. The number of respondents who defined high customer satisfaction as loyalty increased from 47 percent to 52 percent, while the number of respondents who saw loyalty as customer trust based on high value saw the most significant change, increasing from 45 percent to 54 percent of respondents.

Customer satisfaction is not the same as loyalty, according to loyalty experts. Yet poor customer satisfaction can lead to customer defections and damaging word of mouth. Many business leaders ignore this fact and try to skip over customer satisfaction in a rush to build "raving fans." Although customer satisfaction alone does not necessarily lead to customer loyalty (i.e. a positive attitude or such beneficial behaviour as making referrals and increasing spending), customer satisfaction is still a required foundation.

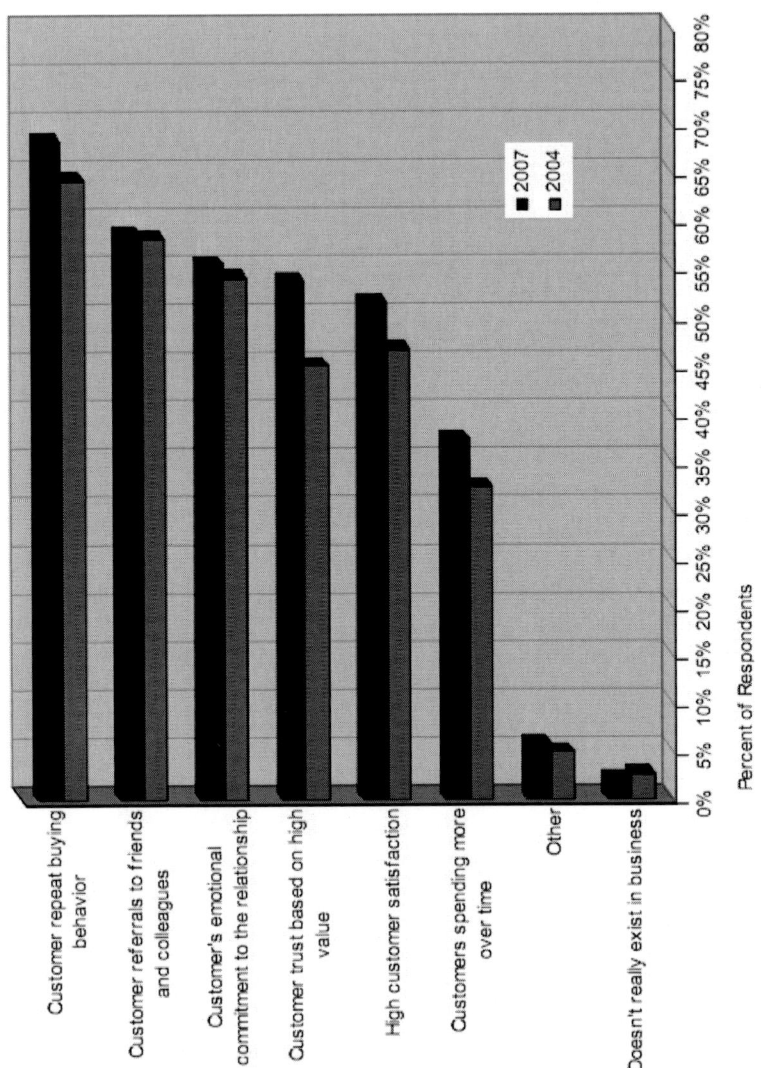

Figure 74: What Is Customer Loyalty? – Perspective of Business Managers
Source (Thompson B. , The Loyalty Connection:Measure What Matters and Create Customer Advocates , 2007)

Factors that Affect Loyalty

1. **Customisation and Personalisation** - Research reveals that customers prefer customised/personalised services (Mattila and Enz, 2002). Personalising the service process is beneficial because it lowers resistance to higher prices, and makes the customer feel important, and hence reduces the negative effects of service failures. Lee and Cunningham (2001) state that service customisation is a viable strategy for organisations to follow. Customisation is important for the development of loyalty among customers.
2. **Convenience** - Convenience is also found to have a positive effect on loyalty (Seiders *et al.*, 2005). Geographical proximity (or a convenient location) is said to have a significant influence on loyalty (Lee and Cunningham, 2001). However, researchers suggest that convenience on its own is not enough to build loyalty. It needs to be accompanied by other variables such as customer satisfaction and high switching costs.
3. **Strategic management focus** - Research has also identified the importance of senior management focus and support in building loyalty (Ennew and Binks, 1996). Some researchers believe that both senior management commitment, as well as customer focused cultures is important for organisations. More research adds the importance of having 'leaders who are dedicated to treating people right [and] drive themselves to deliver superior value to customers' (Reichheld, 2001).
4. **Technology** - Technology is an important tool which organisations can use to improve the quality of their services, and may lead to the development of loyalty. Technology is used to improve services offering, and improve value to customers. Moreover, it is believed that technology is not there to take the place of employees, rather to support them (Lee et al., 2003). Information Technology (IT) can help organisations by allowing them to develop customised solutions for customers. Moreover, it helps in the distribution of information, as well as in gathering information about customers. This helps organisations to target their communications and to customise services in ways that were not possible in the past.

5. **Service recovery** - Service failure may lead customers to become dissatisfied with an organisation. Customers' reaction to dissatisfaction varies from customer to customer (Bearden and Teel, 1983). It has been argued that most customers will not take action, nor will they inform the organisation about an episode of poor service. However, one of the major goals of 'defensive marketing' is to manage customer dissatisfaction in such a manner that its negative and harmful effects on the firm are minimised' (Fornell and Wernerfelt, 1987). Service recovery helps organisations to save face by rectifying the problems that have occurred in the failed service. It has also been thought by some to be an important factor in building loyalty . Service recovery is important because a dissatisfied customer may switch organisations, or he/she may indulge in negative word-of-mouth activities. On the other hand, a good service recovery may convert the negative feelings of the customer to positive feelings. Proper service recovery can build strong positive attitudes, turn dissatisfied customers into loyal ones, and may create more goodwill than if things had gone smoothly in the first place. It has also been stated that the relationship between satisfaction and loyalty is moderated by the type of failure recovery effort in service settings. Not all of the customers in an organisation will complain when they receive poor quality services. Some will leave the organisation without saying a word, while others may stick around for a while, but carry bad feelings in their hearts towards the organisation. Interestingly it was found that those customers who complained exhibited higher levels of loyalty than those who did not complain. Complaining is important for organisations because it provides feedback to organisations. Complaints should be taken seriously, and should be encouraged. Proper complaint handling can help organisations to build loyalty among customers. More recent research indicates that organisations need to develop strategies to cope with cultural factors, since it has been found that culture plays a part in the customers' perception of service recovery efforts (Mattila and Patterson, 2004).

6. **Type of business** - The type of business an organisation is in could affect the loyalty its customers have towards it. For instance, it was discovered that the average consumer is much less trusting of and affectively committed to their mechanic than they are of their doctor or hairstylist. Moreover, it was also found that customers were more emotionally committed to a hairstylist and physician than to an auto mechanic, (Shemwell et al., 1994). This study suggests that there may be industries where customers are more prone to become loyal.
7. **Importance of demographics** - Several demographic variables has been suggested to affect loyalty differently. Caruana found that education and to a certain degree age have an effect on service loyalty for banking customers (Caruana, 2002). Age also affects the perceptions of quality among grocery shoppers. Older shoppers do not prefer a bigger selection of delis as compared to younger shoppers. Age seems to have a positive effect on loyalty. The number of recommendations are said to increase with age. Furthermore, older shoppers claim to be more loyal, and use loyalty cards more frequently (Bellizzi and Bristol, 2004).Besides age, gender also seems to have an effect on loyalty. Women are believed to place a higher degree of importance on trust and commitment. Female customers are more likely to become emotionally attached to a service provider, as opposed to male customers.
8. **Culture** - Culture is said to affect the perceived quality of services. Moreover different cultural groups are said to vary in significance in their perception of satisfaction and dissatisfaction. Culture plays an important role in a consumers' perception of the service recovery efforts carried out by organisations. Customers do perceive service recovery efforts differently. For example, where the American consumers were happy with compensation, those from East Asia were not. Hence, it is suggested that organisations need to understand the cultural differences, so that they can develop more targeted strategies to improve service recovery and loyalty strategies (Mattila and Patterson, 2004).

Developing Loyalty at Different Levels

It has been observed that not all customers should be targeted with similar types of tactics to build loyalty. Yoon and Kim (2000) found that there were differences in the tactics that organisations should use to lure various types of customers to repurchase. Customers who exhibit no loyalty make their decision solely on the basis of an organisation's credibility. Spurious loyal customers make their decisions on the basis of an employee's attitude and favourable recommendations. The loyal customers make their decision on the basis of employee attitudes, organisation credibility and corporate image.

Research suggests a number of factors that can help build loyalty. A number of other variables have been found to play a mediating role on loyalty. However, it is evident from research that no single factor or variable on its own can build loyalty. A number, or all, of these factors are needed to build loyalty. Furthermore, it has been observed that different strengths or levels of loyalty will require different factors. Hence, it is imperative not to think of these antecedents as solutions to a problem, but to think of them as tools, of which many must be used to build that wonderful phenomenon called loyalty.

Loyalty Drivers

Customer loyalty is driven by customers' perception of the value they receive. The core service is part of that value, of course, and let's not forget that price is still a consideration. But increasingly, customer experiences are a substantial part of perceived value, too.

A study of Customer Experience Management, customers ranked quality of experiences as equally important to earning their loyalty as the core product or service they purchased. (Figure 75)

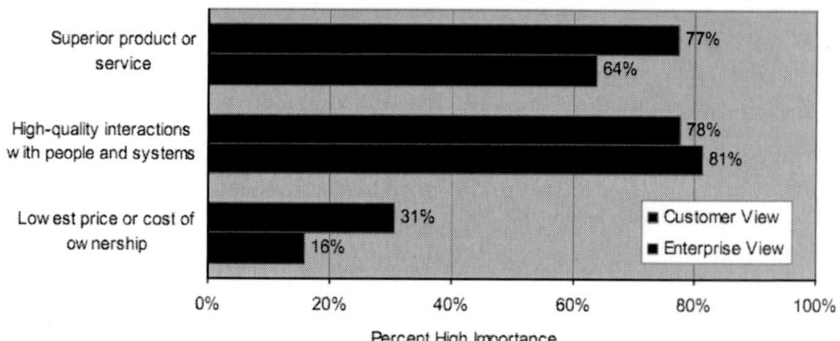

Figure 75: Loyalty Drivers

Source (Thompson B., The Loyalty Connection:Measure What Matters and Create Customer Advocates, 2007)

Choosing a Loyalty Strategy

Customer loyalty is winning the confidence of the customer in favour of an organisation so that the relationship becomes a win-win situation for both the organisation as well as the customer. When the cost of customer acquisition and retention, customers' profitability and loyalty are considered at the same time, it becomes clear that different customers need to be treated in different ways (Reinartz & Kumar, 2002).

Figure 76 contains a matrix shaped roadmap, which can be used for choosing a loyalty strategy based on the type of existing relationship between customers and the organisation. The matrix has two dimensions, the rate of customer profitability and the customer retention period. The matrix has four cells each of which indicate different type of customers from loyalty perspective. However, the word 'profitability' is mostly used for private sector organisations; this can be interpreted as customer's number of interaction with a public organisation when it is to be used for a public organisation. The actions are proposed for each type of customers.

	Short-term customers	Long-term customers
High profitability	**Butterflies** • good fit between company's offerings and customers' needs • high profit potential *Actions:* • aim to achieve transactional satisfaction, not attitudinal loyalty • milk the accounts only as long as they are active • key challenge is to cease investing soon enough	**True Friends** • good fit between company's offerings and customers' needs • highest profit potential *Actions:* • communicate consistently but not too often • build both attitudinal and behavioral loyalty • delight these customers to nurture, defend, and retain them
Low profitability	**Strangers** • little fit between company's offerings and customers' needs • lowest profit potential *Actions:* • make no investment in these relationships • make profit on every transaction	**Barnacles** • limited fit between company's offerings and customers' needs • low profit potential *Actions:* • measure both the size and share of wallet • if share of wallet is low, focus on up- and cross-selling • if size of wallet is small, impose strict cost controls

Figure 76: Loyalty Strategies

Source (Reinartz & Kumar, 2002)

Designing an Optimal Loyalty Program – A Ten Steps Approach

The popularity of loyalty programs has led many organisations to offer loyalty programs that simply imitate the program offered by the leader in their industry. Rather than providing a competitive advantage, this strategy simply creates a competitive stalemate while driving up expenses due to the cost of maintaining the loyalty program. The key point is that an organisation must design its loyalty program to create competitive advantage today and in the future. In addition, when choosing a system to support a loyalty program, it is important to select a system that provides the flexibility to cost-effectively make changes as required. Organisations should start the process of designing the loyalty program, by mapping customer interaction points and identifying key goals and business processes. Once the first part has been completed, these goals and processes should be mapped back to existing systems to identify any technology requirements.

The following is a step-by-step approach for designing a successful program:

Step 1: Identify key customer interaction points – at this stage, an organisation needs to identify all of the points at which a customer interacts with the organisation and then showing them as an integrated process. For example, the Figure 77 shows the continuum of interactions that customers can have with an airline.

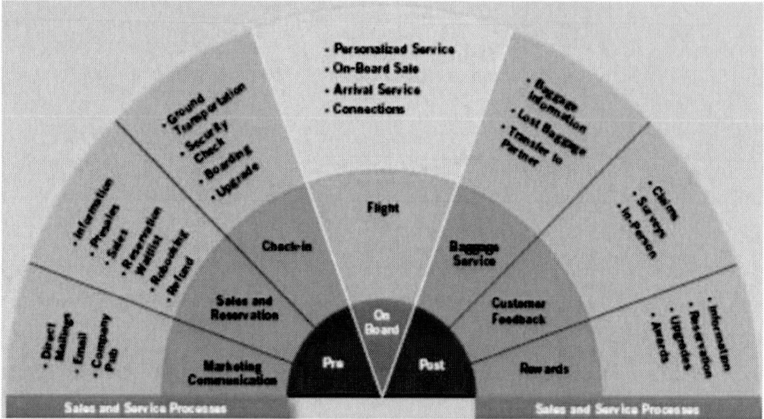

Figure 77: Airline Customer Interaction Map

Source (Oracle , 2005)

Step 2: Map associated business processes – at the second stage, organisations need to ensure that the loyalty program supports all of the business processes used to manage these interactions. Organisations need to ensure that all the key process elements are captured at a reasonable level of granularity, so that all users clearly know what is included.

Step 3: Identify desired business outcomes – organisations at this stage need to articulate a concise set of hard-hitting goals. Clearly articulating specific goals helps ensure that the actions and mind-sets of everyone who contributes ideas to the program are aligned.

Step 4: Identify key profitability drivers - at heart, loyalty programs reward changes in customer behaviour. The specific actions targeted should be the ones that are most likely to increase a customer's profitability, which will vary by both industry and organisation. It is critical to identify not only the profitability drivers but also the underlying factors that drive people's behaviour as it relates to each of these drivers.

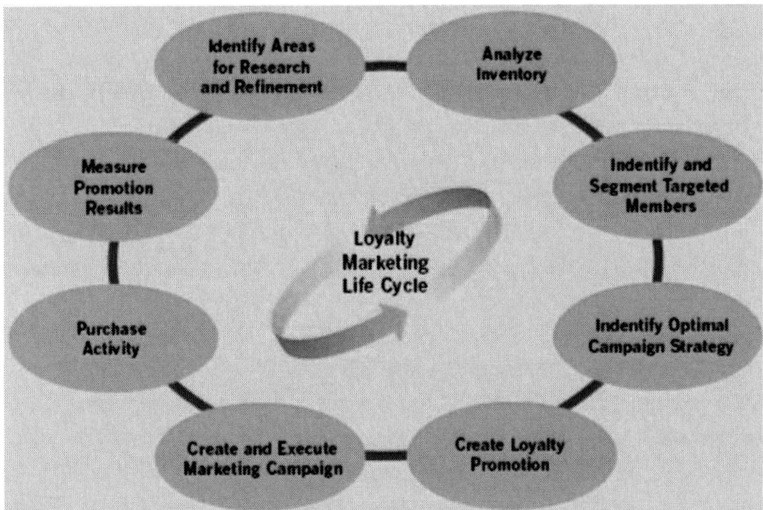

Figure 78: Integrated Loyalty Marketing Life-cycle

Source (Oracle, 2005)

Step 5: Design an integrated marketing strategy – developing and implementing an effective loyalty marketing strategy is critical to generating a positive return from a loyalty program, because marketing promotions will be the primary lever used to get members to change their behaviour and purchase undersold and/or more profitable products or to use more-cost-effective customer service and purchasing channels. Figure 78 shows an integrated loyalty marketing life-cycle. An organisation's loyalty, marketing, analytics, and transactional systems must work together to enable closed-loop marketing.

Step 6: Define loyalty analytics requirements – managers of organisations should leverage data in the design and ongoing management of their loyalty management program. Three requirements have been identified that analytics applications must meet to deliver the greatest value to the business:

- **Insight to action** – this means that the loyalty analytics application provides information in a timely manner and in a form that is understandable to the people who need to act upon it.
- **Embedded analytics** – to get the most value from analytics investments, organisations need analytics that can be embedded in all customer loyalty management processes.
- **Integrated loyalty and marketing analytics** – an organisation should develop the type of program which not only support the organisation's loyalty program and processes but also support other departments in the organisation that plan and execute non-loyalty campaigns.

Step 7: Segment members – members are those customers who has registered with the organisation and willingly given their information to the organisation. Usually, organisations offer incentives i.e. discounts to customers in order to encourage them to become a member. Members are most likely to receive a loyalty card once they have registered their information in the organisation's database. This provides an opportunity for the organisation to track customers purchasing behaviour and be in direct contact with customers. It will help an organisation to realise regular customers.

Step 8: Design the incentive structure - loyalty programs are designed to change members' behaviour by providing a set of incentive structures. An organisation must design and manage each structure, as well as the relationship between the different incentives, in order to ensure that members are motivated to behave in the desired manner.

Step 9: Define the partnering strategy - loyalty programs often involve a web of partners that together create an extended "loyalty ecosystem."

Step 10:Choose the appropriate technologies and vendor - the exact features and criteria that are used to evaluate the potential technologies and vendors will vary. However, they can often be grouped as depicted in Figure 79.

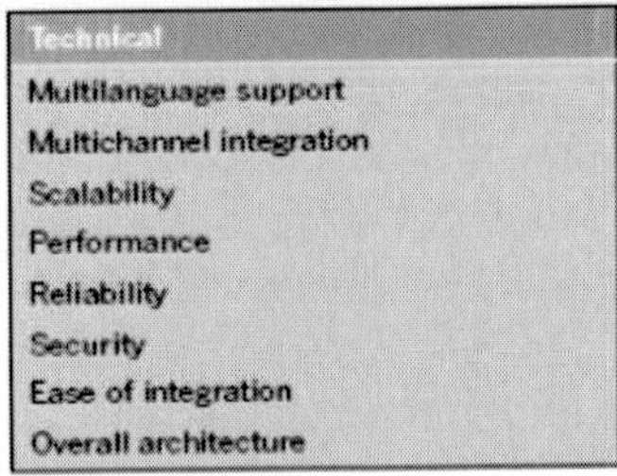

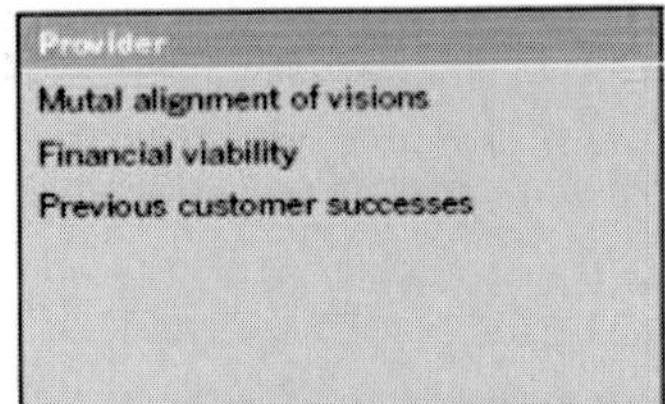

Provider

Mutal alignment of visions

Financial viability

Previous customer successes

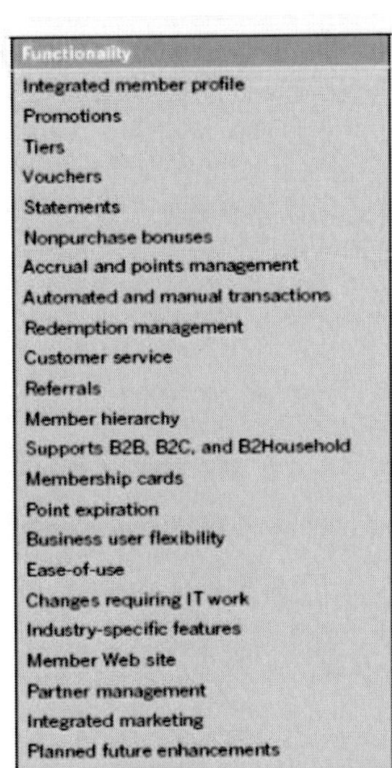

Figure 79: Loyalty System Functionality Evaluation Categories

Source (Oracle , 2005)

Building Loyalty through Customer Experience Management (CEM)

Research has revealed that both a good service quality and high levels of customer satisfaction don't always lead to customer loyalty (Stuart & Tax, 2004). CEM however is one such tool that has shown to build loyalty among customers through the high level of experience it provides to the customer at every step. Schmitt, Customer Experience Management (2003), states that before and even after the delivery of a service, CEM provides value to customer by delivering information, service, and interactions that result in compelling experiences. It thus builds loyalty with customers and adds value to the organisation. For example a report by the IBM Corporation reveals that customer experience is a key factor for organisations to use in building loyalty to channels and services. Research has also shown the importance of interactions with an organisation as one of the most important variables (Figure 80).

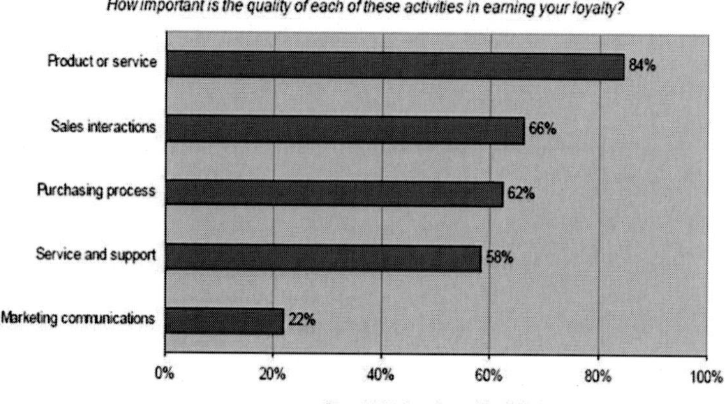

Figure 80: Factors in earning loyalty

Source: Thompson (2006)

When asked about the importance of various factors in earning loyalty, customers responded that sales interactions were the second most important after the service itself. This research links with other research in the industry, which points to organisations earning loyalty though the use of CEM. (Figure 80)

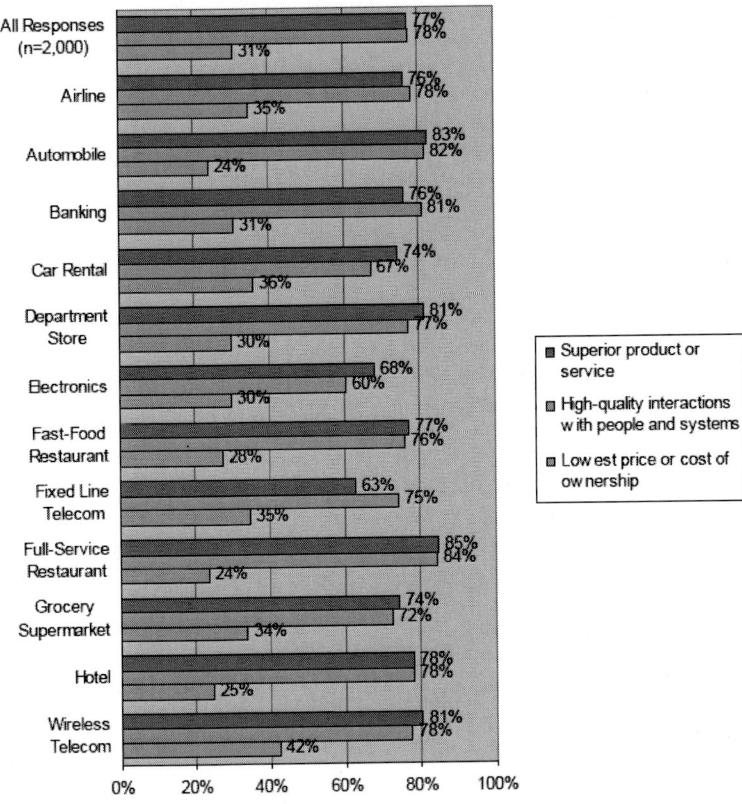

Figure 81: Loyalty drivers by industry

Source: Thompson (2006)

The implication of this research, which spans across different industries, for organisations is to give equal importance to customer experience, in order to win the loyalty of customers (Thompson B. , 2006).

Some researchers argue that not only do organisations need to provide high levels of good customer experiences, but they need to go beyond that and offer 'compelling' customer experiences. This will lead to repeat service orders, positive word of mouth and eventually customer loyalty (Voss & Zomerdijk, 2007). Recently, research has focused on emotional connections of customers with organisations. Berry and Carbone (2007) argue that maintaining an emotional connection requires systematic management of the customers' experience with an organisation and its offerings from the customers' perspectives.

Emotional Dimensions of Loyalty

Research has argued that true loyalty, or the highest level of loyalty can only be developed if an organisation can build emotional connections, in addition to positive attitudes and behaviours (Reinartz and Kumar, 2002; Shoemaker and Bowen, 2003; Mattila, 2001a). For instance, it was found that for casino customers, true loyalty consisted of emotional commitment and trust. The importance of emotional components in building loyalty is even more important for service organisations (Oliver, 1999; Mattila, 2001b; Fournier, 1998). Emotional loyalty (also called attachment, or commitment) has been defined by Baloglu as: 'liking the partner, enjoying the partnership, and having a sense of belonging to the partnership, and having a sense of belonging to the organisation' (Baloglu, 2002). Emotional loyalty goes beyond attachment to an organisation and includes the organisation's employees, its products or services and brands (Gould, 1998).

In order to achieve the best results, an organisation needs to win over a customer's heart as well as the mind (Duboff and Sherer, 1997). In fact emotions are said to be a better measure of true loyalty than the other types (Dick and Basu, 1994). Moreover there seems to be a higher correlation between overall customer loyalty and emotional components than the cognitive components (Yu and Dean, 2001).

A shift in marketing research from 'relational to emotional decision making process' of customers has been observed (Oh *et al.*, 2004). This is primarily due to the importance of emotional loyalty which has been the focus of numerous studies. For example, Mattila found that for restaurant customers, the development of strong emotional ties resulted in greater commitment than any loyalty program (Mattila, 2001a). Shoemaker and Lewis (1999) discovered that this type of loyalty makes customers more resistant to switching. Heskett (2002) agrees with these notions adding, the benefits of this apostle-like behaviour, and ownership among customers is so great that it often outweighs the potential costs. Furthermore, it has been noted that affective factors are more important in those cases where the customer makes decisions on little or inconsistent information (Homburg *et al.*, 2006).

Benefits of Emotional Loyalty

Emotional loyalty is found to have numerous benefits for organisations. It has been found that emotional loyalty leads customers to purchase additional products and spend more money with the organisation (Wong, 2004; Baloglu, 2002). Customers from different service industries (health care, automotive service, and hairstylist) who had strong emotional attachments indicate their willingness to continue their relationship with the firm (Shemwell *et al.*, 1994). Emotional attachment leads customers to not only purchase repeatedly from a service provider, but also purchase exclusively from that particular service provider (Butz and Goodstein, 1996; Kandampully, 1998). These customers also tend to devote a higher share of their wallet to their preferred organisation (Barnes, 2003; Butz and Goodstein, 1996; Kandampully, 1998).

Emotionally attached customers not only spend more, and purchase a larger variety of services, they are said to accept higher prices (Mattila, 2001a). Customers who are emotionally attached are willing to pay premium prices as compared to those who are loyal only in the cognitive sense (Yu and Dean, 2001). Research has also found that emotionally loyal customers are more likely to generate positive recommendations than customers in other forms of loyalty (Mattila, 2001a). These customers will then have longer relationships with the organisation, and are more vocal than customers who are loyal only in the cognitive sense (Shoemaker and Bowen, 2003; Yu and Dean, 2001; Barnes, 2003).

Emotional loyalty leads customers to believe that no other organisations can satisfy their needs better (Palmer *et al.*, 2000). This results in customers not searching for alternatives (Baloglu, 2002; Shoemaker and Bowen, 2003). Customers who are emotionally loyal also resist pressures to switch to competitors (Mattila, 2001a; Yu and Dean, 2001).

Emotionally attached customers are also more likely to cooperate with an organisation (Baloglu, 2002). These customers are vocal when it comes to pointing out service failures (Kandampully, 1998). This is an important factor since it helps organisations identify weaknesses. Truly loyal customers are also more forgiving of service failures (Mattila, 2001a). In the context of private sector, one of the most important benefits of emotional loyalty is its difficulty to copy (Palmer *et al.*, 2000) hence giving organisations a strategic advantage over competition.

How to Build Emotional Attachment

A number of factors have been discovered by research that leads customers to become emotionally attached to an organisation. Heskett (2002) developed a loyalty model, where the highest level of loyalty is one where the customer feels that he is not just a part of the organisation, but is the owner. The idea is to make customers think that they are not only a part of the community, but also can influence the organisation's strategies, or are owners of the organisation. Ownership is a powerful factor which has been successfully used in increasing loyalty among the internal customers (employees) of an organisation.

Communicating with the customer is also found to have made a significant impact in developing emotional attachment. Communication includes all written, oral, and electronic communications, as well as giving the customer appropriate reward/thank you behaviour (Duboff and Sherer, 1997). Communicating with the customer on an intimate level also lets employees of a firm develop emotional connections, and lets the organisation find out about and anticipate customers needs

(Kandampully, 1998). It also enables customers to become more familiar with the organisation's employees, brands, and services. Another important aspect of communication is to provide the customer with accurate, useful, relevant and timely information (Barnes, 2003).

Customers who have strong emotional bonding with an organisation indicated that personal recognition, a feeling of familiarity, or having had a memorable experience' has a positive effect on their bonding experience (Mattila, 2001a). Moreover research has indicated that organisations that pay special attention to customers (Price *et al.*, 1995), that develop trust and commitment and 'does more for the customer than anyone else does' will develop strong emotional bonding.

Human brands that allow customers to achieve autonomy will help in building strong emotional bonds with customers (Thomson, 2006). Other research has indicated that organisations that enable customers to achieve what they wish, will result in positive emotional attachments (Barnes, 2003).

Customers who can relate to an organisation will tend to be more emotionally attached. Organisations need to create ways in which customers can relate to them. The ways include things such as a common history, shared value, interests, cultures and beliefs (Barnes, 2003).

An enjoyable experience is considered by researchers to be a good predictor of loyalty (Wong, 2004). The enjoyable experience can be related to various factors of the service interaction, including enjoyable employee customer interaction (Shoemaker and Bowen, 2003). Making customers happy, is not related to loyalty, but does have a significant effect on the evaluation of service quality (Wong, 2004).

Jones and Sasser (1995) state that 'different satisfaction levels reflect different issues and, therefore, require different actions'.

	Satisfaction	Loyalty	Behaviour
Loyalist/ apostle	High	High	Staying and supportive
Defector/ terrorist	Low to medium	Low to medium	Leaving or having left and unhappy
Mercenary	High	Low to medium	Coming and going; low commitment
Hostage	Low to medium	High	Unable to switch; trapped

Table 6: Loyalty classifications of individual customer

Source: Jones and Sasser (1995)

They have divided customers into groups according to their loyalty strength, and satisfaction. (Table 6)

1. **The hostage:** Hostages have no other alternative but to stick with the organisation. Sometimes 'these individuals experience the worst the organisation has to offer and must accept it' (Jones and Sasser, 1995).
2. **The mercenary:** These types of customers 'may be completely satisfied but exhibit almost no loyalty'. These customers are usually expensive to acquire, but they depart quickly.
3. **The defector/terrorist:** Defectors are those customers who switch. Customers who switch may include dissatisfied, quiet dissatisfied, neutral and merely satisfied customers. The worst of these is the terrorist, who has had a very bad experience and tells others about it.
4. **The loyalist/apostle:** This is someone who is highly satisfied with the organisation. These customers return frequently to the organisation. In certain circumstances, an organisation can have customers whose expectations have been exceeded by a huge margin. These customers actively recommend the organisation to others, and are known as apostles.

Oliver (1999) presented four loyalty strategies. These strategies are based on two factors, individual fortitude and community support.

Individual fortitude	Community/social support	
	Low	High
Low	Product superiority	Village envelopment
High	Determined self-isolation	Immersed self-identity

Table 7: Four loyalty strategies

Source: Oliver (1999)

The Four Loyalty Strategies are:

1. **Self-isolation:** Customers in this state are loyal only to one brand. The customer is so enthusiastic about his/her brand that 'he or she has achieved a state not unlike the concept of love'. The customer seems to be immune from competition, will defend the brand, and recommends it to others.
2. **The village:** In a village the importance is on the community of which a customer feels a part when he/she consumes a particular product or service. The customer in this type of loyalty will voluntarily and willingly submit to the judgment of the group. This is performed by the customer for the rewards of membership to the community. The rewards can be in the form of a friendship. This concept is similar to that of a family.
3. **Individual and social/integration:** A customer, who is in this type of loyalty situation, will feel as if he/she is part of the product/service. Examples of this type of loyalty can be towards 'sports teams, music groups, well-known entertainers,' etc. (Oliver, 1999)

In order to create that extreme love type loyalty, organisations need to firstly provide services that are unique or superior to any other similar services. Secondly, a profitably sized segment of the organisation's customers must find it desirable in this manner. A service must be subject to adoration from the customer perspective. Moreover, the organisation needs to be able to embed this in a social network, and needs to develop and maintain the village. For those organisations that are not able to create any loyalty angles, simply satisfying the customer is their best chance for success.

The theoretical model states that at first a customer will become loyal in a cognitive sense. The customer then moves on towards becoming loyal in an affective sense, later moving on to cognitive and finally into a behavioural loyalty (Oliver, 1999).

Cognitive loyalty is defined as where the customer becomes loyal to a brand solely on the basis of brand beliefs. This is similar to the notion of brand image. Affective loyalty means that the customer develops a liking towards the brand. This is built through the positive experiences that the customer has experienced. Cognitive loyalty is where the customer develops a deeply held commitment to buy. Finally, action loyalty or behavioural loyalty is where the 'intentions are converted to actions'. This is a theoretical model which has received much attention. For example, it has been used to develop a multi-item scale (McMullan, 2005).

A Roadmap for Building Customer Loyalty

The section provides a roadmap for building customer loyalty. It basically explains who your most valuable customers are; how to achieve a high standard of customer care for all your customers; and how to turn your most valuable customers into your most loyal customers.

Activities	***Critical Success Factors (CSFs)***
Make customer care a key part of your business strategy	• List your top key accounts, and give these customers the best service. • Make sure customer-facing employees have access to all the information they need to serve customers efficiently. Give them the power to make certain decisions independently. • Draw up a set of procedures and standards to be used wherever customers have direct contact with your business. For example, set standards for speed and courtesy when answering phone calls.
Learn as much about your different customer segments as you can	• Find out what, when and how customers order, and use this information to improve the service you offer.

Activities	*Critical Success Factors (CSFs)*
	• Use your database to record information about your customer's buying habits so you can tailor your offer and service. • As part of your sales and marketing strategy, set out the levels of service you plan to offer your different customer types. • Find out more about your customers by generating opportunities for feedback
Develop a brand around your company, products or services	• Create a consistent, clearly defined identity for your business or service. • Advertise to build brand awareness of your service or service
Design and deliver a 'customer experience' to address how you handle customers when they contact your business, whether by phone, letter or email	• Do you address customers by their first name or use a more formal form of address? • Follow up queries with a 'thank you' letter, email or phone call.
Encourage employees to deliver high quality customer care	• Make sure employees have good basic communication skills. For example, a poor telephone manner will ruin the credibility of a telesales company. • Train employees in job-specific skills. For example, get sales people to listen to the customer more, so they sell intelligently, not aggressively. • Train all relevant personnel how to answer and deal with telephone calls. • Make sure employees can handle complaints effectively.
Think of ways to make life easier for customers. For example, a retailer might provide customer car parking, and a simple procedure for returning unwanted goods	• Concentrate on providing quality service in key areas. • Try to save the customer inconvenience. • Exceed your customers' expectations. For example, promise delivery in ten days, but actually deliver in seven, always keep your promises. • Keep customers informed about any

Activities	*Critical Success Factors (CSFs)*
	problems, and make it easy for them to contact you. • Use your website to give customers the services and information they want.
Use appropriate technology	• A good database system can help you record, organise and plan your contact with customers. • Make sure information from your website can be transferred to your main database. • Contact management software may be a useful tool if you have a lot of high-value customer accounts.
Give customers a personalised service	• A common way to achieve this is by giving each customer an account manager. • Personalise all communication. • Personalise the email addresses of customer-facing employees. • If you use computerised telephone systems, give customers the option of talking to an operator at any time.
Create opportunities for feedback	• Ask new customers why they chose you over the competition and existing customers what you could do better. • Set up a customer hotline, and make sure the number is on every piece of communication you send out. • Get feedback online by putting an email response form or newsgroup on your website. • Newsgroups may need filtering or editorial control. Make sure you have time to deal with this before setting it up. • Consider making all or part of your website registration-only to allow you to get more. • Encourage customers with a concern to contact you. • Carry out customer satisfaction surveys.
Contact any customer who has stopped buying	• Assign a skilled person to this task, otherwise customers tend to give easy

Activities	*Critical Success Factors (CSFs)*
from you (a lapsed customer) and find out the reason.	answers, such as "you are too expensive", which may hide the real reasons.
Monitor and analyse the contact you have with customers	• Keep a record of customer feedback to help you identify problem areas. Find out what caused each problem. • Use hit analysis software to discover which of your web pages are most popular. • Call analysis software lets you monitor selling and levels of satisfaction.
When marketing – or selling – to customers, divide them into at least three groups, and plan a different type of communication for each.	• Group one is potential customers who have not yet purchased anything. The aim of your communication is to build interest in your service. • Group two is customers who have made a purchase. Your aim is to increase the frequency of their buying and to sell them other products in your range. • Group three is your premium customers, who already make regular purchases. Your aim is to turn them into 'advocates'.
Only offer services that match customers' needs	• Ask your customers which of your services they are interested in. For example, send out a questionnaire. • Regularly mail, email or phone them with special offers, and news about your new services. Suggest services which will enhance or upgrade what they have already bought. • Ideally, you should anticipate when they need to re-order.
Have regular contact with customers	• Telephone key customers regularly to get feedback, or send them a newsletter or e-newsletter. • Send best wishes for Christmas, anniversaries or other occasions.
A cumulative (or 'retrospective') discount gives customers money	• Your accounting system may need to be able to track the purchasing activity of each customer and flag up the discounts as they

Activities	*Critical Success Factors (CSFs)*
back whenever they reach specified spending targets.	are earned. If customers have to ask for the discount, you may achieve less loyalty as a result.
Some schemes offer the customer rewards.	• One danger of discounts and rewards is that your customer might have made the purchases anyway, in which case you are wasting money.

Table 8: CSFs for Building Customer Loyalty

Source: (Zairi M., 2009)

Assessment Toolkit: Loyalty

Customer Service Quality Factor

Q1. To what extent does the organisation allow customisation of services in accordance with individual's needs and preferences?			
Basic	**Developing**	**Maturing**	**Leading**
The organisation's service delivery strategy does not support customisation of services.	Customisation of services is considered by the organisation's strategy; although it lacks the required infrastructure for individualisation of services.	The organisation has a clear strategy and also the necessary capability in place for customising services in accordance with customers' requirements but the organisation views this as a reactive response to service orders. i.e. services are customised after an order has been initiated and received.	The organisation has adopted a proactive and effective strategy for customising services i.e. customers' needs and the required capability for customising services are proactively identified, acquired and utilised.
Q2. Does the organisation acquire a good strategy for improving the quality of services?			
Basic	**Developing**	**Maturing**	**Leading**
The organisation lacks a system for measuring and improving the quality of services.	There is a system in place for measuring the quality of services; although the system is internally oriented (i.e. service quality is measured from	There is a service quality measurement and management system in place; although, the system is not effective in	The organisation owns an effective system in place for measuring service quality from customers' point of view. The gap

	organisation's point of view) rather than externally oriented (from customers' point of view).	measuring the gaps that might exist between services' features and customers' expectations.	between customers' expectations and their perceptions from organisation's services is effectively identified. There is a clear strategy for closing this gap.
Q3. To what extent does the culture of the organisation support employees in building customer loyalty?			
Basic	**Developing**	**Maturing**	**Leading**
People of the organisation put the organisation's and their own interests before customers' interests.	Culture of the organisation communicates the message of 'putting customers first' at a very basic level; although, people are not sufficiently empowered to handle customers' enquiries.	Although, people of the organisation are sufficiently empowered to handle customers' enquiries in order to create a long lasting relationship with customers; their achievements in this regards are not adequately appreciated.	The organisation recognises and fully appreciates individuals' creativity in handling customers' enquiries.

Customer loyalty strategies

Q1. How does the organisation use customers' feedbacks for building customer loyalty?			
Basic	**Developing**	**Maturing**	**Leading**
The organisation lacks a system for collecting customers' feedbacks regularly.	The organisation has a system for gathering customers' feedback; although, the feedbacks are not effectively used for improving customer relationships.	There is an effective system for collecting customers' feedback; although, the feedbacks are only used for recovering service failures.	There is a well-developed customer feedback system within the organisation and the organisation uses the feedbacks for building long lasting relationship with customers as well as improving future services.
Q2. To what extent does the senior management of the organisation focus on building loyalty?			
Basic	**Developing**	**Maturing**	**Leading**
Leaders of the organisation have a lack of or basic understanding about the concept of customer loyalty.	The leaders of the organisation have a basic understanding about the concept of customer loyalty and its benefits; although, they view it as the outcome of overall organisation's strategy. So the organisation lacks a clear	Leaders of the organisation have a good understanding about customer loyalty and its benefits and they view it as a part of overall organisation's strategy; although, they give priorities to other strategic objectives rather than customer	Leaders are fully aware of the benefits of customer loyalty and they view it as an important strategy for achieving a sustainable business growth in the future. There is a great level of commitment for achieving

	strategy for achieving customer loyalty.	loyalty.	customer loyalty among leaders.
Q3. Does the organisation own a clear strategy for building customer loyalty?			
Basic	**Developing**	**Maturing**	**Leading**
The organisation does not appreciate customer loyalty as a way for reaching business sustainability and hence it has not a clear strategy for building customer loyalty.	The organisation has developed a strategy for maintaining customer loyalty if there is any rather than building it since senior leaders view it as the outcome of other strategies.	The organisation has developed and deployed a customer loyalty strategy, although, the strategy seems to be slightly ineffective and outdated due to the lack of review.	Customer loyalty strategy has been effectively developed and deployed on a continual basis. The strategy is to be reviewed and updated regularly.

Customer experience management

Q1. To what extent does the organisation's CEM support loyalty programs within the organisation?			
Basic	**Developing**	**Maturing**	**Leading**
The organisation lacks a system for managing customer experience.	The organisation reactively measure customer experiences i.e. customers are being asked about their experience after the services are delivered.	The organisation maintains a clear strategy and an implementation plan for managing customers' experiences; although, the organisation lacks to measure the emotional side of customers' experience so it is not really effective	The organisation has successfully adopted and implemented customer journey mapping and customer experience mapping. The focus is to emotionally attach customers to the organisation

		in building loyalty.	through an effective CEM.
Q2. How often does the organisation measure customer experiences?			
Basic	**Developing**	**Maturing**	**Leading**
The organisation rarely asks customers about their experiences from organisation's services.	The organisation occasionally seeks customers' feedback about their experiences of services.	Customers' experiences are regularly measured and customers' feedbacks are most of the times gathered.	The organisation has adopted customer experience mapping so that it can constantly measure customer experiences.
Q3. To what extent does the technology capability of the organisation facilitate customer loyalty management?			
Basic	**Developing**	**Maturing**	**Leading**
The organisation lacks the required technology capability in order to manage customer relationships.	Although, the organisation is within the state of technology capability development and hence it fully relies on its partners. It is expected to see the organisation has the required capability on its own in the future.	The organisation has established the required technology for managing customer relationships and building customer loyalty; although, the system is isolated from the outside and hence there is a danger of losing the effectiveness and competitiveness due to lack of networking and partnership.	The organisation has a well-developed and integrated infrastructure and strong technology capabilities for managing customer relationships and building customer loyalty. There is an effective networking with technology partners for acquiring the necessary and advanced technology in the future.

Leadership is about empathy. It is about having the ability to relate to and connect with people for the purpose of inspiring and empowering their lives.

Oprah Winfrey

Chapter 13: Customer Experience

Introduction

Winning new customers is considerably more difficult and much more expensive than retaining existing customers. Many organisations acknowledge this by regularly conducting customer surveys to measure customer satisfaction. However, they often fail to realise that it is not customer satisfaction that is decisive, but rather customer retention. It is vital to monitor continuous and immediate feedback on product delivery, service quality, after sales service and the retail environment so that adjustments to daily customer interactions can be made rapidly. In recent years, there has been an increased interest in organisations around the role of customer experience in achieving competitive advantage and differentiation. The financial impact of improved customer experiences is significant. Customer experience management focuses on creating differentiated experiences at touch points that customers choose to interact with the organisation focuses on CEM as a strategy helps service delivery capability align and adapt to behavioural shifts of the target audience. Benefits realised go well beyond improvements in customer satisfaction (KPMG, 2011).

The Philosophy of Customer Experience

The result shows that there is a flat line, more or less, with very little differences reported between different experiences in different industries. The report concludes that there is a significant gap between the providers' strategic plans and their commitment to how they wish to go about achieving their corporate goals. It shows that there are high levels of ambitions within the providers, without great support on the ground in terms of processes and capabilities and without proper measurement systems for tracking the downstream delivery aspect to their customers and consumers. Furthermore, the research indicates that a big hurdle in achieving true customer centric mentality, is that the culture of the organisations are not geared towards applying customer oriented attitudes and behaviours. As the report concludes, these organisations tend to pay more of a lip service to customer centricity by being more protective of their short term financial targets rather than investing significantly in inducing and creating the necessary change for being customer centric and being customer focused.

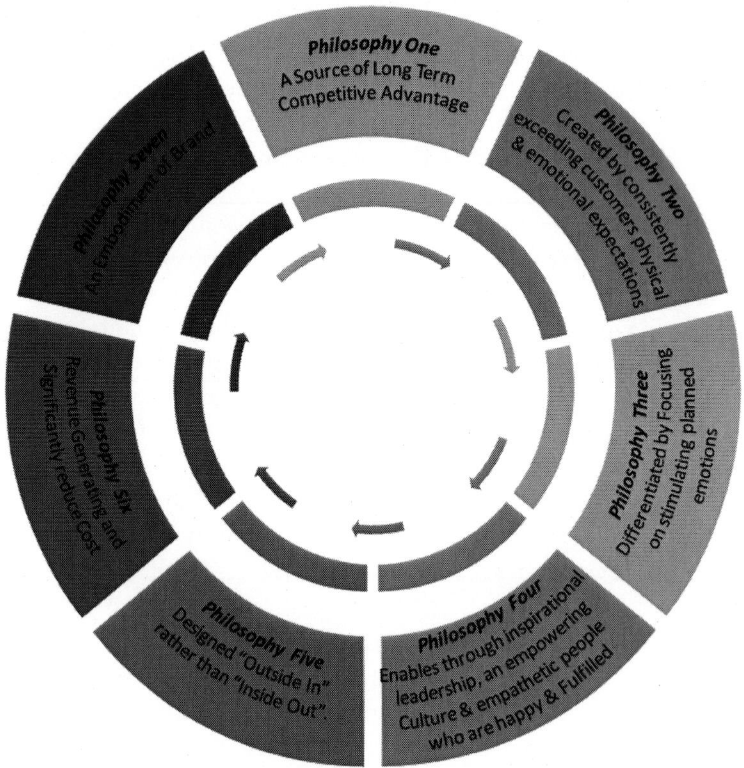

Figure 82: The seven philosophies for building great customer experience virtuous cycle

Source: Shaw and Ivens (2002)

Great customer experiences, it is thought, are achieved when:

1. They are a source of long term competitive advantage. What it means here is that the providers have a firm belief that by giving their customers enjoyable and memorable customer experiences, this will enable them to deliver their own competitive goals and ensure their survivability and prosperity in the long plan.

2. Customer experiences created by an approach that constantly and consistently strives to exceed customers' emotional and physical expectations. This means that the philosophy and the practice is dynamic, which drives through a quality ethos of constant evaluation, measurement, corrective action, improvement, innovation and impact to ensure that the tickling factor of customer experiences will generate the 'wow' and emotional response that is desired by the providers concerned.
3. Customer experiences differentiated by an approach of engagement and empowerment that can stimulate what is referred to as 'planned emotions'. In other words, to ensure that the customer is king and customers are put in the driving seat for manufacturing their own experiences and deciding on the fulfilment aspects that are unique and appropriate to the individuals concerned.
4. That customers' experiences and their uniqueness are gained through an approach to leadership which is inspirational, where people feel empowered, where the culture is based on customer empathy, and where the collective goal is to ensure that experiences are about fulfilment and that the old fashioned mentality of throwing things on the lap of the customers are completely removed.
5. Re-engineering the mindset of value provision by making it more outside in, rather than inside out. In other words, applying more of the pull philosophy as opposed to the product and service push mentality.
6. Using a new ethos to measuring business success by making sure that customer fulfilment, satisfaction and loyalty are really the unique and only source for revenue growth and this can only happen, therefore by internal optimisation and a firm's ability to reduce costs and enhance value.
7. The embodiment of the brand, and this means that the customer experience is really a reflection of what is communicated through the brand, and what is delivered to the customer. Any experience should be equated with what is referred to as the branded customer experience, and this will ensure that for the providers the promise is fulfilled all the time and that there is no gap

between the branding activities on the one hand and the activities of the people involved in the day to day practical delivery of customer experiences.

Total Experience Life-cycle

In online business settings, Minocha *et al.* (2006) stipulated that the total customer experience consists of six stages (Figure 83)

1. **Expectations setting**: during this stage the customer draws upon a number of influences to create his/her personal benchmark of service quality expectations which are going to play a vital role in the decision made later on. Influences can be social, organisational or individual influences and they include the customer's motivations, his needs along with the benefits and costs of shopping online, recommendations, word-of-mouth, advertising, brand, his own experiences of interacting with off-line business channels of that and other organisations, etc.
2. **Pre-purchase stage**: during this stage, the customer chooses a website, carries out the necessary searches for a product or service and makes a decision about whether or not to make a purchase. Decisions are influenced by several factors, such as website usability, information provided, the price, the credibility of the website, the delivery mechanisms and refunds policy, etc.
3. **E-purchase**: during this stage the customer selects the product/service and completes the transaction; this usually involves entering personal details, billing and delivery information, and payment details.
4. **Post-purchase**: this stage involves tracking the order and the receipt of the products/services. During this stage the customer may need to query an order, complain about the state of the delivery, or question his payment handling. He might need to contact the organisation at touch points other than the website.
5. **Consumption**: during this stage the customer consumes and uses the product/service.
6. **Post TCE evaluation**: at this stage, the customer will review his online experiences and compares that with his benchmark of expectations that were set during stage 1, and therefore assess whether or not he/she has received value from this experience.

1: Expectations setting
Expectations set by advertising, recommendations, word of mouth, brand image, personal experiences with other channels of the business

6: Post-TCE evaluation
Review of experiences, and revising expectations

The Total Customer Experience (TCE)

2:Pre-purchase Interactions
Reaching a site, browsing, assessing trustworthiness, searching for, and reading product information

5: Product/ service Consumption
Using and consuming the product/service

3: E-Purchase Interaction
Selection of product, data entry, payment process

4. Post-Purchase Interactions
Tracking orders, contacting customer services, receiving delivery

Figure 83: The total customer experience model
Source: (Minocha, Dawson, Blandford, & Millard, 2005)

For the purpose of this study, the term 'online customer experience' will refer to the pre-purchase, purchase and post-purchase stages as defined by the model in the Figure 84, as they constitute the direct encounter or interaction between the firm and the customer (Minocha *et al.,* 2006).

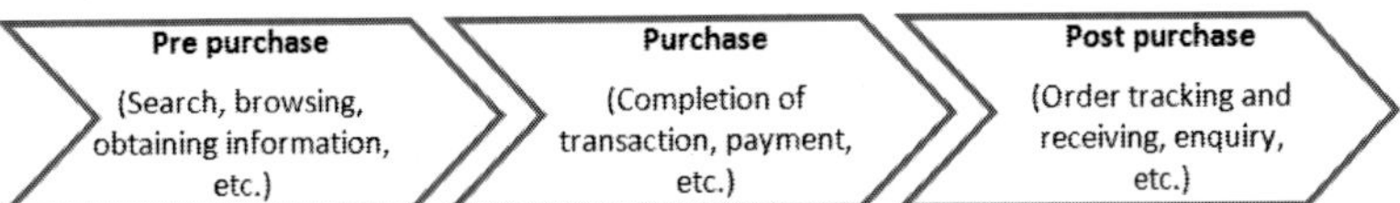

Figure 84: Online customer experience model
Source: (Minocha et al., 2006)

Satisfaction: Transaction Measurement

Oliver (1980) defined satisfaction as an affective, emotional reaction growing and resulting out of confirmation or disconfirmation of product expectations. It is a complex emotional response following experience with a product (Oliver, 1981).

Based on the expectancy-disconfirmation theory, satisfaction is also defined as 'the summary psychological state resulting when the emotion surrounding disconfirmed expectations is coupled with a consumer's prior feelings about the consumer experience' (Oliver, 1997); it is considered a transaction-based measure that is related to a specific exchange with the product/service and is based on the comparison of what consumers would expect.

Anderson and Srinivasan (2003) defined e-satisfaction as 'the contentment of the customer with respect to his or her prior purchasing experience with a given electronic commerce firm'. The understanding of satisfaction in online environments, including the exploration of dimensions and determinations of satisfaction in online environments, is at a relatively nascent stage (Evanschitzky *et al.,* 2004).

The expectancy-disconfirmation model (as explained by Oliver, 1981) has been recognised for its success in explaining the satisfaction dynamics (Phillips, 1999). In brief the model illustrates that satisfaction happens in a series of well-defined steps that start with the consumer forming certain expectations about the likely performance of a product, i.e. consumers are expected to form pre-consumption expectations before they observe the product attribute performance, later the consumer evaluates the product actual performance and then compares the actual performance to his/her own expectations.

Naturally, confirmation happens if a consumer's expectations match (are equal to) the actual performance of the product. Positive disconfirmation takes place if product actual performance was greater than the customer's expectation, and negative disconfirmation is experienced if expectations were greater than the product actual performance.

Affect or emotions have been found to be an important component in the satisfaction judgment process; satisfaction is a function of positive affect and disconfirmation (Oliver, 1997).

As customer satisfaction matters because it affects customers' behavioural outcomes (Zeithaml *et al.,* 1996), considerable emphasis in the literature has been put on linking perceived service quality and customer satisfaction behavioural intentions and financial results (Oliver, 1997). Nevertheless, recent studies have also theorised that there may be other levels, beyond mere customer satisfaction and adequate quality, that could impact customers' behavioural consequences (Oliver, 1997). Recent thinking has begun to focus on delight as a higher level of satisfaction which may create exceptional outcomes (Oliver, 1997) such as unshakable customer loyalty (Arnold *et al.,* 2005).

Although not addressed enough in the literature, satisfaction/dissatisfaction has a uni-dimensional continuum that can entertain extreme positive states of emotional responses and highly positive satisfaction states such as positive surprise (Oliver, 1997). Customers can experience different levels of satisfaction and express different emotional profiles when they evaluate their experience with a product or a service (Westbrook and Oliver, 1991). Customer delight represents an extreme positive emotional state of the satisfaction continuum (Arnold *et al.,* 2005).

Customer delight is defined as a 'profoundly positive emotional state generally resulting from having one's expectations exceeded to a surprising degree' (Rust and Oliver, 2000: 86, in Herington and Weaven, 2007).

Herington and Weaven (2007) stipulated that there is a general agreement in the literature that delight is considered a second level emotion. Delight is characterised by a blend of lower order emotions like pleasure and surprise (pleasant surprise) (Westbrook and Oliver, 1991) or a mixture of joy and surprise (Plutchik, 1980), or a function of surprising consumption, positive affect (joy) and arousal (Oliver, 1997). Westbrook and Oliver (1991) labelled customers with the highest levels of joy and positive surprise as 'delighted customers'.

Oliver (1997) stipulates that 'satisfaction may be best understood as an ongoing evaluation of the surprise inherent in a product acquisition and/or consumption experience'; they then add that unexpected high levels of satisfaction or service performance initiate positive affect (joy), which in turn causes the delight sequence.

Based on the above, the feeling of satisfaction will be presented as a continuum that starts with feeling of fulfilment of basic needs, to feeling of enjoyment to surprise. Customers experience the upgrade of these feeling to reach a feeling of delight as the ultimate feeling.

Customer Experience Management – A Step by Step Approach

Managing customer experience can be a tall order. Every touch point, from advertising campaigns to post purchase support, can effect customer perception and loyalty. To influence on those interactions, organisation often need to go through a significant transformation of their own, adapting their systems and processes, and infrastructure to put the customer at the centre. Positive customer experience can build its own momentum, creating an ecosystem of goodwill that cost relatively little to maintain but can deliver a loyal fan base that generates tangible bottom-line returns. Table 9 offers seven ideas to help organisations drive growth and profitability using customer experience as a service differentiator.

Activity	*Key points to consider*
Step 1: Understand the needs, wants and preferences of your customers	• Has the needs and preferences of your customers changed over time? • What are the growth opportunities in your industry? • What share of growth does your organisation capture? • How do you differentiate your services? • How well aligned is your service roadmap with market trend? • How successful are your renewal, up-sell, and cross sell campaigns?

Activity	*Key points to consider*
Step 2: Establish economic frameworks to understand and prioritise impact of marketing, sales and service decisions	• How do you decide which markets to enter, grow, harvest and exit? • How well do you understand performance within your distributed sale model? • How do you determine which services represent growth categories? • How much cost and pricing volatility in there in the current service portfolio? • What is the cost to service customers using current online and offline support tactics?
Step 3: Track customer behaviour, distil patterns, and adapt to accommodate shifts	• Are current propensity models able to identify emerging trends that represent growth opportunity? • Beyond seasonality and regional factors, what is driving changes in purchase patterns? • How does in-store behaviour affect online purchase decisions? • What are best ways to target your most profitable customers? • Are you reaching your most profitable customers?
Step 4: Develop lead nurturing and customer management plans for customers	• How are past customer and prospect lists managed and leveraged by sales acquisition programs? How effective are your win-back campaigns? • How often does your organisation communicate with its customers? • What is the optimal contact strategy for renewing and up/cross selling customers? • What are your customers preferred communication channels? • What are the most critical touch points in your sales and service life-cycle?

Activity	*Key points to consider*
Step 5: Develop a customer-centric information architecture	• How quickly can new information about a customer disseminate through your organisation? • Was your information architecture designed for services, systems or customers? • How does your information architecture account for relationship hierarchy? • How do you categorise customer data? By life-cycle events, interactions or services? • Are your marketing and customer database integrated?
Step 6: Deploy workflow-based tools to marketing, sales and service customer groups	• How well coordinated are handoffs between marketing, sales and service functions? • How well does your organisation manage customer escalations? • How long does it typically take to resolve? • How is lead nurturing and customer management plans monitored? • What tools are in place to facilitate workflow across business functions? • How much visibility and control do customers have on service issues through online portals?
Step 7: Create a customer experience map to optimise touch points	• Who owns customer experience within your organisation? • If ownership is shared, who drives customer experience tradeoffs decisions? • Are business processes defined, what customer experience factors are incorporated into the planning? • What percentage of workflow ends up on jeopardy paths? • How do you measure the effectiveness of customer experience delivery? • Can your organisation drive growth using customer experience as a differentiator?

Table 9: Seven steps approach for better CEM

Source (KPMG, 2011)

A Guide to CEM Success

Research found that a five-element approach leads to CEM success—as measured by improved business performance. To remember these elements, be SMART: Define a customer-centric Strategy; use appropriate Metrics; ensure your organisation is Aligned with your objectives; Redesign experiences as needed; and use appropriate Technology tools as enablers. Figure 85 depicts these important elements (Thompson B., 2006).

Figure 85: A SMART Guide to CEM Success

Source (Thompson B., 2006)

Model Description

1. **Developing a Customer Experience Strategy – organisations should:**
    - Recognise more valuable customers and treat them differently.
    - Develop a customer strategy using research about what drives customer loyalty.
    - Benchmark customers' experiences vs. those provided by your competitors.
    - Understand how the quality of customer experience is valued by customers.
    - Use brand communications to clearly tell customers the experience they can expect.

2. **Setting Goals and Defining Measurements – organisations should:**
    - Set specific customer experience goals, measurements and objectives.
    - Measure and communicate the quality of customer experiences throughout the organisation.
    - Have top management regularly review customer satisfaction and loyalty measurement.
    - Assess customers' emotional reactions to marketing, sales and service interactions.
    - Use performance measures and rewards to encourage employees to treat customers well.
3. **Aligning the Organisation - organisations should:**
    - Provide sufficient time and resources to train frontline employees to deliver what customers expect.
    - Have leaders that set a good example by putting "customers first".
    - Hire people with the right skills and personalities to interact effectively with your customers.
    - Train your employees thoroughly to be helpful, friendly and responsive to customer needs.
    - Motivate employees to be loyal and committed to the organisation.
4. **Redesigning the Customer Experience – organisations should:**
    - Map customer experiences end to end and identify interactions likely to affect customer loyalty.
    - Use qualitative input from customers, such as individual interviews, shadowing, focus groups, etc.
    - Proactively plan to surprise customers to create a positive feeling about your organisation.
    - Design interactions with your services as part of the total customer experience.
    - Create a vision of the customer experience process with a cross-function team.

5. **Improving Customer Experience With Technology – organisations should:**
    - Use IT systems that enable a complete view of customers' interactions across all channels.
    - Involve both business users and technology experts in IT system planning.
    - Use IT tools to identify and escalate customer satisfaction issues to swift resolution.
    - Consolidate all customer information in databases that are shared across the organisation.
    - Provide front line employees with easy to use tools and information to serve customers.

A Unified CEM Implementation Strategy

This section provides a unified view on CEM implementation strategy. It contains several steps, which helps an organisation to deliver a unique customer experience:

1. **Experience mapping –** creating an experience en map of what is the first thing that an organisation must to do. This will help to identify all of the various points of interactions a customer has with an organisation. It may also be prudent to find out what the customer thinks of the current level of service being delivered for each of the experience points (Figure 86: Example).

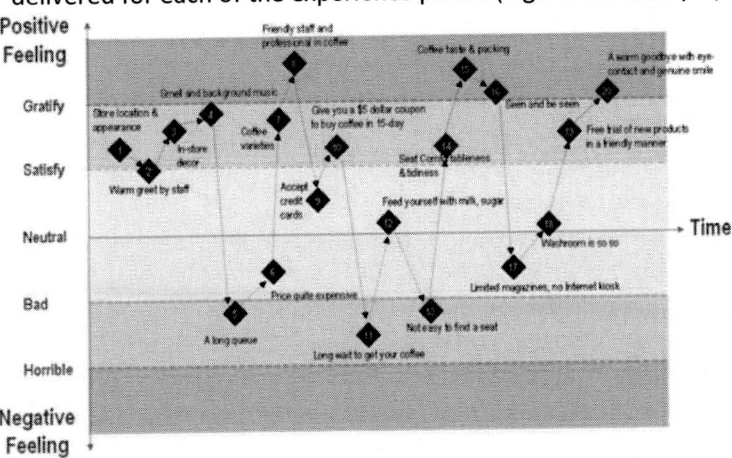

Figure 86: Customer Experience Map: One Starbucks Visit

Source (Thompson B., 2006)

2. **Find out customer expectations** – this will help the organisation to understand what the customer desires, and what is of importance to the customer. Often organisations find it difficult to develop effective CEM strategies because they are unable to understand the requirements of their customers.
3. **Examine the competition** – an organisation cannot work in isolation. Knowing what the competition is offering will only help an organisation to set goals and targets where they can meet and exceed the competition. Customers will always compare an organisation with others, and hence it becomes imperative that the organisation know what its competition is up to.
4. **Analyse and plan** – once an organisation knows what level of service it is providing, the level that customers expect, and the level that the competition is providing, it should be ready to develop its own plan. Organisations should set levels of quality that each experience should deliver to the customer.
5. **Communicate the brand experience** – before a customer actually comes in contact with an organisation, the customer gets to experience the communications about the brand (Schmitt, 2003). Hence, it is imperative that the various marketing communications media should reflect the brand experience that the organisation wants its customers to have.
6. **High quality service** – organisations should ensure that the services on offer meet the customer's expectations.
7. **Motivated employees** – making sure that employees are satisfied and motivated will ensure that in the long run the customer receives a good experience and this can eventually lead to customer loyalty.
8. **Customer interface** – this includes the physical aspects of customer interactions i.e. focusing on right decor, the design of equipment etc.
9. **Senior management focus** – like other areas of management, senior management's commitment to and focus on the desired strategy is imperative for its success. Hence for CEM too, the senior manager's commitment is imperative.

10. **Integrate functions** – this implies that the whole organisation is working towards providing a high quality experience for their customers. The back office as well as front staff needs to effectively work together so that the customer can have the best possible experience.
11. **Post usage** – this entails things such as after sales service, warranties, upgrading or installations.
12. **Continuous innovation** – this is a proven fact that continuously innovating and improving the services is an effective way for maintaining organisation's competitiveness.

Assessment Toolkit: Experience

Internal Factors

Q1. Has the organisation an effective strategy for CEM?			
Basic	**Developing**	**Maturing**	**Leading**
There is no clear strategy for managing customer experiences.	The organisation has spotted the importance of customer experience management in and undertaken few initiatives in order to improve in this area.	The organisation has a well-developed system for managing customer experiences in place.	The organisation has indicated CEM as one area which is strategically important for its growth and hence there is clear objectives, strategy, capability and system in place with regards to CEM.
Q2. How well is the organisation aligned with its objectives of creating unique customer experience?			
Basic	**Developing**	**Maturing**	**Leading**
The organisation does not see CEM as an important management area to focus on. So it is less caring about customers' experiences.	The organisation has set objectives for better implementation of CEM; however, it lacks the necessity means for achieving those objectives such as empowering customers and employees.	The organisation has the necessity processes, systems, infrastructure etc. but it is not fully aligned towards achieving objectives of CEM.	The organisation has established CEM as a strategically important management area and hence it allocates and aligns the necessary resources for achieving its strategic objectives.

Q3. To what extent are the employees of the organisation empowered handling customers' enquiries?			
The concept of employees' empowerment has not been understood or effectively practiced.	The organisation has empowered its employees to certain extent which means they are not really free to use their own initiatives in order to effectively handle customers' enquiries.	The organisation has wide range of training programs with regards how to use empowerment for better handling customers' enquiries; however, the extent to which employees are empowered is still limited.	Employees are sufficiently trained and adequately authorised to contribute in the decision making process, customise customer services and use their own initiative and creativity in order to handle customers' enquiries.

External Factors

Q1. How often does the organisation communicate with its customers with regards to the quality of their experiences from services received?			
The organisation lacks a system for measuring customer experiences.	The organisation occasionally seeks information about their experiences from the services.	The organisation quite often communicates with its customers seeking their opinion about the quality of services and their experiences.	The organisation has established an effective, two-way communication channel for communicating with customers about their perceptions of the quality of services that they have received.

Q2. To what extent does the organisation engage its customers in improving customer service and experiences?			
The organisation sees customers as passive actors so it does not involve them in the process of service delivery.	The organisation has established a communication channel for getting customers feedback and opinions about services.	The organisation to certain extent empowers customers and involves them in the process of customer service. It strives to initiate the concept of service co-creation.	The organisation has effectively implemented the concept of service co-creation. Custoemrs are involved in the process of decision making and they are genuinely involved in the process of service delivery from design to post-delivery of services.
Q3. To what extent does the organisation benchmark customer experience maturity level in order to enhance its capabilities?			
The organisation rarely measures and tracks its customer experiences.	The organisation considers customers' feedbacks, which it receives passively from its communication channel but it has not a clear understanding about the current maturity level of its customer experience management system.	The organisation has clearly established the current maturity level of its customer experience management system and it to certain extent but not at all level benchmarks it against better performers.	The organisation regularly benchmarks its customer experience management system against world-class organisations at different levels: Process-wise, competitive benchmarking, management level etc.

CEM Strategy

Q1. How often does the organisation map customer experiences in order to trace customers' experiences over the number of interaction points?			
The organisation rarely if ever maps customer experiences.	The organisation occasionally maps customer experiences at different interaction points.	The organisation quite often implements customer experience mapping in order to trace customers' experiences over the number of interaction points.	The organisation constantly traces the quality of customer experiences at every touch point areas and always map customer Journey and experience mapping.
Q2. How well can the organisation's technology capability support unique customer experience?			
The organisation's technology capability poorly supports customer experience management.	The organisation's technology capability is in the state of development so to certain extent it can support CEM.	The organisation has a mature and well developed technology capability but due to the lack of review system, there is a risk that the technology capability of the organisation become outdated and consequently loses its, competitiveness.	The organisation has a strong and up-to-date technology capability which fully supports CEM.

Q3. To what extent does the organisation strive toward applying the concept of continuous innovation for enhancing customer experiences?			
The organisation does not see CEM as an important management area to focus on.	The organisation strive to build the fundamentals for CEM and it sees innovation as an effective mean for developing CEM; however, innovation will be considered as a one-off practice during the development phase of CEM at very basic level.	The organisation has a well developed innovation process in place; however, it extensively relies on close innovation and do not seek new ideas from outsiders.	The organisation has an effective, and an advanced innovation process in place, which extensively facilitates the open innovation. Hence, customers will be involved in improving services by generating new ideas.

Empathy is forgetting oneself in the joys and sorrows of another, so much so that you actually feel that the joy or sorrow experienced by another is your own joy and sorrow. Empathy involves complete identification with another.

Dada Vaswani,
Head of the Sadhu Vaswani Mission

Chapter 14: Customer Attraction

Introduction

Research on customer attraction and retention over the past decade has shown that understanding customer needs is critical to success. There are several aspects to this. Firstly, it has been widely accepted that retaining existing customers is much simpler than acquiring new customers. Organisations require less amount of investment for retaining their existing customers. Although, even the expectations of existing customers might be changed over the period of time; organisations can gain more profits from existing customer than new one if they succeed to meet or exceed customers' expectations. This is because of two main factors:

- Organisations have collected in-depth customers' information, which can help in identifying customers' needs or even predicting future needs of customers.
- There is more chance for an organisation to succeed in turning existing customers into satisfied or even loyal customers. Hence, customers become business advocates.

On the other hand, in a highly competitive business environment, organisations should not limit themselves to just serving existing customer segments if they desire to be a head of competition. Reaching out to new customers and delivering services to underserved customers require organisations to continuously develop their capabilities through innovation. In order to attract more customers, organisations should clearly identify what are the needs of new customers and how these needs can be effectively met. Customer attraction requires continuous innovation. Organisations should scrutinise their service delivery life-cycle to see how they can develop further in terms of quality of services provided from customers' perspectives. This requires an effective customer relationship management, customer experience management and customer engagement.

Acquiring and Targeting the Customer

Not every customer is needed; only the profitable customer has to be at the heart of the organisation. CRM is a strategy that identifies and attracts profitable customer, tying them to the organisation or services by efficient relationship marketing to guarantee profitable growth. According to Newell (2000) CRM is a useful tool in terms of identifying the right customer groups, and for helping to decide which customers to serve. The idea that you cannot have a profitable relationship with all customers, and the practice of targeting customers with a differentiated service, is already widespread in many financial services. One method for identifying customer groups is the notion of distinguishing between transaction and relationship customers. For many organisations it would be beneficial to distinguish between the two types of customers and focus on relationship customers.

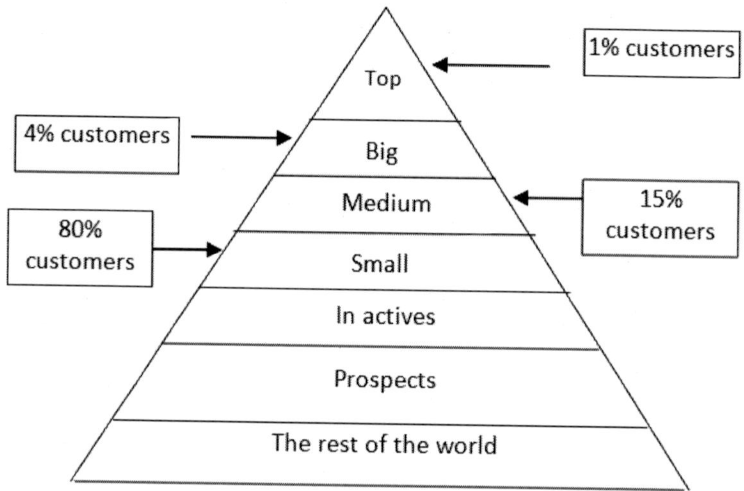

Figure 87: Customer pyramid

Adopted from Curry and Curry (2000)

The customer pyramid (Figure 87) can help an organisation to visualise, analyse and improve profitability of customers. The customer pyramid indicates that there is a differentiation in importance of customers in terms of revenue generation. Based on

Pareto principle, the customer pyramid indicates that 20% of the customers represent 80% of the revenue and incur only 20% of the selling cost. Therefore these customers are profitable. In contrast, small customers (80% of the customer base) are attached to a large portion of the costs, and therefore might not be valuable at all. Improvement schemes have the objective to move customers up the pyramid. If small customers have no growth potential, they should not be served any more. Efforts to try to change their purchasing pattern and have them buy somewhere else could be attempted.

Newell (2000) identified three distinct types of relationship customers: the top, middle and lower groups. The top group (top 10%) consists of customers with excellent loyalty and of high profitability for the organisation. CRM is needed to retain and offer them the best possible services in order to avoid their defecting to other competitors. Middle group customers (next 40-50%) are ones delivering good profits and who show good potential for future growth and loyalty. These customers are probably giving some of their business to competitors.

The idea is to use CRM to target middle group customers effectively as they are the greatest source of potential growth. Lower group relational (bottom 40-50%) customers are those who are only marginally profitable. Some may have potential for growth, but the expense and effort involved in targeting such numbers hinders the effectiveness of servicing existing relational customers in the top and middle groups. CRM should be used to identify this group and seriously consider the response required. Transactional customers contribute either nothing or have an adverse effect on profitability. The consensus therefore is that CRM needs to identify transactional customers to help organisations respond appropriately.

Understanding Customers

The first step in customer attraction is to identify customers' needs and have a true interpretation of their needs and expectations. Organisations should develop a comprehensive customer insight.

Any insight that is developed by using the customer relationship management effectively has to ultimately result in improved service solution provision. Hence, the need of the hour is to manage the customer relationship more effectively and holistically. A customer centric business model has been depicted in Figure 88.

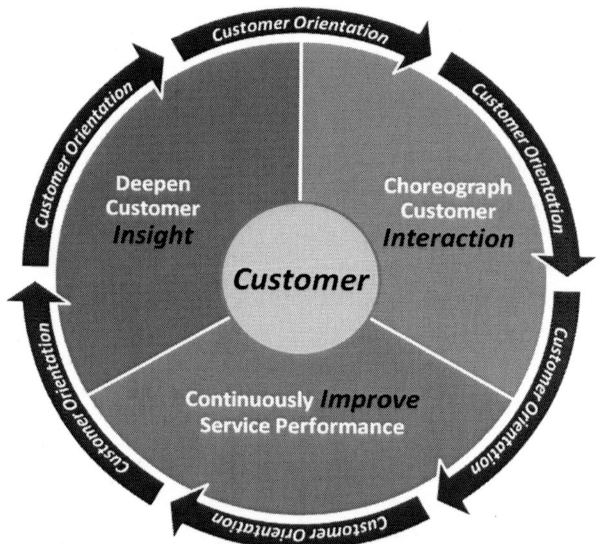

Figure 88: Customer insight, interaction and improvement
Adapted from: (SAS Institute Inc., Peppers and Rogers Group, 2009)

The model suggests a focus on those organisational capabilities and competencies that are most influential in deepening customer insight, choreographing customer interactions, and continually improving the service performance. The model exhorts the organisations to design a unique experience for each customer that is based on the knowledge of that individual, delivering it across services/products and channels, and measuring outcomes to guide ongoing refinements i.e. it is all about citizen/customer centric solution provision. This customer orientation should be embedded deep within the organisation's culture.

Table 10 provides a toolkit in the form of a questionnaire that follows the previously discussed cycle of customer insight, interaction and improvement

Insight					
1. Manage Quality Customer Data	***1***	***2***	***3***	***4***	***5***
• To what extent is information on each customer's or customer segment's service usage readily available?					
• How well developed is the measurement and reporting system for customers' attitudes and perceptions?					
• To what extent is the complete, integrated view of customers' contact history – inbound and outbound – readily available?					
• How well developed the key performance indicators are to measure customer satisfaction or other measurements for customer affinity?					
• How complete and integrated is the view of each customer created across multiple services and channels with a view of the entire customer history?					
• To what extent is there a current view of necessary available to all customers' "touch points"?					
• How proactively are the changes in customer attitudes or perceptions monitored?					
• How robustly are the customer attitudes and perceptions linked to customer behaviour to determine drivers of behaviour?					
2. Profile Customers to Predict behaviour	***1***	***2***	***3***	***4***	***5***
• To what extent are the customers profiled based on both characteristics as well as needs?					
• How well developed the customers' service usage behaviour is anticipated and predicted?					
• To what extent is the likelihood to engage by channel calculated?					
• To what extent is the customer channel behaviour analysed to understand channel preferences?					
• How frequently and customised are the experiences created in response to customer preference?					

• How independent are the customers in self selecting channels for specific activities?					
Interact					
3. Engage with Customers	***1***	***2***	***3***	***4***	***5***
• To what extent is the customer insight used to guide in-bound customer interactions (e.g. pricing, service, et al.)?					
• What is the flexibility level for customers to choose the manner in which they interact or are contacted by the organisation?					
• How well is the outbound customer contact orchestrated across services and channels at the organisation level (versus in silos)?					
• To what extent do the significant changes in customer behaviour create triggers for systematic response?					
• How well developed and trained the employees are in using customer insight information?					
• How customised and individualised the customer interactions are?					
• To what extent is individual "treatment track" created to manage the customer experience across services and channels?					
Improve					
4. Measure and Report	***1***	***2***	***3***	***4***	***5***
• What is the organisational focus in using customer metrics to measure the overall organisational performance?					
• How tightly coupled are the customer metrics and the individual performance?					
• To what extent the employee measurement and incentive programs are aligned to customer metrics?					
• To what extent are the customers' "expressed needs" captured during various customer experiences?					
• To what extent are the customers' profiles continuously updated to reflect the changing needs and expectations?					

• To what extent changes are made to individual customer interactions based on changes in customer's profile?					
5. Learn and Improve	***1***	***2***	***3***	***4***	***5***
• To what extent are the customers' "expressed needs" captured during various customer experiences?					
• To what extent are the customers' profiles continuously updated to reflect the changing needs and expectations?					
• To what extent changes are made to individual customer interactions based on changes in customer's profile?					

Table 10: Questionnaire for Customer Insight, interaction and improvement

Source: (Peppers & Rogers Group and SAS, 2008)

Satisfied Customers

In an increasingly competitive environment, organisations must be customer-oriented. After all, the underpinning of the marketing concept is that identification and satisfaction of customer needs leads to improved customer attraction and retention. It is therefore not surprising that organisations spend substantial resources to measure and manage customer satisfaction.

Customer satisfaction has been related to perceived performance and expectations. If organisational performance in delivering services matches expectations or exceeds them, the customer is satisfied or highly satisfied, respectively. Although customer satisfaction is not the only factor which determine the success of an organisation since the high score of customer satisfaction might be due to a high degree of satisfaction among less profitable customers. Hence, it is imperative for an organisation to firstly, identify who are the most valuable customers and then continuously measure the rate of satisfaction among these customers.

Attracting low profitable customers is not always a waste of resource since some of these customers can potentially be profitable in the future if they are rightly treated by the organisation. Hence, organisations should classify customers based on not only their current value but also the value which the customer can bring to the business in the long term.

Galbreath and Rogers (1999) state that there are three distinct areas that organisations should focus on to satisfy customer needs (Figure 89):

- Customisation of services
- Personal relationships
- After sales service

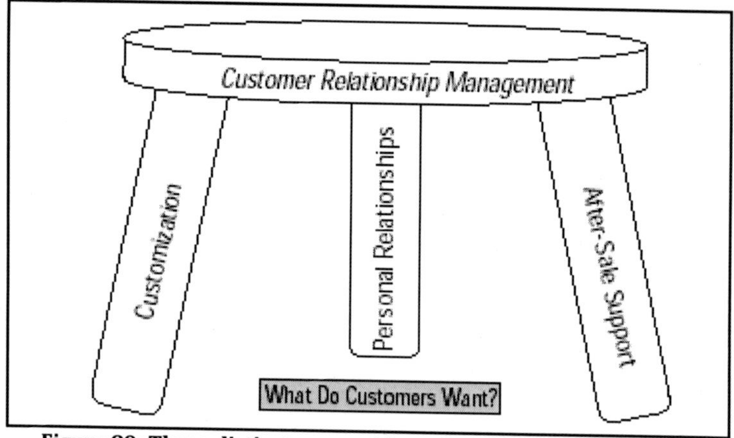

Figure 89: Three distinct areas of focus for customer satisfaction

Source: Adopted from Galbreath and Rogers (1999)

High satisfaction does not necessarily predict attraction and retention since satisfaction has mainly to do with meeting customers' minimum requirements and, in many industries that is simply not enough (Crosby, 2002). Thus, satisfaction is not enough; you have to make your customer a loyal one to ensure future success. As discussed earlier, keeping customers satisfied is a key to success for businesses. Organisations should strive to satisfy their existing customers since it costs five times more for a business to acquire a new customer.

The following is a check-list which can be used for the evaluation of organisation's success in keeping existing customers satisfied (Padgham, 2005).

1. Does the organisation realise the value of its current customers? These are its best accounts. They are quicker to buy and require fewer special deals.
2. Does the organisation communicate to all its customers that they are important?
3. Does the organisation encourage customers to return to its business?
4. Does the organisation tailor its services to its customers' particular needs?
5. Do customers have a direct access to emergency services report a service failure?
6. Does the organisation provide unique services that its customers would find difficult to duplicate somewhere else?
7. Do the customers feel that the organisation is concerned about their interests and welfare?
8. Does the organisation attempt to learn as much about each customer as possible?
9. Does the organisation follow up to make sure orders are filled quickly and accurately?
10. Does the organisation follow up on complaints to make sure the resolution was satisfactory to the customer?

Building a successful, positive image with customers enhances the organisation's overall credibility. Living up to that image creates valuable word-of-mouth publicity. Customers most often base their purchasing decisions on the advice of people they know.

Making the Most of Customer Complaints

Customer complaints should be recognised as constructive criticism that can be used to improve a business. Work with all employees on customer relations regardless of the frequency or type of contact they have with the public. When it comes to attracting customers, organisations have to have a clear, workable strategy. Although, customer complaints can be a reflection of weak performance in meeting customers' needs; it can also be an effective strategy if it is handled correctly and in a systematic manner. Organisation should develop and maintain an effective system for handling customer complaint. The vision for developing customer complaints system should be not only rectifying service failures as reported by customers but also surprising customers through responding to their enquiries promptly and accurately. In fact, customers should be assured that their complaints lead to improvement in the system and future services are to be delivered as per their needs. Customer experience management and feedback management are to be discussed in details in the following sections.

Furthermore, develop a procedure for handling customer complaints based on the following suggestions:

1. Listen to customers and acknowledge complaints. Customers who complain expect action.
2. Develop empathy and show concern for the customer.
3. Ask questions to obtain details; solicit customers alternative solutions.
4. Resolve the action underlying the complaint.
5. When complaints cannot be resolved immediately, update the customer periodically on the progress. Keep a notebook of promised actions.
6. Record the complaints and analyse them periodically to determine trends.

Key Elements of Fair Complaints Handling

Figure 90 describes, in simple terms, some of the key elements of fair complaint handling and how they should link together.

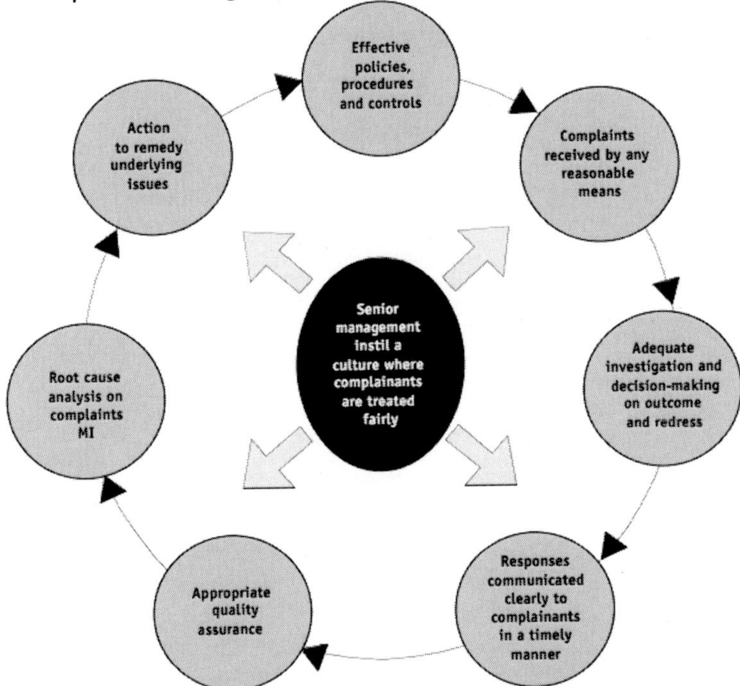

Figure 90: Key elements of fair customer complaints

Source (FSA, 2010)

Table 11 provides a detailed description on the above model.

Key elements	*Description*
Senior management instil a culture where complainants are treated fairly	• Clear responsibility and accountability for complaint handling by member(s) of senior management. • Senior management focused on the quality of complaint handling as well as the volume of complaints. • Complaint handling embedded in the firm's governance structure with senior management actively monitoring standards. • A structured programme of training and development in place for all staff handling

Key elements	*Description*
	complaints (including those in front-line roles) supporting fair decision-making. • The remuneration for complaint-handling staff designed to encourage the delivery of fair outcomes and not encourage inappropriate behaviours.
Effective policies, procedures and controls for complaint handling	• Policies, procedures and controls that are focused on outcomes as well as processes. • Using the two-stage process so that it does not act as a barrier to fair complaint handling. For example, ensuring the complaints framework. • Supports fair handling at both the initial and final stages, and putting in place procedures that avoid the unjustified use of more than two stages.
Complaints received by any reasonable means	• The definition of what constitutes a complaint. • Customers being able to make a complaint by any reasonable means.
Adequate investigation and decision-making on outcome and redress	• Procedures to ensure complaints are passed to the appropriate area for resolution. • Putting in place appropriate support to assist all staff handling complaints in resolving complaints fairly and calculating appropriate redress. • Investigations taking into account all relevant factors.
Responses communicated clearly to complainants in a timely manner	• Aiming to resolve complaints at the earliest opportunity. • The outcome of complaints being articulated to complainants in a way that is fair, clear and not misleading. • Maintaining good quality records of each complaint received, including. • How it was resolved.
Appropriate quality assurance	• Quality assurance focused on the quality of complaint handling as well as process. • The outcome of quality assurance captured that is reviewed by senior management and fed into staff development where relevant.
Root cause analysis carried out	• Complaint-handling that has an appropriate balance between qualitative and quantitative metrics to allow effective root cause analysis to be undertaken.

Key elements	*Description*
	• The output from root cause analysis used to consider whether it would be appropriate to take remedial action for a wider population of non-complainant customers.
Action taken to remedy underlying issues	• Policies, procedures and controls for complaint handling that are adapted to remedy any issues identified. • Taking action to remedy underlying issues within the wider business and/or for wider populations of affected customers where relevant. • The effectiveness of any changes monitored by appropriate analysis.

Table 11: Key elements of fair customer complaints

Adapted from (FSA, 2010)

The Role of CRM

The foremost goal of CRM is to build a long-term relationship with customers to enhance value shares for both parties. Organisations that adopt CRM may do so for a variety of reasons, mostly improving customer retention and customer satisfaction. CRM helps an organisation to profoundly understand customers' needs and then tailor their services to meet or even exceed those needs. A published research found that lifting customer retention rates by 5% of customers could increase organisation profit by 25% to 95%. This is due to the high c cost of acquisition, plus the fact that in the early years, customers are often unprofitable (Reichheld & Teal, 2001). It is only in the latter years, when the volumes purchased increase, that customers become profitable. This leads to the idea that a customer should not be viewed from a single transaction, but as a lifetime income stream (Ang & Buttle, 2002).

From a purely economic point of view, organisations learn that it is less costly to retain a customer than to find a new one. In industrial sales, it takes an average of 8 to 10 physical calls in person to sell to a new customer, but 2 or 3 calls to sell to an existing customer. However, they key driver is to find out more about customers and the way they interact with the organisation. This relationship can then be exploited by cross-selling (of services that the customer has not yet bought from the organisation), by extension selling (of services that relate to those already bought), to by some other transaction offering additional revenue to the organisation.

Managers using CRM software to support their sales, marketing and service activities report several benefits, for example higher levels of customer satisfaction, enhanced customer retention, reduced customer acquisition costs and higher share of customer spend (Ang & Buttle, 2002).

Mohammad, (2001) argues that CRM allows organisations to gather and access information about customers' buying histories, preferences, complaints, and other data, so they can better anticipate what customers will want. The goal is to instil greater customer loyalty. Other benefits include:

- Faster response to customer inquiries.
- Increased efficiency through automation.
- Deeper understanding of customers.
- Increased marketing and selling opportunities.
- Identifying different customers.
- Identifying the most profitable customers.
- Receiving customer feedback that leads to new and improved services.
- Obtaining information that can be shared with business partners.

Thus, CRM is a business philosophy that lets the organisation understand its customers' needs and requirements based on their histories and preferences, which in turn helps the organisation to predict and anticipate their future actions. Today more than before, success in this digital era will rely on those organisations that adopt the CRM strategy efficiency and effectively.

The Role of CEM

Customer Experience Management (CEM) as a strategy for attracting customers has been defined in a number of ways by different researchers. The main focus of these definitions is on the interaction that a customer has with an organisation, and improving that interaction. Berry et al. (2002) has described these interactions as 'experience clue': 'anything that can be perceived or sensed – or recognised by its absence - is an experience clue. Thus the product or service for sale gives off one set of clues, the physical setting offers more clues, and the employees – through their gesture, comments, dress and tones of voice – still more clues.'

(Thompson B., 2006) states that an interaction covers a wide variety of elements from viewing a marketing message to the actual use of a service to a post-purchase service/support activity to solve a problem.' All of these elements and more are part of the interactions/touch points /clues that a customer has with an organisation. A unique customer experience can create a good image about the organisation's capability on customers' mind. Organisations, which constantly strive to please their customers, have a greater chance of winning customers. CEM is the process of strategically managing a customer's entire experience with a service or an organisation. Researchers and managers have argued that organisations now need to focus on building positive experiences for their customers. Management focus has shifted from product orientation to service orientation and more recently to experience management (Voss & Zomerdijk, 2007).

Mascarenhas, Kesavan, & Bernachhi (2006) identify six principles of a total customer experience:

1. Anticipating and fulfilling customer needs and wants.
2. Providing real customer experiences.
3. Providing real emotional experiences.
4. Experiences as distinct market offering.
5. Experiences as interactions.
6. Experiences as engaging memories.

Strategies to Attract and Keep Customers

The following six strategies will help an organisation attract and keep customers.

1. **Offer quality services** - Good quality is the most important reason cited by customers for ordering directly from organisations. Successful marketers keep customers with repeat sales of quality services. Quality can have different dimensions but the widely known dimensions are: accurate, timely, responsive, complete, easy to use, user friendly, relevant, accessible.
2. **Cultivate good people skills** - Attitude is critical to business success. A personal inventory of employee's skills, interests and goals will help determine his/her personality and ability to relate to a wide mix of customers. People skills are essential in building a customer-centric service delivery. Even with a sincere interest and desire to work closely with customers, if employees are not a "people person" the organisation's chance for direct marketing success is slim. Organisations should promote the culture of customer-centricity. It implies employees' empowerment. Employees should be authorised to choose how to handle customer enquiries. It stimulates innovation in service delivery. Employees should be encouraged to make an informal relationship with customers and see what the best way for dealing with individual's enquiries is. This is a part of personalisation of services.
3. **Know customers needs and expectations** – Knowing customers' needs is probably one of the most critical steps in attracting customers. Customers should be acknowledge that, their enquires are received and will be promptly responded. Getting customers insight will help an organisation to tailor their services in accordance with customers' needs and expectations.
4. **Make services attractive through marketing** – This requires promoting current services to new customers and/or new features of existing services to current customers. Organisations should develop and deploy marketing strategies.
5. **Be innovative** – This is a golden rule and a key to success in attracting customers. There are certain parameters, which will be

considered by customers before they become attracted to a business. This may include:

- A business can deliver the required services as per their needs i.e. an organisation is always responsive to customers' needs.
- A business can always give them something extra in delivering services to them i.e. an organisation exceeds their expectations.
- A business can continuously deliver something which they cannot get from anywhere else i.e. innovative services.

6. **Be willing to change –** Customers are always looking for new services. The changes in many of the services, while often minimal, offer something new or different to attract customers. organisations may need to change their services, package, advertising or display to increase their appeal to customers

Attracting Customers through Service Marketing

The key to attracting customers is developing a marketing strategy that forms a solid foundation for your promotional efforts. Implementing promotional activities such as advertising, direct mail or even networking and one-to-one sales efforts along with a marketing plan create greater chance of winning customers.

The following are eight building blocks to attracting customers and developing a strong marketing foundation (Chance, 2004):

1. **Define an organisation's service –** How is an organisation' service packaged? What is it that organisation's customers are really buying? Organisation might be selling web-based software tools but organisation's customers are buying increased productivity, improved efficiency and cost savings. What problem does an organisation's service solve? What need does an organisation's service meet? What want does it fulfil?
2. **Identify an organisation's ideal customer** - Everyone or anybody might be potential customers for an organisation's service. However as organisation probably doesn't have the time or money to market to everyone or anybody. Who is the organisation's ideal customer? What does it make sense for the organisation to spend its time and money promoting service to?

Organisations might define its ideal customer in terms of income, age, geographic area, number of employees, revenues, industry, etc.

3. **Differentiate the organisation from the competition** - Even if there are no direct competitors for organisation's service, there is always competition of some kind. Something besides organisation's service is competing for the potential customers' money. What is it and why should the potential customer spend his or her money with organisation instead? What is organisation's competitive advantage or unique selling proposition?
4. **Find a niche** - Is there a customer group that is not currently being served or is not being served well? Are there customer wants that are not being met? A niche strategy allows an organisation to focus their marketing efforts and dominate organisation's market, even if the organisation is a small player.
5. **Develop awareness** - It is difficult for a potential customer to buy an organisation's service if they don't even know or remember it exists. Generally a potential customer will have to be exposed to an organisation's product 5 to 15 times before they are likely to think of an organisation's product when the need arises. Needs often arise unexpectedly. Organisations must stay in front of their customers consistently if they are going to remember the organisation's product when that need arises.
6. **Build credibility** - Not only must customers be aware of an organisation's service, they also must have a positive disposition towards it. Potential customers must trust that the organisation will deliver what organisation say organisation will. Often, especially with large or risky purchases, organisation need to give them the opportunity to sample, touch, or taste the service in some way. For example, a trainer might gain credibility and allow potential customers to sample their product by offering free, hour long presentations on topics related to their area of specialty.
7. **Be consistent** – In every way and in everything the organisation does. This includes the look of the organisation's collateral materials, the message the organisation delivers, the level of

customer service, and the quality of the product. Being consistent is more important than having the best service. This in part is the reason for the success of chains.

8. **Maintain the Focus -** Focus allows for more effective utilisation of the scarce resources of time and money. Organisation's promotional budget will bring organisation greater return if it uses the budget to promote a single service to a narrowly defined group of customers and if organisation promotes that same service to that same customer group over a continuous period of time

Attracting Customers through Service Innovation

Innovation is a key to success for attracting customers. It is effective exceeding customers' expectations. In a highly competitive business environment, organisations should strive to offer customers something beyond their expectations. Being innovative in order to attract customers requires high flexibility and a willingness to change. Organisations should put service innovation at the heart of their overall strategy. Organisations should exercise certain practices before they adopt service innovation as a strategy for customer attraction: Some of these may be but not limited to:

- Senior management commitment;
- Sophisticated and integrated information management system;
- Employees empowerment;
- Customers empowerment;
- Customer engagement.

Through a people orientated approach to service delivery and the closed loop approach to receiving feedback on service evaluation and service measurement, it is expected that innovation and learning will grow through the culture of improvement to allow freshness to enhance service delivery capability and the embracement of best practice to take place all of the time. Service delivery in the context of the 21st century will be done through e-enablement and that is through having a modern IT infra structure for supporting the value chain at all stages and allowing the free flow of information, upstream, mid stream and down-stream and generating a dynamic approach to service orientations, service enhancement, service impact and service growth and development.

Table 12 illustrates the key enablers for service innovation. These elements have been determined following an extensive research conducted by ECBPM.

Enabler 1: Service Innovation	
Key Elements	***Explanations***
Customer engagement	Collaboration with the customers to innovate.
Top down, bottom up or horizontal	Innovation driven from the top management as well as from the grass root level or at an inter-departmental level.
Employee empowerment and culture of innovation	Desired flexibility for the employees to incentivise innovation and appreciation from top management for encouraging the culture of innovation – ideating, promoting, implementing and measuring the success of innovation.
Leadership	A strong and visionary leadership coupled with the understanding of the fact that the change will inevitably require the allocation of substantial resources.
Solid basics	Fostered on the platform of consistent quality i.e. getting the basics right.
Enabler 2: Service e-enablement	
Key Elements	***Explanations***
Multiple channels	Multiple yet integrated delivery channels (multiple touch points) for citizens.
Digitalising	Digitalising the transactions and empowering citizens to transact deep with the public service providers.
One stop shop	A central (secure) electronic database to provide a one stop solution to the citizens.
Development of IT infrastructure	For the shift to happen from the physical service provision to automated or e-enabled service provision, an affordable IT infrastructure has to be developed.
Training provision	Training staff and citizens on how to use the e-enablement facilities. Help facility for citizens on how to use them.
Managing macro-level issues	Political, cultural, organisational, technological and social issues arising out this change to be managed astutely.

Enabler 3: Service Learning	
Key Elements	***Explanations***
Organisational Culture	Any failure to be seen as an opportunity for improvement, rather than an opportunity to score points.
Right impetus to learning	Excessive command and control from the top management stifles learning.
Sharing and Collaboration	Secrecy stifles feedback and learning process.
Comprehensive evaluation of previous service provision	Comprehensive evaluation of previous policies with regards to the service level agreement and a system in place that ensure that the improvement areas are kept in consideration while doing the service redesign (or design of new services), planning and delivery.
Managing turf wars	The turf wars between the departments and protection of vested interests to be severely targeted by the leadership.
Enabler 4: Service Improvement	
Key Elements	***Explanations***
Philosophy for public service provision	Continuous service improvement – The way of life for any public service providing organisation and the framework to be based on best value (value for money).
Culture of continuous improvement and transformation	Continuously challenging the means of delivery.
	Accountability for delivery standards and value for money.
	Incentives to support service transformation.
	Capability to manage changing delivery systems.
Dynamic monitoring and recording	The real time data analysis of all the aspects of service delivery enables the service provider to plan around the issues before they become problems.
Detailed Analysis	Detailed analysis of data provides real insight into the key factors influencing service quality and provides management with rich information about the systemic improvement opportunities.
Real-time integration of information	Real-time integration of task, time and location based information at the point of action provides the essential context for continuous improvement.

Table 12: Service innovation

With the current climate of cost cutting and budget deficit, innovation has become all the more important in the public service context. In terms of differences between the private and public sector, the following points are important to be noted:

- There are differences in how value is defined. Innovation in public sector is not limited to economic value indicators; it has to be assessed through impact on a range of social values as well.
- There are differences in which organisations operate as well. The public sector organisations operate in a range of different systems and assess the impact of the system conditions on innovation in organisations.

The framework for innovation in public sector organisations has been depicted in Figure 91. The circle represents the aspects that are within the organisational control: these are "innovation capability" which underpins an organisation's "innovation activity", which "impacts on performance". On the other side, there is "wider sector conditions for innovation", that represents the aspects that are outside organisational control but are within the control of policymakers or other sector bodies of strategic influence. These conditions describe how the system, in which an organisation operates, helps or hinders innovation – that is, how the system impacts an organisation's innovation activity and capability. A consideration of these factors also allows comparisons to be made, and lessons drawn, across different systems.

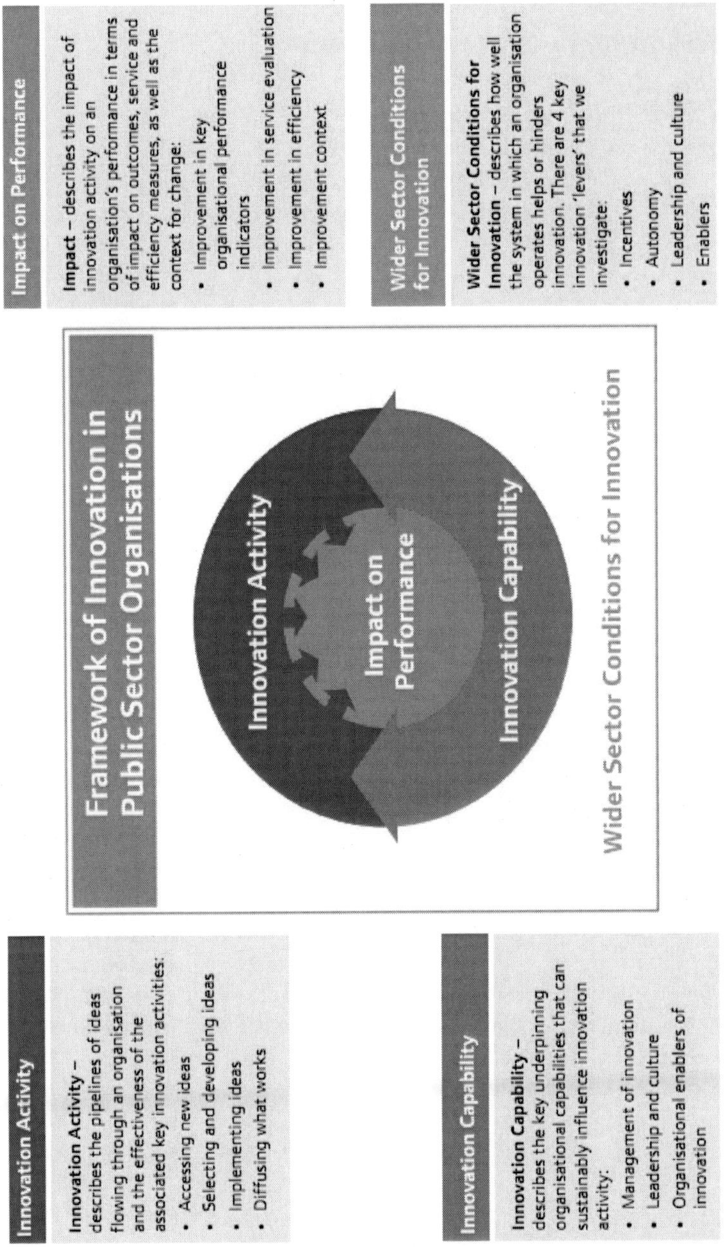

Figure 91: Innovation framework

Source: (Hughes, Moore, & Kataria, 2011)

Assessment Toolkit: Attraction

Customer Relation Management

Q1. Has the organisation a clear strategy for CRM in place?			
Basic	**Developing**	**Maturing**	**Leading**
The organisation does not follow a clear path or strategy for building or maintaining customer relationship.	The organisation has a CRM strategy in place; although, it lacks the required infrastructure and technology capability for deploying the strategy.	The organisation maintains a clear strategy and the required technology capability in place; although, due to the lack of clarity about strategic objectives, the organisation does not fully realise the benefits of CRM.	The organisation sets a clear set of strategic objectives, it has effectively developed and deployed CRM strategy.
Q2. Does the organisation develop and deploy customer Insight to make its services more attractive?			
Basic	**Developing**	**Maturing**	**Leading**
The organisation has particularly focused on push system and it does not seriously consider customers' data for developing future services.	The organisation collects and maintains customers' information; however, translation of these data into insight is not appropriately conducted due to the lack of focus.	The organisation has maintained an enriched customer information data base and customers are clearly segmented; although, the organisation has still applied push system in order to interact with customers.	The organisation has developed a deep customer insight; it has effectively used it for adjusting services with customers' expectations in different segments. (in another word, the organisation has initiated a pull system for its services).

Q3. Does the organisation maintain a clear Service Marketing Strategy for attracting customers?			
Basic	**Developing**	**Maturing**	**Leading**
The organisation has not a clear service marketing strategy in place for promoting new services.	The organisation markets its new services through promotional materials; the focus of its marketing strategy is only on building awareness about existing services. There is slightly ambiguity about target audiences.	The organisation has developed effective marketing communication channels as a part of its marketing strategy deployment. The focus of its strategy is on building awareness about existing and prospective services. Target audiences are clearly identified and communicated.	The organisation has maintained an effective strategy for marketing its services. Target audiences are clearly identified and communicated. The focus of its strategy is on turning customers into service ambassadors, who are voluntarily willing to speak out about organisation's services with other people.

Customer Experience Management

Q1. Does the organisation maintain a Strategy for CEM?			
Basic	**Developing**	**Maturing**	**Leading**
The organisation does not put enough emphasis on CEM.	The organisation views customer experiences as a factor for building customers loyalty and service attraction; however, it does not see it as a top	The organisation views CEM as an effective way for creating service attraction so it has developed a clear strategy for it.	The organisation view customer experience management as The focus of its CEM strategy is on empowering and engaging

	strategic objective. And hence, there is not clear strategy in place.		customers in the process of service marketing i.e. customer advocacy.
Q2. Does the organisation, to some extent, apply the concept of customer empowerment for building service attraction?			
Basic	**Developing**	**Maturing**	**Leading**
The only time customers come to know about the organisation's services is when the services are about to be delivered to the customers, before that the customers having not any clue about services' characteristics.	The organisation seeks customers' opinion about the possible improvements, which can be made in order to make services more attractive. However, customers will not be involved in the process of service design and delivery.	The organisation effectively conducts service sampling, testing and prototyping; it collects customers' opinions about possible service improvements by letting sample of customers actually experience new services at every stage of service design before it started mass production of services.	The organisation has widely applied the concept of service co-creation; it has empowered customers to the extent to which they are actively involved in the process of service design and review. Since services are subject to reviewing and improving services, the concept of service prototyping becomes slightly out-dated.

Q3. To what extent does the organisation strive to fulfilling customer experience from both physical and emotional aspects?			
Basic	**Developing**	**Maturing**	**Leading**
The organisation is even struggling to entirely fulfil customers' expectations of the physical aspects of service quality.	The organisation is less care about emotional aspects of service quality; and, it is very much focus on physical aspects of service quality.	The organisation has successfully fulfilled customers' expectations about physical aspects of service quality and now the organisation even progresses towards fulfilling emotional aspects of customers' experiences.	The organisation keeps surprising customers with regards to the quality of services, which they receive, by exceeding their expectations from both emotional as well as physical aspects.

Customer Service Provision

Q1. To what extent does the organisation focus on service quality as a way of building service attraction?			
Basic	**Developing**	**Maturing**	**Leading**
The organisation has focused on limited number of service quality attributes in order to satisfy customers. It lacks to service quality measurement.	The organisation has a developing list of service quality factors. The list does not include all quality attributes and hence the organisation is to determine which factors have more impact on customers' perceptions. Selecting and	The organisation maintains a comprehensive set of service quality attributes which it constantly review the impacts on these attributes on customers' perceptions.	The organisation not only uses a comprehensive set of service quality attributes which it constantly review the impacts on these attributes on customers' perceptions but also it constantly benchmarking the quality of its

	focusing on limited number of factors is the strategy of the organisation with respects to service quality.		services with world-class organisations.
Q2. Does the organisation uses service innovation for creating service attraction?			
Basic	**Developing**	**Maturing**	**Leading**
The organisation has no system in place for enabling service innovation.	The organisation has conducted limited number of innovation; however, it seeks to build the required infrastructure for enabling service innovation. Management are interested in knowing the impact of service innovation on service attraction.	The organisation has set service innovation as an effective strategy for creating service attraction. The organisation has widely applied the concept of closed-innovation within the organisation. The organisation seeks opportunity for building the capability required for conducting open innovation.	The organisation has successfully established itself as an innovative organisation. Customers are always excited about the organisation's services. The organisation has effectively and widely set up open-innovation within the organisation and hence it effectively engages all groups of stakeholders in the process of service innovation.
Q3. To what extent does the organisation provides service delivery support system after the actual delivery has been conducted?			
Basic	**Developing**	**Maturing**	**Leading**
The organisation does not feel responsible	The organisation, to limited extent, sees itself responsible for	The organisation has established a clear line of responsibilities	The organisation has an effective Service Delivery Support System

about its services once the actual delivery has been occurred.	services, which provided to customers. It seeks to maintain it communication lines with customers even after the delivery; however, there is no clarity about the range after-sales services.	for itself with regards to post-delivery services. It maintains a Service Delivery Support System, which clearly understood by customers.	in place. The system is subjected to a continuous review and improvement. The organisation sees post-delivery customer service as a mean for gaining customer trust and confidence.

Yet, taught by time, my heart has learned to glow for other's good, and melt at other's woe.

Homer

Chapter 15: Customer Intimacy

Introduction

Business success today requires a new depth of customer insight. The right blend of customer-centric strategies and advanced analytical tools delivers it (Peppers & Rogers Group, 2010). Organisations in order to provide support and give shape to their business decisions should focus on one of the three distinct value disciplines: 1) operational excellence; 2) service leadership; and 3) customer intimacy. Although, it is imperative for an organisation to maintain competitive standards within all three disciplines, decision makers should focus on a single discipline of they hope to be a leader in their chosen markets.

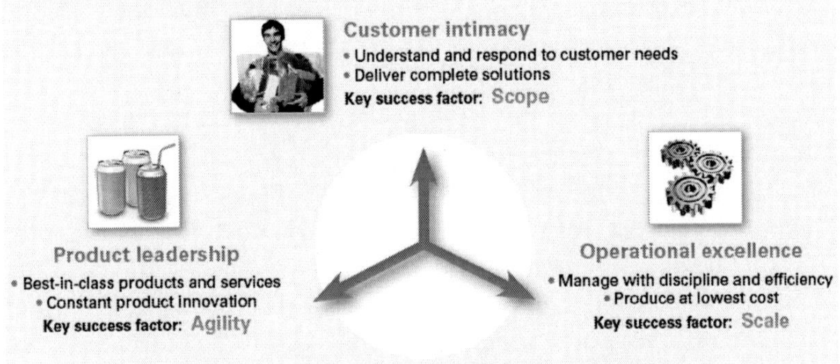

Figure 92: The Dimensions of Competitive Advantage

Source (Peppers & Rogers Group, 2010)

Organisations that have taken leadership positions in their industries in the last decade typically have done so by narrowing their business focus. They have focused on delivering superior customer value in line with one of three value disciplines. Treacy & Wiersema (1993) have identified three value disciplines on which organisations should focus. Adopting these value orientations and aligning them to the overall strategic direction and functioning of the organisation will enable them to meet and exceed customer expectations and thus add "real" value to the customers' experience.

The three value disciplines are described as follows:

1. **Operational excellence** - This means providing customers with reliable products or services at competitive prices and delivered with minimal difficulty or inconvenience.
2. **Customer intimacy** – This means segmenting and targeting markets precisely and then tailoring offerings to match exactly the demands of those niches.
3. **Service leadership** – This means offering customers leading-edge services that consistently enhance the customers' use or application of the service.

Organisations pursuing a strategy of customer intimacy continually tailor and shape services to fit an increasingly fine definition of the customer. Customer intimate organisations are willing to spend now to build customer loyalty for the long term. They look at the customer's lifetime value to the organisation not the value any single transaction (Treacy & Wiersema, 1993).

The importance of customer intimacy as one of the three value disciplines has gained lot of attention in recent years. Organisations, in the 21st century, already realised that the customer is the king. Hence, they continuously strive to build and enhance their competitive positions within this area. This has brought significant change in the way organisations run their day to day businesses for example: the shift from the push system within which organisations tried to sell their products after the products is actually made to the pull system in which entire production line and activity chains is driven by customers' demands.

Organisations strive to become more and more customer focused and try to rationally go extra miles in order to surpass customers' expectations. Organisations that provide customer intimacy do not usually have the best price or the newest innovation; rather customer-intimate organisations try to provide the best total solution for their customers by attending to the broader range of needs. They get to know their customers, as well as the underlying problems that accompany their needs for a particular service.

Customer intimacy means helping customers make the most out of the services they use (Siebert, 2004). With customer intimacy the organisation works to communicate and deliver and product or service experience focusing on the best customer solution for the segment chosen. The activities within the firm and customer selection emphasise processes, activities and messaging stress an intimate or highly emphatic relationship.

Building Blocks of Customer Intimacy

By consistently delivering the types of results and experiences that each customer expects, and by exceeding customer expectations by anticipating their needs in advance, organisations are able to earn that customers trust. These results can vary, from supplying the right products at the right time to customers to improving their interactions and experiences with a company. As Fred Wiersema stated in his 1998 book Customer Intimacy, "building customer intimacy doesn't call for increasing customer satisfaction. It requires taking responsibility for customers' results". "Customer intimacy isn't just about trying to sell more, but is about understanding the needs your customers have, even if the customer herself hasn't articulated that need directly", says Robert Risany, director, product marketing at IBM. In their efforts to build customer intimacy with customers, organisations must learn as much as they can about each customer's behaviour, attitudes and expressed needs and use that to understand where and what their pain points are.

Developing that kind of wisdom about each customer and customer segment ultimately enables organisations to create more customer-centric services and support — potentially growing sales and service in the process. Customer knowledge also allows organisations to craft customised offers and even tailored sales arguments for each customer based on their individual preferences. This approach often leads to increases in close rates, repeat purchases and referrals. Gathering and analysing the data required for customer intimacy will also help businesses to acquire the kind of customer who is likely to be profitable, retain their most valuable customers, and improve operations, products and services based on customers' needs and value. All these outcomes help to increase revenue and reduce costs. The following table depicts the building blocks of customer intimacy

Blocks	Descriptions
Voice of the Customer	A commitment, strategy and process to capture and integrate the thoughts, feelings and emotions of a customer into the ongoing operations of an organisation.
Enterprise Feedback Management	A defined and repeatable approach to integrating customer feedback into all customer-focused aspects of the organisation.
Customer Experience Management	The 360 degree view of the interactions a customer has with an organisation across every touch point and channel.
Exceeded Customer Expectation	The optimisation and standardisation of enterprise-wide business processes to exceed customer expectations at the point of impact.

Table 13: The Building Blocks of Customer Intimacy

Source: (Peppers & Rogers Group, 2010).

Customer Centricity and Intimacy

Sadly, most organisations lack the holistic view of their customers that's required to fully understand and react to customers' needs in a way that will help to forge tight-knit and trusting relationships with them. Decision-makers are impeded by barriers such as silos of customer data, poor data quality and misaligned business strategies that prevent them from developing a comprehensive view of each customer and leveraging the business potential of each relationship. The following are five disciplines that represent key focus areas where customer intimacy is forged (Peppers & Rogers Group, 2010):

1. Customer acquisition, which focuses on attracting the right customers efficiently.
2. Relationship development strategies based on customer interests and what they are most likely to buy.
3. A customer value and satisfaction–based retention strategy.
4. Operational excellence achieved by acting on customer insight.
5. Product leadership based on delivering products customers want.

Customer Insight is at the heart of customer centricity and intimacy.

Customer Insight

To become truly customer intimate, organisation should be able to designing the best possible framework for delivering services. This requires focusing on customers and understanding their needs. Eventually, services provided to customers should be based on customer needs and solutions should be tailored to meet those needs. The availability and usage of customer data and feedback to develop insights into customer preferences, priorities, behaviours and service quality improvement will drive service improvement in public services. Getting customer insight is an ongoing, iterative process that requires adequate resources to refresh the data and analysis. Customer insight is a long term process. Over time you deepen the understanding of your customers. This must be constantly refreshed if it is to improve services and helps to truly meet customer expectations. Figure 93 shows the main pillars of customer insight.

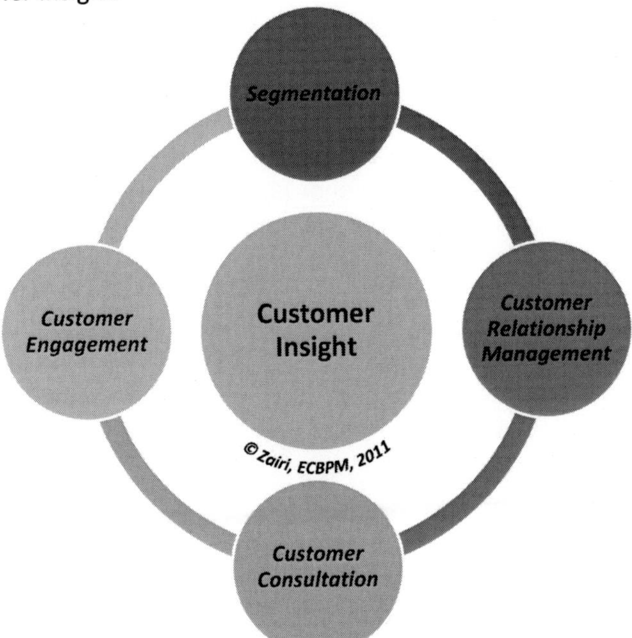

Figure 93: Customer Insight

Customer-intimate organisations should get closer to their customers and develop more robust customer-centric business strategies by leveraging advanced analytics effectively. They take a more holistic approach by applying predictive analytics to historical outcomes such as purchases, responses to offers, defections, etc. A holistic view will enable customer-facing employees to have the right kind of dialogue, leading for example to better sales opportunities with customers and prospects at the point of contact. Capturing the dialogue and the results of these interactions consistently can better inform the business and help to determine future business outcomes.

Customer insight can provide decision-makers with a deep understanding on customer behaviours, attitudes and preferences which can be used to craft the right offers to the right customers at the right time. Customer intimacy can generate numerous business returns, including more efficient customer acquisition; recurring revenue opportunities; increased loyalty and retention to help maximise actual and potential customer value; product innovation to deliver the services customers want and will buy; and operational excellence by applying customer input across the organisation. Maximising profitability and return on investment though building customer loyalty is one of the main drivers for building customer intimacy. Organisation should view this, building customer loyalty through customer intimacy, as a process. The following figure depicts a simple loyalty management process map. This helps organisations identify high-value customers for preferential treatment. In spite of its simplicity, the map helps an organisation to consider appropriate strategy for making customers loyal.

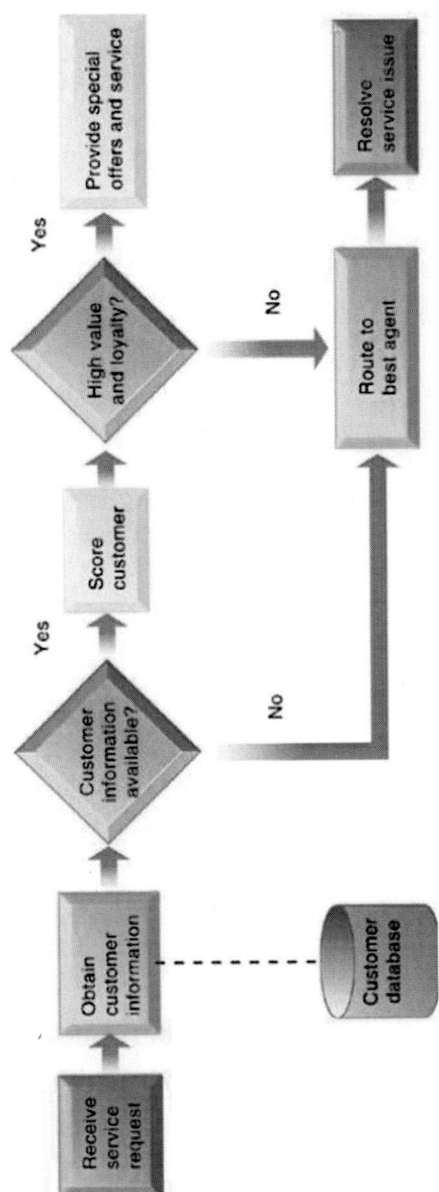

Figure 94: Customer Loyalty Management Process Map

Source (Laudon & Laudon, 2011)

Customer Segmentation

Customer intimacy is about segmenting and targeting customers precisely, and tailoring offerings to match exactly the demands of those niches. For this reason, customer intimate organisations should be able to effectively segment their customers. Customer segmentation is the practice of dividing customers into groups of individuals that are similar in specific ways - such as age, gender, interests, spending habits etc. It is the process of looking at the universe of customers and identifying distinct, manageable segments (sub-groups) that may have similar needs, attitudes or behaviours. In other words, "customer segmentation" is a term used to describe the process of dividing customers into homogeneous groups on the basis of shared or common attributes (habits, tastes, etc.).

Best Practices and Benefits of Customer Insight

A true customer insight can bring considerable benefits for organisations:

- Customer segmentation as a primary step in getting customer insight helps organisations to gain further insight into customer's needs and preferences through segmenting the customer base into groups that share distinguishing characteristics or profiles.
- By using the customer profiling techniques organisations can design their services around the needs of your customers. This enables the organisations to:
    - Record transaction data for all services, including the profile customers accessing each service by different channels.
    - Record the cost to deliver each service through different channels.
- Understanding needs and expectations of customers can enhance the process of decision making through providing important evidences.
- Learning from complaints, contacting dissatisfied customers to discuss their experiences and a customer-led mystery shopping service are useful initiatives for improving customer satisfaction.
- Customer insight data can play a vital role in triggering and shaping service transformation programs. This is because

evidence on the needs and preferences of customers can help to build support for change among managers and staff.

- Greater insight into the needs and preferences of customers can encourage greater uptake of services by making them more accessible. This helps organisations to plug the gap between service need and service delivery.
- Organisations can make customer insight information available to employees in order to ease the process of benefit realisation.
- In order to generate value, customer insight need to be used to deliver better services.
- Getting customer insight is an ongoing, iterative process that requires adequate resources to refresh the data and analysis. Customer insight is a long term process. Over time you deepen the understanding of your customers. This must be constantly refreshed if it is to improve services and helps to truly meet customer expectations.
- Being customer-centric and using insight is not just about being able to collect data and information. It is about having the capability to turn that information into action and it requires a culture which values insight and is willing to act on it.

Adapted from (Improvement and Development Agency , 2008)

Translating Customer Intimacy into Value

Today, this focus on the customer experience has grown to the point where it practically overshadows the services themselves. They have become the doorway to a transformed lifestyle, one that's based on personalised content, rich interactions and new ways to make life more convenient and more enjoyable. It's about what the device allows people to experience, not what the device itself does. That context is essential when considering new ways to innovate and generate revenue. To drive smarter product and service innovation, organisations must know as much as possible about how services are used and how customers integrate them into their lives. A 360-degree view of the customer on how they use a particular device as well as insight into their entire lifestyle is needed (IBM, 2011).

Building new links to customers and leveraging highly interconnected technology allows organisations to shape the interaction with their services and in the process better understand what customers want. Or, with insight into how a game-changing new offering might impact the marketplace, the organisation can even get ahead of customers and redefine how they view the world in ways they never would have imagined. Organisations with a deep understanding of current attitudes and future needs have been able to get ahead of the innovation curve and make an intuitive and visionary leap that redefines the customer experience.

The second important aspect of innovation is that organisations represent entirely new business models and new revenue streams focused on what customers do, rather than the device they buy. Under this kind of business model, the service is a conduit: from the point of view of the customer, its primary value lies in its ability to access “must have” experiences. Today’s organisations need to become businesses that create, orchestrate and manage customer experiences. To do that requires investment in a robust information, analysis and delivery platform. The means to tap into everything from demographics and usage history to point-of-event feedback is essential to creating insight. Service development requires realisation of that insight to drive innovation. And finally, transforming the customer experience requires a partnership strategy with other service providers to create, personalise and deliver new services in real time – to stay in touch and put closer customer relationships to work (IBM, 2011).

Figure 95 depicts a comprehensive capabilities roadmap. Each step builds on the one before to improve both cumulative cash flow and innovation capability. Most organisations have invested in some key capabilities, such as customer information management and/or service life-cycle management, with the aim of enhancing the customer experience. However, it is important to recognise the holistic and interdependent nature of the overall effort. Investing in individual capabilities can produce good returns, but an end-to-end approach offers synergy that can yield the maximum benefit.

Organisations that have made narrowly focused investments may be highly mature in specific areas, while still leaving a considerable amount of financial benefit unrealised.

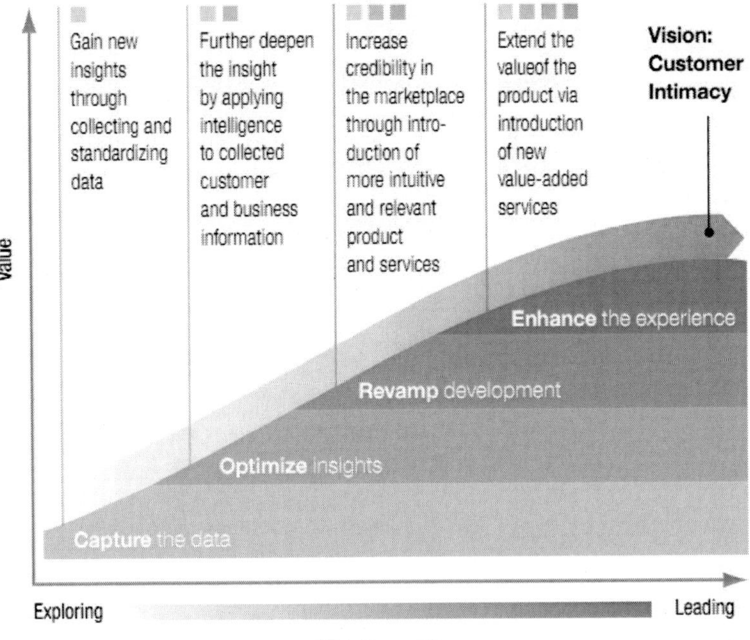

Figure 95: The journey to smarter product and service innovation

Source (IBM, 2011)

Key Principles of Customer Intimacy

Table 14 illustrates five principles of customer intimacy. Implementing these principles help an organisation to effectively enhance its competitive position through maximising value proposition to its customers.

Principles	Descriptions
1. Commit to intimacy	• Deliver mutual results and commit to meeting all customers' needs. • Understand their business better than even they do. • Foster agility to respond to customers' variability and use foresight to minimise unpredictably. • Always be willing to serve the customer.
2. Tailor and deliver the best-fitting solutions	• Craft custom-made solutions to facilitate new ways to do business. • Cooperate with customers to expand and experiment with new forms of tailoring. • Establish and maintain mutual respect and trust between the organisation and its customers
3. Pick the right partners	• Keep an eye out for challenging "stretch" customers ... stretching suppliers to the limit and making them stronger. • Size up attitudinal fit, looking especially for patience and tolerance. • Ask yourself; is there a philosophy of collaboration?
4. Mould and shape the culture	• Strong cultures have memorable credos that permeate the organisation. • The credo must be alive and dominant in facilitating judgement, cooperation and learning. Leaders at every level can contribute to bringing the credo to life.
5. Examine strengths to start organisations journey to intimacy	• Redesign a key process that affects the way customers use organisation's services. • Measure performance and offer rewards in accordance with the goals of the discipline. Customer triage and selectivity can be spearheading forces to intimacy.

Table 14: Five Customer Intimacy principles

Source (WIERSEMA, 2011)

Measuring the Impact

Meeting customer's core service requirements qualifies an organisation only to compete — it does not guarantee it will win loyalty. Increasingly, what creates true and, equally importantly, perceived customer value is the ability to personalise service delivery and convey an aura of understanding and excellence to your customers. Over the past century, there is a significant shift between two extreme paradigms of services, from the service factory model, which emphasises on efficiency, consistency and cost-effectiveness delivered through systems, standardisation and control, to the skilled servitude model, which focuses on responsiveness, customisation and empathy, achieved through a phalanx of skilled and experienced service employees.

A service provider needs to know individual customers being served in order to deliver service that, in addition to being efficient, is also personal and effective in fulfilling their total service requirements. The following seven key design principles help an organisation to effectively deploy its intimacy strategy (Kolesar & Cutler, 2011):

1. **Know your customer** – Having detailed knowledge of the particular customer being served enhances the value and efficiency of service work. Intimate customer knowledge can be harnessed to:
    - Customise the service — tailor service to the precise needs of each individual customer.
    - Foresee customer needs — initiate service based on a tracking of customer history and profiles.
    - Increase perceived value — personalise delivery, project an image of empathy and competence.
    - Improve service recovery — know immediately when service errors occur and respond with customised recovery efforts.
    - Eliminate work — simplify processes; reduce transaction effort because of the communication of data, instructions and need; eliminate repetition of work based on status or history.
2. **Strive for once-and done servicing** – This means eliminating (or at least minimising) the number of handoffs required to complete

a transaction. Ideally, this means completing the transaction or "service event" in real time while interacting with the customer.

3. **Promote value-enhancing self-servicing** - Using information technology, a provider can engineer customer knowledge into self-service tools, greatly expanding their capabilities and hence the possibilities for leveraging self-service options.
4. **Provide one-stop shopping** - Value is created, for both the customer and the service provider, if an organisation can coordinate and simplify the total "service processes." The needs of the customer can then be met through a single service provider, even if the provider is merely acting as an integrator of other branded services.
5. **Let customers design the service** – A key intimacy-enhancing design principle is to offer customers only the services they want — a menu of service features that they can choose from to meet their individual needs. This amount of flexibility increases the cost of operation significantly. Since it is often a lack of information management capabilities rather than a lack of process edibility that prevents service providers from customising delivery, co-creation of services helps the organisations to effectively close the gap between customers' needs and organisations' services.
6. **Engineer competency into service delivery** – The strategy to succeed for service organisations is to build competency into the delivery systems and to rely less on the competency of front-line personnel. This is proven by knowing the fact that due to increasing service complexity, insuring competency through the skills and experience of front-line employees augmented by close management control and supervision is not effective in creating customer intimacy and loyalty.
7. **Build long-term customer relationships** – This is a focusing principle. An intimacy strategy reinforces this logic, that retaining customers is vital in services, by creating an intimate, value-building relationship between an organisation and its customers. This is simply based on competent, convenient, no-hassle delivery of only those services they value — all at a reasonable price.

Organisations that achieve customer intimacy are able to draw upon their knowledge of individual customers and their behaviours, attitudes and preferences to formulate strategies that can generate optimal business returns. Other types of business outcomes that can be influenced by customer intimacy include (Peppers & Rogers Group, 2010):

1. **Customer acquisition** - By knowing the characteristics of their ideal customer, organisations are better positioned to identify and target prospects with the greatest likelihood to purchase and to become high-value customers.
2. **Recurring cross-sell and up-sell opportunities** - Evaluating transaction trends, behaviours and sentiments can help organisations identify the most likely products customers will be interested in purchasing.
3. **Increased loyalty and retention** - Organisations that develop intimate, trusting relationships with customers are able to increase customer loyalty to help maximise actual and potential customer value. They're also able to spot subtle changes in customer purchasing and other behaviours, which may help them to react faster to potential churn, as the European telecom company has.
4. **Operational excellence** - Organisations can use customer insights and other intelligence to help them personalise services for customers. For instance, a leading Australian bank has customised its ATM machines to address each cardholder by name and recommend unique services based on their previous transaction.
5. **Service innovation** - Organisations can detect customer sentiment and analyse their feedback to develop the types of services they're seeking.

Measuring a Customer Intimacy Culture

In today's ever-changing organisational environment, the strategic link to organisational effectiveness and competitiveness is also based on meeting and exceeding the needs and expectations of customers. To enable organisations to do so, they need to understand what the value orientation of their specific customer base is. In simpler terms, what would be perceived as value adding by the customer's specific to their sector and product or service? Organisations that focus their strategic directions and efforts on the provision of an overarching customer service experience are those that become world-class (Potgieter & Roodt, 2004).

Organisations that excel in customer intimacy combine detailed customer knowledge with operational flexibility do that they can promptly respond to almost any needs. World-class organisations not only identify the unique value they can add to their customers, but they also ensure that they strategically align their processes and people practices around the delivery thereof. Organisations that want to align their people practices, processes and products (embedded in a customer service culture) strategically need firstly to determine the value orientation of their customer base. To ensure effectiveness in providing the value the customers prefer, organisations need to have the competency profile; enabling processes and organisational systems to achieve the required results (cf. Dannhauser & Roodt, 2001). Each of the three said value disciplines demand a different core organisational capability. The following table illustrates these core capabilities for customer intimacy value discipline.

The framework presented in Table 15 helps an organisation for the development of the comprehensive Culture Assessment Questionnaire (CAQ) focusing on Customer Intimacy value discipline (Potgieter & Roodt, 2004).

****Core organisational Capability:** Segmenting and targeting precisely, and tailoring offerings to match exactly the demands of those niches. Customer sensitivity and flexibility.

Value Discipline *Customer Intimacy*	
Core Organisational Capability **	**Description**
Dimension 1: Personnel strategy	• Satisfied employees satisfy customer. • Rely on value to shape culture and message. • Promote relationship building as priority.
Dimension 2: Organising	• Customer needs driven but can be individual or team based. • Strong focus on relationship building. • All individuals constantly selling to customers – improving relationship.
Dimension 3: Personnel procurement	• Highly responsive, excellent listening skills, empathetic, consultative, perceptive, flexible values driven • Good communication and technical skills. • Able to assess needs, spontaneous, problem solver, understand motivation. • Long-term relationship focus.
Dimension 4: Development	• Emphasis on organisational values, relationship skills, communication skills, planning, knowledge sharing.
Dimension 5: Achievement	• Measures: relationship productive behaviours. • New customers gained, customers retained and lateral selling.
Dimension 6: Remuneration	• Rewards tied to values. • Based on behavioural, subjective assessments. • Profit sharing (private sector) – individual contribution recognised. • Broad benefits choices.
Dimension 7: Strategy	• Relationship management based.
Dimension 8: Core values	• Customer centricity and sensitivity to customer expectations.
Dimension 9: Core abilities	• Customer relationship building and retention strategies.
Dimension 10: Business model	• Flexible – people centred, 'flat' organisation.

Table 15: Key People Strategies in the Value Disciplines

Source (Potgieter & Roodt, 2004)

Assessment Toolkit: Intimacy

Customer-Centricity

Q1. To what extent does the organisation succeed in creating the culture of customer centricity?			
Basic	**Developing**	**Maturing**	**Leading**
The organisation does not have a clear definition of customer centricity and hence services are designed and delivered solely based on the organisation's requirements.	The organisation strives to build the required capability for building the culture of customer centricity. It occasionally provides training programs about customer centricity; however, there is a lack of clear strategy and objectives for becoming a customer centric organisation.	The organisation constantly promotes the message of customer centricity. It links performance appraisal system, rewards and recognition with individuals' ability in handling customers' enquiries creatively.	The organisation has successfully built and delivered customer intimacy. It effectively encourages people to see things from customers' point of view in everything they do.
Q2. Does the organisation develop customer insight?			
Basic	**Developing**	**Maturing**	**Leading**
The organisation, at a very basic level, seeks information from customers. There is no clarity about the range of	The organisation strives to build the required capability for maintaining customers' information i.e technology	The organisation has an enriched database for maintain customers' information. It uses this information to improve future	The organisation has a deep customer insight supported by an enriched database and a sophisticated data analysis system. The

customers.	required etc. It has identified limited segments of customers and strives to build and maintain its relationship with them. it already established a customer feedback management system.	services. It has clear understanding about the needs of different customers' segments; however, there is a lack of an advanced data analysis system, which make the review of customer insight costly.	insight is subjected to a constant review and continuous improvement.
Q3. To what extent does the organisation engage customers in the process of service delivery?			
Basic	**Developing**	**Maturing**	**Leading**
The organisation does not allows customers to be involved in the process of service delivery. It adjusted a push system for delivering of its services.	The organisation seeks information and feedback once the services have been delivered to customers so that the future services will be improved. The organisation has started its journey from a push system t a pull system but its still far way from an ideal situation.	The organisation actively involves customers in the process of decision making. Particularly, customers are authorised to contribute in the process of service design so their point of view can be incorporated in the system.	The organisation conducts the co-creation of services. Personalisation of services has been facilitated and customers are sufficiently empowered in order to do so.

Customer Intimacy Value Discipline

Q1. Does the organisation maintain a clear strategy for customer intimacy?			
Basic	**Developing**	**Maturing**	**Leading**
Management of the organisation have little or no understanding about the concept of customer intimacy. They much care about the organisation's requirements.	Management of the organisation are familiar with the concept of customer intimacy; however, they put emphasis on some other things at the strategic level so there is a less attention given to customer intimacy. There are number of objectives in relation to customer intimacy at operational level but not at strategic level.	There are some clear strategic objectives in relation to customer intimacy established by the organisation. Management has developed a clear strategy for achieving these objectives; although, deployment of the strategy is not as effective as it is supposed to be because of certain inefficiencies such as lack of employees empowerment, concept promotion etc.	The organisation has a very clear set of strategic objectives in relation to customer intimacy and it has effectively developed and deployed the required for achieving these objectives. The entire organisation is well aligned for achieving customer intimacy.
Q2. To what extent does the organisation build and maintain the culture of customer intimacy?			
Basic	**Developing**	**Maturing**	**Leading**
The organisation has not the required capabilities for building customer intimacy; however, it	The organisation seeks to improve employees' capabilities, knowledge and skills in order to facilitate the application of	Since the organisation views customer intimacy as a way for creating competitive advantage, there is a particular	The culture of organisation fully supports customer intimacy. Individuals are well promoted and

values any improvement customers' satisfaction rate.	customer intimacy throughout the organisation. Hence, it provides limited number of training programs in relation to this.	focus on this at the strategic level of the organisation and hence great commitment from management team. There is a regular set of training programs in relation to customer intimacy provided by the organisation.	encouraged to put customers at the heart of everything they do and see things from customers' eyes. Innovation in handling customers' enquiries is distinctly recognised and highly rewarded.
Q3. To what extent does the organisation empower its employees toward building customer intimacy?			
Basic	**Developing**	**Maturing**	**Leading**
Everything within the organisation is controlled by top management and employees are encouraged to stick to procedures and standards.	The organisation has constantly provided information about management decision making and it occasionally seek employees' ideas about possible improvements, which can be made in relation to customer service.	The organisation has empowered employees to use their creativity in handling customers' enquiries. Employees are permitted to openly discuss any issue with regards to customer service with management; however, they are not involved in decision making.	Employees are given permission to contribute in the decision making process. Processes are designed and adjusted to comfy individual customers. Employees are highly rewarded for innovative thinking in relation to customer intimacy.

Service Delivery Flexibility – Sensitivity to Customers' Needs

Q1. How does the organisation identify customers' needs and expectations?			
Basic	**Developing**	**Maturing**	**Leading**
The organisation completely relies on a reactive and passive process for identifying customers' needs. It adopted a push system in which further improvement in the organisation's services is rarely occurred once services are designed.	The organisation uses a reactive process for identifying customers' needs. The system enables the organisation to seek feedback about their experiences once the delivery has been done. Hence, there is less opportunity for improving services before the actual delivery.	The organisation has shifted away from a reactive to a proactive system for identifying customers' needs. It constantly reaches out to new customers' segments (underserved segments) and seeks new ways of fulfilling customers' needs in more efficient ways.	The organisation successfully adopted a proactive system for identifying customers' needs. It constantly strives to delight customers through offering services' features which are beyond their expectations. The organisation remains totally flexible in meeting customers' needs since it has the required capability for personalising services.

Q2. To what extent does the organisation view service innovation as a means for building customer intimacy?			
Basic	**Developing**	**Maturing**	**Leading**
The organisation does not view service innovation as a means for building customer intimacy. It may be because it has some fundamental agenda, which thinks should have been given more priority compared with customer intimacy.	The organisation started to realise that service innovation can be an effective way for building customer intimacy. Although, it has not the required service innovation capability; it does seek improvements i.e. training programs with regards to service innovation. The organisation needs to establish service innovation system.	There is a good level of understanding about the value of service innovation from customers' point of view. The organisation constantly and thoroughly reviews its service innovation to see how an innovation looks like from customers' point of view does. Customers' feedback and ideas will be collected at the same rate of innovation.	The organisation has successfully adopted open innovation system so any service innovation will include customers' input and consequently acceptable from customers' point of view.

Q3. To what extent is the organisation capable of customising services?			
Basic	**Developing**	**Maturing**	**Leading**
The organisation is either incapable or at the very limited range of customising services.	The organisation does not have the required capability and infrastructure (e.g. IT) for customising services; however, it does collect customers' feedback about services for the next generation of services to be improved.	The organisation has acquired the required capability and infrastructure for customising services; however, customisation of services is still to be done by the organisation as per customers' requirements.	The organisation has maintained the required infrastructure and capability for customising services. It adopted the concept of self service by which customers will be partially or fully authorised to use the required infrastructure and resources and customise services as per their own preferences and needs. In addition, the concept of service co-creation has greatly implemented by the organisation.

Seeing with the eyes of another, listening with the ears of another, and feeling with the heart of another.

Alfred Adler

Chapter 16: Customer Care

Introduction

In today's competitive landscape, senior executives at retail organisations find themselves increasingly under pressure protect their brand, and continuously maximise their customers' to lifetime value. "Know your customer" has been a mantra in the business context for the past several decades, and businesses have started evaluating and segmenting data in order to better understand their customer's likely buying behaviours. Many organisations are rapidly replacing their product-centric programs with strategies centered on the customer experience. They are now focused on enhancing the customer experience to personalise shopping so effectively that it creates an emotional bond with their customer, regardless of the communication channel. Understanding each stage of the customers' life-cycle and recognising the important role that the customer service organisation plays in retaining customers is no longer an option; it is a strategic imperative. By focusing on the causes of consumer behaviour, organisations can make changes that will improve their customer satisfaction and retention rates at each stage of their customers' life-cycle (Sutherland Global Services, 2010).

As depicted in Figure 96 there are several phases for an organisation before it can push a customer up the ladder of satisfaction to the loyalty level, where the customer become also an advocate. For each and every level of satisfaction phases, the organisation should adopt different strategies; however, customer care is the only strategy which will be constant from the first interaction point to the loyalty point. This can be well-fitted within the context of customer experience management. The intensity of customer care shown by an organisation will be different depending on the level of satisfaction and generally it goes up as the customer is getting closer to the loyalty stage; however, once customers become loyal to a business, they have been most likely emotionally attached to the business and hence the intensity of customer care at this stage may decrease. At the loyalty stage, the task for organisations would be to maintain the level of customer care reached rather than improving it further because of the cost issues. Quite rationally, organisations will be more care about their most valuable customers.

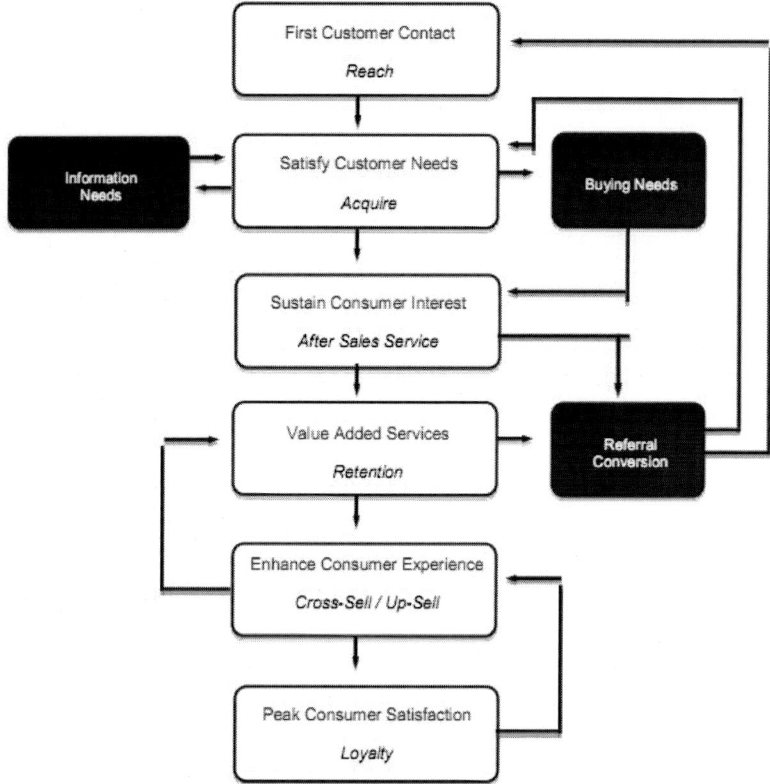

Figure 96: Return on Satisfaction Process
Source (Sutherland Global Services, 2010)

Customer care can be simply defined as 'delivering the best possible service solutions to the customers as per their expectations and then providing comprehensive assurance about post-service delivery support.' This definition, although, seems to be simple to understand but yet complex to implement. It encompasses several parameters and pre-requisites. Customer care is all about showing empathy to the customers i.e. empathy in design of services, delivery of services and also afterward. Customer care is about setting and building the mind-set of customer-centricity in- and out-side of the organisation. It is embedded within the strategy, systems and processes associated with customer experience management of an organisation. It is a mind-set, which an organisation should reflect in everything it does to create a unique customer experience. It means putting customers first always. The outcome of customer care is substantially eyes catching from an organisations' point of view. A true implementation of customer care is a vital element for turning a customer into a loyal one through creating a long-lasting relationship.

Figure 97: Customer Care Management Model

Organisations, in order to successfully deploy customer care strategy should view it as a system and hence they should strive to identify and build its pre-requisites. The customer management model, which is depicted in Figure 97, contains six important enablers of customer care:

1. Strategy, standards and policy;
2. Customer communication;
3. Customer experience management;
4. Customer feedback management;
5. Emotionally attached customers;
6. Service quality.

Customer Care Strategy and Policy

Customer Care is a theme that runs through everything an organisations do; it is at the heart of what it does. A service cannot be seen or touched, only experienced; it is up to all employees of the organisation to provide the personal touch that makes the customer comfortable. A customer care strategy is comprised of three elements:

1. Customer care standards.
2. Customer care skills and knowledge.
3. Customer experience management.

For articulating an effective customer care strategy, it is imperative for an organisation to know exactly what it is trying to achieve and hence set a range of strategic objectives. There might be a range of objectives, which an organisation is trying to achieve from customer care policy. Some of these objectives may include (Harrogate Borough Council, 2006):

- Ensure that services are delivered in a caring and professional way;
- Ensure that staff and members are fully informed about their roles and responsibilities;
- Promote good practice in customer service including service standards;
- Ensure that performance is monitored and that action is taken to address any problems;
- Provide clear guidance on how to deal with customer comments and complaints;

The strategy should truly reflect the following four elements, if it is to provide an organisation with the infrastructure to maintain a high level of Customer Care that is responsive to the experiences that the customers have (North Hertfordshire District Council, 2006):

1. **An effective customer care standards** – Strategy should establish simplified customer care standards that are reviewed regularly to ensure they reflect organisation's Customers' needs. The standards can be used as a framework for all services but should recognise that services may need to set up their own Customer Commitments or Charters to promise to provide their services in a particular way or time period. Customer care should be provided in a professional manner across the organisation by well trained and knowledgeable employees.
2. **Employee training and development** – Strategy should provide the organisation with framework of training and development to continue to build upon the skills our employees have, whilst providing them with access to the latest training, enabling them to deliver excellence in customer care in their jobs. Every employee should give priority to the consideration of the needs of the individual customer, their right to information, to equality of access, to privacy and dignity
3. **Customers' perception evaluation improvement** – Strategy should continue to develop the way in which an organisation evaluates what its customers think of the customer care it delivers.
4. **Customer care standards** - All of the organisations services should consistently seek to attain a defined and published standard of quality and our customers should be informed of their course of redress when these standards are not met.

The main challenges in implementing a customer care strategy may include the following:

- Delivery of new, simplified customer care standards.
- Support the delivery of the customer care standards through best practice in organisation's own service area.s
- Development of an action plan to address the development of customer care for those customers with special needs.
- Development of a portfolio of customer care training for the organisation.

- Development of the organisation's customer care appraisal competencies with the organisational development team.
- Developing the organisation's comments, compliments and complaints system to deliver more management information with the senior managers .
- Development of customer focused consultation with the Best Value team.
- Supporting the establishment of a customer relationship management system through the access to services strategy.
- Project to ensure organisation-wide involvement and adoption of new technology in addition to providing training to promote excellence in customer care.

Source: (North Hertfordshire District Council, 2006)

Best practice example - North Herts District Council Customer Care Strategy

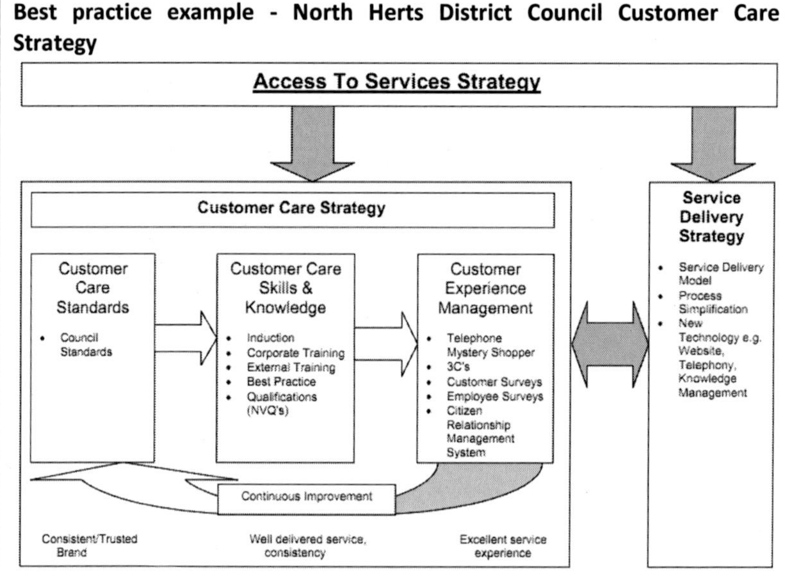

Figure 98: Customer care strategy - A best practice example

Source (North Hertfordshire District Council, 2006)

Figure 98 depicts a best practice example of customer care strategy. Three elements of customer care strategy have been highlighted. The figure shows how customer care strategy has been viewed as a part of the organisation's overall service strategy. This underscores the importance of customer care from senior management's points of view. The fact is that customer care philosophy is a top-down approach, which requires special attention by senior managers in order to be fully understood and effectively implemented throughout the organisation. The figure also demonstrates the link between service delivery strategy and customer care strategy.

The following are some of the best practices for organisations to be able to effectively play their role in delivering a great customer care (Harrogate Borough Council, 2006):

- Give customer care a high organisation priority.
- Develop organisation values and practices on customer care which are shared across the organisation and communicated effectively.
- Set out the good practice necessary to achieve those values in a way that supports a devolved management culture.
- Encourage all employees to optimise their use of existing resources in delivering services and customer care.
- Provide additional resources, where necessary, to supplement the resources provided by individual services in the development and delivery of customer care.
- Provide customer care training for all of its employees.
- Update information to all its employees to add to their knowledge and awareness of customers and their care.
- Regularly monitor its customer care strategy to ensure that the needs of all its customers are met successfully.
- Provide a clear, accessible process for any customer to comment or complain about any aspect of the organisation's service.

The next important aspect of customer care strategy is to establish clear guidelines and procedures for dealing with customers queries. Procedures might be established in different forms and styles depending on the strategic objectives of the organisation from the deployment of customer care strategy. Employees should be well informed about procedures and guidelines and they should be given adequate training for implementing the procedures so that they can deliver great customer care. Some of the most common procedures are customer contact procedure, customer complaints and complements procedures etc. Procedures contain certain guidelines for handing customers' enquiries in specific areas. They will tell employees what to do in specific circumstances and hence they remove confusion. They clearly define roles and responsibilities so that the accountability of individuals will be maintained.

Case study - Swedish airline, SAS

The 1980s was the turnaround of the Swedish airline, SAS. Following a disastrous year when SAS made a loss of $8 million, the organisation promoted a young marketing executive, Jan Carlzon, to the position of president. Just 18 months later, the airline achieved a gross profit of $71 million. While competitors had concentrated on cutting costs in an effort to reduce their losses, Carlzon had focused on customer care. He started by identifying the airline's most important customers — business flyers. He then asked them what would make them want to fly with SAS, rather than a competitor. The answer was loud and clear. They wanted punctual flights. Carlzon put a monitor on his desk, showing the take-off and landing of every SAS flight, around the world. He personally phoned pilots to find the reasons for any delays. Suddenly, SAS flights became extremely punctual and new customers started queuing up

Source (BHP Information Solutions Ltd., 2011)

Customer Care Standards

Standards are an organisation's values that will create satisfied customers, internally and externally. The standards are designed to establish a consistency in output whilst ensuring that the organisation can be responsive to the individual needs and wants of the customer at the time. This is often reliant on the level of care shown by the employee. The organisation should therefore aim to standardise the skills and knowledge that sit behind the service delivery process. The organisation should ensure that these standards are continually reviewed based on customers' feedback so that customer care excellence is maintained through continuous improvement. Organisations should apply customer care standards to all of their services. However the customer care standards should provide a framework that allows individual services to make additional commitments to their customers about the way in which they will deliver their service. By setting and meeting customer care standards customers are more likely to hold the values organisations want them to have in dealings with them (North Hertfordshire District Council, 2006).

Ideally, customer care standards should be in-line with service excellence standards. The aim of the standards is to make customers the focus of service provision. There are five criterions for customer care standards. The following table comprises of these criterions.

Criterions	Action items
Customer Insight	• Have in depth understanding of current and potential customer segments based on current and reliable information. • Develop insight about organisation's customer segments to better understand their needs and preferences via a variety of ways eg: customer feedback surveys. • Identify hard-to-reach and disadvantaged segments and individuals and have developed services in response to their specific needs. • Engages and involves customers using a range of methods appropriate to the needs of the identified groups. • Make customer consultation integral to continual service improvement. • Review strategies and opportunities to engage customers regularly to ensure the methods used are effective and provide reliable representative results. • Uses reliable and accurate methods to measure customer satisfaction on a regular basis. • Analyse and publicise satisfaction levels to the full range of customers about all main areas of service and how they have been improved as a result of feedback. • Sets challenging and stretching targets for customer service to ensure levels are improving. • Makes positive changes as a result of customer feedback analysis improving the customer journey.
Customer-focused culture	• Put customers at the heart of service delivery. • Uses customer insight to inform policy and strategy to prioritise service improvement activity. • Establish policies and procedures that support the rights

Criterions	Action items
	of customers to expect excellent levels of service. • Treat all customer segments fairly and equally. • Maintain the privacy and dignity of all customers. • Actively encourage employees to promote and engage in the customer-focused culture of the organisation. • Put customer-focused service delivery as a priority at all levels of the organisation. • Demonstrate how customer feedback is incorporated into internal processes, policy development and service planning. • Value, recognise and celebrate customer- focused services.
Information and Access	• Make the information of the full range of services and contact details that readily available to customers. • Make all communication to customer is available and appropriate for their needs and understanding. • Ensure all information to customer is current, accurate and complete and provided in a variety of medium. • Ensure services are accessible to customer through a provision of a range of alternative channels. • Review accessibility regularly. Ensure customer feedback will identify possible service improvements and offer better choices. • Interacts and supports the wider community.
Service Delivery	• Keep customers informed about performance. • Ensure customers, partners and employees are consulted and involved in reviewing and raising local standards. • Inform customers what they can expect from organisation's services. • Develop services utilising customer feedback, best practice and benchmarking against similar organisations. • Maintain an easy-to-use complaints procedure which includes a commitment to deal with problems fully and solve them wherever possible within a reasonable time limit. • Provide training and guidance on how to handle complaints. • Ensure that the outcome of the complaints procedure for customers (whose complaint is upheld) is satisfactory.

Criterions	Action items
Timeliness and Quality of Service	• Set appropriate and measurable standards for timeliness of response for all forms of customer contact including phone calls, letters, e-communications and personal callers. • Make information available about the promises on timeliness and quality of customer care service their customers can expect. • Share good customer service practice with colleagues and partners. • Keep customers informed of wait times and any problems. • Monitor performance against standards for timeliness and quality of customer care service and take action if problems are identified. • Publicise and benchmark performance against customer care service.

Table 16: Customer Care Standards - Five Criterions
Adapted from (Portsmouth Hospitals NHS Trust, 2009)

Customer Care Charter

While customer-care standards are a set of values that explain how an organisation treat its customers, customer-care charter explains what organisation's customer-care standards are and what services, customers can expect from the organisation. A customer-care charter may be defined as a public document that sets out basic information on the services provided, the standards of services and customer care that customers can expect from an organisation, and how to make complaints or suggestion for improvement. A customer care charter is formed from different elements. Some of them are:

- **Vision statement** – A statement expressing the long-term vision of customer care;
- **Mission statement** – A statement explaining the purpose of the organisation from providing customer care as an important principle of the whole business;
- **Core values** – A statement or a list of the values that the organisation believes in and which will tell the customers how they will be dealt with by the public service providers;

- **List of the services** – A comprehensive list of services offered by the customer;
- **Customer care standards** – The level of quality of the services that the organisation will deliver to the customers;
- **Advice to customers** – Advice on the steps customers may need to take before they come to the offices for service or before they avail the provided services;
- **Feedback from customers** – Information on how customers can provide the organisation feedback on the quality of services provided;
- **Complaints** – Information to customers on how they can register complaints and the assurance that the complaints will be dealt with confidentially and promptly;
- **Annual reports** – Information to customers that an annual report on the performance of the organisation will be published, and when & how can they access those reports;
- **Contact points** – Information to customers on official address, telephone numbers, web site and internet address etc.

Adapted: (Caribbean Centre for Development Administration, 2004)

A world class service delivery requires that there is a continuous cycle of improvement built around the stated principles and core values of a typical public service.

• **Core principles**	• **Core values**
○ Principle of equality of treatment ○ Principles of neutrality ○ Principle of legality ○ Principle of continuity	○ Accountability ○ Honesty ○ Impartiality ○ Loyalty ○ Integrity ○ Justice ○ Objectivity ○ Selflessness ○ Transparency ○ Excellence

Source: (The Secretary for Public Sector Reforms Management, 2009)

A Checklist – For developing and reviewing a customer-care charter

1. ***Customer-care charter commitment and consultation***
   - Has commitment from management been obtained for the development of the service charter?
   - Has the organisation's purpose been identified in preparing a service charter?
   - Do staff understand what the service charter means to the organisation's business?
   - Have customers, staff and other key stakeholders been consulted during development of the service charter?
2. ***Customer-care charter coverage***
   - Does the service charter state who the organisation's customers are?
   - Has the service charter covered how organisation staff will treat their customers?
   - Does the charter state the services it covers, including those delivered directly to the public, those that are delivered indirectly on behalf of the organisation, and those that are not delivered directly by the organisation, but nevertheless have an impact on the community?
   - Is it clear to customers that the charter covers all of the organisation's overall operations or only certain programs or services for which the organisation is responsible?
   - Should there be more than one charter from the same organisation designed to cover specific customer groups or services?
   - Does the organisation provide online communication strategies and online service delivery?
   - Does the charter cover the specific needs of organisation in rural and regional locations?
3. ***Customer-care charter format***
   - Are the language, format and presentation of the charter understandable, readable and accessible to the organisation's customers, including those with specific needs?
   - Is there more than one version of the charter to suit the needs of customers with particular communication needs?
4. ***Customer-care standards***
   - Are the standards within the service charter measurable (quantifiable) or qualitative?
   - Are the service standards set to encourage improvement in the organisation's performance?
   - Does the service charter set out customers' rights and

responsibilities?

5. ***Complaints handling***
   - Does the service charter state the organisation's complaints handling procedures and encourage customer feedback?
   - Does the organisation have accessible internal complaints handling procedures in place?
   - Does the service charter provide contact details for external dispute handling mechanisms?
6. ***Monitoring and review***
   - Does the charter state the organisation's monitoring and internal review procedures?
   - Does the charter articulate an external review process to measure performance against the service charter standards?
   - Do the monitoring and review procedures provide avenues for participation by customers, staff and other key stakeholders?
   - Has the organisation developed reporting and accountability procedures, including, for example, publication of the Service charter's performance in its annual report?
   - Has a review date been set for the charter?
   - Is the charter consistent with the overall value system of the organisation?
7. ***Service charter promotion***
   - Has the organisation developed procedures to ensure the promotion of the charter, and its availability?
   - Has the organisation considered a broad range of marketing methods so that staffs, stakeholders and customers will all know what the charter is and where to find it?

Source: (Commonwealth of Australia, 2000)

Customer Communication

A communication strategy is the first thing which an organisation should have in place if it is to provide its customers with a good customer care. This is often used to establish and manage on-going communication throughout the customer journey. There is a strong link between how well- informed customers about the organisational services and how satisfied they are overall. Good communication leads to better reputation and stronger relationships with stakeholders. This also helps organisations prove that they are delivering good services that offer value for money. To communicate effectively any issue an organisation need to carefully answer the following questions:

- What is the organisations message?
- Who is the target audience for organisations message?
- What does the organisation's audience know and think now?
- What does the organisation would like them to know, think, and do? If the organisation wants its audience to take action, what action are you asking them to take. If organisation's message focuses on taking action, it should also ask:
    - What are the perceived barriers that prevent the target audience from taking action?
    - What are the perceived benefits they would receive if they changed their behaviour?
    - Why is it in the best interest of the target audience to take action?
    - How can the barriers be lowered and the benefits increased?
    - What is the target audience doing instead of the preferred action?
    - What are the benefits they feel that they would be giving up?
- How can the organisation get its message across to its audience?
- Another way to think about communications is to ask these three questions:
    - How do we get people to think about our services?
    - How do we get them to think about our services in such a way that they want to solve them through public policies as well as individual actions?
    - How do we get them to think about services in such a way that they want to solve them through the specific policies and actions we support?

To gather people's views about the service they receive, organisations have to make it clear that they want to know what users think, they are listening and they want to learn from feedback. In order to make sure that customers will notice organisation's message first time, all of communication channels need to work together to give a consistent message in a consistent tone (Figure 99).

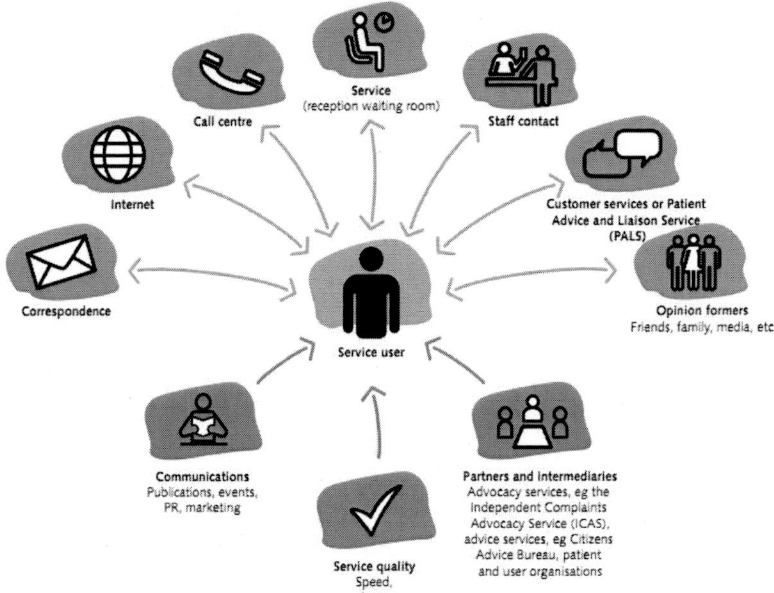

Figure 99: Ways of reaching out customers

Source (DH Department of Health, 2009)

The following is a check list which can be used for a health check of the communication system within an organisation. It should be noted that the following checklist can be developed further and it just conveys the message that an organisation should regularly assess the effectiveness of its communication system in order to make sure that it receives customers' view on the quality of services and their experiences regularly.

Checklist – communication system

- Is the organisation good at letting people know it is listening and want to know what they think?
- When someone first makes contact with organisation's service, does the organisation explain how they can offer feedback or complain?
- Does the organisation regularly ask people who use its services about their experiences of the care the organisation provides?
- If anyone working in the organisation's service was asked about organisation's complaints process, would they be able to explain the basic system and tell the service user where they could get more information and support?
- Is the information the organisation provides accessible to all the people who use its services?
- Is it clear to everyone working in the organisation's service, and the people who use it, what changes the organisation have made in light of ideas or comments it has received?
- Has the organisation ever run, or been part of, a campaign to get people to give their views?
- Does the organisation use other sources of information about people's experiences to help improve service such as surveys and consultations?

Source (DH Department of Health, 2009)

Customer Experience Management

Customer experience encompasses every aspect of an organisations offering - the quality of customer care particularly is important in shaping customer experience. Customer experience is the internal and subjective response customers have to any direct or indirect contact with an organisation. The objective of customer experience management is to capture and distribute what a customer thinks about an organisation and it has to be measured at points of customer interaction: "touch points". CEM helps an organisation to locates places to add offerings in the gaps between expectations and experience (harvard Business review, 2007). Achieving excellence in the delivery and management of customers' experiences requires a focus upon insight, interaction and improvement, each of which is enabled by organisational capabilities and competencies. Together, they reside on an enterprise framework and are guided by a strong customer orientation to form a closed-loop system. As depicted by model in Figure 100, if an organisation is to provide excellent customer care, it should consider the entire customer life-cycle. The organisation should be capable of distinguishing different phases of customer journey and rightly undertake suitable customer care strategies at each different phase. It is a continuous improvement cycle, which provides an opportunity for an organisation to continually improve its customer care and consequently to improve its customer experience maturity level (Figure 101). This require maintaining a great customer insight, interacting with customers effectively (i.e. personalising services), and then optimising customer services through learning from customers' feedback.

Figure 100: The Customer-Centric Service Delivery Model

Source (SAS Institute Inc, 2009)

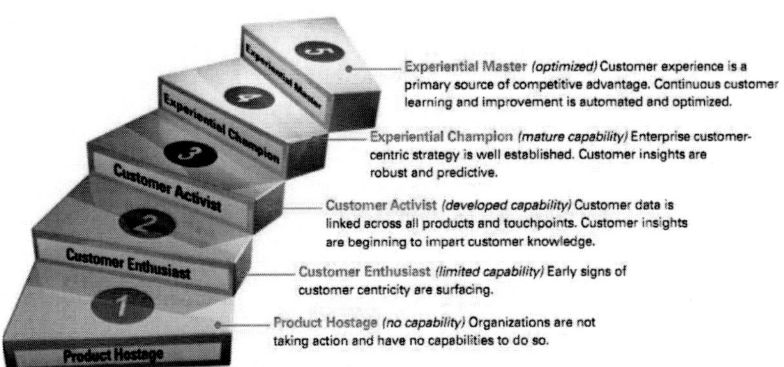

Figure 101: Customer Experience Maturity Model

Source (SAS Institute Inc, 2009)

There are a set of fundamental truths about how customer experience operates. Figure 101 contains the five laws of customer experience and their implications for organisations:

Laws	Implications
Every interaction creates a personal reaction	• Experiences need to be designed for individuals; • Customer segments must be prioritised; • Customer feedback needs to be the key metric; • Employees need to be empowered.
People are instinctively self-cantered	• Asking: "Would our target customers fully understand this?" • Don't sell things, help customers buy them; • Let any front-line employee that needs to explain to a customer how your company is organised.
Customer familiarity breeds alignment	• Don't wait for organisational alignment. use a clear focus on customer needs as a way to align the decisions and actions of individuals; • Broadly share customer insight; • Talk about customer needs, not personal preferences,
Unengaged employees don't create engaged customers	• Don't under-spend on employees training; • Make it easy to do the right thing. Enabling; technologies need to be designed for employees to easily accomplish tasks that help customers; • Develop a robust communications plan that not only tells employees what the organisation is doing, but also

Laws	Implications
	explains why it is doing it; • If employees do things that help customers, then find a way to celebrate those actions; • Measure employee engagement,
Employees do what is measured, incentivised, and celebrated	• Don't "expect" people to do the right thing. So make an explicit intervention on behalf of customer experience i.e. measure employees performance, celebrate achievements and good works etc. get consistent behaviours from employees when all three levers (measurements, incentives, and celebrations) are working together; • Clearly define good behaviour,

Table 17: Five laws of customer experience

Source: (Temkin B., 2008)

Customer Feedback Management

Customer feedback is data from customers about their perceptions and experiences as an organisation's customer. Any customer centric organisation views this as a critical customer engagement touch point; hence it becomes vital for the organisation to encourage the customers to provide the feedbacks (both bouquets and brickbats). Active soliciting of the feedback will result in rich and relevant customer intelligence that will drive the continuous improvement and organisational service delivery excellence agenda forward. The suitability of the feedback channels and the audit of the overall customer complaint (and feedback) system will constitute the bulk of the course. In order to close the strategy planning, development and deployment loop for service excellence, it is also necessary that the customer feedback management system becomes an integral part of the Performance Management System of the organisation. The concept of customer feedback management is entirely built upon communication with customers. For an effective customer feedback management, organisations require a good communication strategy, wide range of communication channels and full senior management commitment. Table 18 provides some useful definitions in relation to customer feedback management.

Terms	Definitions
Feedback	"Customer (and employee) feedback provides the foundation upon which successful organisations are built. It delivers strategic guidance and actionable insights that enable companies to improve marketing and customer service, to deliver better customer experiences, to develop and refine their services over time, and to profitably grow the business." Jeff Zabin – Analyst, Aberdeen Group
Feedback Management	Feedback Management is both a discipline and a set of techniques, processes, metrics and tools for systematically collecting feedback, and systematically and effectively acting on the feedback - putting it to work to help achieve the organisations strategic and tactical business objectives.
Feedback Management Maturity	The degree to which an organisation is effectively practicing the discipline of Feedback Management and realising the associated benefits. Like many other disciplines, Feedback Management capabilities and practices typically progress through stages on the way to full realisation.

Table 18: Terms and definitions of CFM

Source: (customer centricity Inc, 2011)

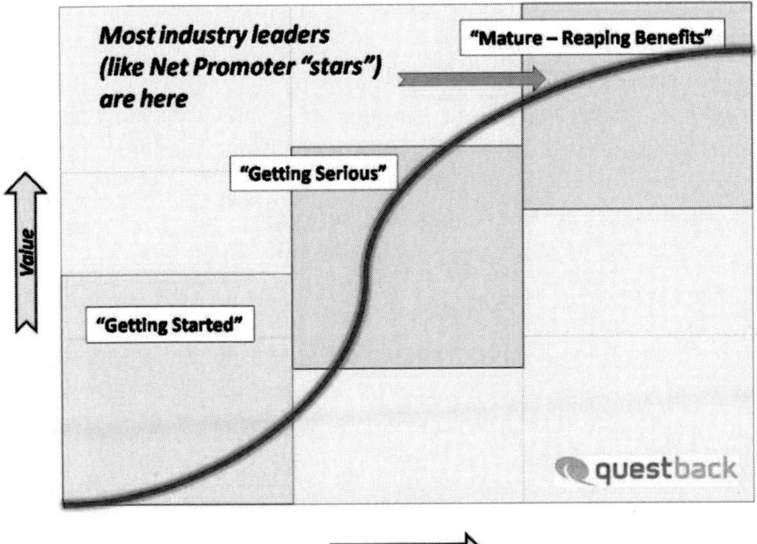

Figure 102: The Feedback Management Maturity Curve

Source (customer centricity Inc, 2011)

From the definitions provided by Table 18, it is quite clear that having an effective customer feedback management with a high maturity level in place is vital for an organisation if it is to provide a great customer care (Figure 102). High maturity level for a feedback management is imperative because it is just at the highest level that an organisation can fully realise the benefits of its feedback management for improving its customer care.

The following are some of the implications from the concept of feedback management maturity curve:

1. It's a journey for any organisation to attain feedback management maturity.
2. There are some recognisable stages on the way.
3. As with people, different firms embrace the journey with different approaches.

The above implications might require further elaboration, but the curve has been introduced here only to showing that at which maturity level, the benefits of CFM is to be fully reaped.

Complaints system as a part of customer feedback management system should be checked to ensure that it is relevant and works properly. There are three simple steps towards an excellent customer care through incorporating customer feedback into the service provision management system.

1. Listening to customers' enquiries carefully.
2. Responding to customers' needs promptly and effectively.
3. Improving continually.

This is a continuous improvement cycle, that if implemented with extra care, it leads to a great customer care. The approach doesn't encourage undertaking big changes, rather it promotes incremental improvement of services driven by customers' feedback. The approach is based on the following practice: 'Organisations will be encouraged to ask people what they think of their care, to sort out problems more effectively and to use the opportunities to learn.' This approach allows an organisation and the person complaining to agree on the best way to get a satisfactory outcome. People, who use services, whatever their background or circumstances, should find it easier to tell what they think or make a complaint. The new system will also encourage services to learn from individual complaints and improve as a result.

Do's and Don'ts for handling a complaint

- *Do's - Handling a complaint*
  - Give your name;
  - Take the person who complains seriously;
  - Tell the person what will happen next and the stages of the procedure;
  - Act quickly once the complainant has left;
  - Get their details, e.g. Names, addresses, telephone numbers, dates
  - Listen, get the facts and make notes;
  - Stay calm even if the person gets angry;
  - Be sympathetic and honest;
  - Whenever, possible use the telephone instead of a letter.
- *Don'ts - Handling a complaint*
  - Argue with the complainant;
  - Get into a blame conversation;
  - Accept abuse from a complainant, e. g. Swearing;
  - Deter people from making a complaint (asking them not do it, to do it in writing, in person or coming back later);
  - Consider the complaint as a personal criticism;
  - Use jargon when writing back to the complainant.

Making Customers Emotionally Attached

A number of factors have been discovered by researchers that lead customers to become emotionally attached to an organisation. Hasskett (2002) developed a loyalty model, where the highest level of loyalty is one where the customer feels that he is not just a part of the organisation, but is the owner. The idea is to make customers think that they are not only a part of community, but also can influence an organisation's strategies, or are owners of the organisation. Ownership is a powerful factor which has been successfully used in increasing loyalty among the internal customer of an organisation. Creating a sense of ownership for an organisation is not an easy task since it requires a genuine customer empowerment. Showing great customer care can be reflected in authorising and enabling customers to make a greater contribution in service delivery. Customers who can relate to an organisation will tend to be more emotionally attached. Organisations need to create ways in which customers can relate to them. The ways include things such as a common history, shared value, interests, cultures and beliefs.

Employees can play an important role in creating emotionally attached customers. Since employees are in direct contact with customers, they can highly influence on organisations' image from customers' perspectives. Customers who have a strong emotional attachment toward employees will have a stronger overall relationship with the organisation and will tend to be more loyal. In light of these facts employees become even more important for service firms because of the central role they play in developing emotional attachment. Organisations should love their customers (Roberts, 2004). Organisations need to design their services to leave space for the love factor, which consists of 'empathy, compassion, emotion, involvement, sense of humour, tacit knowledge and intuition'.

Service Quality

An organisational culture incorporating customer care as its central tenet and involving efforts to understand the needs of customers enables the organisation to provide quality services that satisfy the identified customer needs. Service quality is an important factor in making customers' mind about the level of customer care provided by an organisation because customer experience is about how the organisation is experienced in every channel and at every interaction.

As depicted by Figure 103, there are a range of quality criteria which might have a direct impact on customer experience. In a pull system of service delivery, service quality is defined and measured from customers' point of view. Hence, it is imperative for an organisation to fully understand the exchange of value over the customer journey is a key to success if it is to show a great customer care and consequently, creating a unique customer experience. What the exchange of value means is to clearly understand:

1. Customer value expectation – This derives from customer wants and needs, previous experiences, company communication and word-of-mouth.
2. Service value proposition – An organisation's strategy in terms of unique mix of product, price, place, service and image.
3. Customer value perception - This is the customer evaluation of the interaction with the organisation through channels.
4. An organisation more or less might be able to measure the above three areas; however, there is one more, which is most likely to be hidden from the organisation's sight and this is also difficult to be measured by the organisation itself.
5. Value Realisation - This consists in the outcome (in terms of market share, wallet share and profitability) of relationship between company and customer.

The last one is probably the most challenging one to be identified, measured and managed. Organisations should effectively and clearly measure the gap, which might exist between these four and then develop and deploy a proper strategy to close these gaps.

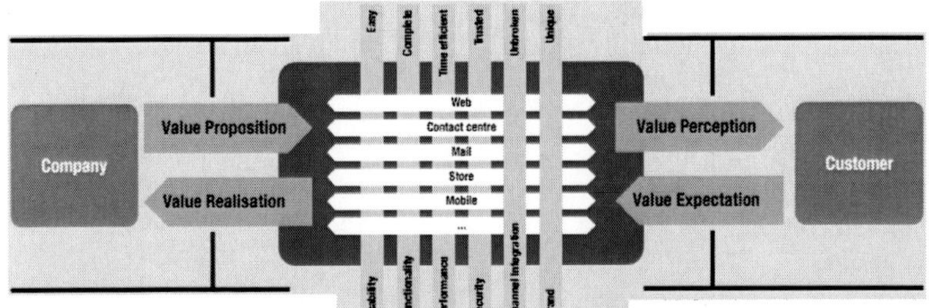

Figure 103: Service Quality - Exchange of Value

Source (IBM, 2005)

Assessment Toolkit: Care

The Culture of Organisation

Q1. To what extent does the culture of the organisation promote customer care?			
Basic	**Developing**	**Maturing**	**Leading**
The organisation has particular focus on financial performance and does not see customer care as an important management area to focus upon.	The organisation, to a limited extent, supports customer care programs and initiatives so it has delivered some of these programs occasionally in order to increase the level of customer care.	The organisation has held an effective customer care system including clear processes, procedures. Individuals are encouraged to show customer care at their works. Post sales service is effectively implemented.	The organisation distinctly recognises and highly rewards caring individuals about customers. It links performance appraisals, incentives and rewards to individuals' level of customer care.

Q2. Does the organisation maintain the required strategy, policy and procedures for delivering an excellent customer care?			
Basic	**Developing**	**Maturing**	**Leading**
The organisation has articulated its strategy to meet its financial expected returns so customer care is given less priority.	The organisation has a set of objectives, which can be effectively achieved through delivering customer care; however, it lacks the support from its policies and procedures.	The organisation has a clear set of strategic objectives in relation to customer care and an effective strategy for achieving those objectives in place. It has established clear policies with regards to customer care,	The organisation has articulated its overall strategy in such a way that to reflect a great customer care. So every policy and procedures are designed while keeping customers' needs on mind. The organisation's intention for

	There is misalignment can be observed.	which are fully communicated with customers and understood by employees.	delivering a great customer care can be traced at the strategy management level of the organisation i.e. vision and mission statement etc.
Q3. How often does the organisation deliver training programs for enabling its employees to deliver an excellent customer care?			
Basic	**Developing**	**Maturing**	**Leading**
Since the organisation does not see a great value in showing customer care, it does delivery very limited or none training programs for enabling its employees in this relation.	The organisation occasionally provides training programs for its employees to enable them in delivering a great customer care and it also constantly conveys the message about the value customer care throughout the organisation.	The organisation has constantly provides employees with a range of training programs in relation to customer care and it also constantly conveys the message about the value customer care throughout the organisation.	The organisation has constantly provides employees with a range of training programs in relation to customer care. Training programs is customised to meet specific needs of individuals performing in different positions within the organisation. .It also constantly conveys the message about the value customer care throughout the organisation.

Communication and Consultation with Customers

Q1. To what extent does the organisation communicate with its customers and seek their feedbacks?			
Basic	**Developing**	**Maturing**	**Leading**
The organisation rarely uses a one way communication channel for giving information about services. it uses limited number of communication tools such as leaflets etc.	The organisation uses different types of communication tools for giving information about its services, it occasionally seeks customers feedback with regards to the level of after sales service. The communication tools can be as wide as printing materials to media.	The organisation uses two ways of communication channels for constantly giving information about and seeking feedback from its customers about the quality of post-delivery customer services.	The organisation always measures the gap that might exist between customers' expectations of and customers' perceptions about post-delivery customer services. There is a wide range of communication channel available for customers to communicate with the organisation. Communication channels are personalised based on the targeted customers.
Q2. What percentage of service improvement is driven by customers' feedback? (Customers' feedback can be considered with some other factors to drive an improvement initiative)			
Basic	**Developing**	**Maturing**	**Leading**
Equal to or less than 10%	Between 11% to 35%	Between 36% to 65%	Between 66% to 100%

Q3. Does the organisation develop a customer complaints management?			
Basic	**Developing**	**Maturing**	**Leading**
The organisation does not have a clear complaints management system in place. So customers are not provided with a clear guidance about how to make a complaint.	The organisation has a system in place for registering customers' complains and also customers are ,at a basic level, guided about how to make a complaint; although, the system is to further improve i.e. customers are not notified about their complaints later on, the results of the complaint etc.	The organisation has a clear customer complaint management system in place which is well communicated with customers. Roles and responsibilities for handling customers' complaints are clearly determined. Customers are issued with sufficient guidelines about how to make complaints. Customers are notified about further action, which is to be taken on their complaints.	The organisation has advanced its customer complaints management system one step further from the maturing phase by compensating for customers' bad experiences. The compensation policy has been jointly developed by customers and the organisation. Other system's qualities are considered to be as same as what customers can expect from a mature complaints management system.

Customer Service Support

Q1. Does the organisation develop service quality measurement and management system?			
Basic	**Developing**	**Maturing**	**Leading**
The organisation has considered the quality of services from its own	The organisation focuses on quality aspects such as service easy to access, user friendly	The organisation focuses on quality aspects such as responsiveness, reliability, service convenient, which	The organisation focuses on quality aspects such as service uniqueness,

perspective.	and availability, which does not really lead to inspiring customers.	can create a positive and significant impact on customers.	customer care, empathy, service excellence, service partnership etc, which can inspire customers.
Q2. Does the organisation maintain customer experience management system?			
Basic	**Developing**	**Maturing**	**Leading**
There is no clear strategy for managing customer experiences.	The organisation has spotted the importance of customer experience management in and undertaken few initiatives in order to improve in this area.	The organisation has a well-developed system for managing customer experiences in place.	The organisation has indicated CEM as one area which is strategically important for its growth and hence there is clear objectives, strategy, capability and system in place with regards to CEM.
Q3. To what extent does the organisation engage customers in the process of post-service delivery?			
Basic	**Developing**	**Maturing**	**Leading**
The organisation does not really give enough value to post-delivery services.	The organisation has a limited and rigid work procedures and policies for handling post-service delivery enquires.	The organisation quite often consults with customers with regards to post-service delivery and seeks further improvement.	The organisation directly involves customers in the process of service delivery including post-service delivery.

Most people do not listen with the intent to understand; they listen with the intent to reply. They're either speaking or preparing to speak. They're filtering everything through their own paradigms, reading their autobiography into other people's lives.

Stephen Cove

Chapter 17: Impression

Introduction

Organisations' impression on customers' mindsets forms an imperative part of organisations' strategies. The impression, which customers get from businesses, can be well described by the strengths of organisations' brands. It is no longer a hidden fact that branding is an effective strategy for organisations if they are to succeed in a fast-paced and highly competitive business environment where customers' preferences and needs are constantly changing. Since organisations started to realise the value of brands, they view brands as not only a tool for measuring customers' loyalty but also a strategy for creating customers' mindsets.

Building and properly managing brand equity has become essential for any business organisations. Customer-based brand equity is a valuable tool in brand positioning and evaluating their marketing strategy. Necessary feedback can be obtained from consumers for this evaluation will aid in: identifying service or product related problems; identifying advertising/positioning problems; and also providing feedback to the employees on where improvements need to be made. Customer-based brand equity scale gives service industry managers a structured approach for formulating their branding strategies. Strong brand increase trust in services, enabling customers to better visualise and understand them (Ahmad & Hashim, 2011).

Any organisation can benefit enormously by creating a brand that presents the organisation as distinctive, trusted, exciting, reliable or whichever attributes are appropriate to that business. In different industry sectors the audiences, competitors, delivery and service aspects of branding may differ, but the basic principle of being clear about what an organisation stand for always applies.

The following three basic reasons, which explain why an organisation should focus on branding strategies as a way of impacting on customers' mindset (Design Council, 2011):

1. **Creating difference** - Branding is a way of clearly highlighting what makes organisation's offer different to, and more desirable than, anyone else's. Effective branding elevates a service or organisation from being just one commodity amongst many identical commodities, to become something with a unique character and promise. It can create an emotional character in the minds of consumers who choose products and services using both emotional and pragmatic judgements.
2. **Adding value** - People are generally willing to pay more for a branded service or product than they are for something which is largely unbranded. And a brand can be extended through a whole range of offers too.
3. **Connecting with people** - Creating a connection with people is important for all organisations and a brand can embody attributes which consumers will feel drawn to.

Case Study – Harley Davidson

The Harley Davidson transformation began with a company that was suffering. In the 10 years to 1983, Harley's market share of the 850 CC plus motorcycle category had dropped from 80% to 23%. The company was haemorrhaging cash and profits. Staff were demoralised. The culture and environment was toxic. Involvement, empowerment and alignment was the secret of success.

The organisation has conducted a multiple-phase strategy includes the following phases:

1. The rationalisation and tough command and control management.
2. The Integrated Marketing, which depends first on uniting everyone around a collective vision of value that connects to the identity and purpose of the organisation/brand. This depends on a profound and shared understanding of customers and an organisation that can deliver value seamlessly throughout all customer experiences across the relationship. This also means connecting and matching spiritual with practical qualities: vision, purpose, values with information, processes, and systems.

The organisation, in order to strengthen its brand, focuses on the following activities:

1. Creates a culture supports the values expressed in the brand.
2. The culture encourages people to release their creative potential.
3. Practices ensure shared learning across the organisation.
4. Ensure that customer management in the organisation focuses on customers over their lifetime.
5. Ensure that treating customers in ways appropriate to them.
6. Ensure that brand recognises individual customers wherever they interact or do business, even when it is appropriate.
7. Ensure that there is a profound shared knowledge of key customer groups.
8. Ensure that quality information about customers for all who need it is provided.

The organisation has transformed its operation from a push system into a pull system where the entire activity chain has been driven by customer demands. Harley-Davidson developed what they call a circle organisation of three overlapping elements concerned with creating demand; producing products and providing after sales support (see the following figure). A leadership and strategy council (LSC) at the centre has members nominated from these circles.

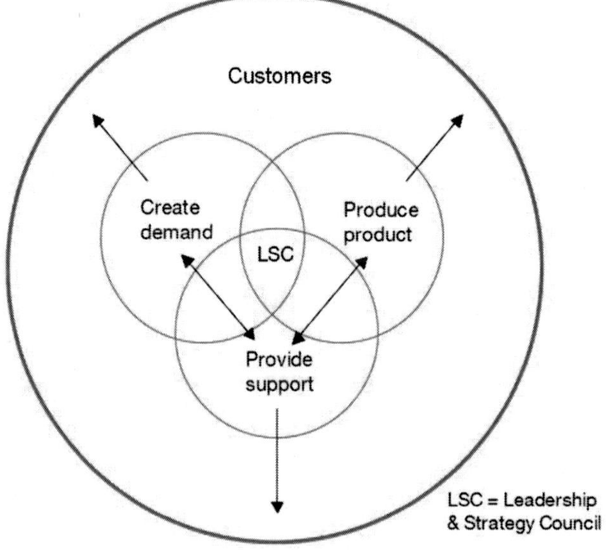

Figure 104: Harley-Davidson Circle organisation

The organisation has constantly ensured that quality is understood to be what is good for the customer, employee and organisation. The organisation successfully implemented an holistic discipline that inspires coherent and creative organisation, culture and customer experience alignment around fundamental truths of the brand to deliver value to customers, employees and the organisation.

Source (Jenkinson, 2005)

Branding in Public Sector

Although all branding is about communicating a clear offer to your customers or users, branding in the public sector is not necessarily as concerned with maximum market stand-out, as it typically is in the commercial/private sector. For public sector organisations, such as the police force and health services, the focus may be on clarity and access to important information. So branding and design may focus on signposting this information or communicating issues clearly in order to change people's behaviour. Clarity can sometimes fall foul of the complex nature of public sector services, which are often run by a network of stakeholder organisations or partners.

In branding terms, putting the logos of all such partners on customer-facing communications can lead to visual clutter, a lack of clarity and confusion. It's important, therefore, to be clear when a brand or branded campaign is needed and to ensure that its identity is distinct and clear for users. Whilst most organisations are providing a service of one type or another, for some businesses customer service is the dominant part of the offer. For these organisations particular attention needs to be paid to how the brand (the big idea and all its components) are reflected in the way the service is provided and the way staff interact with customers.

In essence, service brands are built on the people who deliver them. This means that staff needed to be trained to get an understanding of the organisation's culture, its 'promise' to customers and how they will be put into practice on a day to day basis. In this scenario, the human resources department is closely linked to brand management (Design Council, 2011).

Case let – First Direct: service

First Direct was the first organisation to bring a 24-hour banking service to the market and its level of service was a key message in promoting the bank to potential customers.

To ensure the delivery of high quality service, First Direct recruits people with customer service skills rather than those who are already in the banking industry. This ensures that the organisation's service delivery matches is brand 'promise'.

Source (Design Council, 2011)

Brand Identification

Building a strong brand has been shown to provide numerous financial rewards to organisations, and has become a top priority for many organisations. With true brand quality, customers express a high degree of loyalty to the brand such that they actively seek means to interact with the brand and share their experiences with others. The challenge in building a strong brand is to ensuring that customers have the right type of experiences with services so that the desired thoughts, feelings, images, beliefs, perceptions, opinions and soon become linked to the brand. There are four questions that customers invariably ask about brands. Figure 105 and Figure 106 well depict these questions, brand pyramid and its breakdown. The brand pyramid entails six brand-building blocks (Keller, 2001).

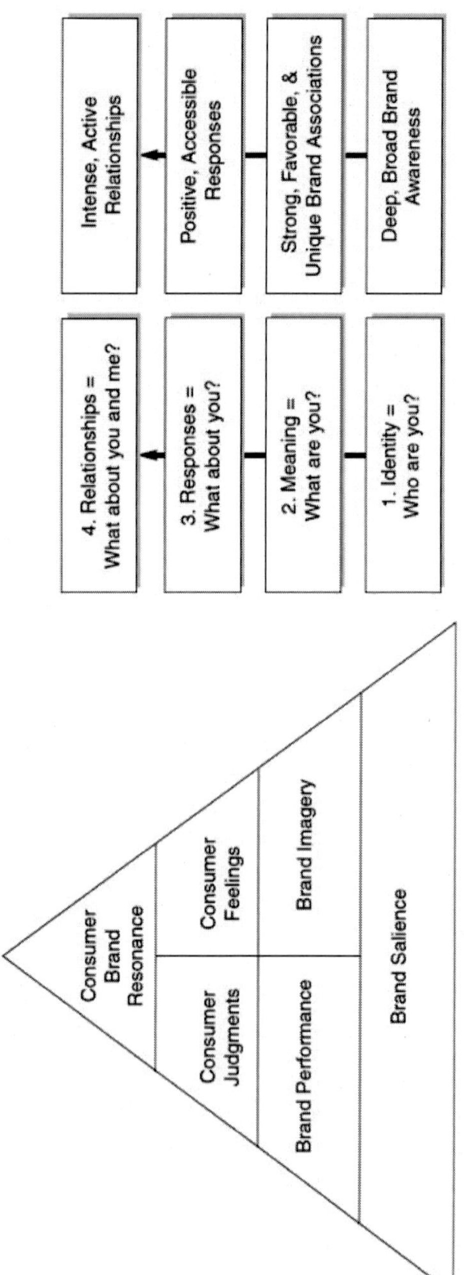

Figure 105: Customer-Focus Brand Equity Pyramid

Source (Keller, 2001)

Figure 106: Sub-dimensions of Brand-Building Blocks

Source (Keller, 2001)

Description of the Brand Pyramid

1. **Brand Salience –** This relates to the aspect of customer awareness of the brand. Brand awareness refers to customers' ability to recall or recognise a brand. Questions such as:
   a. How easily and often is the brand evoked under various situations?
   b. To what extent is the brand top-of-mind and easily recalled or recognised?
   c. What types of reminders are necessary?
   d. How pervasive is brand awareness?
2. **Brand Performance -** The service itself is at the heart of brand equity, as it is the primary influence of what customers experience with a brand, what they hear about a brand from others, and what the organisation can tell customers about the brand in their communications. To create brand loyalty customers' experiences with the service must at least meet, if not actually surpass, their expectations. They are five important types of attributes and benefits that often underlie brand performance:
   a. Service empathy, efficiency and effectiveness;
   b. Primary characteristics and secondary features;
   c. Service reliability and durability;
   d. Style and design;
   e. Price.

3. **Brand Imagery** – This entails the extrinsic properties of the service, including the ways in which the brand attempts to meet customers' psychological or social needs.
4. **Customer Judgments** - This focus upon customers' personal opinions and evaluations with regard to the brand. There are four types of customers judgments:
   a. Service quality;
   b. Service credibility;
   c. Service consideration;
   d. Service superiority.
5. **Customers' Feelings** – This is customers' emotional responses and reactions with respect to the brand. There are six important types of brand-building feelings:
   a. Warmth – The extent to which the brand makes customers feel a sense of calm or peacefulness.
   b. Fun – The extent to which the brand creates the feeling of light-hearted, cheerful, joyous and so on.
   c. Excitement – The extent to which the brand makes customers feel that they are energised and are experiencing something special.
   d. Security – The extent to which the brand creates a feeling of safety, comfort, and self-assurance for the customers.
   e. Social approval – This occurs when the brand results in customers' feeling positively about reactions of others to them; that is when customers feel that others look favourably on their appearance, and behaviour and so forth.
   f. Self-respect – Self respect occurs when the brand makes customers feel better about themselves.
6. **Brand Resonance** – This refers to the nature of the relationship that customers have with the brand. This characterised in terms of intensity or the depth of the psychological bond that customers have with the brand as well as the level of actively engendered y this loyalty (e.g. repeat purchase, etc.). This can be broken down into four categories:
   a. Behavioural loyalty – This entails the extent to which customers repeat purchases or service orders and the amount, or share, of category volume attributed to the brand.

For the bottom line profit results, the brand must generate sufficient frequencies and volumes.

b. Attitudinal attachment – This includes personal attachment of customers to the brand. Customers must go beyond simply having a positive attitude to view the brand as being something special in a broader context.
c. Sense of community – Identification with a brand community may reflect an important social phenomenon whereby customers feel a kinship or affiliation with other people associated with the brand.
d. Active engagement – This reflects the strongest affiliation of brand loyalty when customers are willing to invest time, energy, money, or other resources into the brand beyond those expended during purchases or consumption of the brand.

Source (Keller, 2001)

Measuring Service Impression

The cautious validation of the brand value's psychological facets constitutes the core of the *brand potential index*. In accordance with the relevant literature on brand value measuring this index measures a brand's potential in 10 facets (Figure 107).

Figure 107: Brand Potential Index

Source (Hupp & Henrik, 2002)

In comprehensive empirical quality assessment surveys conducted for fast moving customer goods, service, and customer goods brands, it turned out that these ten facets truly measure the brand attractiveness (compare Hupp 2000).

Unlocking Customer Advocacy

Customer advocacy is a result of deep and extremely positive impression of services from a customers' point of view. The need for a Customer Advocacy function typically results from the reality that a lot of people at a firm affect the customer experience and the perception that a customer has of the organisation (Bailey & Jensen, 2006).

If organisations are not aware of customers' attitudes toward their businesses – and the impact these perceptions have on financial performance – they may be counting on organic growth that simply will not materialise. But by identifying which customers are advocates, apathetic and antagonists, organisations can more precisely target customer experience improvement initiatives based on a more informed understanding of customer preferences and future value.

To boost the bottom line, we believe banks must increase focus on customer attitude. In order for organisations to fully achieve the benefits from organic growth, executives need to understand customer attitude and its impact on customer behaviour. Customers who have a positive attitude toward the organisation are advocates, while those whose experiences shape negative opinions become antagonists. As such, a bank's ability to effectively manage and influence customer attitude becomes paramount to achieving organic growth.

Organisations continue to explore how to create more meaningful customer experiences to enhance their customers' opinions of their organisation. Based on the IBM study, a new approach has been developed for delivering customer experiences – one that enhances customers' perceptions and builds a competitively superior experience, while prioritising resources and investments. IBM calls organisations that excel in the customer experience arena "customer focused enterprises". Figure 108 depicts six characteristics of a customer focused organisation:

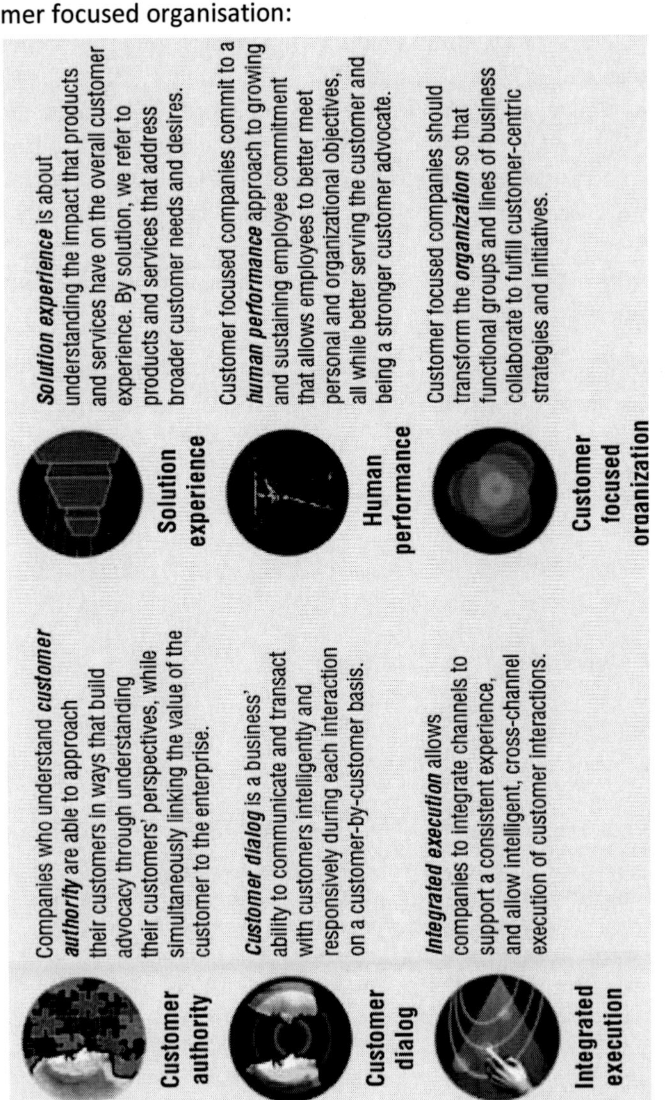

Figure 108: The six characteristics of a customer focused enterprise

Source (IBM, 2006)

The foremost consideration executives need to accept is that improving customer attitude must start at the top. A mindset shift is required, beginning with executive management. Organisations that are successful at building long-lasting relationships with customers typically have charismatic leaders who inspire ongoing innovation and passion for the customer. Consider some extreme examples: Howard Shultz at Starbucks, Richard Branson at Virgin or the late Steve Jobs at Apple. Each of these leaders developed a passionate brand, and motivated their teams to live the brand though every customer interaction.

Case study – Retail Banking - Can a focus on improving advocacy unlock growth potential?

With an understanding of the critical drivers of customer attitude and the economic potential associated with improving those factors, banks *can* begin to position the organisation to realise organic growth potential. IBM study shows that advocates, on average, hold 14 percent more products than antagonistic customers, and the profitability of products held by advocates is 21 percent higher (Figure 109).

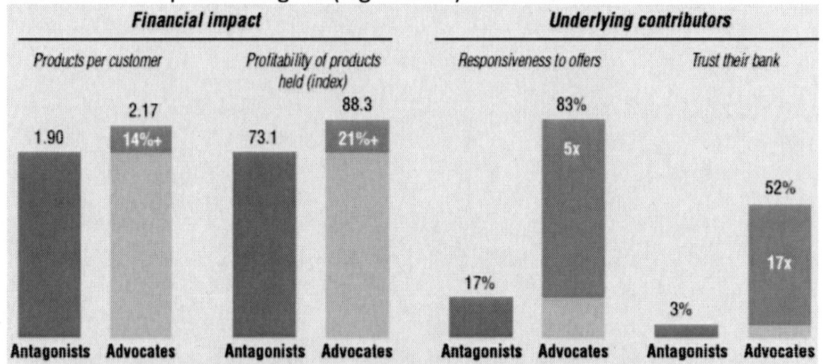

Figure 109: Banks have the potential to unlock significant value by proactively growing their share of advocates

Banks evaluate ways to better manage their customer base. IBM did find significant differences in how each group of, advocate and antagonistic customers, felt about the bank. Advocates of banks gave their bank credit for doing "everything right," while antagonists found fault in almost everything their bank did. Clearly, customers who take on an advocate posture are attune to the actions of their bank and are open, willing and positive toward interactions. Whereas, antagonists are shut off from communications and don't give their bank credit for even fundamental attributes of a bank's delivery system (Figure 110)

	Antagonists *Percent who agree*		Advocates *Percent who agree*	
Larger gap ↑	5%	Bank values my business	73%	
	12%	Employees listen and follow-up	69%	
	16%	Provides consistent knowledge across interactions	73%	
Find fault with "everything" their bank does	11%	Resolves issues fairly	64%	Give the bank credit for doing "everything" right
	23%	Proactively corrects errors	75%	
	41%	Provides me with plenty of ways to bank	90%	
	6%	Provides relevant offers	52%	
	29%	Bank uses the information it already received	68%	
Smaller gap ↓	16%	Bank understands my financial goals	53%	

Figure 110: Banks rarely account for the extreme gap in attitude of their customer base

Source (IBM, 2006)

Building Service Mindset

Service mindset is an unwavering focus on the customer. It is a demonstrable understanding of the customer's needs, wants and expectations. It's an obsessive desire to satisfy customers. Service mind-set creates the total impression of services on customers' minds. It challenges employees to look at the world from the customer's point of view. An organisation, which has a service mindset constantly, conveys the message about positive customer interactions rather than negative. A service mindset enables an organisation to view negative customer interactions as opportunities to learn even more about customers' needs and expectations. It helps an organisation to see things from the customers' perspectives. In an organisation with a service mindset, every function is defined, designed and established with customer in mind. In order to build a service mindset, an organisation requires following simple steps (Smikle, 2002):

1. Measure regularly - Gather regular feedback from customers.
2. Measure internally – While measuring customers' satisfaction, measure employees satisfaction as well.

3. Link – Link bonus plans to measures of customer satisfaction. That kind of bottom-line approach makes everyone take notice of customer satisfaction.
4. Communicate service standards - Build dialogue in the organisation about acceptable levels of service.
5. Strategise for service - Create a strategy and plan for customer satisfaction. Link customer satisfaction goals with other business imperatives.

The primary part of a service mindset is to understand the service quality from a customers' point of view and how a customer judges the quality of a service?

Basically, there are five dimensions that influence customers' assessment of service quality:

1. **Empathy –** The provision of responsive, individualise attention to customers.
2. **Responsiveness –** The willingness to help customers and to provide prompt service.
3. **Assurance –** The knowledge and courtesy of employees and their ability to convey trust and confidence.
4. **Reliability –** The ability to perform the promised service dependably and accurately.
5. **Tangibles –** The appearance of physical facilities, equipment, personnel, and communications materials.

Personnel

An important factor in building service mindset and creating a one-lasting impact on customers' mind is the required infrastructure, particularly, employees' capabilities. Customers interact with employees regularly, so all employees must be aware of, and actively involved in creating service quality, great customer care and unique customer experience. Organisations should create a 'do it right' culture. It should be noted that without the buy-in of employees, it is impossible to achieve a truly customer-focused service quality (Tikkanen-Bradley Consulting Group, 2007).

Service Recovery

Excellent service recovery plan and strategy can generate a deep and positive impact on customers. Winning organisations see service failure as an opportunity to impress customers with an exceptional service recovery and complaints handling. Organisations that provide excellent service recovery have an opportunity to differentiate themselves. The essence of excellent service recovery is good communication and empowering the employee to assess and respond to the service failure. Strong service recovery has a significant impression on customer perception partly because customers pay more attention when things go wrong. Table 19 contains the keys to an excellent service recovery process (Tikkanen-Bradley Consulting Group, 2007):

Steps	***Requirements***
Identify service problems	1. Monitor customer complaints- an effective complaints handling system has two aspects: • Promote internal action to resolve the complaints it receives • Promote external action to apologise to complaining customers, acknowledge the organisation's awareness of the situation, and inform the customer of the situation being taken to resolve the problem. 2. Conduct customer research – seeking complaints demonstrates genuine interest and concern on part of the organisation, and most of the customers are happy to provide their opinion. 3. Monitor service process – proactively anticipate and identify problems before customer experience them.
Resolve problems effectively (people factors)	1. Prepare employees for recovery – providing sufficient training on how to deliver an excellent customer service 2. Empower employees – authorising employees to satisfy customer complaints on the spot. 3. Facilitate employees – providing technology and information for employees to resolve problems effectively. 4. Reward employees – establishing appropriate rewards to persuade employees to excel in problem resolution.

Steps	***Requirements***
Learn from the recovery experience	1. Conduct root-cause analysis – discovering and correcting the underlying problem to prevent future problems 2. Modify service-process monitoring – designing a proactive strategy to identify potential flaws and to suggest changes to service procedures. 3. Set up problem tracking system – identifying opportunities for improving service reliability.

Table 19: Excellent Service Recovery Process
Adapted from (Tikkanen-Bradley Consulting Group, 2007)

Assessment Toolkit: Impression

Service Quality

Q1. To what extent does the organisation consider and measure service quality dimensions?			
Basic	**Developing**	**Maturing**	**Leading**
There is very limited number of service quality attributes considered by the organisation. They mostly include the quality attributes from the organisation's perspectives such as efficiency and effectiveness.	There is a range of service quality dimensions considered by the organisations. The measures include those dimensions which the organisation perceive that they are important to customers such as price, value for money, easy to access and user friendly etc.	The organisation focuses on those service quality dimensions which are required for building customers' trust and confidence such as responsiveness, consistency, continuity etc.	The organisation considers and measures a comprehensive set of service dimensions; although it has a particular focus on those dimensions which helps in building customers loyalty, advocacy and intimacy such as service empathy, service convenient, uniqueness etc.
Q2. Does the organisation maintain a service recovery strategy?			
Basic	**Developing**	**Maturing**	**Leading**
The organisation does not have a clear strategy or a plan for service recovery.	The organisation already realised the importance of service recovery plan in building customers' trust so it has maintained a service recovery	The organisation maintains a clear service recovery plan and strategy. Roles and responsibilities for recovering service failures are clearly defined.	The organisation maintains an effective service recovery strategy, which is quite suitable in handling complex situations for example: when the organisation

	plan, which is only effective in handling service failures at a basic level. For example: it acknowledges service failures; however, it does not provides customers with subsequent actions for rectifying failures.		is facing an unexpected high service demands. The strategy is subjected to a continuous review. It records learning experiences from service failures and use them for future improvements.
Q3. To what extent does the organisation measure the quality of customer experiences?			
Basic	**Developing**	**Maturing**	**Leading**
The organisation does not seek customers' experiences once the services are delivered. It does simply rely on the rate of service failures.	The organisation measures customers experiences based on the number of service complaints and complements. Customers' feedback is occasionally collected.	The organisation constantly seeks customers' feedback about the organisation's services. It has a system in place not only for handling customers' complaints but also for reflecting learning experiences from complaints into the system for future improvements.	The organisation adopted customers experience and journey mapping so that it measures customers experiences at different touch points.

Brand Equity

Q1. In measuring the discrepancy between customer expectations and their perceptions of the service delivered, where the gap or gaps exist?			
Basic	**Developing**	**Maturing**	**Leading**
There are gaps such as: • Customers' expectations versus management perceptions • Management perceptions versus service specifications • Service specifications versus service delivery • Service delivery versus external communication	The following are gaps identified: • Customers' expectations versus management perceptions • Management perceptions versus service specifications	Customer expectation is very close to their perceptions of the service delivered	Customers are delighted because of high quality of services, which is beyond of their expectations.
Q2. Does the organisation maintain a clear brand strategy?			
Basic	**Developing**	**Maturing**	**Leading**
The organisation does not have a clear brand strategy. It does strive to build brand salience.	The organisation strives to build brand imagery and brand performance.	Theo organisation has a clear brand strategy in place for measuring customers' emotional responses and reactions as well as their personal opinions and evaluations	The organisation has an effective brand strategy, which is characterised in terms of intensity or the depth of the psychological bond that customers have with the organisation.

Q3. Does the organisation measure the depth of impression created by its services?			
Basic	**Developing**	**Maturing**	**Leading**
The organisation only measures quality of services and brand awareness as two factors for measuring the depth of service impression.	The organisation uses acceptance of premium pricing, service quality and brand awareness, buying intention and brand identification as main factors for measuring the depth of service impression.	The organisation uses confidence in brand, brand loyalty, willingness to recommend brand in addition to what have been used by a typical developing organisation.	The organisation uses a Brand Potential Index including all of its parameters from brand awareness to brand loyalty, to empathy with brand to uniqueness to etc.

Service Mindset

Q1. Does the organisation develop a customer-centric culture?			
Basic	**Developing**	**Maturing**	**Leading**
The organisation has a focus on internal requirements and what is good for itself.	The organisation has maintained basic requirements for developing a culture of customer-centricity, which includes clear communication channels for interacting with customers; however, the organisation lacks advanced requirements such as customer empowerment.	The organisation has sufficiently empowered employees for dealing with customers' enquires. Rewards and recognition system has been specifically designed to encourage individuals for putting customers at the heart of everything.	The organisation has not only sufficiently empowered its employees to deal with customers enquiries but also empowered customers to actively contribute in the decision making process. Customers are placed at the heart of everything.

Q2. To what extent is the organisation capable of customising services?			
Basic	**Developing**	**Maturing**	**Leading**
The organisation has not the required capability and infrastructure for customising services. There is no clarity about customers segments. Push system has been adopted.	The organisation has clearly determined different customer segments; however, it fails to provide adjust services in accordance with their needs.	The organisation has effective adjusted services in accordance with customers' needs in different segments.	The organisation has adopted self service so that customers are enabled to personalise services as per their own wishes. There is lot of flexibility and adoptability in delivering services.
Q3. To what extent do employees' attitudes support the creation of service impression on customers' minds?			
Basic	**Developing**	**Maturing**	**Leading**
Employees are encouraged to focus on efficiency and cost saving so they give less emphasis on the impact generated by the quality of services on customers' mind.	The organisation has encouraged employees to focus on the quality of services provided to customers; however, emphasis is on those quality parameters which can bring an immediate return for the organisation.	Employees are fully aware of the quality of services on customers' mindset. They are encouraged to see things from customers' point of view.	Employees' efforts, creativity and innovative thinking in creating a positive service impression on customers will be distinctly recognised and highly rewarded. Employees have a positive attitude towards customers and are fully committed to delivering unique experiences.

Man who know little say much.
Man who know much say little.

Unknown

Chapter 18: Innovation

Introduction

While we are trying to improve our quality of life new technologies are revolutionising the way we learn, work and play. Technologies in agriculture are increasing crop yields while minimising the need to spray herbicides and insecticides on our foods and into our environment. Pharmaceutical and biotechnology organisations are coming up with new cures and treatments that help us live longer and healthier lives. Advances in health care have increased life expectancies, while technology used at CAT scans and MRIs make surgery safer, less invasive and more accurate. New computational power has given us the keys to our genetic code, transformed the global economy, and opened a universe of business and community service opportunities. High speed data networks offer great potential to increase productivity, promote and economic growth. Innovation is a key ingredient and driver of competitiveness in the modern economy.

The understanding of innovation as a key driver to competitiveness has its roots in the works of Schumpeter, who described market dynamics as a process of creative destruction. Later he developed further this concept, referring to it as a process of "creative accumulation". In this later model, organisations have different capacity to accumulate technological capabilities and to generate innovation. The accumulated technological competencies are the key determinants and drivers of organisation innovation and competitiveness.

Innovation is a pre-requisite for any successful organisation. That does not necessarily mean product/service innovation – many leading organisations achieve success according to how they run their organisations, not by inventing a better product or service. To achieve success over a long period of time, all organisations need to embrace innovation. Porter believes that it is at the Innovation Driven Stage in which competitive advantage is gained through "the ability to produce innovative products and services at the global technology frontier using the most advanced methods". Research confirms that innovative organisations – those that are able to use innovation to improve their processes or to differentiate their products and services – outperform their competitors, measured in terms of market share, profitability, growth or market capitalisation. This demonstrates that innovation can enhance competitiveness, but it requires a different set of management knowledge and skills.

Success in business today demands constant innovation. Generating fresh solutions to problems and the ability to inherit new products or services for a changing market are part of the intellectual capital market that gives an enterprise its competitive edge. In a dynamic environment, success comes from looking for the next opportunity and having the ability to find hidden connections and insights into new products or services.

The term innovation comes from the Latin word "innovare", which means "to renew or change". Today innovation management is seen as "the creation and capture of new value in new ways". If necessity is the mother of invention, invention is the mother of innovation. Joseph Schumpeter, the Austrian economist who was the first to place innovation at the centre of economic activity, saw innovation as a three stage process:

- Invention – the demonstration of a new idea
- Innovation – its first commercial application
- Diffusion – the spreading of the technology or process through the market.

Subsequent accounts of the innovation process are not so linear, and highlight complex feedback mechanisms between different stages. However, whatever the model used, the basic point remains that innovation is a process which contains many phases, and will therefore draw on a range of different skills, usually provided by a range of people and institutions, even if the original idea comes from one individual.

If innovation is more than just invention, then it is also about much more than just physical technologies. As we are currently in an era defined by innovation in information and communications technology, the popular idea of an 'innovation' might be a new device like an iPad or a 3G phone. However, innovations are constantly happening in all areas of the economy and society, including services (think of Amazon, EasyJet or Ocado, all new services made possible by the internet), cultural products and movements, business models, management practices and institutions. Source: (Lent & Lockwood, 2010)

Innovation and the related management concepts have developed and evolved significantly over the past 25 years. These six management concepts are the ground-breaking shifts in the field of innovation and that have fundamentally changed the way the organisations aim to deliver value to their customers. Table 20 highlights the innovation concepts of a particular zeitgeist and the related questions that should be asked by business leaders.

Innovation Concepts	**Descriptions**	**Pertinent Questions**
1986: Stage-gate product development	• Winning at new products calls not only for the selection of the "right" ideas and products but also for the effective and efficient management of the product development process all the way to launch. • The model divides a new product development project into discrete and identifiable stages, each preceded by a gate that serves as a go-or-kill decision point. • It promotes effectiveness and efficiency; effectiveness as each gate specifies a set of deliverables and a list of criteria enabling informed decision-making and efficiency as each stage consist of a set of prescribed, multifunctional and parallel activities.	How often do we fail to kill a project sufficiently early, before resources and investments have run out?

Innovation Concepts	**Descriptions**	**Pertinent Questions**
1991: Strategic R&D portfolio management	• The main focus here was to align the overall R&D portfolio with the business strategy and ensure balance in terms of risk, reward and time-to-completion. • The leaders have to not only address the question of how to decide which technologies to invest in, but also take into account the question of how to manage and exploit them for maximum commercial benefit.	How can we justify our R&D investment to investors and secure a strong competitive position for the future?
1991: Lean product development	• Lean product development sets out to reduce waste and lead times by adhering to a set of development principles and a specific way of thinking, supported by tools for efficient problem-solving, communication and other tasks. • The lean tools such as set-based concurrent engineering, the chief engineer, value stream mapping and visual planning became prevalent.	How much time and effort do we waste due to needless iterations in our new product development process?
1995: Disruptive innovation	• The launch of new technologies and products in the hitherto disregarded small market segment, which are then improved until they eventually outperform the established technologies and products. • The key here was that the technology in itself may not be radically new, but technology was used by disruptive innovators to offer customers radically improved performance on hitherto neglected product attributes.	How has a hitherto insignificant player surprised us again and grabbed a leading share in this growth market?
1997: Business model innovation	• It emanates from the need of an organisation to rejuvenate systematically the way it does business as disruptive innovations threaten its position. • It is not only about the products or services offered by the organisation, but	How can we turn the economics of a business upside down and enter a market cosily

Innovation Concepts	Descriptions	Pertinent Questions
	the focus area now shifts to the way an organisation does business inherently. • It is about the modification and alignment of the four distinct components - the customer value proposition, the profit formula, key resources and key processes – in order to find new market segments and optimise performance.	carved up by the incumbents?
2003: Open innovation	• The paradigm now shifts towards "the use of purposive inflows and outflows of knowledge to accelerate internal innovation, and expand the markets for external use of innovation, respectively." • The value creation now goes one notch higher from the concept of user innovation to the concept of focusing on value capture and finding the most appropriate business model for commercialising a new offering.	Should we keep our innovation secrets to ourselves or should we create an open platform to accelerate growth?

Table 20: Evolution of innovation management concepts

Source: (Roos & Anemo, 2011)

In the 21st century, organisations are aggressively seeking innovation in order to achieve unexpected values through organisational performance enhancement. Organisations not only build innovation as a core competency but also strive to make it a distinctive capability in order to survive in highly dynamic and competitive business environment. Innovation can be categorised into three different types:

1. Product innovations,
2. Service innovations, and
3. Organisational (procedural or process) innovations

Types of Innovation in the Public Sector

Innovation in the public sector can be divided into several types, for instance:

- A new or improved service (for example health care at home)
- Process innovation (change in the manufacturing of a service or product)
- Administrative innovation (for example the use of a new policy instrument, which may be a result of policy change)
- System innovation (a new system or a fundamental change of an existing system, for instance by the establishment of new organisations or new patterns of co-operation and interaction)
- Conceptual innovation (a change in the outlook of actors; such changes are accompanied by the use of new concepts, for example integrated water management or mobility leasing)
- Radical change of rationality (meaning that the world view or the mental matrix of the employees of an organisation is shifting)

The first two types of innovation can be subsumed under product/service innovation. The innovations can be labelled in the following ways:

- Incremental innovations—radical innovations (denoting the degree of novelty, in industry most innovations can be considered incremental improvements of already existing products, processes or services)
- Top-down innovations—bottom-up innovations (denoting who has initiated the process leading to behavioural changes, "the top" – meaning management or organisations or institutions higher up in the hierarchy – or "the bottom" – meaning "workers on the factory floor", in this case public employees, civil servants and mid-level policy makers)
- Needs-led innovations and efficiency-led innovation (denoting whether innovation process has been initiated to solve a specific problem or to make already existing products, services or procedures more efficient)

Levels of Innovation

- Incremental, i.e. minor changes to existing services/processes
- Radical, i.e. new services or ways of "doing things" in relation to the process or service delivery
- Transformative/Systemic, i.e. new workforce structures, organisational types, and inter-organisational relationships
- Sustaining, i.e. organisations move on an established trajectory by improving performance of existing services/systems
- Discontinuous/Disruptive, i.e. new performance trajectory by introducing new performance dimensions, new services and processes, etc.

Source: (Koch & Hauknes, 2005) (IDeA Knowledge, 2005)

In any organisation, there are certain areas required to be probed prior to innovation:

- Value, culture and leadership
- Business processes, financial, business models and networks
- Market and industry structure
- Technologies, performance, value and context
- Finally and yet important, the competition

To build an innovation platform, the organisation should ensure that it has sufficient amount of information available before it actually starts to articulate a vision or initiate a process. Information needs to be collected in relation to the following areas:

- Strategic locations for driving innovation within the organisation
- The level of senior management engagement
- Visionary mission statement that support innovation with a strong link
- The type of processes applied by the organisation for product/service development as well as deliver mechanism
- Customers insight through customer segmentation
- Organisation's technological capabilities
- Potential pitfalls, stumbling blocks, and barriers for organisational innovation
- Intellectual property rights, rules and regulations which might limit future innovation

Philosophy of Innovation

Micro-managing the process of innovation has been found to be fraught with danger as it may be perceived as a stifling force, not a facilitating force. Certain organisations are better than others at consistently using innovation to achieve high performance and generate profitable growth while continuing to support existing businesses. What do they do differently? One thing is for sure. They don't use a one-size fits all approach. The business leaders agree that there is no magic solution. Rather, the overwhelming majority has been towards a two-staged approach:

1. The business leaders identify the critical constraints within their organisations that compromise innovation, and then
2. They work actively towards relieving the most significant bottlenecks in their existing processes by employing one of a set of approaches.

Source: (Accenture , 2006)

So from a leader's perspective who is trying to pursue excellence by unleashing the full potential of innovation, the key is to identify the root causes of the failures to innovate and intervene specifically to remove the blockages. To overcome the constraints on innovation, leaders have to embrace one of the philosophies as depicted in Figure 111. An in-depth understanding of these philosophies will enable the leaders to weigh the different options and take the approach that is best suited for the specific context.

Building from the previous discussion, Figure 112 depicts the seven innovation philosophy, the stages of innovation and specific constraints that may be expected in those stages. This matrix can be used by leaders to figure out which innovation philosophy is best suited depending on the stage of the life-cycle of innovation. This will ideally equip the senior management team the tool to overcome specific obstacles encountered at each stage of the innovation process.

	Philosophy	Core belief	Related thinking
Organization-based philosophies	Top management-led	Speed to market and overall business effectiveness are improved when senior executives use their power and resources to lead innovation initiatives	*Blue Ocean Strategy*, Kim and Mauborgne
	Internally networked	Innovation flourishes when better linkages across teams and parts of the organization provide greater access to organization resources (e.g., skills, processes, customer channels and funding)	*Medici Effect*, Johansson; *How Breakthroughs Happen*, Hargadon
	Distributed	Innovation opportunities are maximized when responsibility for innovation is driven down into the components of the organization, and ultimately to each individual employee	*The Innovator's Solution*, Raynor and Christensen; *Weird Ideas That Work*, Sutton
Value chain-based philosophies	Supplier-driven	Suppliers are a very important but relatively undervalued and untapped source of rapid, low-cost innovation	"Innovation Sourcing Strategy Matters," *MIT Sloan Management Review*, Linder, Jarvenpaa and Davenport
	Partner-intensive	Innovation processes yield better results when they are opened to external organizations that act as partners in the end results	*Open Innovation*, Chesbrough
	Competitor-driven	Enviable business returns can be achieved by innovating on what first-to-market competitors provide, versus taking the lead	*Fast Second*, Markides and Geroski
	Customer-driven	The most profitable innovation is driven by a close connection to customers that provides a deep understanding of their true wants and needs	*Democratizing Innovation*, Von Hippel; *The Future of Competition: Co-Creating Unique Value With Customers*, Prahalad and Ramaswamy

Figure 111: Seven Philosophies of Innovation

Source: (Accenture , 2006)

Stage of innovation	Specific constraint	Innovation philosophy						
		Top management-led	Distributed	Internally networked	Supplier-driven	Partner-intensive	Competitor-driven	Customer-driven
Ideation	Too few ideas		✓	✓	✓	✓		✓
	Ideas have too little potential value	✓		✓				✓
	Ideas are for things customers don't want or need		✓	✓	✓		✓	✓
Selection	Not able to select the best ideas to pursue	✓						✓
	Timing wrong; either too early or too late							✓
	Too many initiatives get through screen	✓					✓	
	Too few initiatives get through screen		✓			✓	✓	
Development	Can't afford to fully develop ideas				✓	✓		✓
	Quit too soon; lack the will to complete tough projects	✓	✓	✓				✓
	Don't have enough capability (talent and processes) to develop ideas			✓	✓	✓		
	Have good ideas, but competitors come to market first				✓	✓		
Commer-cialization	Customer adoption rates are poor	✓			✓		✓	✓
	Organizational design inhibits effective execution	✓		✓			✓	✓
	Lack credibility in target marketplaces	✓				✓		✓
Cycle-wide	Nature of innovation changing in specific industry; not well positioned	✓	✓			✓		✓
	Don't have enough growth in current domains	✓				✓		✓
	Idea-to-profit cycle too slow	✓	✓	✓	✓	✓	✓	✓

Figure 112: Breaking the constraints on innovation

Source: (Accenture , 2006)

Culture of Innovation

Innovation, by the nature of the beast, is a risky proposition. The risk here is in terms of the expected failures but the lack of having a systemic approach to foster and facilitate innovation poses a greater risk of organisational existence and survival. Because of this inherent conflict, employees in the innovation culture cannot abdicate their responsibility or the need to share some of the risk of innovation. They need to be duly supported by the policies and practices within the organisation. The organisation shares some of the risks and so do the employees with their managers. An innovator never sets out to fail, but certain extent of failure is inevitable. Hence, the culture within the organisation should be one of supportive, rather than of the blame type. Employees should strive for success, but at the same time learn from failures by documenting them and hearing from others about them. In this regard, self-confidence, self-reliance and trust play a hugely important role in the success of information and the sharing of information.

The core process of innovation culture has been depicted in Figure 113. It highlights the systemic and a life-cycle approach to innovation process. It starts from exploring to trying and finally to adopting. New solutions, products and services or even new business processes or strategies are only found through exploration. As new ideas emerge or combine with the existing ideas, the role of innovator is to try them out in a low-risk and low-impact environment. Support system has to be developed around them in order to increase the chances of success and reduce the risk when they are scaled up for full implementation.

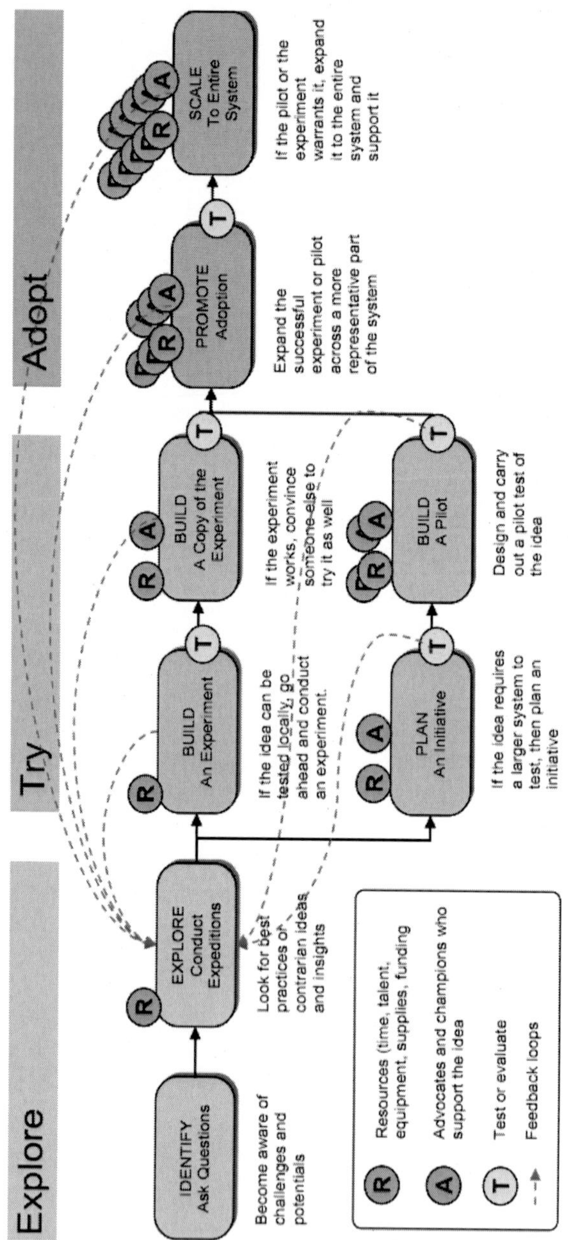

Figure 113: Core process of innovation culture

Source: (Coffman, 2009)

The innovation culture comes to light when people throughout the organisation actively engage in fulfilling three essential roles:

1. Look for insights to develop into ideas, and then into value-adding innovations. This is what innovations creative geniuses do.
2. Support innovation by helping creative people overcome the obstacles that otherwise inevitably impedes their innovation efforts. This is what Innovation Champions do.
3. Define the organisation's expectations and policies to favour innovation. This is what Innovation Leaders do.

Source: (Morris, 2007)

All the three segments of employees when working together in unison will help the organisation in embracing an innovation culture, whose differences with the status quo culture have been, depicted Table 21. Please take cognizance of the fact that the table simplifies many aspects of both cultures, but the purpose here is to just use this for indicative purposes.

Status Quo Culture	**Innovation Culture**
• Predictability • Seek stability • Focus on core competence • High success rate • Reinforce the organisational hierarchy • Fear the hierarchy • Avoid surprises • Focus on inside knowledge • Easy to live with • Corporate politics • Efficiency through standardisation • Extend the status quo • Avoid change • Measure stability • Look for data to confirm existing management models • Look for certainty	• Un-predictability • Seek novelty • Focus on edge competence • High failure rate • Reinforce organisational networks • Focus on creative tension • Embrace surprises • Combine inside and outside knowledge • Hard to live with • Moving the cheese • Efficiency through innovation • Abandon the status quo • Embrace change • Measure innovation • Look for data to contradict existing management models • Embrace ambiguity

Table 21: The innovation culture versus inertia based Culture

Source: (Morris, 2007)

Innovation Myths

Innovation is the new black. In the fast changing and amazingly dynamic world, it is almost a compulsion for organisations to innovate. Innovate or languish forever in mediocrity. But *how* to innovate is a tough question as methods are not as widely known or are as successfully implemented as a lot of other fundamental business activities. It seems magical when it succeeds; however no one sees the hundreds other that had to be discarded or they could not see the light of the day before this idea was actually fructified. This fosters the growth of myths around innovation. To quote a few myths, to be an innovator...

- You have to be a genius (*like Bill Gates*)
- You have to be a charismatic, inspiring leader (*like Steve Jobs*)
- You have to have a lot of resources (*like General Electric*)
- You have to be lucky (*like Post-It inventor Ray Fry*)
- You have to have a special job title (*such as Chief Innovation Officer, or Imaginer*)
- Your innovation has to be secret and proprietary (*like the Stealth Fighter and its "skunk-works"*)
- You have to be in a new field to innovate (*like biotech*)

Source: (Paradis & McGraw, 2007)

The innovativeness level of an organisation can be understood by assessing the organisations on seven main dimensions as depicted in Figure 114. The organisational cultural factors that people experience as enabling or disempowering with regards to innovative thinking are characteristics of a social system, irrespective of industry. The seven dimensions are:

- **Risk Taking** - Leaders in innovative organisations are more interested in learning from failure than in punishing them. It is about establishing an organisational climate where people feel free to try out new ideas. There has to be a balanced assessment of risks in light of the benefits out of innovation. Too much risk taking is also bad; but care ought to be taken that over-estimation of risks does not nip the bud of innovation.
- **Resources** - People ought to understand that they have the "resource" of authority and autonomy to act on innovative ideas. Care is to be practised to ensure that concrete resources are

present to avoid the people from feeling demoralised due to the lack of money and time.

- **Knowledge** - Broad-based knowledge is the fuel for innovation. Information should be widely gathered, easily accessible, rapidly transmitted and honestly communicated.
- **Goals** - Leaders can signal that innovation is highly desirable if they set aspirational goals in specific areas and challenge others to find ways to realise the vision. Linking these to strategic priorities further signals the importance of the call for innovation.
- **Rewards** - Rewards for innovation are symbols and rituals whose main purpose is to recognise innovative behaviour. This demonstrates how much value the organisation associates with the process of innovation that helps the organisation to achieve its strategic goals. The most successful rewards and recognition system debunks the idea of one-size-fits all and are instead based on what appeals to people's intrinsic and individualised motivation.
- **Tools** - Leaders need to consider how they build the capability and capacity of the people and the organisation at large. It is naive to believe that just having the right culture & climate will result in innovative products/services.
- **Relationships** - Innovative ideas are rarely the product/service of a lone sole. Hence, it is important to understand the patterns of interaction between people in the organisation or system. Ideas generally evolve over time and are often a product/service of multiple interactions with others that fuel the process.

Source: (HM Government - Department for Business Innovation & Skills, 2009)

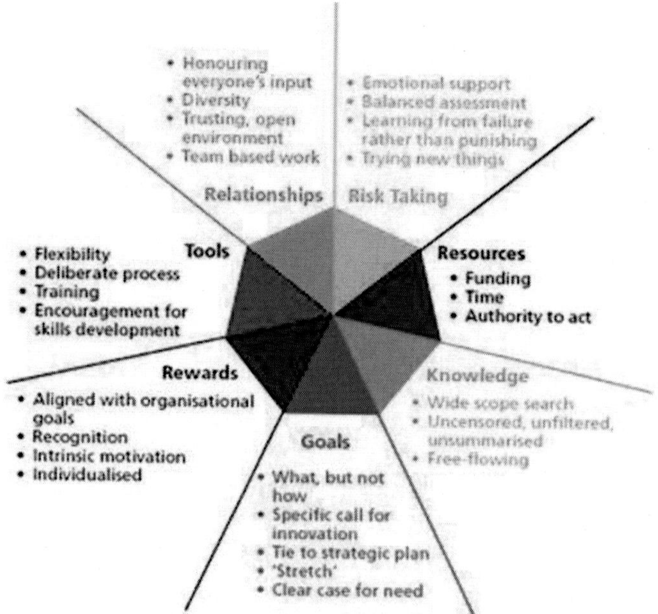

Figure 114: Organisational Dimensions in relation to innovativeness
Source (HM Government - Department for Business Innovation & Skills, 2009)

Employee characteristics and behaviours that contribute towards innovative working include, among other things, openness to ideas, problem solving, motivation, strategic thinking, leadership and management skills, confidence, willingness to take risks, emotional intelligence, tolerance of ambiguity, et al. At an organisation level, these are often the best practices to foster a culture of innovation and creativity:

- Have flat structures and accessible leaders
- Have a no-blame culture
- Recruit for innovative behaviours
- Provide staff with training and tools for innovation
- Provide the time, space and resource to innovate
- Have systems in place to source, develop and evaluate innovations
- Learn from success and "smart" failures.

Source: (HM Government - Department for Business Innovation & Skills, 2009)

Best practices for Building an Innovative Work Culture

- Invest in employee growth and development
- Make training mandatory and based on needs analysis
- Acknowledge innovative contributions and reward them publicly
- Instil ownership and accountability
- Create a sense of belonging
- Build confidence through encouragement
- Leverage the strengths of individuals
- Improve the physical work environment
- Develop a tolerance towards failure but insist on learning from smart failures
- Capture innovative ideas through multiple channels and multiple stakeholders
- Promote a culture of continuous improvement – Challenge the status quo

Source: (CRM Today, 2011)

Model for Innovation

Figure 115 illustrates a model for fostering innovation in an organisation in public sector. The outer membrane consists of the essential pre-conditions for innovation, without which a culture of innovation cannot be fostered and sustained in an organisation. Within this, the core of innovation process has been depicted. It recognises that innovation goes beyond the creation of good ideas. It comprises of the systematic application of the development, implementation, checking and adjustment sub-processes to the innovation process. The essential pre-conditions for innovation are the role of leadership at all the levels within the organisation, understanding the external environment within which the organisation operates, focussing and prioritising the important, building organisational innovative capability and agility, and the incentives and rewards system to recognise and disseminate innovation so that a learning organisation can be developed. These are some of the best practices in the public sector context for sustaining the innovation momentum.

- Public sector leaders are committed to achieving a supportive culture where innovation is encouraged and lessons disseminated;

- Innovation is embedded in corporate strategy and adequately resourced;
- Staff have the requisite skills, training and development opportunities;
- Departments encourage internally-generated innovation and actively engage with customers and stakeholders to garner external ideas and innovations;
- There is a deep understanding of core business, organisational policy and aspirations, the broader external environment and internal and external sources of data and information;
- There are mechanisms in place to assess and respond to new and emerging issues;
- Organisational capabilities and agility are built; and
- Innovation is appropriately recognised and rewarded

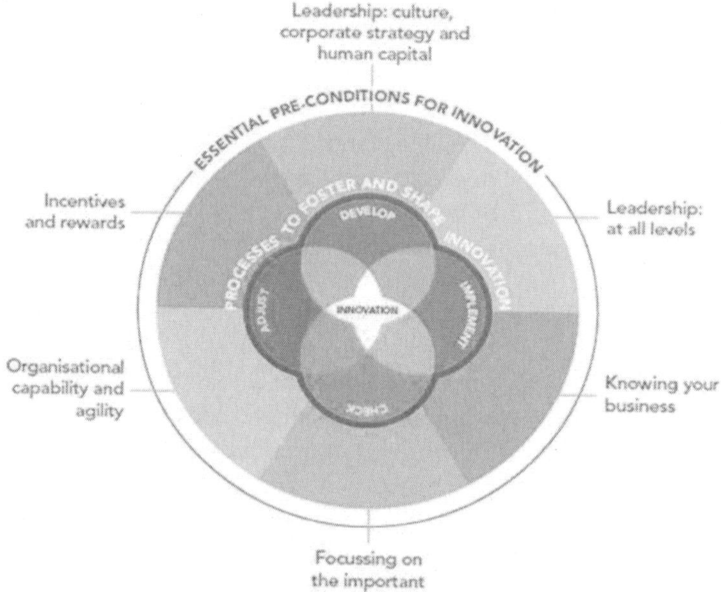

Figure 115: Process to foster and share innovation

Source: (Australian National Audit Office, 2009)

On the other hand, the processes to foster and shape innovation have been illustrated in the core of Figure 115. It is important for organisations to understand and apply the innovation processes to an extent that are fit for purpose depending on the level and extent of risks involved. The Innovation risk matrix as provided in the Table 22 can be used to gauge the relative risk level of innovation.

Features of the Innovation	***Low***	***Medium***	***High***
Is the nature of innovation incremental or transformative?			
Is the organisation's experience with this type or scale of innovation limited or extensive?			
Is the innovation within the organisation's control or will it require the involvement of other stakeholders or partners?			
Expectations regarding the innovation			
Are there sensitivities, as identified by stakeholders, around the impact of innovation?			
Are there sensitivities, as identified by stakeholders, around the means being used to apply innovation?			
Are there expectations, as identified by stakeholders, about the scope of the innovation, its resourcing and the time available to implement it?			

Table 22: Measuring Risk level of Innovation

Source: (Australian National Audit Office, 2009)

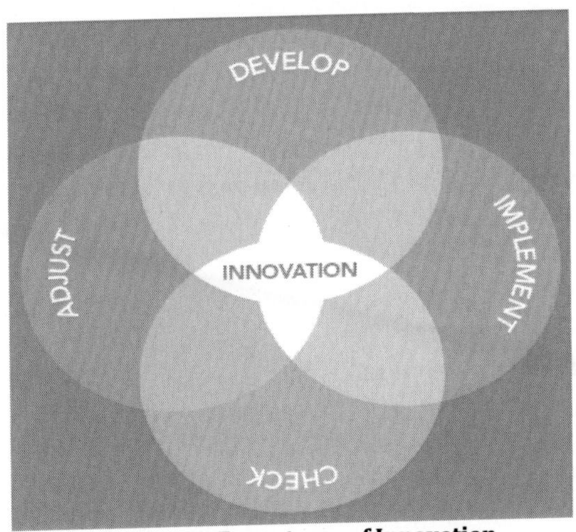

Figure 116: Four stages of Innovation

Source: (Australian National Audit Office, 2009)

Figure 116 depicts the core of the innovation processes and comprises of four main steps, which are

- **Develop options and solutions** - This step is mainly about developing new approaches to old problems and solutions to new and emerging issues. It entails understanding the needs, problems or opportunities for innovation, thinking outside the current paradigm and assessing the options to develop effective solutions. In developing options and solutions, the key steps to consider depending on the circumstances are to:
  - Understand the need, problem and opportunity and the broader context so the issues are appropriately framed;
  - Bring together the best available evidence base so that options development is well-informed and risks are identified early and can be appropriately managed;
  - Think outside the current paradigm to develop innovative solutions based around a strategic insight framework — where are we now? What is the desired end-point? How do we get there?;
  - Undertake early and active engagement with customers and stakeholders, including through establishing alliances and partnerships, to provide new ideas and insights, help identify and mitigate risk and build support;
  - Assess options as rigorously as possible when seeking to develop effective solutions recognising both the costs and benefits from a stakeholder perspective; and
  - Use experimentation, trials and pilots, to learn lessons, build an evidence base, identify and reduce risks and demonstrate proof of concept
- **Implement** - Without efficient, effective and timely implementation, inspirational and forward looking ideas will not be transformed into new processes, products, services or methods of delivery. As such, it comprises of preparing an implementation strategy, considering transitional agreements and monitoring the transition. The key considerations in the implementation phase, depending on the circumstances are to:
  - Ensure that sufficient attention is given to the practical constraints to effective implementation, including the

resources required to meet timeliness expectations. For complex cases, this may require an implementation strategy;
  - Consider the need for a transition plan, particularly where there is likely to be a significant impact on policy settings, service delivery or the regulatory environment; and
  - Monitor the transition process to ensure that the initiative is rolling out as planned and any unexpected issues are promptly dealt with.
- **Check and evaluate** - This phase is about tracking and monitoring the extent of success of innovations. They provide the basis on which judgements can be made about efficiency, effectiveness and appropriateness of the innovations implemented by the organisation. Hence, this phase comprises of preparing an evaluation strategy, monitoring short-run uptake and impact, and evaluating longer-run outcomes. Key steps for the check and evaluate phase are:
  - Prepare a tailored evaluation strategy which includes the collection and analysis of appropriately-targeted information;
  - Monitor short-run uptake and impacts to obtain early indications of the effectiveness of the initiative and whether adjustments are required;
  - Ensure data and information are being collected and early trends analysed, including through customer and stakeholder feedback; and
  - Evaluate longer-run outcomes based on a sound methodology.
- **Adjust and disseminate** - Innovation is not a static process; rather it is dynamic and it involves people learning from experience and sharing the knowledge and lessons learnt within the organisation to build the organisational capability. Depending on the circumstances, this phase may entail reconsidering aspirations and objectives, building on experience and success, preparing for the next development cycle et al. Key issues to consider in this phase may include:
  - Reconsider the initial aspirations and objectives to ascertain whether they are still current;

- Understand the impact of the initiative since first implemented and subsequent developments in the internal and external environment;
- Build on experience and success and take account of lessons learnt;
- Engage customers and stakeholders in the consideration of possible adjustments and new directions;
- Disseminate the results as widely as practicable; and
- Look to the future and prepare for the next development cycle to improve processes or responsiveness.

Source: (Australian National Audit Office, 2009)

Ten Hints for involving Frontline Employees in Creating Innovative Organisations

There are two main conditions that are considered to be of significant importance in order to involve frontline employees in creating innovative organisations:

- **Frontline employees know that their leadership is on their side.** This is important so that a culture of trust and openness can be built. In order to facilitate this, the leaders ought to:
  1. Be immediately responsive to requests for improved working conditions
  2. Support mistakes, but encourage the employees to learn the lessons and continually grow and develop
- **Frontline employees understand the big picture.** In an organisation, where the employees can view the clear line of sight between the organisational objectives and their contributions, it is expected that the motivation and engagement levels of the employees would be higher. In order to facilitate this, the leaders ought to:
  3. Create an explicit mission and related performance measures, giving people a reason to be innovative
  4. Broaden job categories so that an individual can experience multiple perspectives and constraints
  5. Move people around; employee mobility helps in increased intra-organisational learning and knowledge management
  6. Reward team, not individuals or find ways to beat the formal performance-appraisal as it often fosters unhealthy competition
  7. Make the hierarchy as unimportant as possible so that the employees are accountable for their work and not to their supervisors

8. Break down functional units as this silo thinking has resulted in stifled creativity and innovation at workplace
9. Provide everyone all the information and satiate their communication needs; overhead units hoarding critical data can be a killer for employee empowerment and engagement
10. Tell everyone what innovations are working; what is the level of success and what are the outcomes?

Source: (State and Local Government Review, 1995)

Creating a Culture for Innovation and Improvement

To successfully build a culture for continuous improvement and innovation, people need to be actively engaged and empowered and should perceive themselves to be a part of the system. The successful innovation and improvement initiatives share several fundamental cultural components:

- **Have change initiatives linked to what matters most** - People ought to view improvement and innovations as approaches that the organisation can take to move the organisation from where it is to where it wants to be – its vision. The initiatives, when taken in isolation, may be viewed as ways to fix the problems and hence can generate negative consequences. A future-oriented perspective, can link individuals to the organisation and be a crosswalk between day to day work and the broader organisational goals.
- **Remember that organisations are perfectly designed to get the results they get** - One cannot expect to get different results from doing the same things over and over again. Tinkering at the edges of the system without examining the core processes in detail will lead to only incremental changes in the organisation, if any. What gets measured is what gets done, and what's valued is what is rewarded. This needs to be borne in mind while designing the performance measurement system and the rewards and recognition system.
- **Quality is everybody's business** - Leaders need to champion and support the innovation and the improvement initiatives at the organisation. This support from the top cannot be overly stated.

However, at the end of the day there has to be enough empowerment at the grass root levels so that the opportunities of improvement can be actively searched and targeted. Also, there is a case for actively taking inputs from customers and other stakeholders.

- **There is no one best approach –** Be responsive and flexible - Organisations are complex and diverse and so is the external environment. Evidently, responsiveness and flexibility are what separates a world class organisation from also-rans. A common language and common models can be helpful but they are the tools that needed to be adapted to the organisation, its culture contextually.
- **Communicate and celebrate -** Communicate and celebrate the success in a timely manner. That will provide the energy and enthusiasm for the employees to maintain or even increase the momentum of innovation and improvement. Share information about improvements as well as share learning across the functions.
- **Adapt and evolve –** Stay focussed on the long term vision and goals - As the approaches to innovation and improvement become established and systematised, monitor how the organisation internally and the external environment are adapting and evolving. What's crucial is that organisation continues to be a learning organisation and does not rest on its past laurels. Keeping the momentum going by focussing on long-term goals, listening to all the stakeholders, and monitoring the pulse of the organisation.

Source: (Office of Planning and Institutional Assessment, 2009)

Link between Motivation and Innovation

Innovation and motivation have been found to be inextricably linked to one another. A climate of openness that gets employee engaged in the process of organisational innovation is often found to motivate employees to increase their productivity and efficiency, as well as motivate them to learn the best practices, think out of the box, continually learn and develop, etc. The following five practices have been found to be relevant in this context in the public sector:

- **Get to know every employee** - It is important for employees to feel that they are cared for and their voices and perspectives are given due attention. In this regard, one-to-one meeting has been found as an effective tool as it helps managers in understanding the strengths and aspirations of employees. This eventually results in right sort of people doing the right sort of thing, the commitment level rises and people are more likely to contribute ideas in such scenarios.
- **Challenge them to improve the operation** - This is the most difficult phase for managers as the success of this depends on so many external factors. However, right employee profiling with the right innovation culture & climate is found to be the right approach while challenging employees to challenge the status quo and come up with ideas to improve the practice and performance.
- **"Customer for a day"** - This tool has been found to be effective in scenario where the organisations don't have desired level of intelligence for the external and internal customers. Each employee is made a customer for a day and his or her responses may be used as a surrogate measure for the voice of customers.
- **The Great Idea award** - Rewards and recognition system influences the behaviour of the employees. Therefore, careful attention ought to be given to design and develop it so that there is positive behaviour demonstrated by employees, innovation proclivity.
- **Don't forget the implementation** - Lack of implementation of ideas may lead to disgruntled employees who are disillusioned with the organisation's intent on innovation. Resources and time ought to be allocated to ensure that the ideation phase is culminated into the fructification phase.

Source: (GovLeaders.org, 2008)

Drivers of Innovation

Innovation is motivated and driven by a range of short-term and long-term imperatives. Innovative activity in the public sector can be segregated in three main streams:

- **Shaping policy directions –** Role of the public sector is to provide advice and reasoned logic to the government in order to drive fact based decision making in relation to policies and programs.
- **Implementing policies and programs –** Delivering solutions to the customers and citizens effectively and efficiently so that a perceptive value-add can be delivered.
- **Administrative innovations –** Introducing new internal processes and practices to improve productivity/reduce costs.

One of the main drivers for innovation in the public sector is the need for organisations to respond effectively and efficiently to new and changing government as well as customer expectations in the increasingly complex environments. Examples include the consequences of an ageing population, national security, climate change, et al. This is fostered also by the increased awareness of the people facilitated by technology and globalisation.

There have been instances where the innovations have been limited to a particular department or a service. However, now there is an increasing need to transcend the boundaries and work effectively within the cross-functional setting. Collaboration, rather than a silo mentality, has been recognised as the way moving forward. Such coordination involves consultation, negotiation, cooperation and agreement within various entities within the organisations.

Also the time frames within which the public sector organisations ought to respond to the changing needs and expectations of the customers have been getting shorter. At the same time, the stakeholders are demanding a more holistic and customer-centric approach to solution delivery. There is also a constant pressure to do more with less i.e. increasing the organisational productivity. Technology developments however provide opportunities for innovation that were not previously available.

Why Innovate? • To respond more effectively to altered public needs and rising expectations ["one-size-fits-all" approach outdated] • To contain costs and increase efficiency, esp. in view of tight budgetary constraints • To improve delivery and outcomes of public services, including addressing areas where past policies have made little progress • To capitalise on the full potential of ICT
Emergent patterns of Innovation in public services • Provision of client-centred services, e.g. one-stop shops, seamless provision, etc. • Delivery of services through partnerships, e.g. local /regional partnerships, PPPs, etc. • New Public Management, e.g. introduction of private sector business practices; focus on measuring performance, market testing, etc. • Openness to experimentation ***Source: (IDeA Knowledge, 2005)***

Know-How for Innovation Management

Table 23 illustrates some of the pillars of Innovation management. The methodology section provides know-how on how a manager can go about implementing it in his or her organisation.

Knowledge Management	
Methodology	***Common Uses***
• Catalogue and evaluate the organisation's current knowledge base; • Determine which competencies will be key to future success and what base of knowledge is needed to build a sustainable leadership position therein; • Invest in systems and processes to accelerate the accumulation of knowledge; • Assess the impact of such systems on leadership, culture and hiring practices; • Codify new knowledge and turn it into tools and information that will improve both innovation and overall profitability	• Improve the cost and quality of existing products or services; • Strengthen and extend current competencies through intellectual asset management; • Improve and accelerate the dissemination of knowledge throughout the organisation; • Apply new knowledge to improve behaviours; • Encourage faster and even more profitable innovation

Open Innovation	
Methodology	***Common Uses***
• Focus resources on its core innovation advantages. Allocate resources to the opportunities with the best potential to strengthen the core businesses, reduce R&D risks and raise the returns on innovation capital; • Improve the circulation of innovation ideas. Develop information systems to capture insights, minimise duplicative efforts and advance teamwork; • Increase innovation imports. Gain access to valuable new ideas, complement core innovation advantages, improve the organisation's collaborative abilities and build its reputation as an innovative partner; • Increase innovation exports. Establish incentives and processes to assess objectively the fair value of innovations. • Carefully structure strategic alliances to protect the organisation's rights, raise additional cash and strengthen relationships with partners	• Clarify core competencies; • Maximise the productivity of new product/service development without increasing R&D budgets; • Decide quickly and efficiently whether to buy or sell patents and other intellectual capital; • Promote faster, higher-quality innovations
Rapid Prototyping	
Methodology	***Common Uses***
• Identify the most important and risky elements of an innovation project; • Determine what hypotheses must be tested before making substantial investments; • Design the fastest, lowest-cost methods for testing hypotheses; • Test, learn and modify. Redesign prototypes based on customer reactions, consider adding new features suggested by customers and continuously improve the prototype with repeated testing to improve quality and features	• Speed innovation through real-world testing before the product/service launch; • Lower innovation costs with less costly prototypes, freeing up development teams to conduct testing that's more thorough and to explore more ideas; • Reduce risks of failing to meet customer needs by

	incorporating customer feedback early in the product/service development cycle, helping to ensure that a product is delivered on time and on budget

Table 23: Pillars of Innovation Management

Source (Bain & Company, 2011)

Factors that Foster Innovation within the Public Sector

The following table contains factors that will foster innovation within the public sector organisation.

Elements	*Factors that will foster innovation*
Generating Possibilities	• Manifestos and public commitments • Intensive attention to the views of users, frontline staff, and middle managers • Diversity of staff and exploiting differences • Constant scanning of horizons and margins • Developing the capacity for creative thinking • Working backwards from outcome goals • Creating space and time • Breaking the rules • Competition
Incubating, Prototyping and Managing risks	• Probability rules – provide guidelines to aid decisions concerning which ideas merit further exploration and support • Risk Management – A culture of tolerance for "honourable" failures must emerge • Innovation champions – Those individuals who are willing to invest resources and organisational capacity for designing, implementing and evaluating an innovation • Safe space: Pilots, Pathfinders, Controlled Experimentation and "Zones" – These are deliberately designed to suspend some of the rules that normally constrain local agencies and managers • Incubators – Incubators for innovation provide advice and general support, finance and freedom from external

Elements	*Factors that will foster innovation*
	pressure and rules • Modelling – The cost of developing working prototype can be significant, therefore modelling methods may be more appropriate in some scenarios • Funding for early development – For innovations to be progressed from ideas to prototypes, they require financial support • Involving end-users – This increases the likelihood of identifying and remedying weaknesses and problems of innovation implementation
Replication and Scaling Up	• An incentive for individuals and teams – Recognition, particularly by peers has been found to be of more importance than monetary rewards. Pride in contributing to the creation of public value. • Incentives for organisations – Additional funding for the organisation • Scale and innovative capability • Beware "best practice" – One size rarely fits all • Change management – Key skills and competencies in scaling up and spreading innovation are similar to the skills of more general change management
Analysis and Learning	• Metrics for success – Clear and transparent measurement systems for assessing the success of innovations are critical to evaluating what works and creating cultures of learning • Real-time learning – Through formative and summative evaluation • Peer and user involvement – Networks of peers play a critical role in learning from and supporting continuous improvement • Double-loop learning – Process and mechanisms need to be in place to analyse, evaluate and learn about innovation more generally • Requisite variety – The internal diversity in skills and experiences of employees must match the variety and complexity of the environment

Table 24: Factors that foster innovation within the public sector

Source (IDeA Knowledge, 2005)

Creativity and Innovation

"The essential part of creativity is not being afraid to fail."
Edwin H. Lan

Demands for organisational innovation and technological advantage are crucial components of competitive strategy for many organisations Most organisations face serious competitive challenges due to the rapid pace and unpredictability of technology change. Industries dependent on highly sophisticated technologies and organisations engaged in multinational competition are particularly vulnerable to the need for continuous and rapid modification of their product features and the ways in which they conduct business .These conditions have led management theorists and practitioners alike to call for more creativity in management practices, products, and production processes.

Creativity is the ability to make or otherwise bring into existences something new. Whether a new solution to a problem, a new method or device, or a new artistic object or form. Wyckoff defines creativity as new and useful. Creativity is the act of seeing things that everyone around us sees while making connections that no one else has made. Creativity is moving from the known to the unknown. Creativity and Innovation are linked very closely to competitiveness.

There is a firm correlation between new products and market share - what would happen if organisations stopped introducing new products? Microsoft would have almost lost its dominance if it hadn't improved on Windows 95. As product life-cycles decrease organisations have to introduce new products –for example the average life span of a mobile phone is less than a year.

Competitors force the introduction of new products - if Nokia didn't introduce new mobile phones every year then Motorola or Siemens would. Macro changes push innovation - China's entry into the WTO meant that Western organisations would face competitions of scale and scope.

A broad new definition of innovation is proposed. The term no longer just refers to new products and processes, but also to new business processes and new ways of carrying out productive activities. Innovation should not be understood simply as invention or the first use globally of a new technology, but also as the first application of a product or process in a specific setting. Organisations need to think less about invention and more about doing things differently with available knowledge and technology that they can acquire. A three-stranded typology of innovation is proposed—

1. Creation and commercialisation of new knowledge and technology;
2. Acquisition of knowledge and technology from abroad for local use and adaptation; and
3. The dissemination and effective application of knowledge and technology.

Ten Success Factors for effective "Innovation Strategy Framework"

An innovation strategy framework consists of four key elements: innovation proposition, business case, organisation and culture, and competence focus & collaboration. Hence, in the bigger scheme of things, it is important to analyse the current innovation strategy at an organisation according to ISF dimensions. A thorough analysis of the current innovation approach, the competence focus and existing collaborations, the business case of the innovation portfolio as well as the organisation and culture is a crucial step to pinpoint the weaknesses of any organisation's innovation strategy. These are the key success factors for having an integrated and holistic innovation strategy framework that can be implemented.

Innovation proposition

1. **Technological vision:** Top performers constantly scan their environment for long-term trends in the market and in technologies. They develop a long-term innovation vision and stick to it, no matter what the short-term trends are.
2. **Customer knowledge:** Understanding customer preferences enables organisations to better focus their innovation efforts on relevant issues. Customer research needs both a regional and a socio-demographic approach to be of value.

3. **Strategy match:** Successful organisations match their R&D strategies at a very early stage, and very closely with the respective partners.

Competence focus & collaboration

4. **Competence focus:** The best innovators closely match their R&D competencies with their R&D strategy.
5. **Strategic partners:** With their increasing complexity, R&D networks are becoming a crucial success factor. Supplier-supplier and supplier-institution collaborations have increased.

Business case

6. **Investment focus:** R&D funding must be independent of current business needs. In the past, short-term changes in the R&D focus have often led to long-term problems. Catching up with past R&D cuts has often proven to be extremely expensive.
7. **Trend focus:** Relying on megatrends contributes significantly to the soundness of R&D investments, as these trends are highly predictable. Interpreting these trends in terms of an organisation's own business model is a main conceptual challenge.
8. Cost focus: Leaders in innovation always have a strong cost focus, with respect to R&D efficiency and effectiveness.

Organisation & culture

9. **Outside-in strategy:** Top performers concentrate on innovations that the customers need and end low-value projects early. Processes that strengthen this ability are a common understanding of innovation aims within the organisation and a standard quality process.
10. **People involvement:** Organisations that involve people from all levels in their R&D are much more successful innovators. The keys to employee involvement are easy and motivating communications, low hurdles for submission of ideas, and efficient and transparent filters for the incoming ideas.

Source: (car-innovation.com, 2010)

Open and Close Innovation – The Evolution Process

Chesbrough coined the term "Open Innovation." He describes how organisations have shifted from closed innovation processes towards a more open way of innovating. Traditionally, new business development processes and the marketing of new products took place within the organisation's boundaries. However, several factors have led to the erosion of closed innovation First of all, the mobility and availability of highly educated people has increased over the years. As a result, large amounts of knowledge exist outside the research laboratories of large organisations. In addition to that, when employees change jobs, they take their knowledge with them, resulting in knowledge flows between organisations. Second, the availability of venture capital has increased significantly recently, which makes it possible for good and promising ideas and technologies to be further developed outside the organisation, for instance in the form entrepreneurial organisations. Besides, the possibilities to further develop ideas and technologies outside the organisation, for instance in the form of spin-offs or through licensing agreements, are growing. Finally, other organisations in the supply chain, for instance suppliers, play an increasingly important role in the innovation process.

As a result, organisations have started to look for other ways to increase the efficiency and effectiveness of their innovation processes. For instance through active search for new technologies and ideas outside of the organisation, but also through cooperation with suppliers and competitors, in order to create customer value. Another important aspect is the further development or out-licensing of ideas and technologies that do not fit the strategy of the organisation. Open Innovation can thus be described as: combining internal and external ideas as well as internal and external paths to market to advance the development of new technologies. This means that organisations have to become aware of the increasing importance of open innovation. Not all good ideas are developed within their own organisation, and not all ideas should necessarily be further developed within their own organisation's boundaries. Also a shift should take place in the way people look at the organisation and its environment. Involving other parties when developing new products and technologies can be of great added value. Figure 117 and Figure 118 and illustrate the difference between the open innovation and closed innovation processes. While the closed innovation focuses on the existing markets and is constrained by the organisation's boundaries, the open innovation research and development phases go beyond the organisation's boundaries and are not constrained by them.

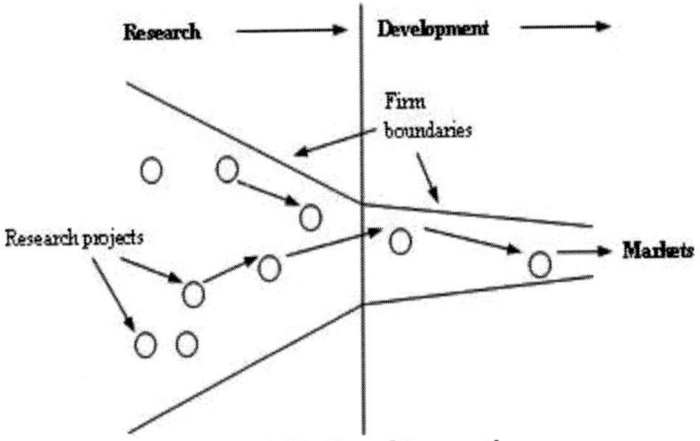

Figure 117: Closed Innovation
Source: (Chesbrough, 2003)

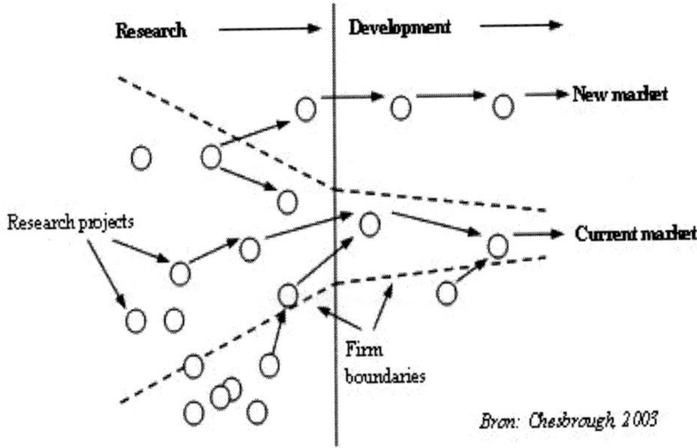

Figure 118: Open Innovation
Source: (Chesbrough, 2003)

The differences in the management thinking in both the principles have been illustrated in Table 25. Obviously, the organisation rooting for closed innovation is an internally focussed organisation which relies on its internal resources and intelligence to come up with innovative ideas; management is generally sceptical that open innovation may lead to the corrosion of intellectual capability of the organisation. On the other hand, the open innovation principles are rather embracing in nature. The managers in such organisations feel that getting more ideas on board is important. They are not in a hurry to be the first to market and they don't feel that their competitive advantage can be simply eroded by opening up the system's boundaries.

Closed Innovation Principles	***Open Innovation Principles***
The smart people in the field work for us.	Not all smart people in the field work for us. We need to work with smart people inside and outside the organisation.
To profit from research and development, we must discover, develop and ship it ourselves.	External research and development can create significant value; internal R&D is needed to claim some portion of that value.
If we discover it ourselves, we will get it to the market first.	We don't have to originate the research to profit from it.
The organisation that gets an innovation to the market first will win.	Building a better business model is better than getting to the market first.
If we create the most and the best ideas in the industry, we will win.	If we make the best use of internal and external ideas, we will win.
We should control our intellectual property, so that our competitors don't profit from our ideas.	We should profit from others' use of our IP and we should buy others' IP whenever it advances our business model.

Table 25: A Comparison of Different Innovation Principles

Source: (Chesbrough, 2003)

Open Innovation – General Concepts

Open innovation has been proven to produce products/services that are better fit with the customers' needs & expectations, that are produced at a lower cost and at a faster pace. However, the fruits of open innovation have not been fully exploited, because of the inherent competitive world where businesses may be secretive by nature and would shy away from embracing the partnership based approach. Some of the typical barriers are:

- ***Intellectual property*** – With organisations working beyond their corporate boundaries, the issue of intellectual property is a hot one. The larger organisations may take the lead in the process and may set the rules of the game often to the discomfort of the partners of smaller size. On the other hand, a stricter IP regime will add to the cost and the time of the process thereby mitigating some of the advantages of the open innovation.
- ***Complexity*** – The collaborative spaces need different managerial techniques. Managing diverse teams and getting the team members to effectively communicate, collaborate and share information is no mean feat. Distance issues, languages, cultural differences etc add to the complexity.
- ***Interdependence*** – Organisations have been found to be reluctant to rely on others. The critics say that placing the fortune in the hands of others is not a smart move. However, they tend to miss the point that the organisations are often heavily dependent on one another in the market place.
- ***Human factors*** – The factors discussed above were the tangible problems, the structural impediments that the open innovation process may expect to find. Nonetheless, the human factors are as important, if not more, for providing a glass ceiling to the innovation potential of an organisation.
  - *Inertia* – Open innovation, which has been found to be rather discontinuous in nature, involves a lot of effort for a potentially exciting but uncertain reward. Taking leaps into unknown requires people to overcome inertia.
  - *Culture and tradition* – Organisations which are risk averse, would rather take a tried and tested approach to innovation. The innovation funnel and the "stage gate" model are often

used as the models to drive the innovation process. These organisations would rather comfort themselves by using the tried and tested approaches rather than challenging themselves to adopt the paradigm of open innovation.

- *Mindsets* – Often in large organisations, there is a climate of suspicion and distrust with the outsiders. Employees are rarely trained to exploit external innovations and open innovation requires different sets of skills and motivations. Often, the "not invented here" cliché can be heard in such scenarios. The role of performance measurement in impeding this process is also important, as short-term financial metrics hinder the adoption of open innovation.

Source: (Nesta (a), 2010)

For leaders in excellent organisations, it is clear that in order to foster and exploit the full potential of open innovation; they will have to look at several aspects, including organisational culture. In order to bridge over the soft and hard barriers that impede the collaborative approach, the following guiding principles can be adopted.

1. ***Strategy***
    - With a win-win business model in mind, the senior management should demonstrate its seriousness about collaboration and its intent to see through a potential partnership to the end by committing the necessary time, money and resources. A clear vision of why the organisation is going for collaborative approach and what it expects out of the process would result in the senior management team asking the right questions to their potential collaborators for their skills, ideas or resources.
    - Suspend judgement and let the ideas flow to you. A premature judgement will not allow unconventional and innovative ideas to develop; this inadvertently will kill the relationships.
    - Try not to manage risks down to zero. "Managing the risk down to zero" approach will stifle the open innovation

process. Remember it is not about minimising the risks; it is about managing the inherent uncertainties.

- Measuring open innovation is still in its infancy state. However, some of the emerging best practices are to ensure that the measurement considers all the direct and indirect measures of innovation benefits and costs from the multiple stakeholders' perspectives. Valuing networks, predictive measures of key relationships and the complementarities of products and processes have to be considered in the innovation measurement.

2. *Communication*

- Organisations often try to take the large leap of faith and try to become open innovators by trying to change the culture, an arduous and long drawn out course of action, to say the least. This may not be the best approach to adopt. Success sells. The momentum has to be created, the low hanging fruits have to be targeted. The first hand evidence of people adopting a new approach and it working will create the necessary buzz and the impetus to move the agenda forward.
- Communicate with the outside world effectively; don't get wrapped in the process of open innovation.
- The open innovation not only requires different structures, but also different way of thinking and communication style. The command-and-control approach will inevitably fail in this context. The new innovators have to be open-minded and communicative.
- The significance of open innovation for an organisation will have to be highlighted by having mechanisms to support the paradigm. Whose responsibility is it? How is open innovation rewarded? When and where does it happen?
- Setting an innovation culture is also about ensuring that the organisation has enough polymath leaders, who are multi-skilled individuals who combine their comprehensive and diverse functional expertise.

3. Networks

- The quantity of networks is important, but what is more important than having a large, diverse and engaged network, is to have people who approach you first with an opportunity before they approach their competitors. It's not whom you know, it's who knows you. Hence, what is important from a leaders' perspective is to ensure that the organisation should be easy to find, the network should understand what it is you want and they should feel that you really would value doing businesses with them.
- Customers are incredible assets that organisations can leverage, but unfortunately not many organisations have used the customers' knowledge about their brand; they see the customers as the passive recipient of products and services. Sometimes, it makes better business sense to buy from the customers as well as sell to them, i.e. establish a two way flow of value.
- Embrace your critics because they would show you aspects/perspectives that you may have missed out because you are in the system. Engaging the critics in a conversation may be challenging but it is highly beneficial.
- Networks need active management. Hierarchies work primarily through command-and-control whereas informal networks work through trust. The management approach that suits best to a particular context should be used; however care must be taken not to mix the two approaches.
- Don't overestimate your capabilities. There are a lot of smart people out there who need to be actively engaged and listened to. It is an unlimited source of innovation which has huge hidden potential.

Source: (Nesta (a), 2010)

Applying Open Innovation to the Public Sector

"Citizen-sourcing" has been recognised by many governments and public service providers as the way forward because in these cases citizens, being the final customers, understand their needs and expectations better than any customer intelligence unit can ever dream of. There has to be a persistent dialogue and interaction between citizens and citizen centric government so that the voice of the customers can truly be engrained in the service design and delivery. This concept of "open government" offers newer and novel ways of interactive public value creation and citizen co-creation by systematically integrating external factors into the governmental and administrative processes.

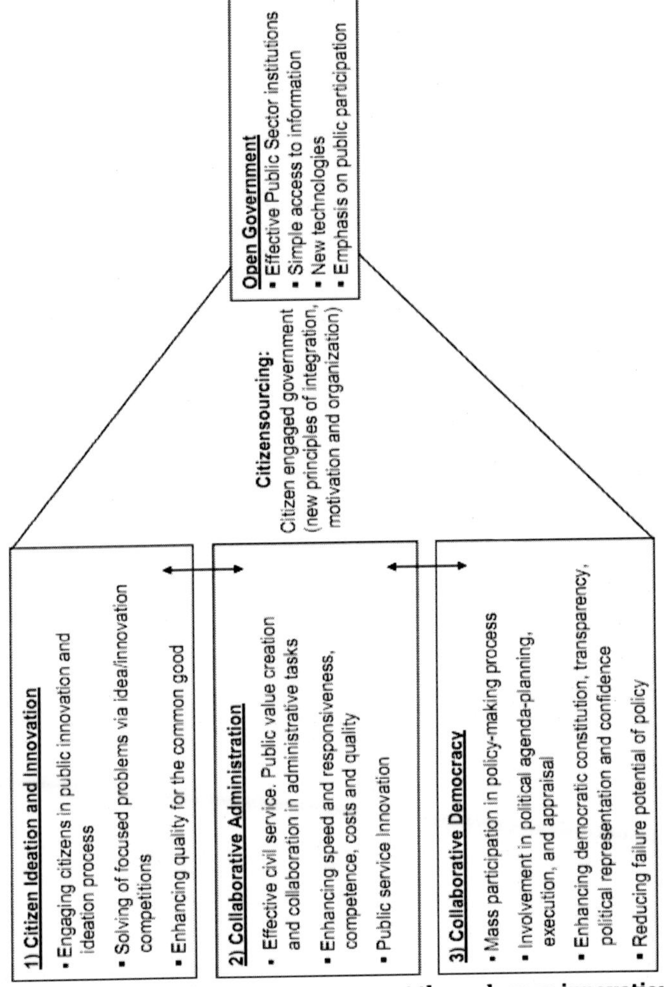

Figure 119: Building open government through open innovation

Source: (IRSPM, 2010)

A framework for citizen-sourcing has been depicted in Figure 119. It includes the following three dimensions:

- **Citizen Ideation and Innovation** - This phase is mainly about actively engaging citizens in public innovation and ideation process for achieving the greater good.
- **Collaborative Administration** - The second tier is concerned about the integration of citizens for enhancing existing public administrative processes.
- **Collaborative Democracy** - Last but not the least, this level summarises new ways of collaboration to improve public participation within the policy process, including the incorporation of public values into decisions, improving the quality of decisions, building trust in institutions and educating and informing the public.

Current examples of successful citizen collaboration and participation in the public sector have been provided in the Table 26 for understanding the better practices and initiatives adopted by some of the leading governments.

Citizen Ideation and Innovation	***Collaborative Administration***	***Collaborative Democracy***
Citizen Feedback and Recommendation Systems: • FixMyStreet.com • Patientopinion.org.uk (patient feedback in UK National Health System) **Innovation Contest Initiated by Public Organisations:** • USAID Development 2.0 Challenge • Inducement Prizes at the National Science Foundation • U.S. Dept. of Energy Lighting Prize	**Urban Planning:** • FutureMelbourne.com.au • Unifiedneworleansplan.com (urban planning for hurricane destroyed New Orleans) **Public Participation in Patent Examination:** • Peer-to-Patent.org • PatentFizz, IP.Com or Patent Debate (no formal connection to USPTO)	**21st Century Town Hall Meeting:** • AmericaSpeaks.org • MoveOn.org **Similar approaches:** • deliberative-democracy.net • calhealthreform.org • californiaspeaks.org • democracylab.org • european-citizensconsultations.eu **Political Recommendation**: • Number 10 Downing Street E-

Citizen Ideation and Innovation	*Collaborative Administration*	*Collaborative Democracy*
General Public Sector Service Improvement: • www.showusabetterway.co.uk • Open U.S. Government Dialog (opengov.ideascale.com) • U.S. Transportation Security Administration's Idea Factory	**Public Security:** • Peoplefinder-Project reveals new public duties • Texas Virtual Border Watch (Texas-Mexico border observation via webcams) • Southern California Wildfire Response	Petitions **Political Monitoring:** • govtrack.us • data.gov **Collaborative Legal Codification:** • New Zealand Wiki Policing Act 2008 • Regulations.gov (eRulemaking)

Table 26: Best practice examples

Source: (IRSPM, 2010)

Co-creation and Innovation

The customer is always a co-creator of value. Co-creation has been considered by many as the magic mantra to drive the organisational innovation engine. It embraces the philosophy of partnership where stakeholders engage for a shared common vision. It is an active, creative and social process, based on collaboration between producers and users that is initiated by the organisation to generate value for customers. It creates value as it helps the organisation in these aspects:

- **Creative:** co-creation is a form of collaborative creativity, that's initiated by organisations to enable innovation with, rather than simply for their customers
- **A rich mix:** co-creation draws on a combination of management and marketing approaches, the psychoanalytic tradition, and processes related to innovation, knowledge and group decision-making
- **A facilitated process:** co-creation thrives on fantasy, play and creativity, but the role of the facilitator or facilitating organisation is often overlooked

- **All about relationships:** we stress the importance of focusing on the quality of the interactions between people rather than on technologies per se
- **A learning process:** we need to intertwine knowledge and processes in an overall co-creation framework, rather than just enabling co-creativity, if we want to achieve wider organisational impact

Source: (Promise Corporation, 2009)

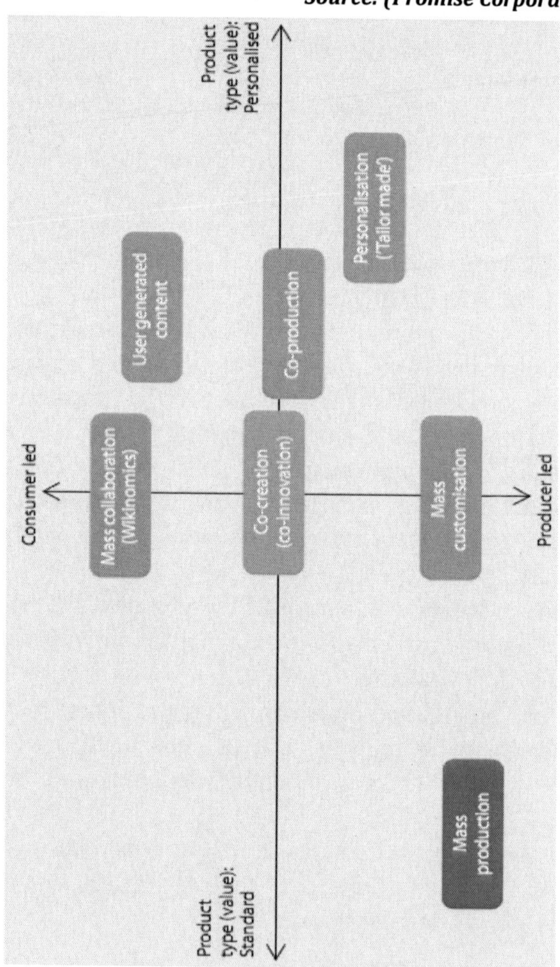

Figure 120: Co-creation Matrix

Source: (Promise Corporation, 2009)

Figure 120 depicts the family of concepts associated with co-creation. The X-axis depicts the extent to which the product/service has been personalised and the Y-axis illustrates to what extent the creation is led by customers or producers. The two dimensions can also be understood from these two perspectives:

- ***The role of the organisation*** – whether the process is consumer-led or producer-led? Mass-collaborations may be mainly user-driven, but the other approaches tend to be led by the organisation.
- ***The type of value created*** – is it standardised value, customised value or personalised value?

Table 27 provides the various approaches adopted by organisations in order to foster partnership and customer engagement & involvement for innovation.

Concept	***Description***	***Examples***
Collaborative innovation	Gaining competitive advantage by expanding the borders of an organisation through widespread involvement and interdependence between actors at all levels, daily based information exchange, integration of business processes and joint work and activities. For radical or discontinuous innovation, joint development and co-design are the most typical forms of networking. In the case of continuous innovation and improvement processes, the most common form of inter-organisation interaction is mutually-beneficial customer-supplier collaboration over an extended period of time.	**Boeing 787** The development of the Boeing 787, ranging from concept to production, was done by Boeing and its global partners.
Consumer / customer Involvement	The concept of consumer/customer involvement has been used in two different ways: **A) Psychological:** a consumer's perceived importance, risk, symbolic value or emotional appeal of a product	

Concept	*Description*	*Examples*
	or product category. **B) Behavioural:** When organisations engage consumers/customers in some way, leading to a benefit for the organisation, customer or both (e.g. as resource in product innovation or co-producer of products).	
Co-production	In co-production, the customer is an active participant in the production and delivery of a service, giving the participant a potential to customise his or her world. A broader perspective of co-production is found in the interpretive marketing literature, suggesting that a fundamental characteristic of the postmodern era is the reversal of production and consumption, requiring marketers to increasingly open up their processes and systems.	**'U-Scan'; Ikea** Self-service checkouts at supermarkets or self-assembly furniture
Mass Collaboration "Wikinomics"	A kind of collaboration model based on collective actions, which occur while large numbers of contributors or participants work independently but in collaboration on a single modular project. Projects typically take place on the internet by means of web-based collaboration tools.	**Wikipedia** Articles on the world's largest online encyclopaedia, written entirely by internet users.
Mass Customisation	Mass customisation refers to organisations applying technology and management methods to provide product variety and customisation through flexibility and quick responsiveness. While the goal of mass production is to produce an affordable standardised product, mass customisation produces enough variety in products and/or services so that nearly everyone finds exactly what he or she wants at a reasonable price.	**Dell; Nike ID** Dell computers allow customers to configure the specifications of the computers that they purchase

Concept	*Description*	*Examples*
Open Innovation	Open innovation occurs when a organisation commercialises its own ideas and innovations from other organisations, and seeks ways to bring its in-house ideas to market by deploying pathways outside its businesses. External R&D can create significant value; internal R&D is needed to claim some portion of that value.	**Linux; Procter & Gamble** P&G's 'Connect + Develop' programme enables a two-way sharing of innovation between P&G and external individuals or organisations.
User Generated Content	User generated content can be defined as content made publicly available through technologies like the internet, reflecting a certain amount of creative input or effort that is created outside of professional practices or routines.	**Youtube** Youtube, the online video sharing service, allows users to upload their own and view content generated by other users.
User Involvement	User involvement occurs when representatives of a target user group participate in the system [software, etc.] development process.	

Table 27: Different approaches to open innovation

Source: (Promise Corporation, 2009)

All the co-creation approaches share the two main features of the expansion of products/services or organisational boundaries and the involvement of consumer. Co-creation, however, as collaborative innovation with customers adds a third dimension which is a focus on co-creating new values with customers that is initiated by the organisation. At the heart of it, co-creation is an active, creative and social process that entails connections and interactions between people, active collaboration and co-creativity, not just co-construction or co-production. Hence, it can be seen as coming-together of aspects of marketing and management theory, psychology and techniques derived from group decision-making, innovation and knowledge processes.

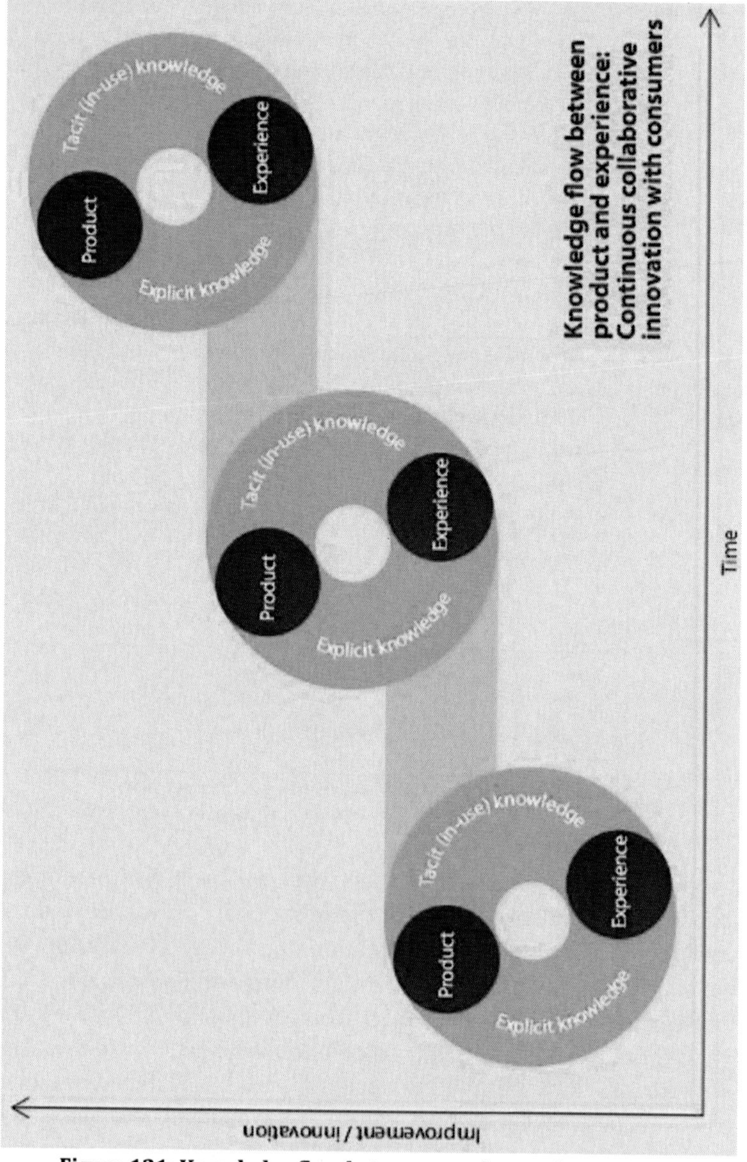

Figure 121: Knowledge flow between product and experience

Source: (Promise Corporation, 2009)

As a knowledge process, co-creation goes through an iterative process, as depicted in Figure 121. This iterative process involves the construction and de-construction of experiences and hence it goes through a cycle of value creation. It is, therefore, seen both as an adaptive framework that facilitates innovation in a 'boundary-spanning' way by connecting customers and other members of the organisation and as a developmental tool that intertwines organisational knowledge and learning processes with relationship building and the creation of new value and meaning.

Outside Innovation – How your customers will co-design your organisation's future

The better an organisation becomes at innovation, the more likely for it to be the leader and set new rules for others to follow and emulate. However, now the rules of the games have changed. Organisations no longer win by hiring the smartest engineers, scientists or designers; rather they win by engaging the smartest customers. This outside-in perspective helps the organisations in co-designing products, services and overall customer experience with the customers. This helps in providing the organisations with the necessary leverage to create solutions that better meet the needs of prospective customers, will revolutionise business models and practices, and will attract fanatically loyal customers.

Drawing from dozens of fascinating stories of outside innovation pioneers such as the BBC, LEGO, Staples, Karmaloop, National Instruments, Hallmark, Koko Fitness, GE Plastics, SEI Wealth, Kraft, Flickr, Mozilla, Zopa and others, Seybold shows how to win the innovation wars by:

- Finding lead users in an industry and commercialising their inventions.
- Engaging with the most visionary customers to co-design new products and new processes.
- Enabling customers to trouble-shoot each others' problems, hack solutions, and modify and extend an organisation's products to meet their needs.
- Providing innovation toolkits to customers to design very specific solutions for themselves —customised solutions that leverage a organisation's deep domain expertise.
- Encouraging customers to "strut their stuff" by contributing their insights, nurturing online customer communities, and allowing customers to redesign a organisation's business strategy.

Source:* *(Patricia Seybold Group, 2006)

Co-production in Public Services

"Co-production changes all this. It makes the system more efficient, more effective and more responsive to community needs. More importantly, it makes social care altogether more humane, more trustworthy, more valued – and altogether more transforming for those who use it." ~ Phil Hope MP, then Minister of State for Care Services, UK.

"The public become, not the passive recipients of state services, but the active agents of their own life. They are trusted to make the right choices for themselves and their families. They become doers, not the done-for." ~ David Cameron, Prime Minister, UK.

Co-production as a means of delivery of public services focuses on equal and reciprocal relationships between professionals designing & delivering the services and customers using the services; hence both the services and neighbourhoods become far more effective agents of change. The key characteristics of co-production are:

- **Recognising people as assets** – It is about transforming the perception of people from passive recipients of services to one where they are equal partners in designing and delivery of the services.
- **Building on people's existing capabilities** – The delivery model of public services has to be changed from a deficit approach to that of one that provides opportunities to recognise and grow people's capabilities and actively support them to put these to use with individuals and communities.
- **Promoting mutuality and reciprocity** – The way forward is to provide people with ample opportunities and range of incentives to engage, which will enable to work in a reciprocal relationship, where there are mutual responsibilities, expectations and accountabilities.
- **Developing peer support networks** – The networks – built around peers, personal networks and professionals - are the backbones on which this agenda will move forward. It is the best way to transfer knowledge and support change.

- **Breaking down barriers between professionals and recipients –** The reconfiguration of the services has to be conducted in a way that the distinction between producers and consumers of services is blurred.
- **Facilitating rather than delivering –** This is the paradigm shift where the public service agencies are no longer the central providers of services themselves, rather they become catalysts and facilitators of change. Figure 122 demonstrates the critical middle ground that co-production occupies when user and professional knowledge is combined to design and deliver services.

Source: (Boyle, Coote, Sherwood, & Slay, 2010)

Figure 122 depicts roles and responsibilities for professionals who are involved in designing and delivering of services within the public sectors.

		Responsibility for design of services		
		Professionals as sole service planner	Professionals and service users/ community as co-planners	No professional input into service planning
Responsibility for delivery of services	Professionals as sole service deliverers	Traditional professional service provision	Professional service provision but users/communities involved in planning and design	Professionals as sole service deliverers
	Professionals and users/communities as co-deliverers	User co-delivery of professionally designed services	Full co-production	User/community delivery of services with little formal/ professional
	Users/communities as sole deliverers	User/community delivery of professionally planned services	User/community delivery of co-planned or co-designed services	Self-organised community provision

Figure 122: User and professional roles in the design and delivery of services

Source: (Boyle & Harris, The challenge of co-production, 2009)

Customer-Centric Innovation

"Tomorrow's successful consumer product organisations will likely be those that have leveraged consumer insights to create nationally recognised brands that are worthy of their price. Effective consumer-centric innovation can often be the path to this outcome because it can help create products that capture the consumer's imagination, provide entertaining brand experiences, or offer solutions to previously unmet needs." ~ Deloitte.

In the reality of empowered customers, customer centric innovation (CCI) has almost become indispensible in order to survive in the ultra-competitive market place. With the open flow of information made readily available real-time and on demand by internet technologies, the customers have more informed choices now and the decision making is impacted by a range of factors hitherto unknown. Organisations which see the customers as external to them are bound to miss the finer details and the broad brushing/generalisation will impact them negatively. For example, there has been an emerging group of socially conscious customers who would like to see how their consumption pattern impacts the world. For example, Nike has been blamed with using unscrupulous practices read lower payment to the employees and violation of human rights. This has negatively impacted the brand image of Nike.

As consumer product organisations embrace the reality of empowered consumers and the Internet-enabled world, many have been moving to an "open innovation" product development model. This model is based on the idea that information can now be gathered on a mass scale by using both external (end users, suppliers, academia, etc.) and internal (employees) sources as inputs into the new product development process. The proponents of open innovation hold the view that locking the intellectual property within the organisation is not going to have significant benefit. In fact, once the organisation embraces the culture of open innovation by partnering, engaging with the customers' et al, they can leverage from others' expertise and can access the deep customer insight. Moving beyond just creating collaborative, external opportunities around innovation, CCI puts the consumer at the core of the innovative process. Figure 123 depicts the CCI continuum ranging from consumer-tested innovation to consumer-centric innovation.

	Consumer-tested innovation	Consumer-focused innovation	Consumer-centric innovation
Consumers' role	Mostly uninvolved	Reactive	Champions
Degree of company control	Interactions controlled by company	Consumers given freedom to express aspirations	Company can empower end users and others throughout the innovation process
R&D philosophy	Closed innovation	Consumer-guided	Dynamic open innovation
Organizational design	Organized by manufacturing process	Organized by product purpose	Organized by consumer segment
Role of Computers/Internet	Computer-aided design, Quantitative testing of concepts & advertising	Testing, but also used for product information, advertising	Mining blogs and social networking sites for insights, leveraging virtual private communities, enabling co-design/ customization of final product
Critical issues	Lack of ideas, conviction, for most innovation	Tendency towards incremental innovation, easily copied	Right system and structure for R&D, marketers, and consumers enables use of consumer insights across the process

Figure 123: Implementation of CCI - A continuum

Source: (Deloitte Development LLC, 2009)

The key difference is the role that consumers play in the three main categories of CCI as depicted in Figure 123. This varying level of intensity of embracing consumer-centric innovation is evident in the organisations with varying degree of customer centricity. Consumer tested Innovation use consumer input sparingly, if at all, in their product development processes. At the other end of the spectrum are organisations that walk hand in hand with consumer down the innovation path.

Source: (Deloitte Development LLC, 2009)

Procter & Gamble demonstrates this "customer is boss" philosophy and hence adopts the consumer-centric innovation as its strategy to maintain its competitive advantage in the ultra competitive market place. There is a organisation-wide emphasis on design thinking, co-creating with customers is the norm, use of "influencer marketing, and commitment to have 50% of its innovation coming from sources outside the organisation differentiate the organisation from its competitors.

The question arises – How can organisations drive the philosophy of consumer centric innovation forward? What are the drivers and enablers that leaders in excellent organisations have to be wary about and take steps to facilitate the process?

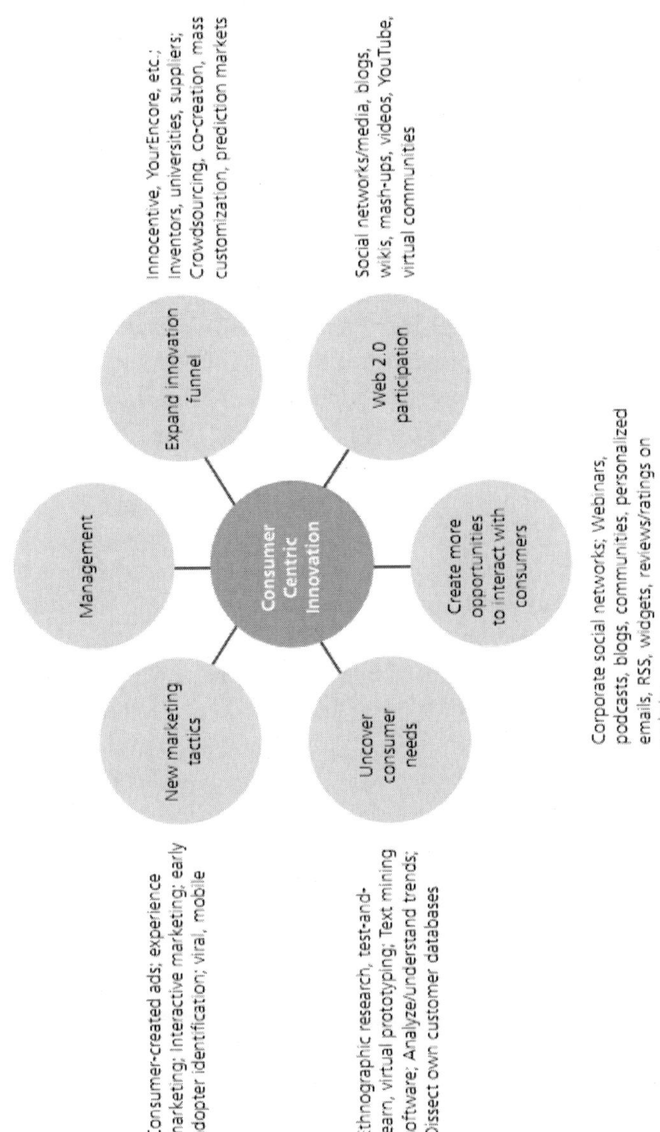

Figure 124: Inputs into customer centric innovation

Source: (Deloitte Development LLC, 2009)

Figure 124 depicts some of the inputs that are required to have world-class consumer centric innovation. These are:

- ***Management commitment*** – Management commitment and constancy of purpose are absolutely necessary. Commitment need not be at the top most level; however champions are often needed through the organisations so that different departments work towards the common goal. "Build it and they will buy it" philosophy has already been abandoned by CCI focussed organisations. Now the innovation process starts from the deep understanding of the customers and their needs, both met and unmet. The value comes from the focussed attention on the target group of customers and engaging and empowering them will drive the CCI process in the right direction.
- ***Expand your innovation funnel*** – Excellent organisations engaged with CCI has started moving beyond their human capital and employees' expertise for wider range of ideas. Many are employing open innovation processes that seek answers from a vast global talent pool eager to share knowledge. Others are using co-creation to good effect in order to reduce the associated risks as well as to build the brand loyalty – a win-win scenario for the organisation as well as the customers.
- ***Increase your Web 2.0 participation*** – Online marketing and intelligent mining of information related to consumer preferences and product critiques have resulted in significant benefits to the organisations. In particular, user-generated content (UGC) – including videos, social networks, blogs, and wikis - has provided a wealth of knowledge around consumers' interests at a lower cost.
- ***Create more opportunities for your consumers to interact with you*** – Organisations are looking at innovative means to have a meaningful engagement with the customers. Multiple channels have been opened up and effort is on to make the interaction easy, smooth and hassle free. Most notable among them being the organisations' effort to develop their websites into a two-way interaction medium that suits the specific needs of the target customer group. By creating areas on their websites where consumers can write online reviews, sign up for personalised

emails, participate in contests, or read or contribute to blogs, organisations are gaining vast amounts of knowledge.

- ***Uncover consumer needs*** – Technology has greatly expanded the ability of organisations to better understand consumer sentiments around brands and products. Tools such as ethnography, consumer targeting, virtual prototyping, and in-market experimentation to better understand interest in new products have been adopted by organisations to successfully pursue consumer centric innovation. The key here is to extract and analyse the buried and hidden consumer information. Organisations are using cutting edge filters and excellent data analytics to zoom in on the relevant information.
- ***Employ new marketing tactics*** – Organisations are using new marketing tactics such as using customers as their brand ambassadors and evangelists to generate the authentic buzz about the newer products/services. Word of mouth marketing, viral dissemination of customer review about the products, widespread use of mobile and web technologies have improved the customer's engagement with brands or products, organisations often develop closer relationships with those individuals, thereby gaining even greater insights.

Source: (Deloitte Development LLC, 2009)

Assessment Toolkit - Innovation

Philosophy of Innovation

Q1. Does the organisation develop the culture of learning and innovation?			
Basic	**Developing**	**Maturing**	**Leading**
The culture of organisation does not support or little facilitate innovation and learning i.e. there is a fear among employees to share their failure experiences,	The organisation does not sufficiently empower employees, there is still a culture of blame for sharing failure experiences; although, the organisation started its journey towards a learning organisation by modifying some of its policies and work procedures.	The culture of organisation fully support innovation and learning i.e. employees are encouraged to share their learning experiences with others and there is no fear of blame.	The culture of organisation fully support and facilitate innovation and learning. Employees are empowered to use their creativity and innovative thinking for handling customers' experiences. Any innovation is distinctly recognised and highly rewarded. There is a strong link between innovation and rewards and recognition system.
Q2. Does the organisation maintain a clear innovation strategy?			
Basic	**Developing**	**Maturing**	**Leading**
The organisation does not have a clear strategy or process for innovation.	The organisation has a system in place for collecting new ideas for further improvement; although, it is not conducted in	There is a clear process for innovation. Individuals' roles and responsibilities with regards to innovation are	The organisation has established a set of strategic objectives in relation to innovation and it has articulated an effective

	a systematic way.	clearly defined and determined.	strategy for achieving these objectives. The organisation sees innovation as a way for achieving competitive advantage.
Q3. Does the organisation sufficiently empower employees to use their creativity?			
Basic	**Developing**	**Maturing**	**Leading**
Everything within the organisation is controlled by top managers, supervisors.	There is a clear and two ways communication channel between managers and employees so that any good ideas will be collected at the operational level and will be communicated to the strategy level for further consideration; although, policies and procedures are not adjusted to sufficiently empower employees to act creatively. Employees are still encouraged to followed work procedures.	Employees are highly rewarded for generating any good idea, which leads to an innovation. Work procedures and policies are supportive and adjusted to give more authority to employees.	Employees are encouraged to use their own initiatives, and creative thinking in handling customers' complaints. Policies and procedures are adjusted to give more freedom to employees. Employees' representatives are allowed to contribute in the decision making process.

Innovation System

Q1. Does the organisation adopt open innovation?			
Basic	**Developing**	**Maturing**	**Leading**
The organisation does not have a clear innovation processes neither of close or open innovation.	The organisation is internally oriented in relation to any possible innovation created. It does not involve different groups of stakeholders in the process of innovation, in particular, from outside of the organisation.	The organisation has a proven track record of conducting close innovation; it recently started its journey towards adjusting open innovation by establishing partnerships with other organisation. There are number of R&D partnerships.	The organisation has successfully adopted open innovation, it extensively seeks innovative ideas from both inside as well as outside of the organisation. It has several R&D partnerships. Customers are involved in the process of innovation.

Q2. Does the organisation empower customers to actively contribute in the process of innovation?			
Basic	**Developing**	**Maturing**	**Leading**
The organisation does not maintain any system for seeking customers inputs.	The organisation heavily relies on customers' feedback for improving services but it does not directly involve customers in the process of innovation.	The organisation has run several conferences, meetings, open discussion board etc. about its recent innovation in order to involve customers in the process of innovation. Customers are occasionally allowed to attend in the process of decision making but not given right to contribute.	The organisation has successfully implemented the concept of service co-creation. Customers are empowered to actively contribute in the service delivery from service design to delivery to post-delivery etc.

Q3. What percentage of innovation within the organisation is generated through partnership? (Partnership includes partnering with other organisation as well as customers.)			
Basic	**Developing**	**Maturing**	**Leading**
Equal to or less than 10%	Between 11% and 35%	Between 36% and 65%	Between 65% and 100%

Innovative Service Delivery

Q1. To what extent does the organisation rely on designing new and innovative services in order to create the greater impact?			
The organisation completely focuses on building its basic capability requirements so there is less room left for further investment on innovation.	The organisation has realised the importance of being innovative and hence it started to shift its attention on advancing its existing technologies. There are limited by growing number of innovation programs, initiatives has been implemented.	The organisation has acquired an advanced level of capabilities requirement for designing new and innovative services. It constantly benchmarks itself against world-class organisations in order to catch up with the latest innovations.	The organisation has established a world-class status for itself. It is widely known as an innovative organisation, which constantly introduce new and innovative services.
Q2. What are the drivers of innovation (internally vs. externally driven) for the organisation?			
The organisation highly focuses on meeting its budget plans so the main drivers can be found internally and they are mostly	However, the organisation has realised the importance of open innovation, due to the limited resources, the main drivers of innovation can be	The organisation has the sufficient resources available to start its journey toward a leading organisation so its constantly compare its	The main objective of the organisation to keep its world-class organisation. It is highly customer oriented so

related to efficiency and cost saving.	found internally such as HR management, resource management, capacity management etc.	performance against best performers so the main driver for its innovation is to increasing market share and customer satisfaction etc.	that the main drivers will come from outside of the organisation.
Q3. To what extent is the organisation capable of E-delivery of services?			
The organisation does not have the required capability or technology infrastructure for e-delivery of services.	The organisation can deal with a limited number of online application; however, it does not have the required infrastructure or capability to manage the entire service life –cycle. For example: customers are given opportunities to send their request online; however, further communication with customers would be through other channels such as post, or over the phone.	The organisation has the required capability for delivering online services; however, it lacks an integrated technology infrastructure for e-delivery of services at one-stop.	The organisation has successfully adopted one-stop shop. It also adopted the concept of self-service so that customers can personalise e-services as well.

Know that you believe you understand what you think I said, but I'm not sure you realize that what you heard is not what I meant.

Robert McCloskey

Chapter 19: Impact

Introduction

Customer empathy is far different from customer service. Customer empathy is the art of seeing the transaction through the customer's eyes. It's thinking about the customer's fears, anxiety, and trying to understand their previous transaction. Empathetic organisations create long term relationships with customers. So, listen carefully. Look inside their hearts before they respond. Then, respond with kindness, thoughtfulness, and understanding. Customers are rewarded with trust, friendship, and loyalty (Shafer, 2005).

Customer empathy is the ability to reach outside of ourselves and walk in someone else's shoes, to get where they're coming from, to feel what they feel. Widespread empathy is about getting every single person in an organisation to have a gut-level intuition for the people who buy their products and services. Increasingly, organisations strive to determine what drives their profit and in particular, how much customers can create impact on their profitability and business growth. Customers often become more profitable over time and loyal customers account for a high proportion of the sales and profit growth of successful service providers. Customer empathy has a direct impact on building customer loyalty. It has a direct and an immediate impact on the perception of customers about the quality of services.

Another important effect of customer empathy, apart from building customer loyalty and increase business profitability, is on stimulating innovation. Customer empathy entails seeing organisation's services from customers' perspectives. Hence, empathetic organisations truly empower customers to actively contribute in the process of service delivery. Involvement of customers will be widened across the process of service provision, from service design to service delivery to post-service delivery. Organisations constantly seek customers' ideas at each and every step of service delivery and genuinely incorporate new and innovative ideas into the system in order to improve services. This can be well encompassed within the context of open innovation.

In addition, customer empathy greatly helps an organisation in increasing the effectiveness of services and efficiency of activities. Once an organisation has begun to see things from the customers' point of view, it will incorporate customers' ideas in the process of service delivery. Services' characteristics and features become close to customers' needs. Employees' attitude towards customer service will be highly influenced as a result of the culture of customer empathy. They no longer see customer service as a one way interaction with customers and strive to build a deep relationship with customers. They focus the depth and the length of the relationship. They understand that it is important to find out not only where defectors go but also what they defect, was it because of poor service, price, or value? In addition to handle customer problems, service providers must have the latitude to resolve any situation promptly.

Customer empathy improves service value. Value as a function not only costs to the customer but also of the results achieved for the customer. Value is always relative because it is based both of perceptions of the way a service is delivered and on initial customer expectations. Because value varies with individual expectations, organisations can get huge benefit from customer empathy and to move all levels of management closer to the customer and give frontline service employees the latitude to customise a standard service to individual needs. Likewise, customer empathy can generate a huge impact on service quality.

Service quality is a function of the gap between perceptions of the actual service experiences and what a customer expected before receiving that service. Differences between experiences and expectations can be measured in generic dimensions such as reliability and timeliness of service, the empathy and authority with which the service was delivered (Harvard Business Review, 1994).

Turning Customer Service into a Sustainable Advantage

Customer service is important to an organisation's success. The majority of corporate executives embrace it, and almost all customers demand it. But achieving a high level of customer service – and sustaining it over the long haul – is a goal that has eluded all but a relatively small number of organisations. In order to create a sustainable competitive advantage through an exemplary customer service, organisations embrace customer empathy. To capture the broader conception of customer empathy, organisations should promote senior leaders, managers and frontline employees work together to collectively stand in their customers' shoes in order to better understand and resolve customer needs. Organisations with great customer empathy consistently strive to (booz&co., 2007):

- Understand and resolve customers' problems at minimum cost to customers
- Create an organisation-wide culture of empathy
- Empathise with and give decision-making power to their frontline employees so
- They can focus on generating excellent customer service
- Sustain an organisation-wide service ethos through storytelling
- View the frontline as a driver of customer service innovation
- View customer service as a profit-generating activity and important contributor to shareholder value, rather than "just a cost centre".

These organisations have nurtured long-term customer relationships that set them apart from their competitors, and which will be difficult for their competitors to disrupt. Such relationships have quantifiable long-term benefits for the organisations that possess them.

Superior customer service is important first and foremost because it helps generate customer loyalty. Studies have shown that the best customer service generates – and has a real, measurable impact on – customers' emotional satisfaction. It is emotional satisfaction that is especially important and it is very much attainable through customer empathy. One study showed that reducing customer defections by 5% (i.e., increasing customer loyalty by 5%) enabled businesses to increase the lifetime value of the average customer significantly.

Case study- retail banking

One major retail bank found that its emotionally-satisfied customers had lower attrition and higher spend rates than other, less satisfied customers (see the following figures)

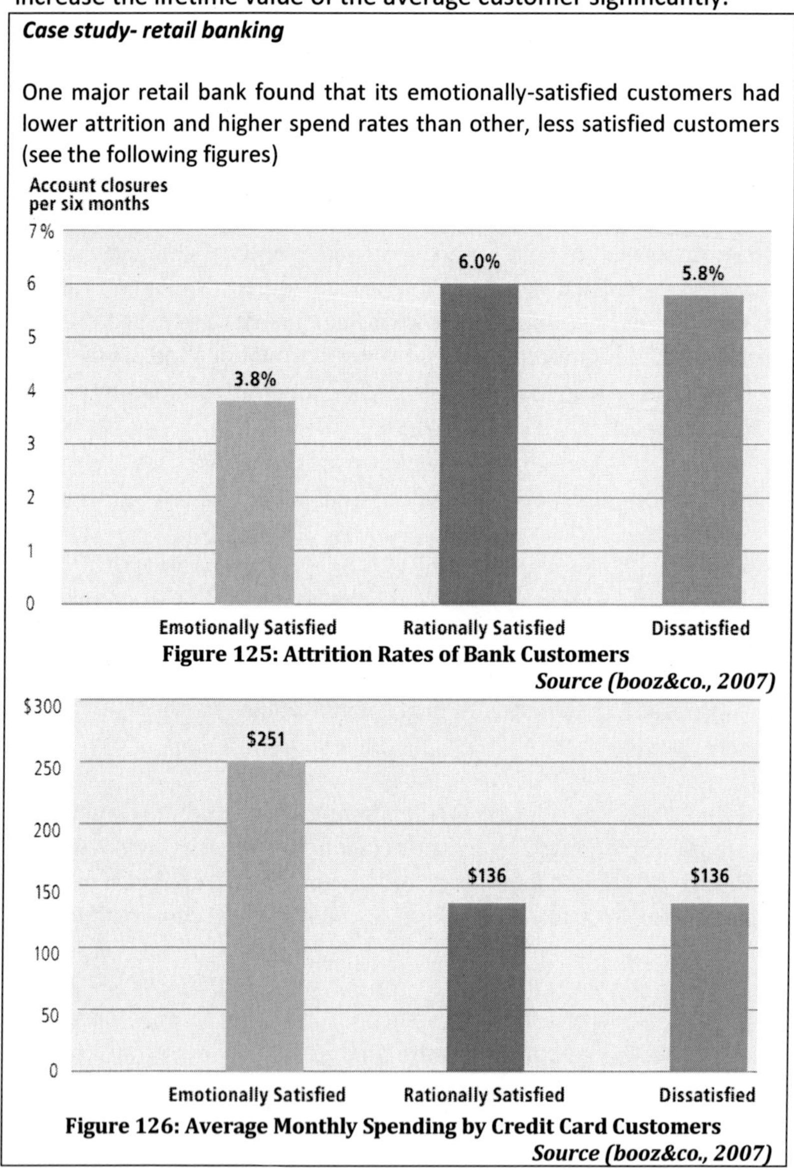

Figure 125: Attrition Rates of Bank Customers

Source (booz&co., 2007)

Figure 126: Average Monthly Spending by Credit Card Customers

Source (booz&co., 2007)

In service industries, customer relationships are a critical driver of sustainable advantage because they are difficult to imitate or replace. Multiple studies have shown that these relationships can have a measurable impact on organisations' economic performance. In addition, studies have shown that excellent customer service also generates increased returns to shareholders. For example: A portfolio constructed by purchasing shares in organisations with high scores in the American Customer Satisfaction Index (ACSI) has gained 75% in value whereas an investment portfolio in short-selling organisations with low scores in the Dow Jones Industrial Average (DJIA) has lost 5% (see Figure 127).

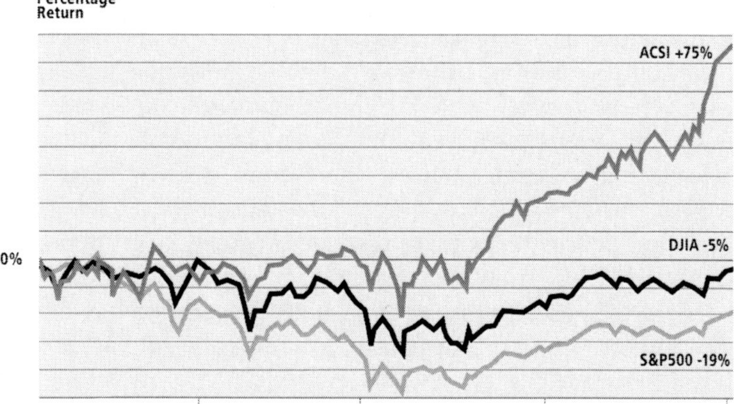

Figure 127: Comparative Performance of American Customer Satisfaction Index Portfolio with Major Indices

Source: (booz&co., 2007)

Great customer empathy can be a way to attract, retain and even win back customers in an penetrated market place with an increasing competition and faster commoditisation of products and services. A great deal of the thought on how to achieve a sustainable strategic advantage through customer empathy has focused on exceeding customer experiences. Exceeding expectations certainly delights customers, but a customer service strategy that relies on constantly exceeding expectations is likely to fail a test of sustainability. Organisations that have achieved sustainable strategic service believe that instead of trying to generate individual "wow!"

experiences for thousands of customers, the better approach is to consistently meet their customers' high expectations. In the long run, this builds trust and reaffirms, rather than inflates, their expectations, thus forming the basis for long-term customer relationships that translate into a sustainable strategic advantage for the organisation. Creating a strategic point of differentiation is not only a question of how an individual representative reacts to an individual customer, but also how the organisation as a whole understands and reacts to its customers.

When an organisation can consistently sense and solve its customers' most difficult problems – when it exhibits consistent empathy – it creates unique, sustainable customer relationships that are difficult for its competitors to replicate. Delivering sustainable strategic service starts with an empathetic frontline – one that consists of service representatives who can sense customers' problems and needs by putting themselves in their customers' shoes. In customer service interactions, this means feeling and anticipating a customer's distress, excitement, frustration, or desires. Achieving truly sustainable competitive advantage also requires an organisation that is, as a whole, aligned with its frontline and customers so that the frontline can put empathy into action.

Putting empathy into action means having a frontline that lives in the customer's shoes and can improvise in the moment to solve customers' problems; it also means having an organisation that can empathise with customers and employees and invest in changes to avoid a problem occurring again (booz&co., 2007).

Customer Loyalty and Profitability

Once an organisation targets its customers and begins to meet and exceed their expectations, customer satisfaction rises. Loyalty follows, bringing with it a significant and measurable impact on the bottom line. Earl Sasser and Fred Reichheld studied a wide range of service industries, and they discovered that relationships with typical customers grew increasingly more profitable over time in all cases—regardless of industry. Figure 128 clearly demonstrates that the longer the customer relationship lasts, the more profitable it tends to become. In one study of service organisations, extending the customer relationship from five years to six years resulted in a 25% to 85% increase in profitability.

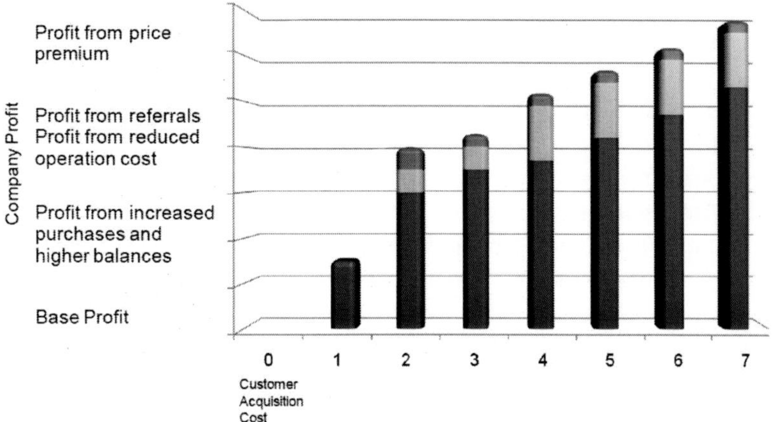

Figure 128: Customers profitability over time

Source (The Pert Group, 2011)

Putting Empathy into Action

In order to put customer empathy into action, organisations require a set of processes and behaviours. This term 'Empathy Engine' introduced by booz&co. (2007) encompasses the whole package required for implementing customer empathy. It entails sensing customers' problem *(empathy) and consistently act on them (engine). As depicted in Figure 129, the empathy engine consists of five components (booz&co., 2007):

1. ***Information*** – This includes the key insights learned by the frontline during their interactions with customers. Harnessing that flow of information and using it to bring the organisation ever closer to its customers is what the Empathy Engine must do consistently to succeed.
2. ***Values*** – An organisation can have complete information about what its customers want, but unless it actually places value on meeting those demands, it can never develop genuine, valuable customer relationships. The Empathy Engine values its

relationships with customers. It establishes, lives, and shares these values that shape its long-term strategy, day-to-day decisions, and frontline improvisation.

3. ***Senior leaders*** – Senior leaders realise the bottom-line impact that customer care can have and rally the organisation around customer service and the importance of living in the customers' shoes.
4. ***Managers*** – They make caring for their employees their priority, so their employees can focus on taking care of their customers. To accomplish this, managers need the freedom to make decisions about their staff and how service is delivered.
5. ***The frontline employees*** – Frontline staff maintains the delicate balance between the customers' demand for a "just for me" experience, and the need to deliver efficient customer service in a cost-effective manner.
6. ***Customers*** – Customers provide constant feedback to the organisation and how well it is doing. Healthy customer empathy creates the right experience for customers at each point of contact – and gains knowledge through each interaction.

While the first two, like the blood flowing throughout the body, must be kept flowing throughout the organisation, the last four are chambers which play an important role in establishing the potential, empathetic customer relationship. When the Empathy Engine circulates information and values throughout an organisation, senior leaders, managers and the frontline are able to harness empathy to understand their customers and each other, creating and sustaining a cohesive organisation devoted to developing valuable relationships with customers.

Organisations that employ the Empathy Engine approach represent a shift away from a linear, hierarchical concept of customer service to a more holistic approach that involves senior leadership, management, the frontline, and customers. This approach sustains interactions with a constant flow of information and shared values. These organisations realise distinctive and sustainable competitive advantages based on customer relationships that cannot be easily replicated by their competitors. The result: increased market share, shareholder value and profitability (booz&co., 2007).

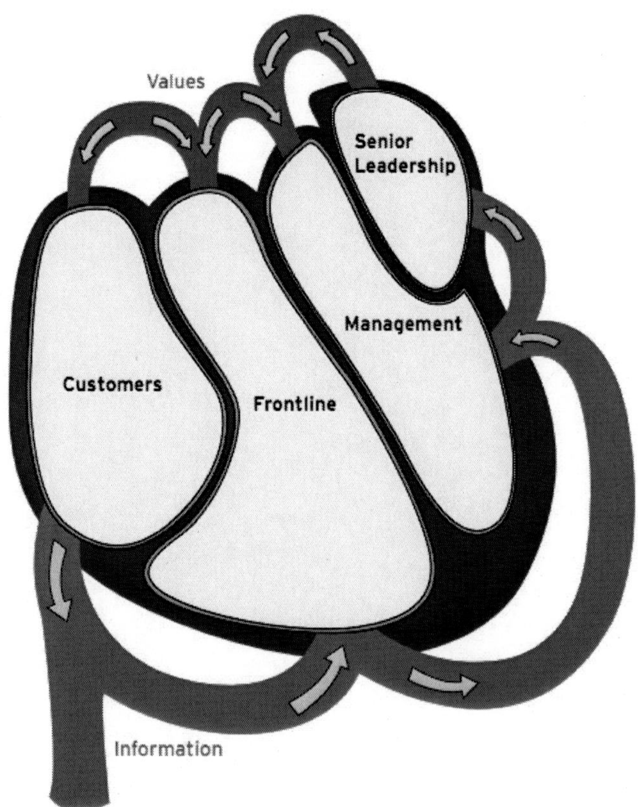

Figure 129: The Empathy engine

Source: (booz&co., 2007)

Service Profit Chain

The life time value of customer loyalty can be enormous, especially when referrals are added to the economics of customer retention and repeat orders and purchases of related services or products. Service profit chain establishes the overall impact generated from Customer loyalty and the relationships between profitability, business growth, and customer and employee satisfaction (see the following figure). Figure 130 depicts profit and business growth is stimulated by customer loyalty. Customer loyalty itself is a direct result of customer satisfaction. Satisfaction is largely influenced by the value of services to customers. Value of services can be enhanced by the degree of customer care shown by an organisation.

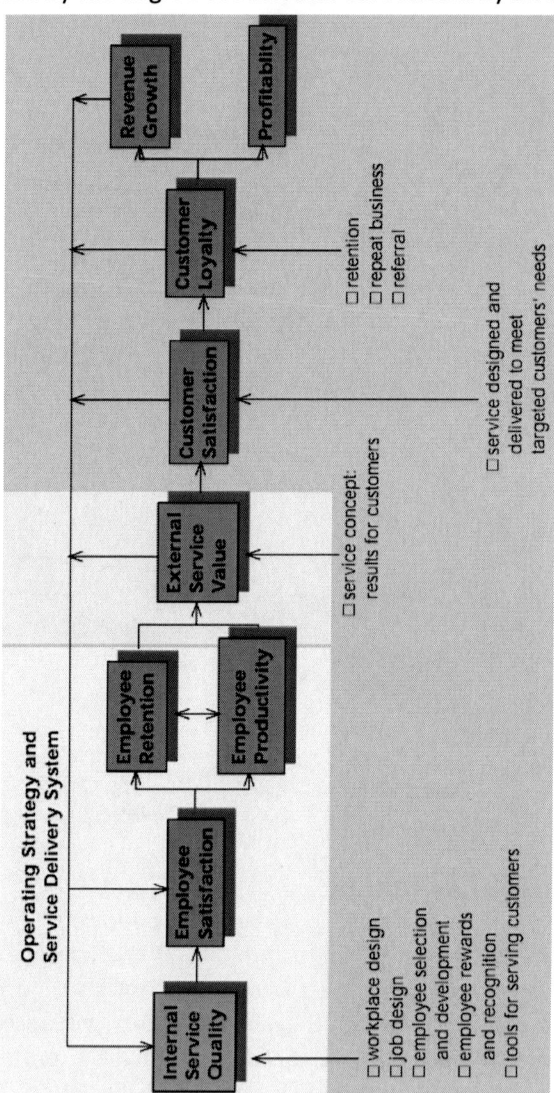

Figure 130: The links in the service profit chain

Source (Harvard Business Review, 1994)

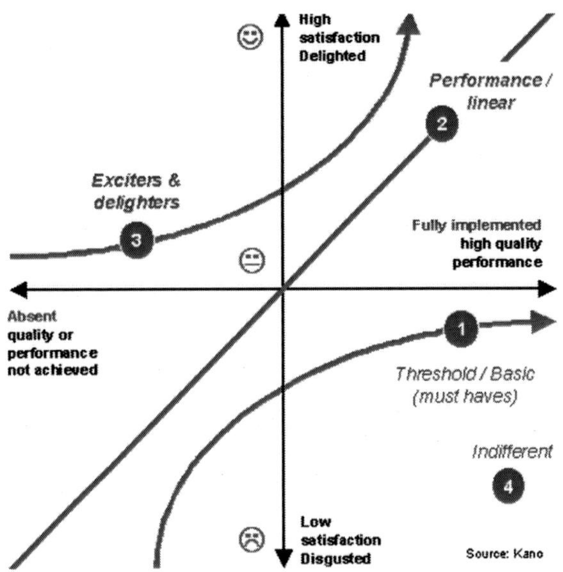

Figure 131: Kano Model

Source (University of Cambridge, 2010)

As depicted by the Kano Model in Figure 131, service differentiation can only happen when an organisation can reach to the level of customer excitement through not only fulfilling customers' needs but exceeding these needs. This requires differentiating organisation's services from competitors' services through offering something extra on top of what actually customers need and what they can get from others. The Kano Model can describe this well. It offers some insight into the service/products attributes which are perceived to be important to customers. Product/service differentiation can either be gained by a high level of execution of the linear attributes or the inclusion of one or more 'delighter' features. Since customer expectations change over time, and it is substantially difficult and costly for an organisation to proactively identify customers' needs and then tailor its services accordingly, organisations require a tolerance for meeting customers' needs. Emotionally attached customers create the required tolerance for organisations, which keeps them ahead of any change that might occur in customers' needs.

Most organisations can offer services that greatly fulfil basic needs of the customers; however, this can hardly lead to a sustainable competitive advantage for any organisation. Even if organisations succeed to achieve high customer satisfaction through delivering excellent service quality (which is mostly comprised of tangible, physical and hard service attributes), they still require sustaining this level of satisfaction, which put the justifiability of this strategy, in terms of the associated cost, under a big question mark.

The implication of the above discussion for organisations is to strive towards engaging customers emotionally and deeply through delivering great customer empathy. This creates customer loyalty and leads to a sustainable competitive advantage and consequently high profitability & flexibility and sustainable business growth.

The philosophy of customer empathy should be well embedded in the culture of an organisation if the organisation is to succeed in achieving customer loyalty. Recently, organisations started to realise customer empathy as an important value, which require be building and well promoting among employees throughout the organisation. This is because unless employees have a true sense of customer empathy, they cannot effectively contribute in delivering it.

Once customer empathy has been recognised as a value within the organisations, it is everyone responsibility to effectively promote such a value to the customers. Individuals' performance like organisational performance is highly influenced by the value system of an organisation and hence, customer empathy as a component of value system can greatly influence on the employees' performance and productivity.

Employee factors produce an indirect effect on customer loyalty and profitability. For example, employee capability—built by hiring the right people, giving them training, support, latitude, and rewards—promotes employee job satisfaction. When employees enjoy their work and believe they are making a difference they tend to stay longer, to become more productive and knowledgeable – in short, they become loyal employees. Such employee loyalty, in turn, creates greater customer satisfaction.

After all, customers are more likely to be happy when they are being served by motivated employees who take the time to get to know their specific needs and circumstances. Not surprisingly, happy customers tend to buy more from the company and also to refer other customers to the company more frequently. Thus, customer satisfaction breeds customer loyalty. And there is a dramatic cause-and-effect relationship between customer loyalty and profitability: in some industries, a small percentage of a company's most valuable and loyal customers can account for more than half of total profitability (The Pert Group, 2011).

The links between customer empathy and the level of customer satisfaction is well underscored by the fact that employees' productivity generates direct and significant impact on the level of customer satisfaction.

Case study – Southwest Airlines – Employees productivity and Customer satisfaction

At southwest, customer perception of value is very high and though the airline does not assign seats, offer meals, or integrate its reservation system with other airlines. Customer place high value on south west's frequent departures, on-time service, friendly employees, and very low fares. South west's management knows this because its major marketing research unit is in daily contact with customers and report its finding back to management. The airline has the highest level of on-time arrivals, the lowest number of complaints and the fewest lost-baggage claims.

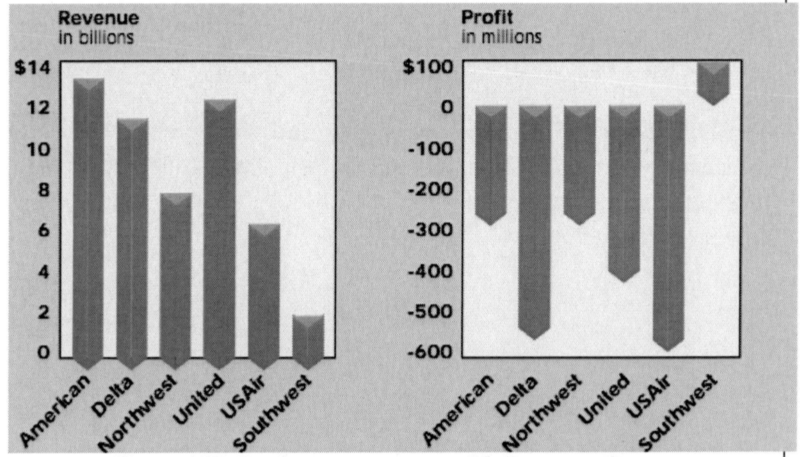

Figure 132: Southwest compares with its competitors

Source (Harvard Business Review, 1994)

Stimulating Innovation

Recent research among service organisations across industries is providing evidence for the types of business process factors associated which enhanced innovation performance. The innovation processes used by organisations with high new product/service success rate are considerably different than those by less successful organisations. The best innovators make customer needs discovery a key part of their-end of innovation process. That leads to better idea generation, concept development, new service success rate, and profitability. Table 28 highlights top five factors for innovation success and failure.

Success	*Failure*
• Understanding customer needs	• Ineffective process
• Systematic process	• Not understanding customer needs
• Management support	• Resource management
• Cross functional teamwork	• Insufficient funding
• Right skills	• Lack of clarity in objectives

Table 28: Top reasons for innovation success and failure

Source: PDMA Foundation's CAPS (2005)

Great customer empathy enables organisations to focus on understanding customer needs as part of a systematic front-end of innovation process. As depicted by the above table, understanding customer needs is the primarily factor for innovation success. Leading innovation experts insists that customer needs knowledge is 'sticky' – it is deeply embedded in the customer's environment and hence, the best approach for getting customer knowledge is to truly dissolve in customer's environment through building customer empathy. Emphatic design helps an organisation to identify needs that customers themselves may not recognise. The technique of empathic design is built upon not only to effectively gathering, analysing and applying information gleaned from observation of customer's behaviour but to proactively find out about customers' thought process and what customers might need in the future (Ross, 2009).

When an organisation develops a shared and intuitive vibe for what's going on in the world, it is able to see new opportunities faster than its competitors. The organisation has the courage of its convictions to take a risk with something new. And it has the passion to stick with it even if it doesn't turn out right the first time.

Organisations with widespread empathy can even ensure the quality of what they make when every part of the organisation isn't firing on all cylinders. At Nike, people who work on running shoes tend to be runners themselves. So even if the market research isn't that great, the shoes end up being awesome anyway. This isn't about market research. It's not about the Voice of the Customer. It's about strategy and culture. Imagine a place where every person has the same intuitive connection to the world — not just the employees in particular departments such as in marketing and design, but the people who work in finance, too and in HR and legal.

The line between inside and outside the organisation starts to blur. Rather than seeing itself as a separate body from its customers, the organisation starts to see itself as part of the same tribe. It starts to think like customers and feel confident enough to rely on its intuition. The organisation finds itself anticipating what real people are up to and what they're looking for from the organisation. The effects can be profound (Patnaik, 2011).

Especially in tough times, empathy is one competency that companies can't afford not to develop. It can help them to move more quickly, make better decisions, and create new businesses that can fuel their growth. It can even secure the future of their organisation. And all that innovation can start with empathy.

Case study- IBM Operation Bear Hug

In the early 1990s, IBM was in crisis. The organisation was laying off employees by the thousands as its profits and revenues collapsed for the first time in its history. Most experts agreed that the organisation as it had been — a technology integrator with its hands in everything from giant data centres to consumer printers — had to go. In fact, by the time Lou Gerstner was installed as CEO, just about everyone believed his job would be to divide Big Blue into a dozen Baby Blues. Everyone, that is, except Gerstner, who believed the company needed to survive.

To figure out how to make that possible, he sent his top 50 managers into the world to each visit at least five customers in person. He called it Operation Bear Hug, a culturally appropriate name for an empathy program at one of the least emotionally demonstrative organisations in the Fortune 500. The managers weren't supposed to sell product in those meetings. Instead, they were to listen to customer concerns and think about how IBM might help. Those executives' 200 direct reports then had to do the same thing. Bear Hug immediately led to quicker actions to resolve customer problems, as well as greater attention to new market opportunities.

That empathic connection to real-world customers helped managers to see whether a particular decision added value for customers or destroyed it. It also revealed some major opportunities. Managers discovered that large corporate clients were fascinated by the Internet but unclear about what they should do about it. Beyond selling product, IBM realised that it could make a major impact by providing the infrastructure needed to help large enterprises leverage the power of the Web. The resulting e-business initiative was wildly successful and helped put IBM on the path to long-term growth.

Over time, the dogged attention Gerstner gave customers started to shift the organisation, making it less insular, less arrogant, and more outward-looking. By his second year at IBM, the organisation was back in the black, setting off a decade of uninterrupted double-digit revenue and earnings growth. Its leaders had the courage to take on that challenge because they had seen their customers face-to-face.
Source (Patnaik, 2011)

Assessment Toolkit: Impact

Profitability & Business Growth

Q1. Does the organisation focus on customer life-time value measurement?			
Basic	**Developing**	**Maturing**	**Leading**
The organisation has a focus on short-term profitability. (up to 1 year)	The organisation has a focus on short- to – middle term profitability. (between 1 and 3 years)	The organisation focuses on medium to long term customer value. (Between 3 to 7 years)	The organisation focuses on customer life-time value. (Over 7 years)
Q2. To what extent does the organisation seek service effectiveness through delivering customer empathy?			
Basic	**Developing**	**Maturing**	**Leading**
The organisation gives more priority to achieving efficiency and cost saving rather than effectiveness.	The organisation strives to achieve service effectiveness through determining customer segments.	The organisation strives to achieve service effectiveness through establishing a deep customer insight and customising services.	The organisation strives to generate significant impact, achieve multiple objectives including delivering genuine customer empathy.
Q3. Does the organisation maintain customer satisfaction and loyalty measurement system?			
Basic	**Developing**	**Maturing**	**Leading**
The organisation has occasionally collected customer satisfaction rate and the measurement is	There is a system in place for measuring and improving customer satisfaction; however, the	The organisation has a customer loyalty measurement and management system in place.	The organisation has a loyalty management system in place and it has also focused on customer

not done in a systematic way.	organisation does not have a strategy, system or plan for measuring and managing customer loyalty.		intimacy and advocacy management.

Employees' productivity and performance improvement

Q4. Does the organisation consider employees' skills in managing customer empathy as a selection criteria during recruitment process?			
Basic	**Developing**	**Maturing**	**Leading**
The ability to show customer empathy is not considered as a selection criteria for employees. The organisation look into sales skills of candidates during the assessment process.	The ability to handle customers' enquires quickly in a complex situation is a sort of skills, which will be considered by the organisation during the assessment process.	The organisation looks into employees' ability to build and maintain a god relationship with customers during the assessment process.	The ability to deliver customer empathy, build and maintain one-lasting relationship with customers and innovative thinking is sort of skills, which will be considered by the organisation during the assessment process.
Q5. How often does the organisation delivers employees training program with regards to customer empathy?			
Basic	**Developing**	**Maturing**	**Leading**
The organisation rarely delivers training programs in relation to customer empathy. The organisation	The organisation occasionally delivers training programs in relation to customer empathy.	The organisation quite often delivers training programs in relation to customer empathy.	The organisation constantly delivers training programs in relation to customer empathy. The main aim is to boost employees

focuses on increasing employees productivity in terms of number of services delivered.			ability to delivering a great customer care and intimacy.
Q6. Does the organisation link its reward and recognition system to the individuals' skills for delivering customer empathy?			
Basic	**Developing**	**Maturing**	**Leading**
There is a poor/ no link between individuals' incentives and their ability for delivering customer care/ empathy. Employees are incentivised based on the number of sales they made.	Individuals are rewarded in accordance with their performance in achieving higher customer satisfaction.	Employees' ability to deliver a great customer care and make a great use of customers' relationship with the organisation will be the base for performance appraisal.	Employees' creativity and innovativeness in delivering an excellent customer service, which enhance the depth of customer relationship will be highly rewarded.

Service Innovation

Q1. Does the organisation measure the rate of innovative services - Open innovation?			
Basic	**Developing**	**Maturing**	**Leading**
The organisation does not have a clear innovation processes neither of close or open innovation.	The organisation is internally oriented in relation to any possible innovation created. It does not involve different groups of stakeholders in the process of innovation, in particular, from outside of the organisation.	The organisation has a proven track record of conducting close innovation; it recently started its journey towards adjusting open innovation by establishing partnerships with other organisation. There are number of R&D partnerships.	The organisation has successfully adopted open innovation; it extensively seeks innovative ideas from both inside as well as outside of the organisation. It has several R&D partnerships. Customers are involved in the process of innovation.
Q2. To what extent does the organisation strive to deliver co-created services with shared responsibilities?			
Basic	**Developing**	**Maturing**	**Leading**
The organisation does not allow customers to be involved in delivery of services.	The organisation, to limited extent, collects and incorporates customers' inputs for designing and delivering services; although, it does not directly involve them in the process.	The organisation, to limited extent, has shared responsibilities with customers in relation to design and delivery of services; however, customers are mostly involved in delivery side rather than design.	Customers are given a significant role and responsibility over the process of service delivery from deign to delivery and post-delivery. They are directly involved in the decision making process.

Q3. Does the organisation develop a service improvement measurement system?			
Basic	**Developing**	**Maturing**	**Leading**
The organisation does not have a clear service improvement measurement system in place; although, it uses limited number of performance metrics for establishing its performance status. Metrics are designed to measure performance aspects such as cost saving, efficiency etc.	The organisation has a performance measurement system in place, which helps the organisation to measure the current level of its performance; however, it lacks to support performance improvement cycle.	The organisation has a clear service improvement measurement system in place.	The organisation has service improvement measurement system in place and the system is subjected to a continuous review.

So when you are listening to somebody, completely, attentively, then you are listening not only to the words, but also to the feeling of what is being conveyed, to the whole of it, not part of it.

Jiddu Krishnamurti

Chapter 20: Inspiration

Introduction

The Customer Service environment is changing constantly and rapidly in order to cope with a lot of challenges and to respond to the many new needs and demands in the marketplace. The place and the role of the customer have become of very high importance in these changes and reforms. Managing customer satisfaction is therefore indispensable for organisations in order to see if they are doing the right things and if they are doing things right. Customers have different faces and different roles; sometimes they are customers of service delivery and sometimes they act like citizens when paying taxes, having to obey the rules, etc. This is also translated in a difference in public and private service delivery. Moreover most organisations are delivering services. Services have some clear characteristics which make them special and not the same as products. Expectations have a central role in influencing satisfaction with services and these in turn are determined by a very wide range of factors. It is arguable that the range of influences on expectations is even wider for public services. The service quality literature usually attempts to categorise the factors that influence attitudes towards the service on a number of different levels. At the highest level this involves a small number of service quality dimensions. As with the models for measuring satisfaction and identifying priorities, there are also a number of different constructions of the service factors that are most important in influencing perceptions of the service.

This changing role of customers has an impact on the policy and management cycle as a whole. Traditionally, the policy and management cycle is dominated and controlled by managers and administrators. Now, customers are increasingly involved in this policy and management cycle at different stages (design, decision, implementation and monitoring; and evaluation). Customers become co-designers, co-deciders, co-producers and co-evaluators. Managing satisfaction is therefore more than only measuring satisfaction at the end of the line in the evaluation stage. Having insight into and an impact on the needs and expectations of customers at the start or at a much earlier stage (the citizen/customer as "co-designer", "co-decider" or "co-producer") is also very important (EUPAN, 2008).

Service Excellence has a strong emotional impact upon customers, creating intense feelings about the organisation, its staff and its services, influencing customers' loyalty to it. Yet many organisations seem to find service 0excellence elusive, hard to grasp, and often difficult, if not impossible to deliver. To be a winner, organisations have to continually strive to provide the very best service when compared with any industry. That is why it is quite challenging. It takes lot of times and energy and requires significant investment in terms of money and time. Whatever best in class organisations do, they are in search of excellence and never willing to settle for what they have already achieved. Innovation Departments continuously looks at trends and why people behave in a certain manner, why they do certain things. They strive to create the new things that create the 'wow', the things that customers never expected, and a whole realm of things that customers don't know they want (Wirtz & Johnston, 2001).

Case study- Singapore Airlines

Singapore Airlines (SIA) is internationally recognised as one of the world's leading carriers. It has been consistently one of the most profitable airlines in the world, and it is routinely voted the 'best airline', 'best business class', 'best cabin crew service', 'best in- flight food', 'best for punctuality and safety', 'best for business travellers', 'best air cargo carrier', even 'Asia's most admired company'. Mr Yap Kim Wah, SIA's Senior Vice President responsible for Product and Service, explained "We have a high reputation for service and that means that when someone flies with us they come with high expectations. But still we want them to come away saying 'Wow! That was something out of the ordinary'." Mr Sim Kay Wee, the Senior Vice President responsible for Cabin Crew added, "Customers adjust their expectations according to the brand image. When you fly on a good brand, like SIA, your expectations are already sky-high. And if SIA gives anything that is just OK, it is just not good enough."

SIA uses the feedback from its staff together with information about other airlines and from major surveys to help them come up with new ideas. SIA recognises that whilst all the components of a service are important, there is a difference between the hygiene and enhancing factors. So the organisation constantly strives to personalise services and deal with customers' enquiries individually. Organisation has a list of the things that passengers expect when it comes to good service; flight schedules, punctuality, seat comfort, functional, and technical skills such as safe ty, or just pouring a cup of coffee without spilling it all over the place. Certain procedures must be followed. These are all hygiene factors. The enhancing factors are the softer skills, such as warmth, caring and anticipation of needs. SIA has very elaborate feedback mechanisms to help its staff not only listen to customers, but also understand them better. The organisation tracks and analyses all the feedback it receives so that it can improve future services.

Managers, in SIA, do a lot of 'Management by Walking Around', so there is plenty of opportunity for staff to give feedback. Managers will also actively solicit feedback. If someone has an idea, they will pull a few people to one side and talk about it. It's about injecting a sense of ownership and letting everyone see the big picture."

Source (Wirtz & Johnston, 2001)

Service Excellence

In the context of service excellence what organisations need to demonstrate is the global development of service management, evolutions and radical changes that are taking place, the understanding that customers are at the heart of service design and service delivery and the sustainable aspects of service management as a global phenomenon the provision of public services has moved away from the traditional aspect of producing higher levels of efficiency to producing high levels of quality and to the provision of compliance to standards of service and in the 21st century through e-governments, for example, service management has moved by putting the customer in the driver's seat, the customers now through one stop shop can enter government portals and design and configure services to be highly customised. So the emphasis on service management is the number one aspect that we will bring into our approach.

Figure 133: Service Excellence Model

Source (Goleman Consulting, 2011)

Model Description

Figure 133 depicts a model for service excellence.

1. ***Service leadership*** – This is based on the notion that customer service contains three key variables: a promise, a process, and people. After going through the step-by-step process of service management, the reader will have the necessary understanding and skill to choose the right strategy for the right circumstances, to design service processes, to identify the means and methods to implement these processes, and to measure the outcome. Service leadership can be defined as enabling or empowering others to accomplish something worthy. The following are six dimensions of service leadership (wendy-hewlett, 2010):
   a. Vision and Values – Service leaders have a clearly defined vision for their team's success. Service leaders are role models for the values that they represent.
   b. Direction – Service leaders set goals for the team. They are able to delegate to capable team members and they ensure that the tasks and priorities are sufficiently explained.
   c. Persuasion – Service leaders are able to persuade others to believe in their vision.
   d. Support - Leaders ensure that everyone functions well as a team and provides the team with the tools and resources required to achieve the desired outcome.
   e. Development – Service leaders are aware of the needs and goals of the team members and are able to provide opportunities for team members to accomplish these goals.
   f. Appreciation – Service leaders show team members that they care by showing respect and appreciation for their efforts.
2. ***Service agility*** – Agility is vital in today's volatile environment; it comprises two important components (Voss & Wang, 2009):
   a. Responsiveness – The ability to respond to externally-induced change

   b. Multi-competence – The capability to excel simultaneously in multiple criteria so that the organisation can rapidly realign itself to meet changed customer demands
3. ***Customer experience*** – Customer experience management (CEM) is the process of managing events and personal interactions that make up a customer's experience. A total customer experience can be seen as a totally positive, engaging, enduring and socially fulfilling physical and emotional customer experience across all levels of one's consumption chain and one that is brought about by a unique and individualised service offering that calls for active interaction between customers and providers.
4. ***Customer delight*** – This entails providing unique customer experience through introducing innovative service's features and keeping customers surprised in a positive ways. Organisations require five important capabilities if they are to delight customers:
   a. Woo – The ability to win others over.
   b. Empathy – The ability to understand the mood of others and see things from customers' perspectives.
   c. Discipline – The ability to work systematically and consistently.
   d. Command – The ability to control the situation though communication.
   e. Responsibility – The ability to own a problem until it is resolved.
5. ***Customer focused strategy*** – Organisations who aim to become customer-centric must demonstrate the following six winning traits (Booz Allen Hamilton, 2004).
   a. *Customer life-cycle view* - Organisations should have broad insights what is the true need of customers. They should clearly define what the level of customer/citizens expectations is and how do they meet or even exceed that level. The comprehensive, precise and reliable information

about changing and future needs of customers/citizens should be collected.

b. *Solution mindset* - The objective is to design a suit of service/product bundles, that when coupled with an advisory relationship can deliver cost-effective tailored solutions to customers'/citizens' specific problems.
c. *Advice bundling* - Effective communication strategy is an underlying pre-requisite for customer-centric organisations. Customer has to be engaged in a continuing dialogue with organisations.
d. *Can-Do customer interface* - Winning organisations offer integrated, multi-channel services in which the outlets serve as the hub. Self-service channel (e-Government e.g. website, telephone, kiosks etc.) are able to effectively deal with customers'/citizens' routine needs, thus, skilled customer care personnel can deal with more complex customers' needs and consultation transactions.
e. *Fit-for-purpose processes* - Customer-centric organisations deliver their most basic and stable products/services through the most efficient, least expensive business streams while more complex and less predictable services/product (or elements of services/products) will be diverted to more customised streams.
f. *Collective, cross functional efforts* - This entails tailoring solutions to customers' ever-changing needs, which requires a deep level of cooperation across all functions, service lines and organisations' boundaries.

6. ***Customer intelligence*** – Customer intelligence gives organisations the opportunity to leverage data to improve customer experiences, and to use deep customer knowledge to boost business performance. While the first of the two following figures depicts the customer Intelligence maturity model; Figure 134 shows the building blocks of customer intelligence.

Figure 134: The Key Elements of a Customer Intelligence Centre
Source (Frankland, 2009)

As depicted in Figure 135, there are three levels of Customer Intelligence within organisations. In the context of service excellence, organisations are encouraged to develop customer intelligence at the strategic level.

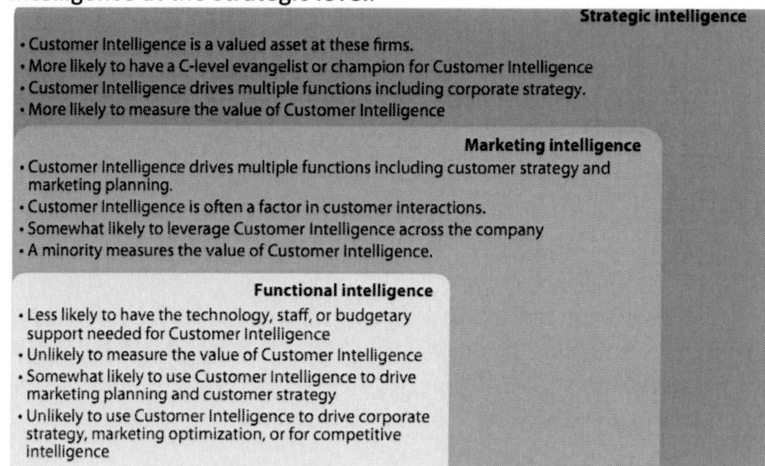

Figure 135: Customer Intelligence Maturity Model
Source (Frankland, 2009)

7. ***Customisation of services*** – This entails moving away from one size fits all to a new emerging concept called service individualisation or for me only kind of mindset. Mass customisation refers to the ability of providing customised services through flexible processes and at reasonably low cost with high quality. In light of new capabilities brought by Web service, customers will soon be able to directly input and interact with service providers.
8. ***Managing multiple touch-points*** – This explains how an organisation can effectively manage its customers' touch points used for transactions, interactions and information provision. Channel strategies must reflect the balance between customer and business needs and demonstrate clear value to both the organisation and its customers, underpinned by an understanding of end-to-end delivery costs. It also includes Customer experience mapping and measurement are an integral part of customer experience management, which is focussed towards enhancing the entire customer experience at various touch points. It is a process of tracking and describing all the experiences the customers have as they encounter a service or a set of services, taking into account not only what happens to them but also their personal responses to the experiences in terms of their level of satisfaction and to what extent their needs and expectations were met.
9. ***Service delivery through partnership*** – As depicted in Figure 136 partnership can occur at different states of service delivery.

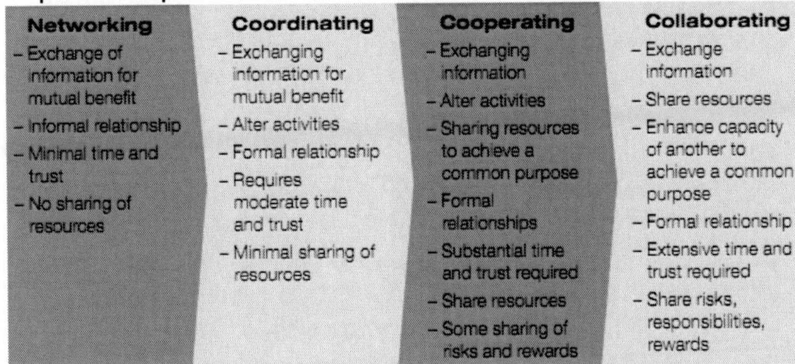

Figure 136: Continuum of relationships

Source (Himmelman, 2001)

10. **Delivering services through partnering with customers** - This can be well fitted within the context of service co-creation. This is a relationship between customers and organisations to achieve valued outcomes. Such partnerships empower customers to contribute more of their own resources (time, will power, expertise, effort) and have greater control over service decisions and resources (UK-Cabinet Office, 2009).
11. ***People development*** – This encompasses four important areas:
    a. *Talent management* – This includes recruitment process and selection criteria, employees' retention strategy etc.
    b. *Employees' engagement and empowerment* – This includes engaging employees in the process of decision making and empowering them to be creating in handling customers' enquiries.
    c. *Employees development* – This entails skills training and development programs
    d. *Rewards and recognition* – This entails recognising employees' innovative thinking and great performance in handling complex customers' enquiries
12. ***Service performance*** – This entails segmenting customers, developing customer insight and meeting or even exceeding customers' expectations through delivering appropriate services.
13. ***Customer results*** – This entails moving beyond customer satisfaction to customer loyalty and advocacy.
14. ***Executive leadership*** - Good leadership follow ethical and moral-based principles and values; the leaders act with integrity, courage and dedication to their mission. Leading with integrity has distinctive qualities, other than the commonly known themes of leadership. It begins with intention, personal responsibility, preparation and competence: a clear sense of personal identity, capacity and values and taking action without regard to personal gain or glory. Leadership with integrity requires personal and collective accountability and responsibility, which begins with reflection and results in correcting the gaps between what is said and what is done. It includes positive, value-based decision making which considers

all perspectives. Figure 137 illustrates the characteristics required of a 21st Century Leader.

Figure 137: Profile of Executive Leadership

Source: Leader Profile (Konczal, 2004)

Table 29 illustrates executive leadership pillars and a list of best practices for each of these pillars.

Leadership Pillars	Indicative List of Best Practices
Commitment to integrity	• Observe the highest ethical standards of behaviour in performing duties. • Foster a culture where ethical conduct is expected, encouraged, valued and recognised. • Avoid any activity or associations that creates a conflict between the personal interests and the organisation's interests. • Provide education and training in the legal and ethical standards that directly affect the organisation's objectives and the job responsibilities. • Achieve legal compliance by making the decisions and

Leadership Pillars	Indicative List of Best Practices
	carrying out duties in accordance with the spirit and letter of applicable laws and regulations. • Using the organisation's resources, time and facilities only for lawful purposes not for unauthorised personal benefit. • Protecting the organisation's confidential, privileged and competitive information. • Be honest, fair and trustworthy in all the activities and organisational relationships.
Commitment to employees	• Complying with the applicable labour and employment laws and regulations. • Working together to provide a workplace free from discrimination, harassment, retaliation and violence. • Recruiting, hiring, training, compensating, and promoting employees fairly and impartially based on job-related criteria without regard to race, colour, age, sex, religion, disability, veteran's status, national origin, or other characteristics recognised by law. • Preventing workplace injuries by adhering to applicable workplace safety laws and regulations and organisations' standards. • Maintaining a workplace free from the influence of illegal drugs and abuse of alcohol or prescription drugs. • Promoting trust, pride and camaraderie in the workplace. • Treating each other courteously and respectfully. • Giving employees timely information concerning organisation operations and results. • Giving employees work-related information necessary for them to effectively perform their responsibilities.
Commitment to customers and suppliers	• Providing high quality solutions competently and efficiently. • Protecting customers' information from unauthorised use or disclosure. • Respecting the proprietary rights of others, including patents, copyrights and trademarks. • Not entering into illegal or written agreements to limit competition.

Leadership Pillars	Indicative List of Best Practices
Commitment to Communities	• Promoting environmental stewardship by complying with or exceeding environmental regulations and striving to reduce harmful wastes and emissions. • Promoting public safety by not creating unreasonable risks to public health and safety. • Communicating with the community by responding appropriately and accurately. • Encouraging employee involvement in community activities and professional organisations.

Table 29: Main element of leadership and associated best practices
Source: (MDU Resources Group, 2009) (Equifax, 2004)

Figure 138 illustrates the virtuous circle of customer satisfaction. The figure well depicts the result of service excellence, which is creating customer loyalty, business growth and profitability (private sector organisations.

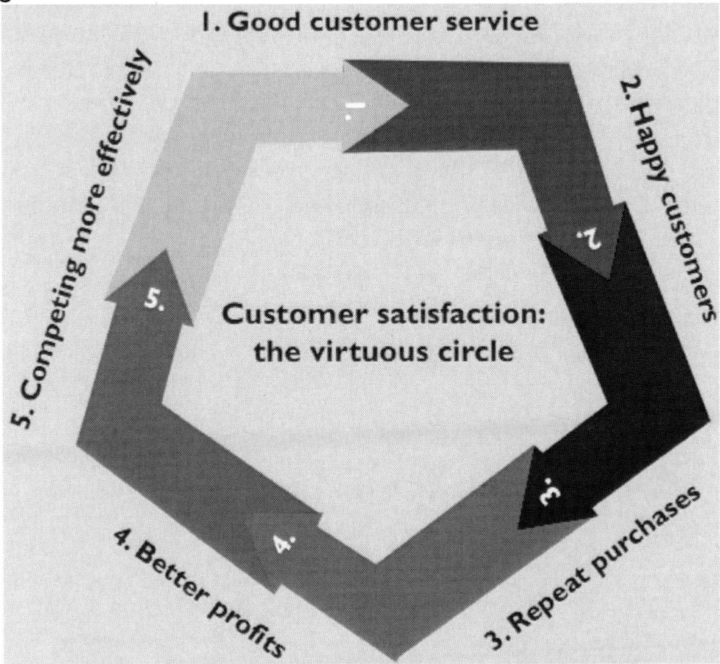

Figure 138: The Impact of world-class Customer Service
Source (The Times 100, 2011)

World-Class Customer Service Management

Customers do not always get exactly what they want. However, successful organisations use customer needs and expectations as a starting point, developing proposals around their customers' needs and expectations, also meeting other corporate imperatives. Managing satisfaction therefore has to do with managing services and/or products, but also with managing expectations and perceptions of the citizen/customer. Measuring satisfaction seems to be just one element in this overall satisfaction management approach. The dynamic way of getting customers involved in delivering of services so as to enhance their perceptions, expectations and commitment through active participation, has been a common strategy to obtain a legitimate level of quality of and satisfaction with services. Understanding and measuring satisfaction is a central concern. Satisfaction is a widely accepted concept despite real difficulties in measuring and interpreting typical approaches to its assessment. Customer satisfaction with a service is related to the size of the disconfirmation experience; where disconfirmation is related to the person's initial expectations. If experience of the service greatly exceeds the expectations clients had of the service, then satisfaction will be high, and vice versa. As depicted in Figure 139, the gap between the two, P(erceptions) – E(xpectations), provides a measure of service quality and determines the level of satisfaction (EUPAN, 2008).

Figure 139: Service quality gap

Source (EUPAN, 2008)

Sources of Customer's Expectations

Figure 140 comprises the sources of expectations:

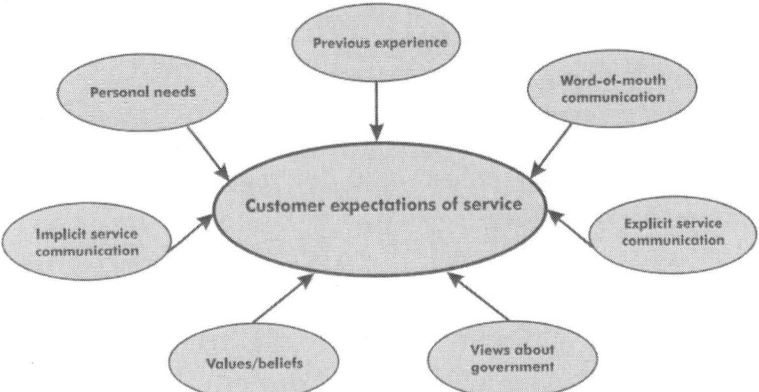

Figure 140: Sources of customer expectations

Source (EUPAN, 2008)

The basic key factors most commonly seen to influence expectations are described as (EUPAN, 2008):

- **Personal needs:** any customer or user of a service will have what they regard as a set of key personal needs that they expect the service to address. These will vary from service to service and from customer to customer. A clear understanding of these needs is necessary to design an appropriate service.
- **Previous experience:** many will have had service encounters before. Their previous experience will in part influence their future expectations of the service. This can include their past experience of the service in question, but also of other services – for public services, expectations will be influenced by experience of similar private services.
- **Word of mouth communications:** expectations will be shaped by communications from sources other than the service provider itself. This can include family, friends and colleagues, but more widely the media and other organisations, such as audit agencies.
- **Explicit service communications:** statements from staff or from leaflets or other publicity material can have a direct impact on expectations.

- **Implicit service communication:** this includes factors such as the physical appearance of buildings e.g. renovation may lead the customer to expect other service aspects to be of higher quality.

Perception and the SERVQUAL model

SERVQUAL is a service quality measurement tool that assesses both service perceptions and expectations across a range of different service characteristics. Figure 141 depicts SERVQUAL model and its gap analysis (EUPAN, 2008):

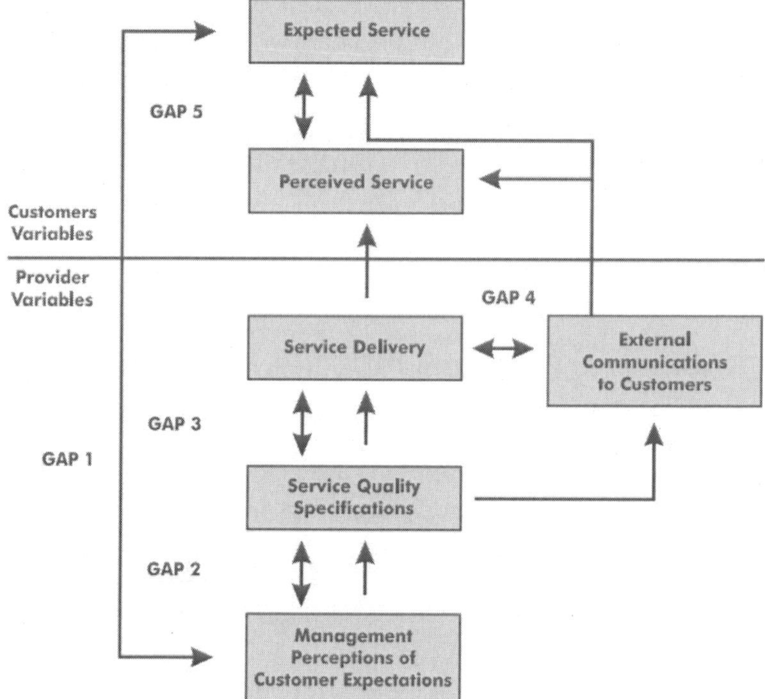

Figure 141: SERVQUAL model

Source (EUPAN, 2008)

The SERVQUAL-model is also known as the "gap-model", by analysing the four underlying gaps, insight is given into the final gap between perceptions and expectations (gap 5). Table 30 illustrates the underlying gaps, which might exist over the process of service delivery.

Gaps	*Underlying cause*
Gap 1: Customers' expectations versus management perceptions	• The lack of a marketing research orientation. • Inadequate upward communication. • Too many layers of management.
Gap 2: Management perceptions versus service specifications	• Inadequate commitment to service quality • A perception of unfeasibility. • Inadequate task standardisation. • An absence of goal setting.
Gap 3: Service specifications versus service delivery	• Role ambiguity and conflict. • Poor employee-job fit and poor technology-job fit. • Inappropriate supervisory control systems • Lack of perceived control. • Lack of teamwork.
Gap 4: Service delivery versus external communication	• Inadequate horizontal communications. • Propensity to over-promise.
Gap 5: The discrepancy between customer expectations and their perceptions of the service delivered	• The influences exerted from the customer side. • The shortfalls (gaps) on the part of the service provider.

Table 30: SERVQUAL the underlying gaps

Adapted from (EUPAN, 2008)

Inspiring customers by incorporating service quality factors

Table 31 contains a comprehensive set of service quality factors or determinants.

Factors	*Description*
Aesthetics	Extent to which the components of the service package are agreeable or pleasing to the customer.
Assurance	Inspiring trust and confidence.
Attentiveness/ Helpfulness	The extent to which the service, particularly of contact staff, either provides help to the customer or gives the impression of interest in the customer and shows a willingness to serve.
Availability	The availability of service facilities, staff and goods to the customer.
Care	The concern, consideration, sympathy and patience shown to the customer.
Commitment	Staff's apparent commitment to their work, including the pride and satisfaction. They apparently take in their job, their diligence and thoroughness.
Communication	The ability of the service providers to communicate with the customer in a way he or she will understand.
Competence	The skill, expertise and professionalism with which the service is executed.
Courtesy	The politeness, respect and propriety shown by the service, usually contact staff, in dealing with the customer and his or her property.
Empathy	Providing a caring and individual service to customers
Flexibility	A willingness and ability on the part of the service worker to amend or alter the nature of the service or product to meet the needs of the customer.
Friendliness	The warmth and personal approachability of the service providers, particularly of contact staff, including cheerful attitude and the ability to make the customer feel welcome.
Functionality	The serviceability and fitness for purpose or "product quality" of service facilities and goods.
Integrity	The honesty, justice, fairness and trust with which customers are treated by the service organisation.

Factors	***Description***
Reliability	Performing the promised service dependably and accurately.
Responsiveness	Helping customers and providing a prompt service
Security	Personal safety of the customer and his or her possessions while participating in or benefiting from the service process.
Tangibles	The physical facilities and equipment available, the appearance of staff, how easy it is to understand communication materials.

Table 31: Service quality factors

Adapted from (EUPAN, 2008)

World-class customer satisfaction management uses customer needs and expectations as the starting point, developing propositions around their customers' needs and expectations; this also answers other corporate imperatives. Managing satisfaction therefore has to do with managing services and/or products, but also important are the management of expectations and perceptions in the final satisfaction of the citizen/customer (Figure 142).

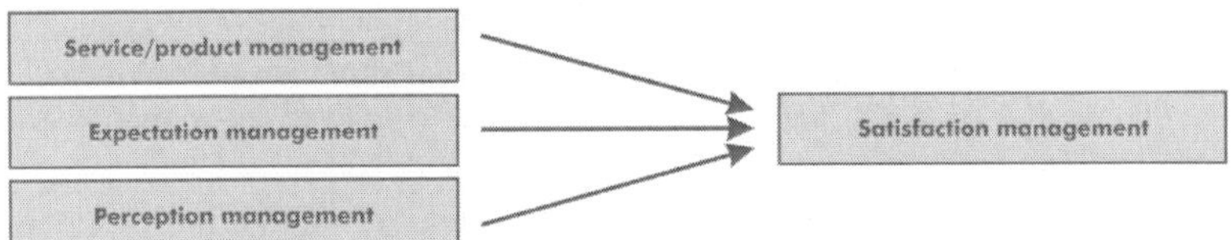

Figure 142: Customer Satisfaction Management

Source (EUPAN, 2008)

Auditing Service Excellence

The new government standard for Customer Service Excellence builds on the legacy of the Charter Mark standard that has been used by thousands of public sector organisations to improve customer service. The fundamentals of good customer service remain the same and will continue to underpin the new Customer Service Excellence standard. But in addition it will have a particular focus on delivery, timeliness, information, professionalism and staff attitude. There will be more emphasis on developing customer insight, understanding the user's experience and robust measurement of service satisfaction. Leadership and culture will move to the fore, whereas financial management and corporate social responsibility will be largely outside of the scope of the new standard

The following section includes the full Customer Service Excellence standard. The guide is presented in two columns, the first being the element of the standard; and the actual requirement to which the organisation will assess; while the second column is guidance that give organisations an indication of the area, which they should look into (SGS, 2006).

1. ***Customer insight*** - This criterion focuses on the importance of developing an in-depth understanding of your customers. This includes consulting customers and using the information you receive to design and provide services. It also covers the importance of monitoring the outcomes of your services and whether customers are satisfied with them.

Sub-criterion	***Element***
Customer Identification	1.1.1 We have an in-depth understanding of the characteristics of our current and potential customer groups based on recent and reliable information.
	1.1.2 We have developed customer insight about our customer groups to better understand their needs and preferences.
	1.1.3 We make particular efforts to identify hard to reach and disadvantaged groups and individuals and have developed our services in response to their specific needs.
Engagement and consultation	1.2.1 We have a strategy for engaging and involving customers using a range of methods appropriate to the needs of identified customer groups.
	1.2.2 We have made the consultation of customers integral to continually improving our service and we advise customers of the results and action taken.
	1.2.3 We regularly review our strategies and opportunities for consulting and engaging with customers to ensure that the methods used are effective and provide reliable and representative results.
Customer satisfaction	1.3.1 We use reliable and accurate methods to measure customer satisfaction on a regular basis.

Sub-criterion	*Element*
	1.3.2 We analyse and publicise satisfaction levels for the full range of customers for all main areas of our service and we have improved services as a result.
	1.3.3 We include in our measurement of satisfaction specific questions relating to key areas including those on delivery, timeliness, information, access, and the quality of customer service, as well as specific questions which are informed by customer insight.
	1.3.4 We set challenging and stretching targets for customer satisfaction and our levels are improving.
	1.3.5 We have made positive changes to services as a result of analysing customer experience, including improved customer journeys.

Source: (SGS, 2006)

2. ***The culture of organisation*** - In building a customer focused culture, organisations look at how those that work within the organisation demonstrate the necessary values and understanding as well as how the operations and procedures meet customer needs and expectations.

Sub-criterion	*Element*
Leadership, policy and culture	2.1.1 There is corporate commitment to putting the customer at the heart of service delivery and leaders in our organisation actively support this and advocate for customers.
	2.1.2 We use customer insight to inform policy and strategy and to prioritise service improvement activity.
	2.1.3 We have policies and procedures which support the right of all customers to expect excellent levels of service.
	2.1.4 We ensure that all customers and customer groups are treated fairly and this is confirmed by feedback and the measurement of customer experience.
	2.1.5 We protect customers' privacy both in face-to-face discussions and in the transfer and storage of customer information.
	2.1.6 We empower and encourage all employees to actively promote and participate in the customer focused culture of our organisation.

Staff professionalism and attitude	2.2.1 We can demonstrate our commitment to developing and delivering customer focused services through our recruitment, training and development policies for staff.
	2.2.2 Our staff are polite and friendly to customers and have an understanding of customer needs.
	2.2.3 We prioritise customer focus at all levels of our organisation and evaluate individual and team commitment through the performance management system.
	2.2.4 We can demonstrate how customer-facing staff's insight and experience is incorporated into internal processes, policy development and service planning.
	2.2.5 We value the contribution our staff make to delivering customer focused services, and leaders, managers and staff demonstrate these behaviours.

Source: (SGS, 2006)

3. ***Information and access*** - Information is vital to customers. They particularly value accurate and detailed information, and this criterion aims to make sure that organisations have this in mind in everything they do.

Sub-criterion	***Element***
Range of information	3.1.1 We make information about the full range of services we provide available to our customers and potential customers, including how and when people can contact us, how our services are run and who is in charge.
	3.1.2 Where there is a charge for services, we tell our customers how much they will have to pay.
Quality of information	3.2.1 We provide our customers with the information they need in ways which meet their needs and preferences, using a variety of appropriate channel.
	3.2.2 We take reasonable steps to make sure our customers have received and understood the information we provide.
	3.2.3 We have improved the range, content and quality of verbal, published and web based information we provide to ensure it is relevant and meets the needs of customers.
	3.2.4 We can demonstrate that information we provide

Sub-criterion	*Element*
	to our customers is accurate and complete, and that when this is not the case we advise customers when they will receive the information they requested.
Access	3.3.1 We make our services easily accessible to all customers through provision of a range of alternative channels.
	3.3.2 We evaluate how customers interact with the organisation through access channels and we use this information to identify possible service improvements and offer better choices.
	3.3.3 We ensure that where customers can visit our premises in person facilities are as clean and comfortable as possible.
Collaboration	3.4.1 We have made arrangements with other providers and partners to offer and supply co-ordinated services, and these arrangements have demonstrable benefits for our customers.
	3.4.2 We have developed co-ordinated working arrangements with our partners that ensure customers have clear lines of accountability for quality of service.
	3.4.3 We interact within wider communities and we can demonstrate the ways in which we support those communities.

Source: (SGS, 2006)

4. ***Delivery*** - this criterion relates to how an organisation carries out its main business, the outcomes for the customer, and how it manages any problems that arise. Research shows that many customers are satisfied with the outcome of their contact with public services but fewer are satisfied with the way the service kept promises and handled any problem

Sub-criterion	*Element*
Delivery standards	4.1.1 We have challenging standards for our main services, which take account of our responsibility for delivering national and statutory standards and target.
	4.1.2 We monitor and meet our standards, key departmental and performance targets, and we tell our customers about our performance.
	4.1.3 We consult and involve customers, citizens, partners

Sub-criterion	*Element*
	and staff on the setting, reviewing and raising of our local standards.
Achieve delivery and outcomes	4.2.1 We agree with our customers at the outset what they can expect from the service we provide.
	4.2.2 We can demonstrate that we deliver the service we promised to individual customers and that outcomes are positive for the majority of our customers.
	4.2.3 We can demonstrate that we benchmark our performance against that of similar or complementary organisations and have used that information to improve our service.
	4.2.4 We have developed and learned from best practice identified within and outside our organisation, and we publish our examples externally where appropriate.
Deal effectively with problems	4.3.1 We identify any dips in performance against our standards and explain these to customers, together with action we are taking to put things right and prevent further recurrence.
	4.3.2 We have an easy to use complaints procedure, which includes a commitment to deal with problems fully and solve them wherever possible within a reasonable time limit.
	4.3.3 We give staff training and guidance to handle complaints and to investigate them objectively, and we can demonstrate that we empower staff to put things right.
	4.3.4 We learn from any mistakes we make by identifying patterns in formal and informal complaints and comments from customers and use this information to improve services and publicise action taken.
	4.3.5 We regularly review and improve our complaints procedure, taking account of the views of customers, complainants and staff.
	4.3.6 We ensure that the outcome of the complaint process for customers (whose complaint is upheld) is satisfactory for them.

Source: (SGS, 2006)

5. ***Quality of services*** - This criterion looks in more detail at the standards organisations have relating to how they carry out their main business. It draws heavily on what service users have identified as the most important factors of excellent customer service.

Sub-criterion	***Element***
Standards for timeliness and quality	5.1.1 We set appropriate and measurable standards for the timeliness of response for all forms of customer contact including phone calls, letters, e-communications and personal callers.
	5.1.2 We set comprehensive standards for all aspects of the quality of customer service to be expected in all dealings with our organisation.
Timely outcomes	5.2.1 We advise our customers and potential customers about our promises on timeliness and quality of customer service.
	5.2.2 We identify individual customer needs at the first point of contact with us and ensure that an appropriate person who can address the reason for contact deals with the customer.
	5.2.3 We promptly share customer information with colleagues and partners within our organisation whenever appropriate and can demonstrate how this has reduced unnecessary contact for customers.
	5.2.4 Where service is not completed at the first point of contact we discuss with the customer the next steps and indicate the likely overall time to achieve outcomes.
	5.2.5 We respond to initial enquiries promptly, if there is a delay we advise the customer and take action to rectify the problem.
Achieve timely delivery	5.3.1 We monitor our performance against standards for timeliness and quality of customer service and we take action if problems are identified.
	5.3.2 We are meeting our current standards for timeliness and quality of customer service and we publicise our performance against these standards.
	5.3.3 Our performance in relation to timeliness and quality of service compares well with that of similar organisations.

Source: (SGS, 2006)

Assessment Toolkit: Inspiration

Service Excellence

Q1. To what extent does the leadership of the organisation support excellence in service delivery?			
Basic	**Developing**	**Maturing**	**Leading**
The leadership team focuses on short term profitability through saving costs and improving productivity rather than quality of services delivered.	The leadership of the organisation focuses on improving technology capability of the organisation.	The leadership of the organisation focuses on gaining competitive advantage through internal capability improvements and employees skills development.	The leadership of the organisation focuses on maintain the leadership position in the market and enhancing their position through delivering excellent customer service.
Q2. Does the organisation conduct customer experience mapping?			
Basic	**Developing**	**Maturing**	**Leading**
The organisation rarely seeks customers' feedback.	The organisation collects customers' feedbacks after the actual delivery is done.	The organisation seeks further improvement of services through CEM; however, it does not constantly trace customers' experiences at every touch points.	The organisation constantly implements customer experience and journey mapping to measure customer experience at every touch points.
Q3. Does the organisation strive to inspire customers through customising services in accordance with customers' expectations?			
Basic	**Developing**	**Maturing**	**Leading**
The organisation strives to inspire customers by offering services	The organisation strives to inspire customers through a	The organisation strives to inspire customers through showing	The organisation strives to inspire customers through offering

at the lower prices.	consistent delivery of services and improve availability of services.	a good customer services and maintaining its promises in delivering services with good quality.	new and innovative services.
Q4. To what extent does the organisation strive towards employees' development for the purpose of enabling them to inspire customers?			
Basic	**Developing**	**Maturing**	**Leading**
The organisation focuses on increasing employees' productivity.	The organisation has delivered training programs for employees on several occasions in order to improve their skills for dealing with complex customers' enquires.	The organisation regularly delivers employees training programs in order to enable its staff to establish lasting relationship with customers and make the most of these relationships.	The organisations entirely focuses on developing employees' soft skills required for delivering excellent customer service.
Q5. Which aspects of customer results are important for the organisation?			
Basic	**Developing**	**Maturing**	**Leading**
The organisation gives value to customers' spending budgets.	The organisation gives value to customer satisfaction rate.	The organisation gives value to customers' repeatability and repeated purchases.	The organisation gives value to customer advocacy.
Q6. To what extent does the organisation uses partnership with customers in order to keep them motivated and inspired about services?			
Basic	**Developing**	**Maturing**	**Leading**
The organisation does not usually involve customers in the	The organisation communicates with customers about services in	The organisation strives to collaborate with customers for	The main intention of collaboration with customers

process of service delivery. Customers are passive receivers.	order to keep them informed.	enhancing services and closing the gaps between their expectations and their perceptions.	for the organisation is to let them to see that they are able to influence on the organisation's operations and service delivery and consequently inspire them.

Customer Satisfaction Management

Q1. To what extent does the organisation use service quality management for inspiring customers?			
Basic	**Developing**	**Maturing**	**Leading**
The organisation has considered the quality of services from its own perspective.	The organisation focuses on quality aspects such as service easy to access, user friendly and availability, which does not really lead to inspiring customers.	The organisation focuses on quality aspects such as responsiveness, reliability, service convenient, which can create a positive and significant impact on customers.	The organisation focuses on quality aspects such as service uniqueness, customer care, empathy, service excellence, service partnership etc, which can inspire customers.
Q2. To what extent do the organisation measure customer expectations for designing and delivering services?			
Basic	**Developing**	**Maturing**	**Leading**
The organisation heavily relies on a push system so it does not seek customers' inputs before	The organisation uses a push system; although, it strives to improve future	The organisation already adjusted a pull system for its service delivery. This enables the	The organisation successfully implements the co-creation of services so that customers will

the actual delivery is conducted.	services based on customers' feedback.	organisation to clearly establish customers' needs and expectations in different segments and then modify its services in accordance with their needs.	be able to directly incorporate their needs into the system.
Q3. Customer perception measurement			
Basic	**Developing**	**Maturing**	**Leading**
The organisation rarely seeks customers' feedback.	The organisation seeks customers' feedback so that on a limited basis, it can measure customers' perceptions about the quality of services delivered.	The organisation engages customers in the process of service delivery; although, the engagement is limited to customer consultation.	Since the organisation uses the co-creation of services and customers are directly involved in the process of service delivery, ideally there should not be any gap between their expectations and perceptions.

Appendix 1: SE Audit Tool

Deficiency

How good is your organisation at minimising, avoiding and preventing the following?

Commonness	**1**	**2**	**3**	**4**	**5**	**6**	**7**	**8**	**9**	**10**
• Predictable Standard Offerings										
• Lack of Unique Features										
• Inability to customise offerings										
• Low perceived value										
• Stale Brand Name (Poor Positioning)										
• Culture that reinforces status quo										
Casualness	**1**	**2**	**3**	**4**	**5**	**6**	**7**	**8**	**9**	**10**
• Poor understanding of customer needs, and an inability to be responsive										
• Arrogant attitude (assumed superiority)										
• No proper dialog with customers										
• No drive for ensuring customer loyalty and retention										
• Lack of appreciation of customer value										
• Lack of competitive monitoring										
Complacency	**1**	**2**	**3**	**4**	**5**	**6**	**7**	**8**	**9**	**10**
• Inability to ensure quality of servicing customers										
• Deficient process										
• Lack of continuous monitoring and improvement										
• Poor response to complaints and grievances										
• Poor understanding of Best Practices										
• Determined to apply and ethos of win-lose										
Total Score out of 180										

(1 = Extremely poor, 10 = Excellent)

Drivers

How good is your organisation at the following?

Competence	**1**	**2**	**3**	**4**	**5**	**6**	**7**	**8**	**9**	**10**
• Clear understanding of customer needs										
• Ability to serve based on true competencies										
• Skills and expertise deployed for optimum service excellence										
• Understanding of market competition based on facts										
• Future plans based on skills and market needs										
• Ability to create a differentiated approach										
Commitment	**1**	**2**	**3**	**4**	**5**	**6**	**7**	**8**	**9**	**10**
• Leadership for service excellence										
• Employees well versed with importance of customer										
• Resources abundantly available to serve customer										
• Closed loop monitoring system, ensuring total customer satisfaction										
• Clear emphasis on importance of customer through vision / mission										
• Breakthrough goals for delivering service excellence										
Concern	**1**	**2**	**3**	**4**	**5**	**6**	**7**	**8**	**9**	**10**
• Customer oriented approach										
• Values stress on importance of customers										
• Open dialogue with customers										
• Endorsement of Best Practices that enhance service ability										
• Culture of continuous improvement and learning										
• Reward and recognition schemes for service excellence										
Total Score out of 180										

(1 = Extremely poor, 10 = Excellent)

Deliverables

How good is your organisation at the following?

Customisation	1	2	3	4	5	6	7	8	9	10
• Ability to deliver to exact customer needs										
• Having flexibility, adaptability and responsiveness										
• Displaying a value based approach to delivery										
• Replenishment of needs through innovative approach										
• Ability to address 'unmet needs' through innovation										
• Service with speed reliability & optimum cost as key drivers of excellence										
Care	**1**	**2**	**3**	**4**	**5**	**6**	**7**	**8**	**9**	**10**
• Exhibiting urgency in dealing queries										
• Carrying customer satisfaction beyond the transaction										
• Having an adequate support and back-up resource										
• Monitoring customer satisfaction and loyalty on a continuous basis										
• Striving to excel at quality delivery to the delight of the customer										
• Managing beyond transactional relationships exhibiting loyalty, retention										

Communication	1	2	3	4	5	6	7	8	9	10
• Continuously inform customers of new products / services										
• Capturing needs and changes on a regular basis										
• Supporting relationship through a process of effective communication										
• Sharing / protocols										
• Combining different media to leverage positioning										
• Reinforcing the power of the corporate brand name.										
Total Score out of 180										

(1 = Extremely poor, 10 = Excellent)

Delectation

How good is your organisation at the following?

Customerisation	1	2	3	4	5	6	7	8	9	10
• Believing in 'Customer is King'										
• Putting customer in 'Driving Seat'										
• Operating as an 'Open System' for the flow of ideas and suggestions										
• Using Customer Experience Management Mindset										
• Measuring Customer Value in different ways and approaches										
• Encouraging the culture of 'tribal customer'										
Co-Creation	**1**	**2**	**3**	**4**	**5**	**6**	**7**	**8**	**9**	**10**
• Stimulating Customer Input in Design and Development Activities										
• Allowing Customers to have direct involvement										
• Providing customers necessary information for their contribution										
• Supporting customers with guidance and technical support										
• Adopting an 'Open Innovation Process' Approach										
• Changing the mindset from Product Push to Customer Pull										
Consecration	**1**	**2**	**3**	**4**	**5**	**6**	**7**	**8**	**9**	**10**
• Moving from Satisfaction to Loyalty Measurement										
• Measuring beyond Utilitarian and Hedonic Dimensions										
• Understanding The Emotional Impact of Quality										
• Encouraging Advocacy and Intimacy Customer Practices										
• Encouraging Customer to Customer Networks										
• Extending Brand Ownership Concept										
Total Score out of 180										

(1 = Extremely poor, 10 = Excellent)

Actual Index Score

1. Deficiencies ***Actual Score /180 *10 =***	
2. Drivers ***Actual Score /180 *10 =***	
3. Deliverables ***Actual Score /180 *10 =***	
4. Delectation ***Actual Score /180 *10 =***	

Efficiency Impact Model (EIM)

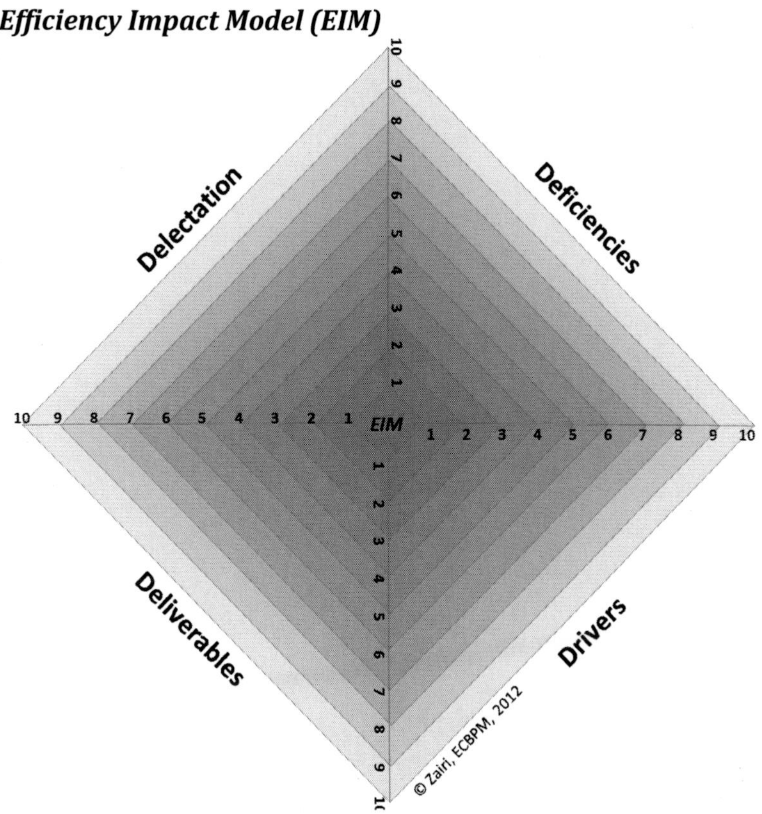

Empathy is the soul and heart of another person...

Fritz William

References

- Aberdeen Group Inc. (2006). The Lean Six Sigma Benchmark Report. Boston, Massachusetts: Aberdeen Group Inc.
- Accenture. (2006). Innovation Unbound. Retrieved 07 12, 2011, from http://www.accenture.com/SiteCollectionDocuments/PDF/Innovation.pdf
- Ahmad, Z., & Hashim, R. (2011). Customer's Brand Equity and Customer Loyalty: A Study on Hotel's Conference Market. World Applied Sciences Journal, 44-49.
- Alavi, M., Kayworth, T. R., & Leidner, E. L. (2006). An empirical examination of the influence of organizational culture on knowledge management practices. Journal of Management Information Systems, 191-224.
- Ang, L., & Buttle, F. A. (2002). ROI on CRM: a customer-journey approach,. Perth, Australia: IMP-Conference, Industrial Marketing & Purchasing.
- APQC. (2002, July). Rewards and Recognition in Knowledge Management. Retrieved October 20, 2010, from http://www.providersedge.com: http://www.providersedge.com/docs/km_articles/Rewards_and_Recognition_in_KM.pdf
- Arveson, P. (1998). The Deming Cycle. Retrieved October 08, 2010, from http://www.balancedscorecard.org: http://www.balancedscorecard.org/thedemingcycle/tabid/112/default.aspx
- Australian National Audit Office. (2009). Better Practice Guide. Retrieved 02 07, 2011, from Innovation in the Public Sector: http://www.anao.gov.au/bpg-innovation/1_introduction.html#1_3
- B. Mitchell, R., Kim, S.-k., & Lim, S. (2004). Building a Knowledge Model: A Decision-Making Approach. Knowledge Management Practice.
- Bailey, C., & Jensen, K. (2006, march). Customer Advocacy. Retrieved November 2011, from http://www.customercentricity.biz: http://www.customercentricity.biz/PDF/Customer_Advocacy.pdf
- Bain & Company. (2011). Management Tools 2011. Retrieved 02 07, 2011, from An Executive's Guide : http://www.bain.com/bainweb/PDFs/cms/Public/Bain_Management_Tools_2011.pdf

- Berry, L. L., & Carbone, L. P. (2007). Build Loyalty through Experience Management. Quality Progress, 26-32.
- Berry, L. L., Carbone, L. P., & Haeckel, S. H. (2002). Managing the total customer experience. Sloan Management Review, 85-90.
- Berson, Y., Nemanich, L. A., Waldman, D. A., Galvin, B. M., & Keller, R. T. (2006). Leadership and organizational learning: A multiple levels perspective. The Leadership Quarterly, 577-594.
- Bhatt, G. (2000). Organizing knowledge in the knowledge development cycle. Journal of Knowledge Management, 15-26.
- BHP Information Solutions Ltd. (2011, June). Customer care. Retrieved November 2011, from http://www.icaew.com: http://www.icaew.com/~/media/Files/Library/collections/online-resources/briefings/start-up-briefings/11CusCar.ashx
- Bland, T., Bruk, B., Dongshin, K., & Lee, K. T. (2010). Enhancing Public Sector Innovation: Examining the Network-Innovation Relationship. Retrieved 02 08, 2011, from http://www.innovation.cc/scholarly-style/bland_enhancing_public15v3a3.pdf
- Bommert, B. (2010). COLLABORATIVE INNOVATION IN THE PUBLIC SECTOR. Retrieved 02 07, 2011, from http://www.idt.unisg.ch/org/idt/ipmr.nsf/0/f77a463b0bf687a7c12577050044a661/$FILE/Boomert_IPMR_Volume%2011_Issue%201.pdf
- Booz Allen Hamilton. (2004). The customer-centric organisation. Retrieved February 02, 2011, from http://www.booz.com: http://www.booz.com/media/file/141263.pdf
- booz&co. (2007). The Empathy Engine. Retrieved November 2011, from http://www.booz.com: http://www.booz.com/media/upload/The_Empathy_Engine.pdf
- Boyle, D., & Harris, M. (2009, 12). The challenge of co-production. Retrieved 08 10, 2011, from http://www.nesta.org.uk/library/documents/Co-production-report.pdf
- Boyle, D., Coote, A., Sherwood, C., & Slay, J. (2010, 07). Right here, right now: Taking co-production into the mainstream. Retrieved from http://www.nesta.org.uk/library/documents/coproduction_right_here_right_now.pdf
- Bryson, J. M. (1995). Strategic Planning for Public and Nonprofit Organizations. San Francisco: Jossey-Bass.
- Burt, A. (2007, March 5). Citizen Relationship Management in Public Administrations. Retrieved February 4, 2011, from

http://zrm.behdasht.gov.ir: /uploads/270_909_pres-CARMEN-white-paper.pdf

- Butterworth, M. (2009, September 15). Barclays receives most complaints from bank customers, Financial Ombudsman Service reveals. Retrieved October 5, 2011, from The Telegraph: http://www.telegraph.co.uk/finance/personalfinance/borrowing/mortgages/6188357/Barclays-receives-most-complaints-from-bank-customers-Financial-Ombudsman-Service-reveals..html
- Buttle, F. (1997). ISO 9000: marketing motivations and benefits. International Journal of Quality & Reliability Managemen , 14 (9), 936-947.
- Calleja, J. (2008, May 23). Learning Organisations: Case Study: ABN AMRO Bank. Retrieved October 21, 2010, from http://www.speedyadverts.com: http://www.speedyadverts.com/SATopics/html/learning_organisation3.html
- car-innovation.com. (2010). Innovation Management. Retrieved 02 08, 2011, from http://www.car-innovation.com/pdf/strategy_and_organization_en.pdf
- cecmi.org. (2010). How does Toyota manage to implement one million new creative ideas each year? Retrieved 02 07, 2011, from http://www.cecmi.org/files/article-toyota-implementation.pdf
- Center for Ledelse og Fremtidstanken. (2005, 03 28). The Seven Circles of Innovation - A Model for Innovation Management. Retrieved 08 09, 2011, from http://www.sevencirclesofinnovation.com/Seven%20Circles%20-%20Complete%20Edition.pdf
- Chance, J. (2004, february 17). 8 Building Blocks to Attracting Customers. Retrieved Novemberq 16, 2011, from http://www.powerhomebiz.com: http://www.powerhomebiz.com/vol31/blocks.htm
- Chesbrough, H. (2003). Open Innovation. Retrieved 02 04, 2011, from http://www.openinnovation.eu/openinnovatie.php
- Coffman, B. (2009). Building the Innovation Culture. Retrieved 07 12, 2011, from http://www.innovationtools.com/pdf/Building_the_Innovation_Culture.pdf
- Cognitive Design Solutions, Inc. (2003). Conscious Competence Learning Matrix. Retrieved November 11, 2011, from Cognitive Design Solutions:

http://www.cognitivedesignsolutions.com/Instruction/TestingEvaluation.htm

- Commonwealth Ombudsman. (2009, April 01). Better Practice Guide to Complaint Handling. Retrieved November 15, 2011, from Commonwealth Ombudsman: http://www.ombudsman.gov.au/docs/better-practice-guides/onlineBetterPracticeGuide.pdf
- Coombs, R., Hull, R., & Peltu, M. (1998). Knowledge management practices for innovation: an audit tool for improvement. Manchester: Centre for Research on Innovation and Competition: The University of Manchester.
- Cooper, R. G., & Mills, M. S. (2005). Succeeding at New Products the P&G Way: Work the Innovation Diamond. Retrieved 02 07, 2011, from http://www.prod-dev.com/pdf/Succeeding_at_New_Products_the_PG_Way.pdf
- Corbett, C. J., Montes-Sancho, M. J., & Kirsch, D. A. (2005). The Financial Impact of ISO 9000 Certification in the United States: An Empirical Analysis. Management Sciences, 51 (7), 1046-1059.
- CRM Today. (2011). Best Practices for Building an Innovative Work Culture. Retrieved 02 07, 2011, from http://www.crm2day.com/content/t6_librarynews_1.php?id=EEEpklkkZFpbvcbYBw
- Crosby, L. A. (2002). Exploding some myths about customer relationship management. Managing Service Quality, 5.
- Crossan, M. M., Lane, H. W., & White, R. E. (1999). An organizational learning framework: From intuition to institution. Academy of Management Review, 522-537.
- Cura Consulting Group. (2004). The Competition/Innovation Cycle. Retrieved 02 08, 2011, from http://www.cura-cg.com/pdf/competition_innovation.pdf
- customer centricity Inc. (2011). The Role of Feedback Management in Becoming Customer Centric. Retrieved November 2011, from http://www.customercentricity.biz: http://www.customercentricity.biz/PDFs/Customer%20Feedback%20Management.pdf
- Daft, R. (2001). Organization theory and design. Ohio, USA: South Western College.
- Davenport, T., De Long, D., & Beers, M. (1998). Successful Knowledge Management Projects. Sloan Management Review, 43-57.

- David Skyrme, A. (2008). The Learning Organization. Retrieved October 20, 2010, from http://www.skyrme.com: http://www.skyrme.com/insights/3lrnorg.htm
- Dell Computer Corporation. (1998, June 05). Dell Computer Corporation Annual Report. Retrieved November 10, 2011, from Dell Computer Corporation: http://www.dell.com/downloads/global/corporate/annual/nar.pdf
- Deloitte Development LLC. (2009). Consumer-centric innovation - Tapping into consumer insights to drive growth. Retrieved 07 11, 2011, from http://www.deloitte.com/assets/Dcom-Mexico/Local%20Assets/Documents/m(es-mx)CostumerCentricInnovation09nov09.pdf
- Design Council. (2011). The power of branding: a practical guide. Retrieved 2011, from http://www.designcouncil.org.uk: http://www.designcouncil.org.uk/Documents/Documents/Publications/Power_of_branding.pdf
- DH Department of Health. (2009). A guide to better customer care . Retrieved 2011, from http://www.oxfordshire.gov.uk: http://www.oxfordshire.gov.uk/cms/sites/default/files/folders/documents/socialandhealthcare/general/complaints/listeningrespondingimproving.pdf
- DMM. (2010, March). Dynamic Modular Management. Retrieved October 08, 2010, from http://wcunning.com: http://wcunning.com/DMM/PM/OrgChange.html
- Dolan, S., & Draba, R. (1992). Resource Management through Measurement. Retrieved October 13, 2010, from Rasch Measurement Transactions: http://www.rasch.org/rmt/rmt61b.htm
- Drucker, P. (2002). The Desciplin of Innovation. Massachusetts: Harward Business Review.
- dti.gov.uk. (2003, 12). Innovation Report. Retrieved 02 08, 2011, from Competing in the global economy: the innovation challenge: http://webarchive.nationalarchives.gov.uk/tna/+/http://www.dti.gov.uk/files/file12093.pdf/
- Dyer, J. H., Gregersen, H. B., & Christensen, C. M. (2009, 12). The Innovator's DNA. Harvard Business Review, 87 (12), p. 66.
- Eckerson, W. (2007). Ten Characteristics of a Good KPI. Retrieved October 19, 2010, from http://www.gerke.com: http://www.gerke.com/documents/ten_characteristics_of_a_good_kpi_pd_dw.pdf

- Elliot Davis, B. (2007/2008). Harnessing knowledge market innovations for business advantage. Retrieved October 26, 2010, from http://www.kikm.org: http://www.kikm.org/downloads/LeveragingKnowledgeMarketsStudy.pd f
- EUPAN. (2008). Customer satisfaction management. Retrieved 2011, from http://new.eupan.eu: http://new.eupan.eu/file/repository/20101215131727_EU_Primer_Engli sh__FINAL_LR.pdf
- Experian. (2011, June). Customer Engagement: A new paradigm? Retrieved October 21, 2011, from http://www.experian.co.uk: http://www.experian.co.uk/assets/business-strategies/white-papers/wp-customer-engagement-a-new-paradigm.pdf
- Financial Services Authority. (2010, April). Review of complaint handling in banking groups. Retrieved November 15, 2011, from Financial Service Authority: http://www.fsa.gov.uk/pubs/other/complaint_review.pdf
- FIS KM, I. (2000, February 23). Knowledge Management Framework. Retrieved October 21, 2010, from http://choo.fis.utoronto.ca: http://choo.fis.utoronto.ca/KMIottawa/default.html
- Forrester Research. (2008, September). Measuring The Total Economic Impact of Customer Engagement: A Multi-Company ROI Analysis. Cambridge, MA 02139, USA: Forrester Research, Inc.
- Frankland, D. (2009, October 16). The Intelligent Approach to Customer Intelligence. Retrieved November 28, 2011, from http://www.sas.com: http://www.sas.com/resources/whitepaper/wp_16060.pdf
- Fredericks, J. O., & Salter II, J. M. (1998, January). What Does Your Customer Really Want? Quality Progress , 63-68
- FSA. (2010, April). Review of complaint handling in banking groups. Retrieved 2011, from http://www.fsa.gov.uk/: http://www.fsa.gov.uk/pubs/other/complaint_review.pdf
- Fukuyama, F. (1996). Trust: The social virtues and the creation of prosperity. New York: The Free Press.
- Fuller-Love, N., & Cooper, J. (2000). Deliberate versus emergent strategies: a case study of information technology in the Post O$ce. International Journal of Information Management, 209}223.
- Fulmer, R., & Goldsmith, M. (2000). Future leadership development. Executive Excellence, 18.

- Galbreath, J., & Rogers, T. (1999). Customer relationship leadership: a leadership and motivation model for the twenty-first century business. The TQM Magazine, 3.
- Genesys. (2009). Customer Engagement. Retrieved October 2011, from www1.vtrenz.net: https://www1.vtrenz.net/imarkownerfile/ownerasset/1076/DCEStratGuide093009.pdf
- Genesys. (2009, September). The Cost of Poor Customer Service: The Economic Impact of the Customer Experience and Engagement in 16 Key Economies. Daly City, CA 94014, USA.
- Giber, D., Carter, L., & Goldsmith, M. (2000). Linkage Inc.'s Best Practices in Leadership Development Handbook. San Francisco, CA: Jossey-Bass/Pfeiffer.
- Goleman Consulting. (2011). Singapore Service Class (S-Class) Programme. Retrieved 2011, from http://www.goleman.com.sg: http://www.goleman.com.sg/Newsletter%20Apr04/Goleman%20Newsletter.htm
- Government of Canada. (2009, May 20). A Practical Guide to Handling Consumer Complaints. Retrieved November 11, 2011, from i-Signt: http://www.complaintsoftware.com/Handling_Customer_Complaints_-_A_Best_Practice_Guide.pdf
- GovLeaders.org. (2008). The Link between Motivation and Innovation. Retrieved 02 07, 2011, from http://govleaders.org/motivation.htm
- Greijn, H. (2008, April). Organisational learning. Retrieved October 07, 2010, from www.capacity.org: www.capacity.org/en/content/download/.../33_Capcity_ENG.pdf
- Grundlagen, R. (n.d.). Steps in the innovation process. Retrieved October 15, 2010, from http://www.kmu.admin.ch: http://www.kmu.admin.ch/themen/01254/01262/index.html?lang=en
- Gutner, T., & Adams, M. (March 2009). A Leadership Prescription for the Future of Quality. New York: The Conference Board, Inc.
- Hagen, P., Manning, H., & Peterson, J. (2010). How to Build a Customer-Centric Culture. New York: Forrester Research Inc.
- Hanson, R. (2007). Empathy. Retrieved 11 1, 2011, from http://www.wisebrain.org/Empathy.pdf
- Haroon, F. (2007). Role of knwoledge management in decision making. Retrieved October 26, 2010, from http://www.slideshare.net:

http://www.slideshare.net/haroones007/role-of-knowledge-management-in-the-decision-making-presentation

- Harris, M., & Albury, D. (2009, 03). The Innovation Imperative. Retrieved 10 07, 2011, from www.nesta.org.uk: http://www.nesta.org.uk/library/documents/the-innovation-imperative.pdf
- Harrogate Borough Council. (2006). Corporate Customer Care Policy & Procedures. Retrieved November 2011, from http://www.harrogate.gov.uk: http://www.harrogate.gov.uk/Documents/CSU%20070215%20Customer%20Care%20Policy.pdf
- Harvard Business Review. (1994). Putting the service profit chain to work. Retrieved November 2011, from http://pagesetup.com: http://pagesetup.com/images/content/hbr-article.pdf
- Harvard Business review. (2007, February). Understanding customer experience. Retrieved November 2011, from http://www.dea.univr.it: http://www.dea.univr.it/documenti/Avviso/all/all845856.pdf
- Hasskett, J. L. (2002). Beyond Customer Loyalty. Managing Service Quality, 355-357.
- Hatten, e., Knapp, D., & Salonga, R. (1997). Action Research: Comparison with the concepts of 'The Reflective practitioner' and 'Quality Assurance'. Retrieved October 08, 2010, from http://www.scu.edu.au: http://www.scu.edu.au/schools/gcm/ar/arr/arow/rdr.html
- Hendrick, K. B., & Singhal, V. R. (1999, October). New research proves that TQM is alive and well: The link between Total Quality Management and financial performance. Advance Manufacturing, 33-38.
- Hernez-Broome, G., & Hughes, R. (2004). Leadership development: past, present, and future. Human Resource Planning, 24-32.
- Heskett, J. L., Jones, T. O., Loveman, G. W., Sasser, J. W., & Schlesinger, L. A. (1994, March-April). Putting the Service-Profit Chain to Work. Harvard Business Review , 72 (2), pp. 164-174.
- Heskett, James L., Jones, Thomas O., Loveman, Gary W., Sasser, W. Earl, and Schelsinger, Leonard A. "Putting the Service Profit Chain to Work", Harvard Business Review, (March-April 1994) 164-174
- Hildreth, P., & Kimble, C. (2002). The duality of knowledge. Information Research, 8.

- Himmelman, A. (2001). On coalition and the transformation of power relationships: Collaborative betterment and collaborative empowerment. American Journal of Community Psychology, 277 – 284.
- HM Government - Department for Business Innovation & Skills. (2009). Seven dimensions of culture in an innovative organisation. Retrieved 02 07, 2011, from http://publicsectorinnovation.bis.gov.uk/resources/creating-an-innovative-culture/seven-dimensions-of-culture-in-an-innovative-organisation
- HM Government - Department for Business Innovation and Skills. (2007). Top Tips for Innovation. Retrieved 02 08, 2011, from http://publicsectorinnovation.bis.gov.uk/resources/top-tips
- Hovland, I. (2003). Knowledge Management and Organisational Learning: An International Development Perspective. London: Overseas Development Institute.
- Hughes, A., Moore, K., & Kataria, N. (2011, 03). Innovation in Public Sector Organisations. Retrieved 08 09, 2011, from http://www.nesta.org.uk/library/documents/Innovation_in_public_sector_organisations_v9.pdf
- Humble, J., Jackson, D., & Thompson, A. (1994). The strategic power of organisational values. Long Range Planning, 28-42.
- Hupp, O., & Henrik, S. (2002, August). Evaluation of the Financial Value of Brands. Retrieved 2011, from http://www.uni-hamburg.de: http://www.uni-hamburg.de/fachbereiche-einrichtungen/fb03/ihm/rp7.pdf
- I&DeA. (2008). Improving customer service: London Borough of Lewisham. Retrieved 10 07, 2011, from http://www.idea.gov.uk/idk/aio/87366
- IBM Business Consulting Services. (2005, October 25). 20:20 Customer Experience: Forget CRM – Long Live the Customer! Retrieved November 11, 2011, from IBM: http://www-935.ibm.com/services/de/bcs/pdf/2006/20-20-customer-experience.pdf
- IBM. (2005). 20:20 Customer Experience. Retrieved November 2011, from http://www-935.ibm.com: http://www-935.ibm.com/services/de/bcs/pdf/2006/20-20-customer-experience.pdf
- IBM. (2006). Unlocking customer advocacy in retail banking. Retrieved November 2011, from http://www-935.ibm.com: http://www-935.ibm.com/services/us/gbs/bus/pdf/g510-633-00-unlock-cust-advocacy.pdf

- IBM. (2011, June). The road to customer intimacy. Retrieved November 2011, from http://www.ibm.com: http://www.ibm.com/smarterplanet/global/files/us__en_us__product__cai_electronics_b.pdf
- IDeA Knowledge. (2005). Innovation in Public Services. Retrieved 02 08, 2011, from http://www.idea.gov.uk/idk/aio/1118552
- Improvement and Development Agency. (2008, May). Developing Customer Insight. Retrieved February 28, 2011, from http://www.idea.gov.uk: http://www.idea.gov.uk/idk/aio/8341236
- IRSPM. (2010). Open Innovation Management for the Public Sector. Retrieved 02 04, 2011, from http://www.irspm2010.com/workshops/papers/G_openinnovation.pdf
- Jarrar, Y. F., & Zairi, M. (2010). Knowledge Management: Learning for Organisational Experience. Retrieved October 11, 2010, from http://www.ecbpm.com: http://www.ecbpm.com/files/Knowledge%20Management/Knowledge%20Management%20Learning%20for%20Organisational%20Experience.pdf
- Jenkinson, A. (2005). Harley Davidson: Organisation-led Integrated Marketing. Retrieved 2011, from http://www.centreforintegratedmarketing.com: http://gfx/documents/_harley-davidson-organisation-led-im.pdf
- Jensen, M. (2009, 05 10). Google's 9 principles of Innovation. Retrieved 02 07, 2011, from http://fatagnus.com/googles-9-principles-of-innovation/
- Johnston, R. (2001). Linking complaint management to profit. International Journal of Service Industry Management, 12 (1), 60-69.
- Kambil, A., Friesen, G. B., & Sundaram, A. (1999). Co-creation: A new source of value. Retrieved 02 23, 2011, from http://www.accenture.com/SiteCollectionDocuments/PDF/cocreation2.pdf
- Kaplan, R., & Norton, D. (1996). The Balance Scorecard: Translating Strategy into Action. Harvard Business Review Press.
- Kaplan, R., & Norton, D. (1996a). Using the Balanced Scorecard as a Strategic Management System. Harvard Business Review.
- Keiser, A., Beck, N., & Tainio, R. (2001). Rules and Organizational Learning: The Behavioral Theory Approach. In M. Dierkes, A. Antal, J. Child, & I. Nonaka, Handbook of organizational learning and knowledge (pp. 598-625). London: Oxford University Press.

- Keller, K. L. (2001). Building Customer Base Brand Equity. Retrieved November 2011, from http://mktg.uni-svishtov.bg: http://mktg.uni-svishtov.bg/ivm/resource/CustomerBasedbrandEquityModel.pdf
- Koch, P., & Hauknes, J. (2005). Innovation in the Public Sector. Oslo: Publin.
- Kolesar, P., & Cutler, W. (2011). CREATING CUSTOMER VALUE through Industrialized Intimacy. Retrieved November 2011, from http://www.aug.edu: http://www.aug.edu/~sbajmg/quan6610/Waiting%20Lines/kolesar%20s-b%203q98%20cust%20value%2098304.pdf
- KPMG. (2011). Seven Step Approach for Better CEM. Retrieved November 14, 2011, from http://www.kpmg.com: http://www.kpmg.com/US/en/IssuesAndInsights/ArticlesPublications/Documents/seven-steps-better-customer-experience-management.pdf
- Laudon, K. C., & Laudon, J. P. (2011). Management Information system. USA: Pearson Education Inc.
- Lawrence, E. J., Shaw, P., Baker, D., Baron-Cohen, S., & David, A. S. (2004). Measuring Empathy: Reliability and Validity of the Empathy Quotient. Psychological Medicine, 34, 911-924.
- Lee, H., & Choi, B. (2003). Knowledge enablers, processes and organizational performance: An integrated view and empirical examination. Journal of Management Information Systems, 179-228.
- Legal Ombudsman. (2011, September 03). Guide to good complaint handling. Retrieved November 15, 2011, from Legal Ombudsman: http://www.legalombudsman.org.uk/downloads/documents/publications/LeO_GGCH_v1.pdf
- Leiringer, R. (2004). The Scope for Innovative Thinking within Public Private Partnerships. Retrieved 02 07, 2011, from http://cic.vtt.fi/lean/singapore/LeiringerFinal.pdf
- Lent, A., & Lockwood, M. (2010, 12). Creative Destruction: Placing Innovation at the Heart of Progressive Economics. Retrieved 07 13, 2011, from http://www.bctrust.org.uk/wp-content/uploads/2011/01/ippr-Creative_Destruction-Placing_Innovation_at_the_Heart_of_Progressive_Economics-2010.pdf
- Leskiw, S.-L., & Singh, P. (2007). Leadership development: learning from best practices. Leadership & Organization Development Journal, 444-464.
- Levine, D. I., & Toffel, M. W. (2008). Quality Management and Job Quality: How the ISO 9001 Standard for Quality Management Systems

Affects Employees and Employers (09-018), Working Paper 2008-2010. Bostan: Harvard Business School.

- Lopez, S., Peon, J., & Ordas, C. (2004). Managing knowledge: the link between culture and organizational learning. Journal of Knowledge Management, 93-104.
- Lowenstein, M. (2004, 11 11). Leverage the Marketing Power of Customer Advocacy. Retrieved 10 11, 2011, from http://crmguru.custhelp.com/: http://crmguru.custhelp.com/app/answers/detail/a_id/1391/~/leverage-the-marketing-power-of-customer-advocacy
- Magretta, J. (1998, March - April). The power of Virtual Integration: An Interview with Dell Computer's Michael Dell. Harvard Business Review , 76 (2), pp. 72 - 84.
- Malhotra, Y. (2002). Knowledge Transfer. Retrieved October 26, 2010, from www.yogeshmalhotra.com: http://km.brint.com/CBK/WorkingKnowledge5.pdf
- Marsden, P., Samson, A., & Upton, N. (2005, 09 13). Advocacy Drives Growth. Retrieved 10 24, 2011, from http://www.waltercarl.neu.edu/PDFs/colleagues/LSE_AdvocacyDrivesGrowth.pdf
- Mascarenhas, O. A., Kesavan, R., & Bernachhi, M. (2006). Lasting customer loyalty: a total customer experience approach. Journal of consumer marketing, 397-405.
- McKenna, E. (2000). Business psychology and organizational behavior. Hove: Psychology Press.
- McKinsey & Company. (2007, 06). Three Paradigms of Public Sector Reform. Retrieved 02 08, 2011, from http://www.mckinsey.com/clientservice/publicsector/pdf/TG_three_paradigms.pdf
- Melum, M. (2002). Developing high-performance leaders. Quality Management in Health Care, 55-68.
- Mohammad, A. B. (2001). CRM implementation an empirical study of best practices and a proposed model of implementation. Bradford: TQM.
- Morris, L. (2007). Creating the Innovation Culture. Retrieved 07 12, 2011, from http://www.innovationtools.com/PDF/CreatingInnovationCulture.pdf

- Patricia Seybold Group. (2006, 10). Outside Innovation: How Your Customers Will Co-Design Your Company's Future. Retrieved 07 12, 2011, from http://www.psgroup.com/download/Outside_Innovation_Release.pdf
- Pearlson, K., & Yeh, R. (1999, March 03). Dell Computer Corporation: A Zero-Time Organization. Retrieved November 10, 2011, from http://cyberlibris.typepad.com/news/files/dell_case_study.pdf
- Peppers & Rogers Group and SAS. (2008, 04 29). *Customer Experience Maturity Monitor*. Retrieved 02 23, 2011, from http://www.sas.com/offices/europe/france/pdf/CEMM_France_Handout_17Apr09.pdf
- Peppers & Rogers Group. (2010). The Customer Intimacy Imperative. Retrieved 2011, from www.siliconrepublic.com: www.siliconrepublic.com/download/fs/.../ytw03078usen.PDF - Ireland
- Pervaiz, A., & Zairi, M. (2000). Innovation: A Performance Measurement Perspective in Joe Tidd (ed.) From Knowledge Management to Strategic Competence; Measuring Technological, Market and Organisational Innovation. London: Imperial College Press.
- Politis, J. (2003). The Connection between Trust and Knowledge Management: What are its implications for team performance? Journal of Knowledge Management, 55-66.
- Portsmouth Hospitals NHS Trust. (2009, December). Customer Care Strategy 2010-2012 . Retrieved November 2011, from http://www.porthosp.nhs.uk/: http://www.porthosp.nhs.uk/Customer%20Care%20Strategy%202010-2012.pdf
- Potgieter, A., & Roodt, G. (2004). Measuring A Customer Intimacy Culture In A Value Discipline Context. Journal of Human Resource Management, 25-31.
- Promise Corporation. (2009). Co-creation: New pathways to value - An overview. Retrieved 07 08, 2011, from http://personal.lse.ac.uk/samsona/CoCreation_Report.pdf
- Rafaeli, A., Derfler, R., Ravid, S., & Rozillio, R. (2008, April 04). The Effects of Angry Customers. Retrieved November 10, 2011, from Wharton University of Pennsylvania: http://fic.wharton.upenn.edu/fic/call%20center%2008/Anat%20Rafaeli%20Anger_Effects_Wharton_Feb_2008.pdf
- Ramalingam, B. (2008, April). Organisational learning for aid, and learning aid organisations. Retrieved October 07, 2010, from

http://www.capacity.org: http://www.capacity.org/en/journal/feature/organisational_learning_for_aid_and_learning_aid_organisations

- Reichheld, F. F., & Teal, T. (2001). The loyalty effect the hidden force behind growth, profits and lasting value. Boston, Mass: Harvard Business School.
- Reinartz, W., & Kumar, V. (2002). The Mismanagement of Customer Loyalty. Harvard Business Review.
- ResponseTek Networks Corp. (2008). Why Advocacy is Not Enough - White Paper. Retrieved 10 24, 2011, from http://www.responsetek.com/downloads/why_advocacy-wp.pdf
- Roberts, K. (2004). Love in the desert - being trusted and respected is not enough for US brands in the Middle East. Financial Times.
- Rodríguez Cervera, L. (n.d.). Knowledge Process Management. Retrieved October 21, 2010, from http://hosteddocs.ittoolbox.com: http://hosteddocs.ittoolbox.com/LC071805.pdf
- Roos, D., & Anemo, M. (2011, 01). Ground-breaking Innovation Management Concepts from the Past 25 Years. Retrieved 08 11, 2011, from http://www.adl.com/uploads/tx_extprism/Prism_01-11_Breaking_Innovation.pdf
- Roos, J., & Von Krogh., G. (1996). Five claims on Knowing. European Management Journal, 423-425.
- Ross, D. (2009). Customer needs and innovation effectiveness. Retrieved November 25, 2011, from http://www.innovare-inc.com: http://www.innovare-inc.com/downloads/Customer_Needs_Innovation_Effectiveness.pdf
- SAS Institute Inc. (2009). The State of Customer Experience Capabilities and Competencies. Retrieved November 2011, from http://www.sas.com: http://www.sas.com/ads/377505/report.pdf
- SAS Institute Inc., Peppers & Rogers Group and Jubelirer Research. (2009). Customer Experience Maturity Monitor: The State of Customer Experience Capabilities and Competencies. Cary: SAS Institute Inc.
- Satmetrix Systems, Inc. (2011). How to Calculate Your Score. Retrieved 10 21, 2011, from Net Promoter: http://www.netpromoter.com/np/calculate.jsp
- Savage, C. (2000). The development of knowledge management and why it is important; in Knowledge Management for Development

Organisations. University of Sussex: Canada: Bellanet International Secretariat.

- Schein, E. (1992). The Learning Leader as Culture Manager' in Organizational Culture and Leadership. San Francisco: Jossey-Bass Publishers.
- Schmitt, B. H. (2003). Customer Experience Management. Hoboken, NJ: John Wiley & Sons Inc.
- Senge, P. (1990). The Fifth Discipline: The Art and Practice of the Learning Organization.
- Serrat, O. (2009, September). Harnessing Creativity and Innovation in the Workplace. Retrieved October 14, 2010, from Asian Development Bank: www.adb.org/knowledgesolutions
- SGS. (2006). CUSTOMER SERVICE EXCELLENCE. Retrieved 2011, from http://www.uk.sgs.com: http://www.uk.sgs.com/ssc_5292-0508_customer_service_excellence_booklet.pdf
- Shafer, R. (2005). Customer Empathy. Retrieved November 2011, from http://www.speakersoffice.com: http://www.speakersoffice.com/CUSTOMER%20EMPATHY%20E%20Boo k.pdf
- Siebert, E. (2004). Striving for Customer Intimacy. Retrieved November 2011, from http://www.imalink.com: http://www.imalink.com/pdfs/Customer%20Intimacy.pdf
- Singh, S. K. (2008). Role of leadership in knowledge management: a study. Journal of Knowledge Management, 3-15.
- Sinkula, J. (1994). Market information processing and organizational learning. Journal of Marketing, 46-55.
- Skyrme, D. J. (2002). BUSINESS VALUE FROM KNOWLEDGE MANAGEMENT. Mobilising Knowledge for Business Performance. London: Aslib.
- Smikle, J. L. (2002, September). Creating the Service Mindset: Where Does it Start? Retrieved November 2011, from http://www.smiklespeaks.com: http://www.smiklespeaks.com/file/articles/Create%20the%20Service%2 0Mindset.pdf
- Sonnenwald, D., & Pierce, L. (2000). Information Behavior in dynamic group work contexts: Interwoven situational awareness, dense social networks and contested collaboration in command and control. Information Processing and Management, 461-479.

- Springer, T., Azzarell, D., & Melton, J. (2011, July 8). What it takes to win with customer experience: The secret to profitable organic growth? Deliver a customer experience that your competitors can't match. Retrieved November 10, 2011, from Bain & Company: http://www.bain.com/Images/BB_What_it_takes_to_win_in_customer_experience.pdf
- State and Local Government Review. (1995). Creating an Innovative Organization. Retrieved 02 07, 2011, from Ten Hints for Involving Frontline Workers: http://govleaders.org/behn_innovation3.htm
- Stewart, T. (1997). Intellectual Capital: The New Wealth of Organizations. London: Nicholas Brealy.
- Storey, J., & Barnett, E. (2000). Knowledge management initiatives: learning from Failure. Knowledge management, 145-156.
- Stuart, F. I., & Tax, S. (2004). Toward an integrative approach to designing service experiences: lessons learned from theatre. Journal of Operation management, 609-627.
- Sutherland Global Services. (2010). Creating an Emotional Bond with Your Customer. Retrieved November 2011, from http://www.shop.org: http://www.shop.org/c/document_library/get_file?folderId=177&name=DLFE-706.pdf
- Syncresis, L. (2009). Emergent Strategy Processes. Retrieved October 12, 2010, from http://www.syncresis.co.uk: http://www.syncresis.co.uk/emstrat.html
- Tahir, S., Basit, T., Anis-Ul-Haque, M., Mushtaq, A. H., & Anwar U., C. (2010). Knowledge Management Practices: Role of Organizational Culture. Asbbs Annual Conference (Pp. 1027-1036). Las Vegas: Asbbs.
- Temkin, B. (2008). The 6 Laws of Customer Experience. Retrieved November 2011, from http://www.rightnow.com: http://www.rightnow.com/files/whitepapers/6-Laws-of-Customer-Experience-White-Papers.pdf
- Temkin, B. D., & Geller, S. (2008). The Customer Experience Journey. New York: Forrester research Inc.
- Temkin, B. D., Dorsey, M., Chu, W., & Beckers, A. (2009). Customer Experience Boosts Revenue. Cambridge, MA: Forrester Research Inc.
- The British and Irish Ombudsman Association. (2007, April 03). Guide to principles of good complaint handling: Firm on principles, flexible on process. Retrieved November 11, 2011, from The British and Irish Ombudsman Association: http://www.bioa.org.uk/docs/BIOAGoodComplaintHandling.pdf

- The Centre for Rural Pennsylvania. (2008, April). Developing Effective Citizen Engagement: A How-To Guide for Community Leaders. Retrieved February 23, 2011, from http://www.rural.palegislature.us: http://www.rural.palegislature.us/Effective_Citizen_Engagement.pdf
- The Economist. (2007, March). Beyond loyalty Meeting the challenge of customer engagement. Retrieved October 21, 2011, from http://www.adobe.com: http://www.adobe.com/engagement/pdfs/partII.pdf
- The Pert Group. (2011). How Does Customer Loyalty Effect Profitability? Retrieved November 2011, from http://www.thepertgroup.com: http://www.thepertgroup.com/_file_/How%20Does%20Customer%20Loyalty%20Effect%20Profitability.pdf
- The Times 100. (2011). The importance of excellent customer service. Retrieved 2011, from http://www.thetimes100.co.uk: /downloads/portakabin/portakabin_11_full.pdf
- Thompson, B. (2005, March). The Loyalty Connection: Secrets to Customer Retention And Increased Profits. Bozeman, Montana.
- Thompson, B. (2006). Customer Experience Management: Accelerating Business Performance. Retrieved November 14, 2011, from http://retaintogain.com: http://retaintogain.com/pdf/customer_exp2.pdf
- Thompson, B. (2006). Customer Experience Management: Accelerating Business Performance. Right Now Technologies, Customer Think Corp.
- Thompson, B. (2006, May). Customer Experience Management: The Value of "Moments of Truth". Bozeman, Montana.
- Thompson, B. (2007, October). The Loyalty Connection: Measure What Matters and Create Customer Advocates. Retrieved November 2011, from http://www.rightnow.com: http://www.rightnow.com/files/whitepapers/The_Loyalty_Connection__Measure_What_Matters_and_Create_Customer_Advocates.pdf
- Thorburn, L. (2005). Knowledge Management and Innovation in Service Companies – Case studies from Tourism, Software and Mining Technologies. Australia: Innovation Dynamics Pty Ltd.
- Tikkanen-Bradley Consulting Group. (2007). Winning customers through superior service. Retrieved 2011, from http://www.aaronwallis.co.uk: http://www.aaronwallis.co.uk/Win%20New%20Customers%20Through%20Excellent%20Service.pdf

- Tracey, J. B., Tannenbaum, S., & Kavanagh, M. J. (1995). Applying trained skills on the job: The importance of the work environment. Journal of Applied Psychology, 239-252.
- Treacy, M., & Wiersema, F. (1993). Customer Intimacy and other value discipline. Harvard Business Review, 84-93.
- Tsai, M.-T., & Lee, K.-W. (2006). A Study of Knowledge Internalization: From the perspective of learning cycle theory. Journal of Knowledge Management, 57-71.
- UK-Cabinet Office. (2009). Coproduction in public services. Retrieved 2011, from http://webarchive.nationalarchives.gov.uk: http://webarchive.nationalarchives.gov.uk/+/http://www.cabinetoffice.gov.uk/media/207033/public_services_co-production.pdf
- UKCES. (2010, June). Applying the Learning from Customer Empowerment Models. Retrieved October 11, 2011, from www.ukces.org.uk: http://www.ukces.org.uk/assets/bispartner/ukces/doc/publication/applying-the-learning-from-customer-empowerment-models.pdf
- University of Cambridge. (2010). Kano model. Retrieved November 2011, from http://www.ifm.eng.cam.ac.uk: http://www.ifm.eng.cam.ac.uk/dmg/tool/definition/kano.html
- University, W. S. (n.d.). Student Association of Supply Chain Management. Retrieved October 13, 2010, from http://organizations.weber.edu: http://organizations.weber.edu/sascm/
- Urban, G. L. (2005). Customer Advocacy: A New Era in Marketing? Retrieved 10 13, 2011, from Journal of Public Policy & Marketing: http://ebusiness.mit.edu/urban/papers/customer%20advocacy%20-%20a%20new%20era%20(jm%202005).pdf
- Verado, D. (2000). Managing the Strategic Planning Process. Info-line: American Society for Learning & Development, p. 2.
- Voss, C., & Wang, C. (2009, October). Agility in services capabilities for difficult times. Retrieved November 2011, from http://www.aimresearch.org: http://www.aimresearch.org/uploads/File/Publications/Executive%20Briefings%202/Agility_in_Service.pdf
- Voss, C., & Zomerdijk, L. (2007). Innovation in Experiential Services. London: Innovation in Services, DTI.
- Watson, J. (2003). The impact of TQM adoption on SME financial performance. 16th Annual Conference of Small Enterprise Association of

Australia and New Zealand (pp. 1-9). Ballarat: Small Enterprise Association of Australia and New Zealand.

- Watt, R. (2007). Unlocking Innovation - Why citizens hold the key to public service reform. (S. Parker, & S. Parker, Editors) Retrieved 10 07, 2011, from Demos: http://www.demos.co.uk/files/Unlocking%20innovation.pdf
- wendy-hewlett. (2010). Essentials of Service Leadership. Retrieved 2011, from http://wendy-hewlett.com: http://wendy-hewlett.com/essentials-of-service-leadership/
- WIERSEMA, F. (2011). Key Principles Of Customer Intimacy. Retrieved November 2011, from http://www.leighbureau.com: http://www.leighbureau.com/speakers/fwiersema/topics/keys.pdf
- Wigg, K. M. (1993). "Knowledge Management Foundations: Thinking About Thinking: How People and Organizations Create, Represent and Use Knowledge". Arlington: Schema Press.
- Williamson, B., & Hyde, P. (2000). The Importance of Organisational Values: Part 1: Is your organisation value congruent? Focus on Change Management, 14-18.
- Wilson, James Patrick (2004). An Examination of the Economic Benefits of ISO 9000 and the Baldrige Award to Manufacturing Firms. Master's Thesis, University of Pittsburgh. Retrieved from http://d-scholarship.pitt.edu/6758/1/JamesWilsonThesis.pdf
- Wirtz, J., & Johnston, R. (2001, December). Singapore Airlines: What It Takes To Sustain Service Excellence – A Senior Management Perspective. Retrieved November 2011, from http://homepage.ntlworld.com: http://homepage.ntlworld.com/duc_huynh/PDF%20File/SIA_What%20it%20takes%20to%20sustain%20service%20excellence.pdf
- Zairi, M. (Ed.). (2009). Emotionally Attached - Wooing and Taking Vows with Customers. Keighley, West Yorkshire, United Kingdom: European Centre for Best Practice Management Publishing House.
- Zairi, M., & Letza, S. (1994a). Passing fad or indispensable tool? Strategic Insights in Quality (2), 23-25.
- Zairi, M., & Letza, S. (1994b). Performance measurement - a challenge for the quality and accounting professions. Asia Pacific International Journal of Quality Management, 3 (2), 26-41.
- Zairi, M., & Letza, S. (1994c). TQM and Business Performance - Is there a Link? Journal of Business Executive, 8 (46), 10-11.

- Zairi, M., Oakland, J. S., & Letza, S. (1994). TQM and its Impact on Bottom Line. TQM Magazine, 6 (1), 33-48.
- Zenger, J., & Folkman, J. (2003). Developing leader. Executive Excellence, 5.
- Zoltayne Paprika, Z. (2001, August). Knowledge management support in decision making. Retrieved October 26, 2010, from http://edok.lib.uni-corvinus.hu: http://edok.lib.uni-corvinus.hu/29/1/Paprika4.pdf

Index